THE BENDER-GESTALT TEST

THE BENDER-GESTALT TEST

QUANTIFICATION AND VALIDITY FOR ADULTS

By

GERALD R. PASCAL, Ph.D.

Research Psychologist, Western Psychiatric Institute and Clinic; Associate Professor of Psychology, University of Pittsburgh

and

BARBARA J. SUTTELL, M.S.

Associate Research Psychologist, Western Psychiatric Institute and Clinic

Foreword by David G. Wright, M.D.

Grune & Stratton
A Subsidiary of Harcourt Brace Jovanovich, Publishers
New York London
Paris San Diego San Francisco São Paulo
Sydney Tokyo Toronto

Grune & Stratton, Inc.
111 Fifth Avenue, New York, New York 10003
Distributed in the United Kingdom by Academic Press, Inc. (London) Ltd. 24/28 Oval Road, London NW1

Library of Congress Catalog Card Number 51-3749
International Standard Book Number 0-8089-0358-6

Printed in the United States of America (G-B)

FOREWORD

The studies, of which this text is the exposition, are of unusual interest from several points of view. They make it quite clear, I believe, that a test and a quantified system for scoring responses to it have been devised by which the presence and the immediate severity of psychiatric disorder in a person of adult years frequently can be discovered, with rapidity and with a surprising measure of dependability. The potential scope of useful application of such a test and scoring method, if used only for rough "screening" purposes, is very wide.

But if this is so, these studies must also provoke one to explore further into those most rich and unmapped areas of human psychology—those of the functions and the structuring of the ego. If this is so, the responses of each person to a single test situation must be definitively determined, indeed, by the totality of psychic activity at that time; and the ego, as we conceive it, is the interpreter and actively working intermediator between inner psychic pressures and the circumstances of external reality.

A satisfying definition of mental or nervous illness or disorder has never been made; nor have "wellness" or "normality" been adequately defined. It has been said many times, in more or less earnestness, and with more or less thoughtfulness, that the only workable definition of a psychosis is that which one has if he is behind locked doors in an asylum; and of a neurosis, that which one has if he goes to see a psychiatrist.

All efforts at classification of such disorders thus far have shown themselves to be inadequate frameworks into which the living material does not fit in a meaningful pattern (strikingly unlike the Periodic Table, or even large portions of the "evolutionary tree"); and this too applies for the varieties of psychic "wellness," although I think a most valuable beginning has been made here by Karl Abraham in his "Psychoanalytische Studien zur Charakterbildung" (1925). In 1806, Arnold, in his "Observations on the Nature of Insanity," said "of causes, we know too little to make them a foundation of the arrangement of diseases"; and Tuke, in 1879, said:

> "Could we determine, with certainty, distinctly separated faculties of the mind, we might then, and only then, hope to possess a detailed and symptomatic nomenclature, according as one or more of them are involved.

> Did we possess a perfect knowledge of the physiology of the organ of the mind, we should naturally, as in other diseases, endeavour to adapt our terms to the structure affected—assuming that there are different parts of this organ correlated with different psychical powers; but in the absence of this knowledge, it would seem reasonable to adapt them to the affected functions."

These observations seem equally valid as applied to our level of knowledge today. It is necessary, then, to inquire into the "affected functions" in psychic disorders.

Many of the great observers and clinicians in psychiatry, before the present century (including Isaac Ray, at Butler Hospital), whatever their speculative biases, and perhaps in spite of believing that they occasionally saw "healthy and diseased mental manifestations in combination," agreed generally that "usually the intellect, the emotions, and volition, are all in disorder," whether the illness were basically classed as "amentia," "melancholia," "mania," "oneirodynia," or whatever. These conclusions are thoroughly confirmed, I take it, and to a very considerable measure have been made understandable, by the intensive explorations of the dynamics of personality development which have been made by psychoanalytic and other clinical studies through the present century.

Are, then, all psychic functions affected when a person suffers from a "mental" or "nervous" or "emotional" disorder? I believe that we can postulate that at least those are which are controlled by the ego, that is to say those through which the person deals with external reality and with the interaction of instinctive pressure with external reality. I think that it is this, in addition to our simply knowing too little, that has led to our continuing inability to define psychic disorders satisfactorily and to classify them very usefully, as well as our inability to understand their meanings and the meanings of therapy.

The ego must begin its growth in infancy (or perhaps before) by evolving the differentiation of the individual from all external objects and influences. The ego's prototypical, continuous, necessary, and defining function is "reality-testing." Beginning life with biological needs, instinctual energies, and some receptor and effector apparatus, the infant person is satisfied and is frustrated; and through these experiences he comes to feel emotions, to recognize himself, to differentiate himself from the rest of the world, to relate to others persons, and to learn ways and means of dealing with himself, his feelings, the world, and other persons. The person becomes aware of parts of his ego functions, but certainly the greater part of the ego's work is kept unconscious. The ego strives to arrange to gratify instinctual desires, directly and indirectly, and to arrange to avoid pain and anxiety. In avoiding pain and anxiety particularly, it may use patterns of action and feeling that are defensive and self-restrictive.

These patterns it tends to use when threatened, again and again in later life, during which period these patterns may by no means be fitting to new sets of existing realities, and may no longer succeed in defending and protecting. When this occurs, as it does in the neuroses, both immediate and very old anxieties are aroused, which further militates against the ego's ability to deal comprehensively with reality. In psychotic states feeling is withdrawn from actual external objects back into the self—a situation which recapitulates levels of ego development of early infancy, and is therefore truly "regressive." At such levels the ego's reality-testing is at best very fragmentary.

But if all this is a reasonably valid conceptual formulation, and if it does in fact indicate that the results of Dr. Pascal's studies are fundamentally consistent with century-old clinical experience, it re-emphasizes, I hope, all that we *do not know* about the ego. We do not know enough about the sources of its strengths, inherent or derived from external endowment. We do not know enough about its growth and evolution, and about its critical stages of vulnerability and crystallization. We do not know how changeable its structure is toward positively adaptive ends, nor by what means such changes can be promoted, through the vicissitudes of growing and living.

David G. Wright, M. D.
Superintendent, Butler Hospital,
Providence, Rhode Island.

ACKNOWLEDGMENTS

Most of the work described in this book was accomplished while the authors were employed by Butler Hospital, the senior author as chief psychologist and the junior author as research assistant. To Dr. Arthur H. Ruggles, former superintendent, under whom the work was started, and to the staff of the hospital, we express our gratitude for help and encouragement. Special thanks are due to Dr. David G. Wright, present superintendent, for his constant support during the course of the project and for his critical reading of the manuscript. Mr. Herbert Ruesch, psychologist at Butler Hospital, has helped in the gathering of data from hospital patients. Miss Vera Toppi, departmental secretary at Butler Hospital, has by her loyalty, hard work and cheerful interest aided us greatly.

At the University of Pittsburgh the authors wish to acknowledge the timely and kindly assistance of Dean Herbert Longenecker of the Graduate School, and Professor Wayne Dennis, Head of the Department of Psychology.

Acknowledgment is made to the American Journal of Orthopsychiatry and to Dr. Lauretta Bender for permission to reproduce the Bender-Gestalt designs and to quote from Dr. Bender's monograph. Permission was granted by the Ronald Press and Dr. J. McV. Hunt to reproduce figure 2.

Permission was granted by the *Journal of Abnormal and Social Psychology* to reproduce figures 6, 7 and 8.

CONTENTS

APPENDIX

SCORING MANUAL

LIST OF GRAPHS AND ILLUSTRATIONS

LIST OF TABLES

PART I:

QUANTIFICATION

1: INTRODUCTION

The Bender-Gestalt test consists of nine simple designs, each of which is presented to a subject for him to copy on a sheet of paper. These designs, along with several others, were originally used by Wertheimer (51) in his studies of visual perception. Dr. Lauretta Bender selected from Wertheimer's designs the nine shown in figure 1 and incorporated these into a test for clinical use.[1] The results of her studies with the nine designs are presented by her in a monograph, *A Visual Motor Gestalt Test and Its Clinical Use,* published in 1938 (9). Since the publication of her monograph, Bender's test has come into widespread use as a clinical instrument. It has been used to estimate maturation, intelligence, psychological disturbances, and the effects of injury to the cortex, and to follow the effects of convulsive therapy (9, 11, 30, 39, 46). At least two manuals have been issued by the armed services (4, 30). In 1946 in response to demand, Bender published a separate manual of instructions (10). The test has come to be called the *Bender-Gestalt* (B-G) or simply the *Bender*, and we shall adhere to that usage.

Although the Bender-Gestalt test has, as we have indicated been extensively used, the history of attempts at quantification is surprisingly meager. Bender, in her original monograph made some effort to quantify the records of children, but her very suggestive approach was not carried on by other investigators. Hutt's study (30) presents several factors which, according to him, differentiate between the records of psychoneurotics and "normals." Glueck (21), on the other hand, was unable to find differences between the records of normals and psychotics. Recently, in a fairly exhaustive study, Billingslea attempted a rigidly objective approach to the measurement of Bender-Gestalt performance (12). The variables used by Billingslea, however, indicated little validity when the records of normals and psychoneurotics were compared. And except for a preliminary report of the work to

[1] The test cards may be obtained from the American Orthopsychiatric Association, New York.

be presented in this book (37), we know of no other published attempts to quantify the Bender-Gestalt test.

The test has a considerable literature with respect to its use as a repetitive visuo-motor test. This literature is systematically reviewed by Bender (9) and Billingslea (12), and we shall not consider it in any great detail here. Very little published literature is available, however, about the use of the test as a diagnostic clinical instrument. A mimeographed manual by Hutt (30) suggests some aspects of performance which are said by him to be of diagnostic significance. Bender (9) illustrates the kinds of reproductions obtained from

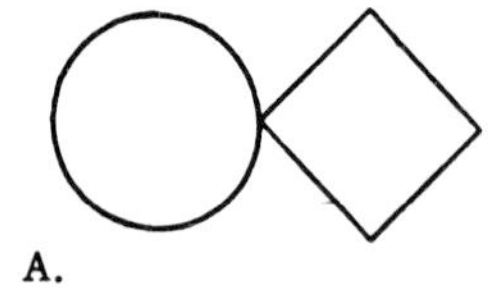

FIG. 1. Designs of the Bender-Gestalt test.

patients of various diagnostic categories, but she does not, in any great detail, discuss the drawings of adults with psychogenic disorders. Nowhere in the literature, as far as we know, is there a systematic presentation of the differences in performance between the records of psychiatric patients with psychogenic disorders and nonpatients. Use of this potentially valuable instrument has, therefore, been handicapped by the lack of a backlog of data as a basis for clinical experience. An important deterrent to the accumulation of data has been the absence of a feasible method of scoring the test, one valid and not too time consuming. It was the necessity of accomplishing this task which prompted the present research.

Our interest in the test began some years back under the enthusiastic influence of Dr. Max Hutt who was then teaching at the Adjutant General School, where the senior author was a student. For Dr. Hutt the test was rich in interpretative value and he instilled in his students a deep interest in it. With increasing experience the test became a valuable clinical tool. Continued use of the test suggested that reproductions made by psychiatric patients tended to deviate more from the stimuli than those of nonpatients, and the more psychologically disturbed the patient the greater the number of deviations. A quantitative approach along these lines, therefore, seemed feasible. A study accomplished in collaboration with Dr. Arthur Irion (5) while the senior author was a member of the armed services indicated that it was possible to grade the B-G reproductions in terms of neatness and accuracy of execution, and that such a grading distinguished significantly between the reproductions of patients and nonpatients. Although this study lacked some obvious controls the results were encouraging and suggested the possibility of a method of scoring the test, hitherto lacking.

Presentation of the scoring method developed and results obtained by its application to the records of normal adults (nonpatients) and adults with psychogenic disorders (psychiatric patients) is the primary purpose of this work. The book is divided into three parts. Part I presents quantitative data on the reliability, validity, and standardization of the test. Part II is a clinical section in which the quantitative and qualitative approaches are combined in the consideration of the individual case. Part III contains the manual proper, where methods of scoring each deviation are presented, and an atlas of scored records.

In the course of administering several hundred B-G tests we naturally developed some ideas about the functions measured by the test. We should like to present these for what they are worth and relate them to evidence from other sources.

The theoretical assumptions which guided Bender are stated by her as follows (9; p. 3): "The Gestalt function may be defined as that function of the integrated organism whereby it responds to a given constellation of stimuli as a whole; the response itself being a constellation, a pattern, or Gestalt." Later, in the same volume, she writes (p. 4): "The whole setting of the stimulus and the whole integrative state of the organism determine the pattern of the response."

We would, in general, agree with this formulation. The overwhelming mass of clinical evidence gathered with the Rorschach test has served to fashion current opinion regarding the positive effects of experience on responses to perceived stimuli (36). To substantiate this view a good deal of experimental evidence has been forthcoming (13, 32, 33, 40). Study of the drawings of psychiatric patients has a considerable history, and the evidence available suggests that when these are compared with those of normal controls discriminating differences can be found (2, 3, 22). Thus, one would expect that on a task such as copying B-G designs, performance would not only be a function of the individual's capacity to perceive correctly and execute the figures but also of the individual's interpretation of them, i.e. what they and the task mean to him in the light of his own experience.

If we accept as given the ability to perceive and execute the designs, deviant performance should, then, be a function of the interpretative factors which obtrude between perception and execution. It is this aspect of performance that we wish to consider.

Prolonged psychological stress often results in a disturbed organism. This disturbance, measured in terms of deviations from normative data, is reflected at several levels of organismic functioning. Hoskins (26) and Gellhorn (20) discuss this subject at the physiological level. More specifically, and representative of studies in this area, Hoagland et al (25) have shown a disturbed lymphocyte reaction in psychotics. At a different level of organismic functioning there is evidence to indicate disturbed reaction time in psychogenic as well as so-called organic disorders (29). Deviations from the number of popular responses on the Rorschach and Word Association tests are a concomitant of psychological disturbances (42). Several writers have reported a relationship between Wechsler-Bellevue Scatter and severity of psychological disturbances (38, 42). It seems, therefore, that when the organism is disturbed by psychogenic factors the disturbance can often be measured at various levels of the response mechanism. We shall postulate, however, that where symptoms are predominatly psychological, disturbances in cortical functioning tend to be more prominent than disturbances at other, lower levels of functioning.

To illustrate our point we present a figure prepared by Hunt and Cofer (27) from data in papers by Huston, Shakov, and Riggs (28,29). In figure 2, the origin of the ordinate is the average time for the normal reaction. The bars represent the differences in milliseconds between the mean times of schizophrenics and controls for reactivity at three levels of complexity. We see, here, that as complexity of reaction increases from latency of patellar tendon reflex to visual discrimination the difference in response time between normal controls and schizophrenics becomes increasingly greater. Unfortunately for niceness of representation, data on strictly comparable populations are not available for more complex responses so that, for instance, we could plot along the same abscissa differences on the word association test. Available evidence (27), however, indicates that extrapolation from the trend indicated in figure 2 is warranted if the baseline is accepted as representing a continuum of increasing complexity of task.

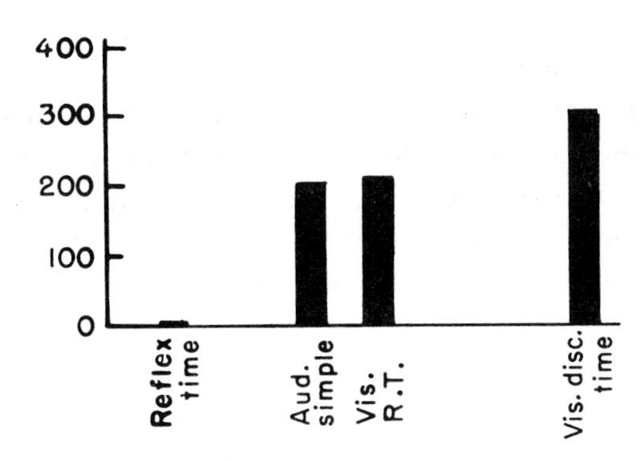

FIG. 2. Differences in reaction times between normal controls and schizophrenics related to complexity of task.

We would suggest that execution of the B-G test is a complex task belonging out to the right on the baseline of a theoretical figure 2 in terms of complexity of task. Its position on the baseline, however, would depend on the measures used to estimate the response. Thus, if we are only interested in whether or not the essential Gestalten are reproduced, then the level of complexity of the task is not as high as it would be if finer nuances of execution were taken into consideration. At this relatively low level of complexity, i.e. measurement of whether or not the essential Gestalten are reproduced, the test would, according to our theoretical figure 2, have less discriminating power for psychogenic disorders. This expectation is borne out in actual practice. All of the designs of the test are correctly reproduced, in their essential aspects, by the age of eleven years (9).

Bender (9), in her original monograph, gives several clinical examples of the effect of cortical damage on the reproduction of the Gestalt designs.

With increasing damage to the cortex there seems to be greater disturbance in reproductive capacity resulting in primitivation of forms and destruction of the Gestalten. She also presents data showing the effect of maturation on the reproduction of the designs. Stainbrook and Lowenback (46) administered the test at various intervals after convulsive therapy and have shown that reproductions parallel the postconvulsive reintegration of the organism. Pascal and Zeaman (39) administered the test to several patients 24 hours after shock and were able to demonstrate that mounting confusion during a series of electroconvulsive treatments was paralleled by deviant performance on the test. Orenstein and Schilder (35), and Schilder (44) used the test immediately after insulin reaction, and after Metrazol convulsion, and found disturbances as follows: perseveration, substitution of circles and loops for points, curves for angles, rotation and separation of parts of the Gestalt. In the light of this evidence, we believe that an essential aspect of cortical functioning is reflected in performance on the B-G test. Reproductions resulting in fragmentation, destruction or primitivation of the Gestalten are regularly obtained from children below the age of six, from patients immediately after convulsive therapy, from brain-damaged individuals, paretics, and seniles; in other words, wherever there is cortical deficit or damage.

Thus, measurement at the level of complexity indicated by estimation of whether or not the essential Gestalten are reproduced does not seem to be of sufficient discriminating power to distinguish between normal adults and those with psychogenic disorders. Adults of normal intelligence without known cortical damage do not, in our experience, fail to reproduce the essential Gestalten. Deviations from the stimuli in these latter individuals do not seem to be a function of ability to perceive or execute the designs. We believe, therefore, that what is being measured by us in the scoring of the B-G of individuals of normal intelligence is some factor other than the ability to perceive or execute the designs. (We shall show later that scores are not a function of drawing ability.)

We may think of B-G performance as a work sample, which involves certainly the cortical capacity to perceive the designs as presented and the psychomotor capacity to reproduce them; but it involves also, and most importantly with subjects of normal intelligence, a factor that seems to be best described as an attitude. The test situation for the individual, once he is subjected to it, becomes a bit of reality with which he has to cope. We would expect, therefore, that in those persons in whom the attitude toward reality is most disturbed, we will find greater deviations from the stimuli. Our findings corroborate this expectation. In the populations tested by us, of normal intelligence and free from brain damage, the greatest number of deviations were found in psychotic subjects, fewer in psychoneurotic subjects, and least in nonpatients.

Deviations from B-G stimuli in our scoring system run from faithful reproductions with low scores to extremely deviant reproductions with very high scores. This continuum is correlated with a progression from less to greater psychological disturbance. Clinical observation and objective tests combine to suggest that this progression is, in turn, correlated with decreasing ability to respond adequately to stimuli in the environment. (By adequately here we mean within the confines of statistical norms.) This enabling capacity of the organism, i.e. to respond adequately to stimuli in the environment, is sometimes referred to as a function of the ego (1). If, for the purposes of this discussion, we limit our definition of ego functioning to the ability to reproduce faithfully the B-G drawings as presented, then we may say that ego strength lies on a continuum from very low to very high B-G scores. This quantitative continuum may, then, in a very limited way, be thought of as an aspect of ego strength—the lower the score the greater the ego strength. To substantiate this hypothesis we find, for instance, that there is a significant tendency for those patients who improved with hospital care to get lower B-G scores when tested on admission to the hospital than those patients who seem not to have improved.

We may, for the moment, recapitulate. The evidence is, we think, sufficiently clear so that we may make the statement that the greater the damage to the cortex through convulsive therapy, amentia, lack of maturation, trauma, etc., the greater the deviations from the stimulus, and on our scoring system the higher the score on the B-G test. What may not be so clear is that deviations resulting in high scores are also a function of what we have reason to believe is attitude toward the task. These latter deviations are, as our data will show, a function of the severity of psychological disturbance as indicated by diagnostic category. We believe that deviations in individuals of normal intelligence without demonstrable brain damage reflect the individual's attitude toward reality. This attitude we believe to be a function of the integrative capacity of the organism, the ego.

2: ADMINISTRATION AND SCORING

Test Administration

In order to reproduce the results to be reported in this book it is necessary, insofar as possible, to adhere to the same general setting as well as instructions used by us. If, as we suspect, the test is measuring, among other things, the subject's attitude toward the task, then the general situation under which the test is administered becomes an important variable to control.

The test is administered to each subject individually in a room free from distracting stimuli. The general tone of the setting is such as to imply a serious test of the subject's capacity. This caution is important because the very ease with which the test is administered and accepted, i.e., the fact that it is so innocent appearing, may easily induce a careless "it doesn't mean anything" attitude. One worker, for instance, attempted to gather records from individuals in a waiting room, asking them for help in this simple task. The designs were reproduced with so little care that they had to be discarded as obviously not representative.

The method of administration, in general, follows that proposed by Bender (10) and Hutt (30), but with some important modifications. The subject is seated at a table, given a blank white piece of paper, 8½ x 11, and a sharp pointed pencil with an eraser. The table top should be hard-surfaced and smooth, free from indentations or scratches which will be reflected in the drawings. The subject is told that he is to copy nine designs or figures. It is important to tell the subject the number of designs he is to copy so that he may plan the size and arrangement; deviations in ordering the designs on the page are scored.

Subjects should also be told not to sketch the designs, but to make single-line drawings. This instruction is obviously important for people with training in drawing. Thus, if a skilled artist is told to reproduce the designs he may, without this instruction, and with painstaking care, exactly reproduce the stimuli.

The instructions are not rigid. Something like the following has generally been used: "I have here nine simple designs (or figures) which you are to copy, free hand, without sketching—on this paper. Each design is on one of these cards which I will show you one at a time. There is no time limit to this test."

Subjects will frequently ask the examiner what he means by "sketching." The explanation here has been that sketching refers to the little lines that artists sometimes use to outline a drawing before making solid lines, or something on that order. In general, however, questions about actual performance are referred back to the subject for his own judgment. Thus, if the subject asks, "Do I have to count the dots?" the examiner should counter with something like, "It's up to you," or "Just as you please." Questions about erasing, using both sides of the paper or additional sheets of paper are handled in the same way, the subject being provided with more paper on request. The subject is not allowed to use a ruler or any such object as a guide for his drawing.

The nine designs are numbered as shown in figure 1. Designs are always presented to the subject oriented as shown in figure 1. After the instructions have been given, and the subject's questions answered, he is given design A, the other cards being held face down. Upon completion of design A, the subject is given design 1 and so on until he has copied all nine designs. Since time is not a factor in scoring we have not systematically recorded the time on all our subjects, but our experience has been that nonpatients take about five minutes or less to complete the test. Patients average about 10 minutes, some patients taking as long as one-half hour to copy the drawings.

During the administration of the test it is important to note the direction in which the paper is held. Orientation of designs on the page as well as deviations are scored. The top of the page is usually indicated by an arrow. Usually one arrow suffices since most subjects keep the paper oriented in the same direction for all nine drawings. Occasionally, however, some subjects will turn the paper to fit in a drawing. This fact should be noted by an arrow as suggested. Subjects will sometimes rotate the card or without rotating the card invert their drawing. This fact is noted. Such notations are made after the subject completes the test.

Scoring

The reproducibility of our results depends primarily on two broad factors: (*a*) the testing situation which we have already disscused, and (*b*) the reliability of the scoring system. We shall, in this section, consider factors making for reliability in scoring.

The scoring procedure is simple, perhaps even deceptively simple. With the exception of design A which is not scored, each design is inspected to determine whether or not scorable deviations occur. Scorable deviations are defined in the scoring manual. The deviations to be scored are given on the score sheet with their assigned weights. Scores are accumulated by designs, plus the scores which have to do with the test as a whole, called *Configuration Scores*, and a final raw score obtained. The raw score is then taken to the appropriate conversion table (depending on the subject's education) and a Z score obtained. With practice it takes about two or three minutes to score a record.

The Score sheet or some such device is important. (See page 209 for a copy of the score sheet). It has been found that with increasing familiarity with the scoring manual it becomes progressively easier to overlook scorable deviations without having at hand a check list such as is provided by the score sheet. We have, typically, had at hand when doing a great amount of scoring, a transparent combination ruler, a protractor, and a six-power magnifying glass. These were occasionally used to check on questionable angular rotation or fine tremor. They were not, however, necessary for reasonably accurate scoring, assuming normal eyesight.

The term "reasonably accurate" is used deliberately. We do not claim our scoring method to be entirely objective. It depends, as a matter of fact, a good deal upon judgment; but judgment, which we have found can easily be selftaught with the aid of the manual provided. Each scorable deviation is defined in the manual accompanied by appropriate illustrations. These should be studied until thoroughly understood. The beginner should then attempt to score the several illustrative records given in the manual and compare his scores with those given. Where judgment is a factor in scoring, subjective certainty is emphasized, i.e., when in doubt do not score. Thus, for instance, design 1 which consists of a horizontal line of 12 dots is scored for wavy line (item 1). We might have defined this in terms of angular deviation from the straight edge of a ruler. We did not. We scored by inspection in a small fraction of the time it would take to make the necessary measurements (a fine discrimination, indeed, considering the grossness of our criteria!). When, then, does a line become a wavy line and scored? We aim for a communality of judgment by the use of illustrations, and for safety add the caution *when in doubt do not score.*

The scoring system is practical. It is not, however, as we have stated, entirely objective or rigidly accurate in measurement. It is most certainly not foolproof. Training, therefore, is essential. It is necessary to understand what is meant by each deviation. It is necessary to study the manual thoroughly and to work through the sample records before attempting to use the scoring system in actual practice. Investigation has shown that thorough study of the manual leads to reasonable reliability in scoring when score sheets are used.

Development of Scoring System

The scoring methods described in the manual are based entirely on empirical findings. The reproductions of psychiatric patients were compared to those of presumably normal individuals. In thus comparing records of "normals" and "abnormals" it was found that the abnormal individuals generally tended to deviate from the stimulus more than normals. A list was made of those deviations which seemed to discriminate between the two groups. Nearly 200 deviations were tried at one time or another. Of these 105 have been retained either on the basis of an item analysis, or, if a deviation occurred too infrequently for quantitative estimate of its discriminating power, on the basis of the fact that the deviation occurred only with patients and practically never with nonpatients. Phi coefficients were calculated from an *abac* presented by Guilford (23). Weights were given on the basis of a modification of an *abac* for weights given by Guilford (23). Where the deviation occurred too infrequently to calculate the phi coefficient, and appeared for our population only in the records of patients, this deviation was given the maximum weight.

A final item analysis (the third) was accomplished on the basis of the records of 260 nonpatients varying in age from 15 to 50 and in education from first year high school to college graduate. These were matched for age, education, and sex by the records of 260 psychiatric patients, 110 of whom were psychotics and 150 psychoneurotics. Table I in the Appendix shows the frequency of occurrence, phi coefficient (where calculated) and weights assigned to the items.

Perhaps a word should be said here in defense of the practice of weighting. In weighting items we were guided by the fact that so many deviations occurred rather infrequently, yet when they did they were invariably found only in the records of patients. It seemed to us, then, that such deviations ought to have more weight than those which occurred both in patients and nonpatients although occurring less frequently in the latter group. Weighting has the spreading effect of multiplying by a constant, the weight being roughly proportionate to the discriminating power of the item. We are satisfied that for our population weighting has had the effect of increasing the diagnostic validity of our scores for the individual case.

Table 1 summarizes the findings of our item validity study. It shows the simple frequency of scored deviations for each design. Chi-square was calculated on the assumption of a 50-50 hypothesis, i.e., that there is no difference between the patient and nonpatient populations with respect to frequency of deviations. For each design, and for the total test, this hypothesis is rejected, based on the significance of chi-square.

Table 1
Frequency of Deviations in Item Analysis Populations
(260 Nonpatients, 260 Psychiatric Patients)

Design	Frequency Non-pt.	Pt.	x^2	P
1	126	251	42.22	< .01
2	165	321	50.07	< .01
3	199	323	118.90	< .01
4	224	410	54.57	< .01
5	237	414	48.74	< .01
6	189	424	89.17	< .01
7	219	485	100.50	< .01
8	195	404	73.75	< .01
Whole	63	136	27.66	< .01
Total	1617	3168	501.98	< .01

Table 2
Reliability of the Scoring Systems
(r= .90, N= 120) (40 nonpatients, 40 neurotics and 40 psychotics)

	Scorer A	Scorer B
Mean Total	33.1	29.3
S. D. Total	20.3	19.2
r_{bis} normal versus psychotic	.79	.76
r_{bis} normal versus neurotic	.71	.70
r_{bis} neurotic versus psychotic	.39	.32

3: RELIABILITY

In encountering the problem of reliability we were faced with the need to estimate not only the reliability of the test, but also, because of its subjective nature, the reliability of the scoring system—the two being, of course, interdependent. We shall deal with the relatively simple task of estimating scorer reliability first, and then take up the more difficult problem of test reliability.

Scorer Reliability

To get some estimate of the reliability of the scoring system 120 records, not previously used in any study, were collected. These consisted of 40 nonpatients, 40 patients diagnosed neurotic, and 40 diagnosed psychotic. All identifying markings were removed from the test records and they were shuffled. The records were then scored by each of the authors in turn. A reliability coefficient of .90 was obtained with a mean raw score of 33.1 for scorer A and 29.3 for scorer B. In order to ascertain whether or not the difference between means reflected an important difference in the discriminating power of the scoring system, biserial correlation coefficients were calculated for both scorers between normal and psychotic, normal and neurotic, and neurotic and psychotic. There were no significant differences between the validity coefficients. Table 2 shows these data.

These results suggest that although there were minor deviations in the scoring for the two scorers, these did not, in general, affect the scoring validity for the population tested. The results, also, confirm those obtained in previous studies, elsewhere described (31). On the basis of three different studies of scorer reliability involving three different pairs of scorers we believe that a reliability coefficient of .90 represents a fair estimate of the scorer reliability which can be attained with practice. Experience has shown that in order to achieve scoring reliability, careful study of the Scoring Manual is required with special attention being paid to illustrative designs.

We have found that when this is done and the 25 completed records provided in the Manual are scored in agreement with the given scores the beginning scorer can attain reasonable reliability. By reasonable, here, we mean reliability such that there is no significant difference between the validity coefficients of two independent scorers.

Test Reliability

The problem of the reliability of a test which purports to be a measure of something which is correlated with whether a person is a psychiatric patient or not is a difficult one. It depends on what variables are being measured. Billingslea (12), in a very detailed objective approach to measurement of Bender performance, found little test reliability. If we measure only the aspects of performance which have to do with whether or not the subject reproduces the essential Gestalt (e.g., makes twelve dots for design 1, produces two crossed hexagons for design 7, etc.) then test–retest reliability is perfect. But, if we include in our score all the deviations which we have found to be related to the patient–nonpatient dichotomy, then our reliability coefficients seem to fluctuate with a number of variables, some of which we know about.

The test seems to be measuring some aspect of behavior which is related to the dichotomy, psychiatric patient vs. nonpatient, which we assume to be a continuum. That there is intra-individual variation on this continuum is obvious; psychiatric patients were not always thus. Various experiences can affect a given person's position on this continuum, such as, threat of loss of position, family strife—in fact, all the things which make for psychiatric illness. Scored performance, then, is affected by experiences, which may intervene between test and retest, if we use the test–retest method of estimating reliability.

If this test is measuring adjustment, attitude toward reality, or what have you (we only *know* that scores are correlated with a patient-nonpatient dichotomy), then the more stable the individual, presumably, the more apt he is to score the same from day to day. This expectation is, in general, borne out by our findings. If we give the test daily over a period of several days to two patients, one of whom is excited and fluctuating in his adjustment and during his course in the hospital undergoes a series of electroconvulsive treatments, and the other of whom although somewhat excited upon admission soon settles down to the hospital routine and is fairly stable in his adjustment, we obtain from the first a fluctuating graph of performance, and from the second, a fairly stable graph (see Chapter 4). We have found, in general, that subjects who score low on the test tend to give the same performance (same score) on successive testing. Thus, for instance, test–retest reliability is higher for nonpatients than it is for patients, higher for low scoring normals than for high scoring normals.

Most of the methods of estimating test reliability have been tried by us. Thus, several splittings of odd–even design comparisons were tried resulting in generally unsatisfactory reliability coefficients. For instance, designs 1, 3, 5, and 7 were correlated against designs 2, 4, 6, and 8 on 97 college students yielding a coefficient of .51. The difficulty here, of course, is that the subjects tend to react differently to each design. (We shall have something to say about this in a later section.) This same difficulty argues against the use of methods advocated by Richardson & Kuder (43). Therefore, in spite of its obvious drawbacks we have decided upon the test–retest method for reporting reliability. We selected a group of normals (nonpatients) with a wide range of test scores, covering, in fact, the entire range of normal scores. This emphasis upon range is necessary if the reliability coefficient is to have any meaning in actual practice, for, as we have noted, the reliability coefficient can be made to vary with the "adjustment" of the subjects of the population. Forty-four subjects ranging in raw scores on initial test from 3 to 42 and in education from first year high school to graduate school were given the test twice with an interval of 24 hours elapsing between tests. When these test scores were correlated a reliability coefficient of .71 was obtained with a raw score mean of 17.3 for test one and 17.5 for test two. We report this particular study as representative of several attempts at test–retest reliability which we have made.

As one would expect, of course, test–retest reliability decreases with an increasing time interval between test and retest. As an extreme in time interval we retested 23 normal subjects after 18 months, correlated their scores and obtained a reliability coefficient of .63.

As test reliabilities go our reliability coefficient is not high. It is attenuated, of course, by the fact that scorer reliability is not perfect. Consideration, however, of the factors that can intervene between test and retest and what, in actual fact, our test is measuring, leads one to a new view of the significance of the test–retest reliability coefficient obtained. Although as a reliability coefficient, *per se*, it is not high, we suggest that it indicates a remarkable consistency of individual adjustment. As users of the test we have not been primarily concerned with reliability as long as validity has been maintained. We do not, in reporting this data on reliability, feel that we have arrived at an accurate estimate of the reliability of the test.

The Effect of Practice.

We find it difficult to make any positive statements about the effect of practice. The same factors influencing test reliability are also, of course, important here. Thus, we have found, as we have noted, no practice effect with low scoring normals. With a subject with a raw score of 3, for instance, there is a surprising consistency of performance over several days. Yet, some normals, depending upon their attitude to the task, will fluctuate in daily performance. Thus, one normal scored 30 on the first test and 16 on the retest, another scored 18 on test and 20 on retest. When, for instance, we compare mean scores for our test–retest population we find no effect of practice.

Since our scores, as we shall show, are not a function of drawing ability one would not expect on logical grounds that score would be affected by practice. Scores depend on essential duplication of the stimuli, not on nicety of drawing. Within the limits of our scoring, therefore, it is difficult to see how practice of the psychomotor functions involved, of themselves, could affect the individual's score. On these and other grounds we believe that changes in performance as reflected in scores are a function of something other than practice, except, of course, insofar as practice in the testing situation is a factor. We would recommend the use of the test wherever repeated performances on a psychomotor task are required. We shall show, in a later section, such use of the test.

4: TEST STANDARDIZATION

Having set up a fairly reliable method of scoring B-G records, with some notion of the validity and reliability of the scoring method, we now set about collecting normal records. With the exception of 84 records obtained from college undergraduates and 56 from a graduating high school class, all of the records were obtained either from Butler Hospital employees or from students attending adult evening classes in various schools and universities in Providence.[1] Four hundred and seventy-four individually administered records were thus obtained. We were fortunate in being able to obtain one hundred percent samples for all the evening classes tested. Table 3 shows our normative population, giving sex, age, education, and mean raw B-G scores.

Table 3

Sex, Age, Education and Mean Raw Score For Nonpatient Population

	High School						College					
	Women		Men		Age Total		Women		Men		Age Total	
Age	N	Mean Score	N	Mean Score	N	Mean Score	N	Mean Score	N	Mean Score	N	Mean Score
15-19	50	18.5	34	19.8	84	19.0	9	12.3	12	11.3	21	11.7
20-24	51	17.7	32	18.2	83	17.9	21	15.9	81	12.7	102	13.3
25-29	16	14.9	24	15.8	40	15.5	6	6.2	38	12.9	44	12.0
30-34	11	16.1	19	17.4	30	16.9	4	12.3	14	12.9	18	11.5
35-39	10	17.3	5	27.6	15	20.7	4	18.0	12	13.2	16	14.6
40-44	6	19.0	5	20.6	11	19.7	1	12.0	1	1.0	2	12.5
45-50	4	17.5	4	17.7	8	17.6	—	—	—	—	—	—
Totals	148	17.6	123	18.5	271	18.0	45	13.7	158	12.5	203	12.7
S. D.						9.4						8.8
Median						15.0						10.0
Q_1-Q_3					11 - 24						6 - 18	

[1] Thanks are due to Mr. Balch, Dean of the R.I. School of Design; Y.M.C.A.; Dr. Wood, Principal of Hope High School; and various instructors of the Brown University Extension Division.

We are unable to state, whether or not our population is representative of a larger population for the Providence area. We know that we have sampled a wide range of vocations, religious backgrounds, and nationality groups in obtaining records from night classes of various kinds. Strictly speaking, of course, our results are only applicable to our population, but then they would be of little practical use. Credence in the applicability of our results derives from two suppositions. On the one hand, previous studies suggest a fairly sizable proportion of the "normal" population to be in need of psychiatric assistance and therefore possible psychiatric patients, the very dichotomy on which our estimate of validity is based (17). (This fact may, in part, account for the positive skewness of the frequency curve shown in figure 4.) On the other hand, we have reason to believe that the selective process making for attendance at some night school classes tested by us, and included in our normal population, has as a characteristic an increased B-G score. Thus, for a night class in "personality" consisting of 34 individuals, the mean raw score was considerably above the average for a comparable group not attending the "personality" class or other night classes in psychology. We believe, in other words, that our population may underestimate the larger population of comparable age and education. This point is, however, debatable, and, in the end, the representativeness of our sample must await confirmation. It is for this reason that we have presented our normative data in raw score form hoping that it may serve as a basis for comparison for other workers with other populations.

A glance at table 3 will show that our data is particularly lacking in records for the age groups 40–50. (We have a few records of individuals of over 50 which we shall discuss later.) There are, in all, only 21 cases for this age group. Another lack in our normative population is that of data on people of only grammar school education. We were able to obtain a few records but not enough to include in our population; most were above the age of 50. For eight subjects of only grammar school education with a mean age of 37 we obtained a mean B-G score of 19.6, with scores ranging from three to 27.

Table 3 includes all the records we were able to obtain of normal subjects (not psychiatric patients) between the ages of 15 and 50 and with at least some high school education. We have tabulated under "High School" all subjects with some high school education, i.e., from one year of high school to high school graduate. Under "College" we have tabulated all subjects with one year or more of college including all persons with graduate training.

Sex Differences

In order to combine the scores of men and women it was obviously necessary to ascertain whether or not there was a difference in score due to sex.

For this study we took, at random, from our files the records of 87 women, 55 of whom were high school educated and 32 college educated. These records were then matched with the records of 87 males of similar age and education. No significant difference between means was found when the "t" test was applied. Logically, there seems to be little basis for the expectation of a sex difference. In addition, this study confirmed a smaller, previous study. We concluded, therefore, that the B-G scores were not a function of sex of the subject, and combined the records of our male and female subjects.

Drawing Ability

A serious obstacle to the use of the B-G test in clinical practice would have been a differential effect of drawing ability. To check on this very obvious possibility we compared the records of a class of 34 advanced fine arts students, attending an art school, with those of a group of college undergraduates matched for age and sex. The undergraduates, not art students, obtained a significantly lower mean score than the art students with score means of 11.1 and 18.3, respectively. We concluded, therefore, that drawing ability has little effect on B-G score. This finding may come as a surprise to some readers but it should be remembered that the instructions are specific about *not* sketching. In fact, our early experience with subjects of some drawing ability lead to the inclusion of the "no sketching" injunction.

What the significantly higher scores for the art students mean is a matter of conjecture. The art school was one of high scholastic standards, comparable to those of the college from which the matched undergraduates were obtained. Is there a process with respect to what the B-G is measuring making for the selection of art as a vocation? At any rate the higher scores for the art students, rather than the reverse finding, gave us greater confidence in our results.

The Effect of I.Q.

There is little doubt in our minds that B-G performance is correlated with I.Q. In fact, the records of mental defectives show marked deviations in performance (9). There was reason to believe, however, considering the development of the scoring system, that given normal intelligence, and normal ability to perceive and execute the designs, scores should be little affected by I.Q., within the age range of our normative population.

We collected records from a class of fourth year high school students and one adult evening class on whom Otis S.A. I.Q.'s were available (36). The age range of the subjects was from 17 to 27, the I.Q. range from 90 to 128, the number of subjects 64. Correlation of raw B-G scores with I.Q. yielded a correlation coefficient of —.16, which is not significant at the five per cent level of confidence.

An interesting confirmation of this relationship between I.Q. and B-G score for adults of I.Q. within normal limits is found in a study of the records of above average children. We had at hand the records of 46 children attending private school. Their age range was from 6 years 3 months to 9 years 3 months. Their Binet I.Q. ranged from 101 to 142. The correlation between B-G score and I.Q. was minus .05. We shall have more to say about the records of children later, but for the moment we wish to point out the similarity of relationship between I.Q. and B-G score both for adults and children.

These results are, we feel, in line with expectation based on the results of previous investigations (15, 47). Thus, we know that copying a circle and diamond drop out very early in the Stanford-Binet tests. Although the copying of simple designs may be an important index of maturation warranting its use as an item in an intelligence test for young children, it is not, and we would not expect it to be, a discriminating test of intelligence for normal adults. These considerations plus our finding, and those of Bender (9), lead us to the conclusion that for our population scores on the B-G are not a function of I.Q.

The Effect of Age

Previous studies (37) had suggested that a relationship exists between age and B-G score for an adult population of wide age range, but that, within limits, there was little effect of age, more specifically, that the range within which age had little effect on score seemed to be between the ages of 15 and 50. For our normal population of 271 subjects with high school education we obtained a correlation of .02 between age and B-G score, and for our normal population of 203 subjects of college education, a correlation coefficient of .03.

Qualitatively, we feel certain of a definite relationship between age and B-G score for the older age groups although we do not have sufficient data to prove our point. We have, for instance, four records of subjects with high school education as follows:

Age 55,	B-G	score	13
Age 63,	"	"	36
Age 65,	"	"	24
Age 68,	"	"	47

These, and the records of other older age subjects with only grammar school education indicate that our scoring system penalizes the subject for some aspects of performance common to old age, e. g., tremor.

For the 46 children's records previously mentioned in connection with I.Q., ranging in age from 6 years 3 months to 9 years 3 months, we obtained a correlation coefficient of minus .58 between B-G score and age in months. (Undoubtedly the restricted range in age attenuated the obtained correlation coefficient.)

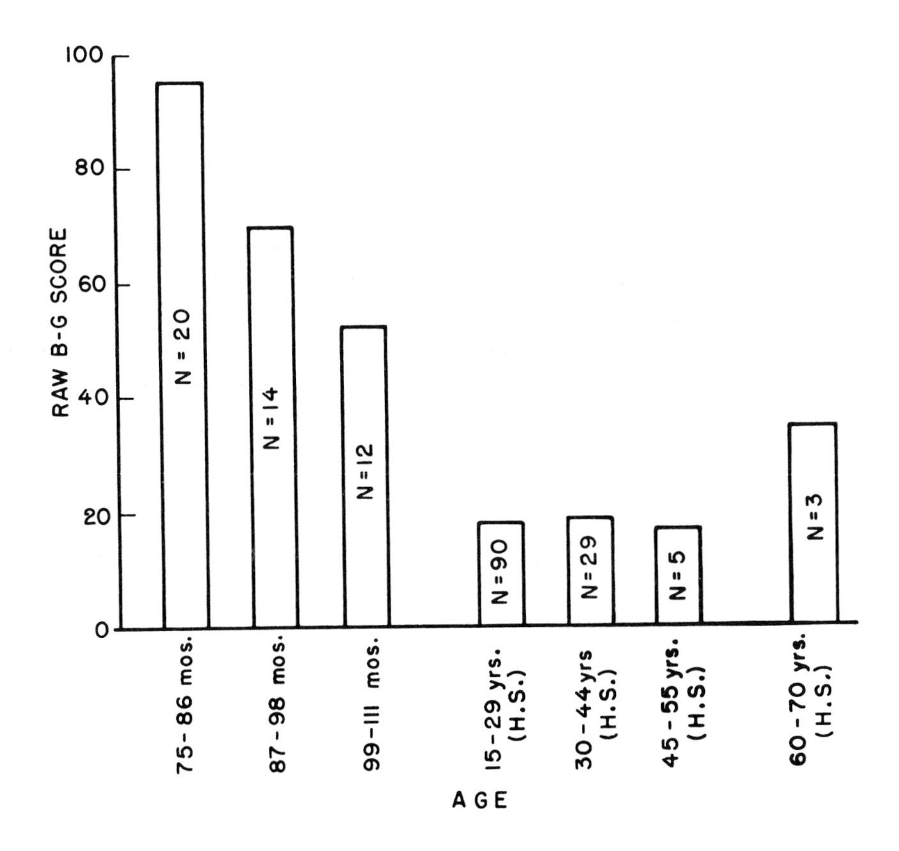

FIG. 3. Bar graphs suggesting relationship between age and B-G scores.

For what it is worth, in the light of our rather meager data, we present figure 3 which is suggestive of the relationship which may exist between B-G score and age. There seems to be little doubt, on a qualitative basis (9), of the maturational factor involved in reproducing the designs. Our data bear this out for the age ranges 6 years 3 months to 9 years 3 months. Our data also suggest that there is a leveling off between the ages of 15 and 50. Whether or not there is a decline in functions measured by us on the B-G test beyond the age of 50 is not known positively, but, as we have indicated, because of the nature of our scoring system it is very probable that the old age group would score higher than the means we have presented for the age group 15–50. This combination of data, qualitative and quantitative, leads us to the not unreasonable expectation that the reciprocal of B-G scores would, if we had sufficient data, make a function similar to that obtained for mental growth, with a decline in the curve for the old age groups (48).

We have taken the trouble to speculate somewhat on this point because of its theoretical interest. The test, as we score it, is measuring something which has to do with whether or not a subject is the patient of a psychiatrist, something which could be, perhaps, the ability to get along in the world without becoming psychologically ill. To put this in the terms we used in the first chapter, we might call it ego strength. It would be of some interest to be able to demonstrate that this is a lawful development.

The Effect of Education

Previous study with a smaller population had led us to hope that we might safely count on a lack of relationship between education and B-G score once we were past the first year of high school. In fact, this expectation influenced us somewhat in the data we gathered and the information we obtained as we gathered the data. Thus for a good many of our records we merely noted whether or not a person had been to college and whether or not he had one or more years of high school training. This unfortunate circumstance makes it impossible for us to calculate anything but a biserial correlation coefficient between education and B-G score. This we did for our entire normal population, obtaining a biserial correlation coefficient of .38, which is clearly significant.

The data in table 3 bear out the estimate of relationship suggested by the correlation coefficient. The raw scores of subjects with some college education are lower in every age grouping than those of comparable subjects with some high school education. Other statistics, the medians and interquartile ranges, bear out the difference between the high school and college populations. In addition, when we plotted our total distribution of raw scores we were confronted, much to our surprise, with a bimodal curve. It was this last, the plotting of the distribution, which gave us our first inkling of the difference between the high school and the college groups. It took some time and a good deal of statistical maneuvering before we came to accept the fact that there is a real difference between the groups.

We are at a loss to explain why this difference should be there, especially in the light of the relationship between B-G score and I.Q., and can only speculate upon its significance. It may be that the college group was generally more test-wise and thus less disturbed by the testing situation. It may be, as suggested by a psychiatrist friend of ours, that going on to college in our competitive society is, in general, an adaptive act related in some way to what we are measuring. Anyhow, the fact remains that we had two different populations based on education.

Z Scores

Fortunately, the shapes of the distributions and variances for the high school and college populations were similar. It seemed, therefore, that the best scheme for combining our populations was to convert the raw scores for each group separately into Z scores with mean of 50 and a standard deviation of 10. This we did and figure 4 shows the distribution of the total normal population. The smoothed frequency curve shown in figure 4 is somewhat skewed. We calculated skewness (g_1) according to a formula given by McNemar (34) and found it to be .6, which is considered moderate.

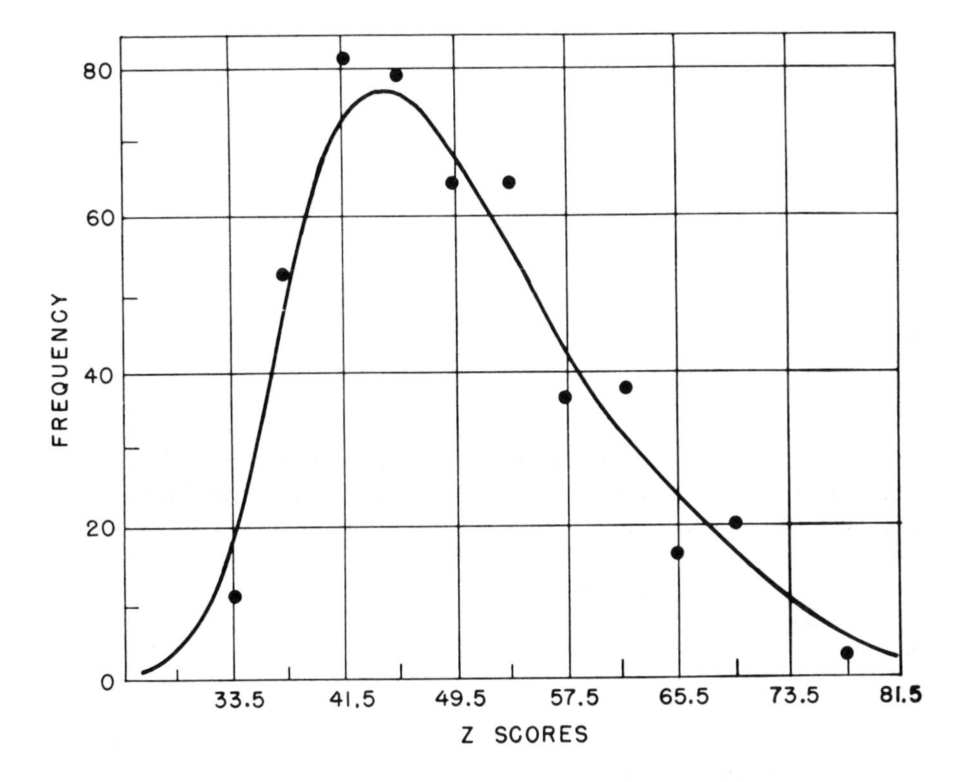

FIG. 4. Distribution of Z scores for normative population. N = 474.

Tables II and III in the Appendix give raw and Z scores for the high school and college populations, respectively. We have computed Z scores for raw scores up to 150, which, we feel, should take care of all scores apt to be encountered in practice. The necessary formulae are given in the Appendix for converting raw scores higher than 150 to Z scores.

Since our data have indicated that the B-G score is not a function of sex, drawing ability, and within limits, I.Q. and age, it is only necessary to know that an individual is between the ages of 15 and 50 and has at least one year of high school education to use our Z scores for comparative purposes. To get the corresponding Z score for an individual within these limits the appropriate table (in the Appendix), depending on whether the subject has a high school or college education, is consulted with the raw score and the Z score read off.

5: TEST VALIDITY

Records were obtained of psychiatric patients from various institutions and outpatient clinics in and about Providence. Table 4 shows the age, education, and mean raw score for the records of 323 patients thus obtained. With respect to diagnostic category patients were classified according to clinical diagnosis. For inpatients, most of whom were psychotic, clinical diagnosis was the result of a conference of two or more psychiatrists. For the outpatients, most of whom were neurotic, the diagnosis was usually made by one psychiatrist. In spite of the known unreliability of psychiatric diagnosis (6) there are two important facts about the patient population which we wish to emphasize: (*a*) they *were* patients of psychiatrists and had either voluntarily or otherwise obtained psychiatric care, and (*b*) they could be classified as either inpatients (primarily psychotic) and outpatients (primarily neurotic). There were so few inpatients who were not psychotic and so few outpatients who were, that we found it just as valid to retain the psychotic–neurotic dichotomy rather than to change to an in–versus–outpatient dichotomy. We would suggest that inpatients are generally in greater need of psychiatric care than outpatients. This consideration becomes important in the light of the increasingly

Table 4

Age and Education and Raw Score Means of Patient Population

	High School				College			
	PN f	Psychotic f	Tot. f	H.S. Mean Score	PN f	Psychotic f	Tot. f	Coll. Mean Score
15-19	15	11	26	41.6	2	0	2	49.0
20-24	30	13	43	38.6	16	11	27	36.0
25-29	51	21	72	37.8	5	11	16	31.3
30-34	17	19	36	38.3	8	7	15	32.9
35-39	9	7	16	40.8	10	6	16	36.5
40-44	7	5	12	37.3	5	6	11	39.5
45-50	8	13	21	47.0	4	6	10	46.5
Totals	137	89	226		50	47	97	
Mean Raw B-G Score	34.5	47.2		39.5	31.5	42.0		36.6
S.D.				21.3				20.5

greater scores from nonpatient though neurotic and psychotic. Of chief importance, however, for our validity study is the reliable fact that all our patients were patients of psychiatrists, and it is upon this dichotomy, patient versus nonpatient, that we primarily base our tests of validity.

No individuals with known organic involvement were included in our patient population. The chief fact influencing selection of cases was availability. For the outpatients the records are for the most part from consecutive cases, and constitute, with few exceptions, a hundred per cent sample of cases referred for treatment over the period during which we collected records. With regard to the inpatient population, we were somewhat selective in that we refrained from including the records of chronic, deteriorated cases. Thus, we only collected records from the intensive treatment wards of the State Hospital.[1] At Butler Hospital we began by testing all but the chronic and deteriorated patients in the hospital and then routinely obtained records from all new admissions to the hospital.

All the records of patients were scored by the authors. Some were scored with knowledge of the fact that they were the records of patients. We were, in scoring, aware of probable bias and attempted, insofar as possible, to maintain the same objective attitude as in scoring the records of nonpatients. Our scoring system is, however, partly subjective in the sense that the scoring of some items is a matter of judgment. We do not doubt, therefore, that it is possible the records of some patients may have received a higher score than they might have had we not known that they were patients. Our studies of validity with smaller groups in which all identifying data on the records were either removed or blocked out and the records of patients shuffled in with the records of nonpatients indicate, however, that such was not the case.

Table 4 should be compared with table 3. The mean scores for patients are higher in every age and educational category than the mean scores for the nonpatients. It should be noted that the standard deviation for the patients is about twice that for the nonpatients. When the two populations are tested for homogeneity of variance a significant F ratio is obtained, precluding the use of analysis of variance technique in our validity study.

Validity Studies on Matched Groups, Using Raw Scores.

In a previous study (37) validity coefficients were reported for two different samples of matched patients and nonpatients. In the first study, 23 patients were matched for age, sex, and education with hospital employees. All identifying information was removed from the 46 records. They were shuffled and given

[1] Thanks are due to Dr. J. Regan, Superintendent and Dr. H. Cronick, Chief of Intensive Treatment, for permission to test the patients of that institution.

to our departmental secretary to score.[2] From her scoring a biserial correlation coefficient of .83 was obtained. In a similar manner a second study was conducted with 126 normals matched against 71 patients for mean age and education. This study yielded a biserial correlation coefficient of .77.

A third study, previously mentioned in connection with reliability, in which the authors, separately, scored the records of 40 nonpatients, 40 patients diagnosed psychotic, and 40 diagnosed neurotic, all matched for age, education, and sex, yielded the following biserial correlation coefficients:

	Nonpt. vs. Psychotic	Nonpt. vs. Neurotic	Psychotic vs. Neurotic
Scorer A	.76	.70	.32
Scorer B	.79	.71	.39

In this study, as in the previous ones, all identifying marks were removed or blocked out on the records which were then shuffled. None of the subjects used in these validity studies were included in the item analysis. They were, in each case, separate groups not used by us in any other study of validity. They represent three separate population samples.

Validity using Z Scores

We now converted the raw scores of all the patients to Z scores based on our normative population. The mean Z score of the total patient population was 73.6 with a standard deviation of 22.4. The mean scores of psychotics and neurotics was 81.1 and 68.2, respectively. Total nonpatient versus total patient population yielded a biserial correlation coefficient of .74, nonpatients versus neurotics .73, nonpatients versus psychotics .91, and neurotics versus psychotics .35. All of these coefficients are comparable to those obtained from the previous studies of validity using raw scores, except that between nonpatient and psychotic, which we feel has been markedly influenced by the fact that a few psychotic patients obtained very high scores; this raised the mean of the psychotic population which, in turn, influenced the size of the biserial correlation coefficient. The fact that the test scores discriminate significantly between the scores of psychotics and neurotics contributes, in our estimation, to confidence in the validity of the scoring, and bears on the supposition that the test may be measuring something which has to do with the subject's ability to cope with his environment, as suggested in the first chapter. This follows if, as we suppose, psychotics (mostly inpatients) are less able to take care of themselves than neurotics (mostly outpatients).

---

[2] Miss Vera Toppi

Table 5
Cumulative Frequencies of Patient and Nonpatient Populations

Z	Nonpts. N = 474			All Pts. N = 323			PN N = 187			Psychotic N = 136		
	f	% Total	Cum. %	f	% Total	Cum. %	f	% Total	Cum. %	f	% Total	Cum. %
32-35	11	2.3	100.0	1	.3	100.0	1	.5	100.0	0	0	
36-39	53	11.2	97.7	3	.9	99.7	3	1.6	99.5	0	0	
40-43	83	17.5	86.7	8	2.5	98.7	5	2.7	97.8	3	2.2	100.0
44-47	79	16.7	69.2	10	3.1	96.2	7	3.7	95.1	3	2.2	97.8
48-51	64	13.5	52.5	16	5.0	93.1	10	5.3	91.4	6	4.4	95.0
52-55	64	13.5	39.0	20	6.2	88.1	14	7.5	86.1	6	4.4	90.6
56-59	35	7.4	25.5	23	7.1	81.9	16	8.6	78.6	7	5.1	86.2
60-63	37	7.8	18.1	40	12.4	74.8	26	13.9	70.0	14	10.3	81.1
64-67	16	3.4	10.3	34	10.5	62.4	24	12.8	56.1	10	7.4	70.8
68-71	20	4.2	6.9	24	7.4	51.9	15	8.0	43.3	9	6.2	63.4
72-75	10	2.1	2.7	32	9.9	44.5	17	9.1	35.3	15	11.0	57.2
76-79	3	.6	.6	14	4.3	34.6	10	5.3	26.2	4	2.9	46.2
80-83				10	3.1	30.3	8	4.3	20.9	2	1.5	43.3
84-87				18	5.6	27.2	7	3.7	16.6	11	8.1	41.8
88-91				9	2.8	21.6	3	1.6	12.9	6	4.4	33.7
92-95				8	2.5	18.8	3	1.6	11.3	5	3.7	29.3
96-99				12	3.7	16.3	7	3.7	9.7	5	3.7	25.6
100-103				6	1.9	12.6	2	1.1	6.0	4	2.9	21.9
104-107				8	2.5	10.7	5	2.7	4.9	3	2.2	19.0
108-111				9	2.8	8.2	2	1.1	2.2	7	5.1	16.8
112-115				5	1.5	5.4	0	0	1.1	5	3.7	11.7
116-119				2	.6	3.9	0	0	1.1	2	1.5	8.0
120-123				1	.3	3.3	0	0	1.1	1	.7	6.5
124-127				1	.3	3.0	0	0	1.1	1	.7	5.8
128-131				1	.3	22.7	0	0	1.1	1	.7	5.1
132-135				2	.6	2.4	2	1.1	1.1	0	0	4.4
136-139				2	.6	1.8				2	1.5	4.4
140-143				0	0	1.2				0	0	2.9
144-147				1	.3	1.2				1	.7	2.9
148-151				1	.3	.9				1	.7	2.2
152-155				2	.6	.6				2	1.5	1.5

Table 5 shows the Z score frequencies of the patients and nonpatients. Figure 5 shows ogives plotted from this table. The ogives were smoothed by inspection. Since we are unable to write regression equations from biserial correlation coefficients these ogives are the best we can offer as to the predictive power of the test, but we shall have more to say about this matter in a later section about the test as a screening device.

Z Scores and Wechsler-Bellevue Scatter

Several studies (38, 41, 42, 49) have shown that Wechsler-Bellevue scatter is correlated with extent of psychological disturbance. Two commonly used measures of Wechsler-Bellevue scatter are: (1) the difference between verbal and performance I.Q.'s, and (2) vocabulary I.Q. minus full-scale I.Q.

There were, in our files, the B-G records of 26 psychotics on whom we also had complete Wechsler-Bellevues. The records for this study were selected on the basis of availability and no other. We do not feel, therefore, that our findings with respect to the relationship between B-G scores and Wechsler-Bellevue scatter can stand as representative for the relationship, but we do believe that these findings contribute to confidence in the validity of our method of scoring the B-G.

Verbal and performance I.Q. differences were calculated for each of the 26 psychotic patients of this study. These were then correlated with B-G Z

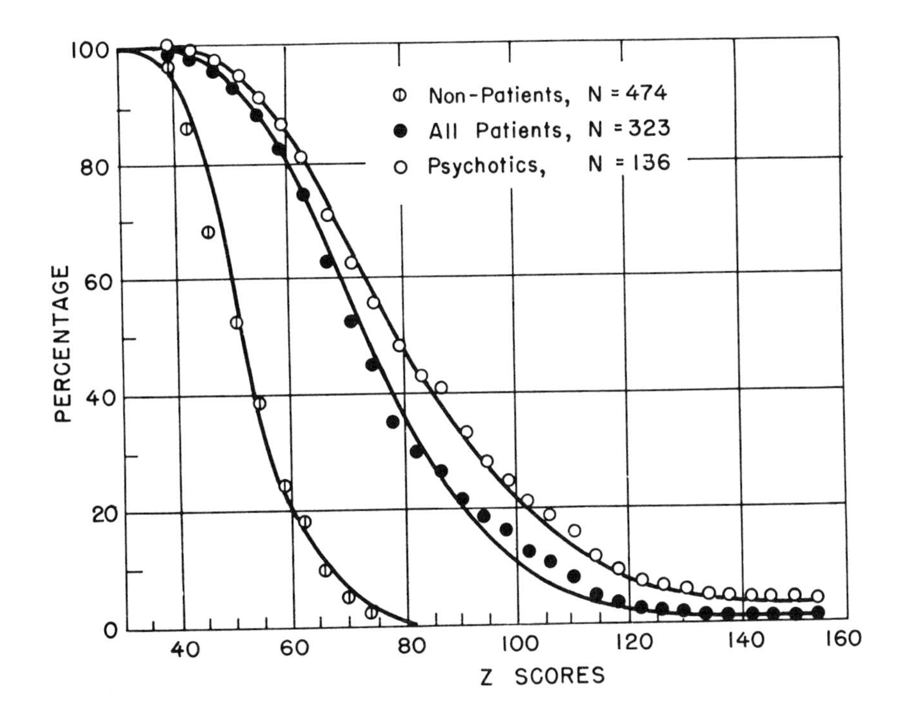

FIG. 5. Ogives of nonpatients and patients.

scores and a product moment correlation coefficient of .37 was obtained (P equals .05). When vocabulary I.Q. minus full-scale I.Q. scores were correlated against B-G Z scores a correlation coefficient of .55 (P less than .01) was obtained.

Z Scores and Prognosis

We were fortunate in being able to follow the course, through the hospital, of 65 inpatients to whom we had administered the B-G on admission.

It is customary at Butler Hospital when a patient is formally discharged to indicate on his record whether or not he has improved. If the patient has recovered from symptoms and seems capable of facing the problems of living which he has to encounter on leaving the hospital, or in other words, has affected what is usually called "social improvement," he is considered improved and it is so indicated on his record. If, on the other hand, he has not affected this social improvement and in the judgment of the psychiatrist his prognosis for coping with problems of living outside the hospital is poor, then he is considered unimproved, and it is so indicated on his record.

By the time we were ready to write this report we had, as we have mentioned, accumulated 65 records of inpatients tested by us on admission, who had been discharged from the hospital. The average stay of the patients was about three months. No attempt was made to control what happened to the patients during their stay in the hospital. Some had electroconvulsive therapy, others psychotherapy, some both and still others very little but routine hospital care. As far as we could determine no systematic factors with respect to treatment were operative within this population of 65 patients.

Of the 65 patients 43 were discharged "improved" and 22 discharged "unimproved." The mean Z scores of B-G's administered on admission were 61.0 for the improved and 81.8 for the unimproved, a mean difference of 20.8, significant at the one per cent level of confidence when the "t" test was applied. These records had been scored routinely as part of the total patient population. Scorers had no knowledge of whether or not a patient was to be discharged as improved or unimproved at the time of scoring.

The plain fact seems to be that the patient who, upon admission, gave a low scoring B-G record, had a better chance to improve as the result of hospitalization than the patient who produced a high scoring record. The significance of such a finding is a matter of some theoretical interest. We recognize the oversimplification involved in the concept of "ego strength" at this time, but for want of better terminology, we should suggest that those patients with low scoring records have greater ego strength than those with high scoring records, if, as we have indicated, ego strength is one factor making for successful coping with the problems of living in our society. (By successful, here, we mean without becoming psychiatrically ill.)

Our criteria in this study leave us open to criticism and, rigorously speaking, we are defenseless. Very practically, however, we have little doubt about the significance of our results. Anyone who has seen an acutely ill, confused, hallucinated patient change, during the course of hospitalization, to one free from symptoms, with some awareness of how ill he has been, and grateful at being once more restored to sanity, will understand what it means to discharge a patient as improved. We might add, also that the designation "improved" is not given lightly.

The B-G and Electroconvulsive Therapy (ECT).

Several investigators (35, 44, 45) have used the B-G to follow the effects of ECT and have been able to show marked impairment of performance with mounting psychological confusion as result of shock treatment. At Butler Hospital we have used the B-G as scored by us along with other tests to estimate the effects of ECT (39). We shall present some of our findings in a series of graphs.

Figures 6, 7, and 8 show B-G raw scores before, during, and after a series of electroshock treatments for three cases. Figure 6 contrasts B-G scores on two matched patients, case A undergoing an ECT series and case B with no particular therapy other than routine hospital care. The B-G was administered

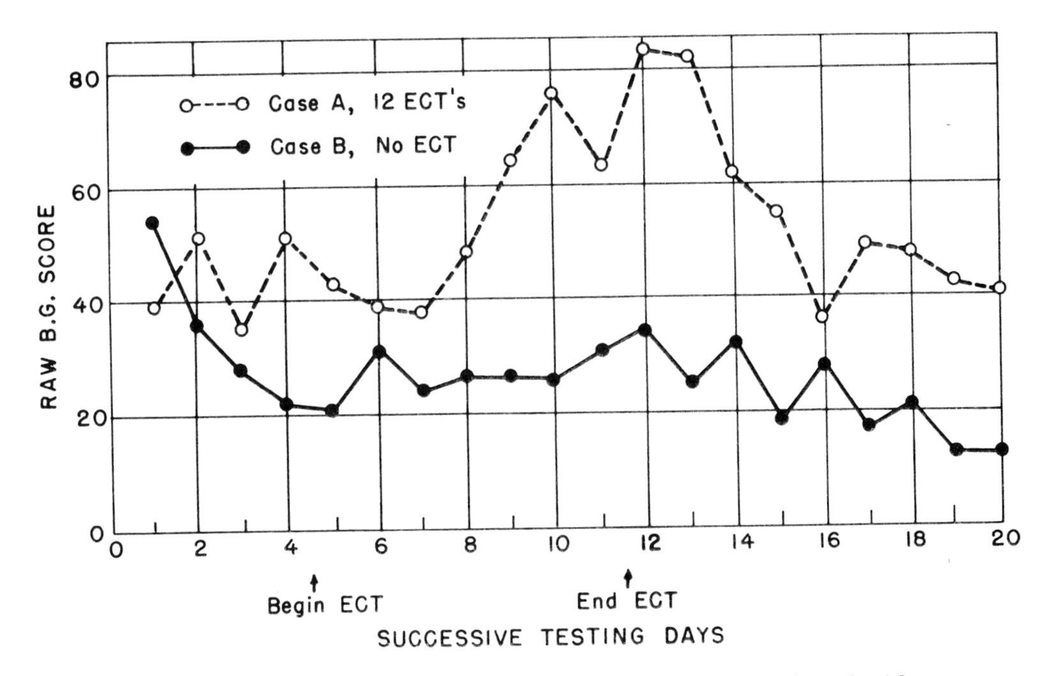

FIG. 6. Contrasting performance on two matched cases, with and without ECT.

every other day before and after the ECT series and twenty-four hours post-shock during the ECT series to case A, and to case B at the same time. Both patients were admitted to the hospital about the same time. Both were psychotic. Case B, the nonshock patient, made a fairly rapid adjustment to the hospital and a few days after admission was transferred to a convalescent ward. This improvement is reflected in lowered B-G score. Two months after admission the patient was discharged improved. Case A received a series of twelve electroshocks. The B-G score reflected the initial improvement observed clinically after the first three treatments. Thereafter continued treatment resulted in mounting confusion, observed clinically and reflected in increasing B-G scores. Some days after the cessation of treatment the patient became more tractable, showing clinical improvement, which was reflected in a lowering of B-G score.

Figures 7 and 8 show the raw B-G scores of two other patients, each given a series of 12 electroshocks. In each case the B-G was administered as for cases A and B. For all three shock patients, cases A, C, and D, intial clinical improvement as a result of ECT is shown in lowered B-G. Mounting confusion with continued ECT is shown in increased B-G score. Improvement after ECT is shown in lowered B-G score. These graphs are representative of our findings when using the B-G test to follow the effects of ECT. We feel that this ability of B-G scores to reflect the patient's reaction to ECT contributes to confidence in the validity of the method of scoring.

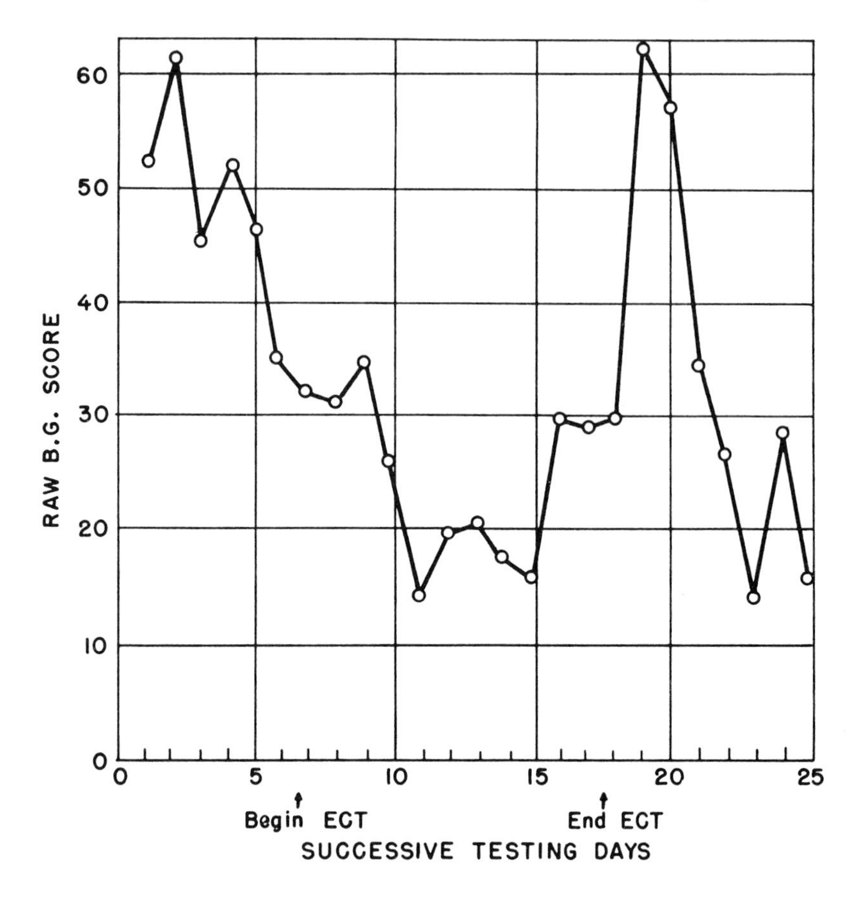

FIG. 7. B-G test scores and ECT (case C).

The B-G as a Screening Device

The B-G test as we score it is a fallible instrument whose validity is based on fallible, very gross criteria. The best that we can say for it is that it seems very crudely to be estimating some aspect of behavior which has to do with whether or not an individual is apt to be the patient of a psychiatrist. The test should, it seems to us, be used in conjunction with other estimates of proneness to psychiatric illness. It is easily administered and easily scored and could profitably be used as a rough check of other procedures. In the absence of other procedures the test does considerably better than chance in its ability to screen out individuals who are apt to be psychiatrically ill. We do, therefore, recommend its use as a screening device, providing its limitations are known.

A glance at the ogives of figure 5 will show that no matter how low a cutoff score is set it is bound, for our populations, to include some patients. On the

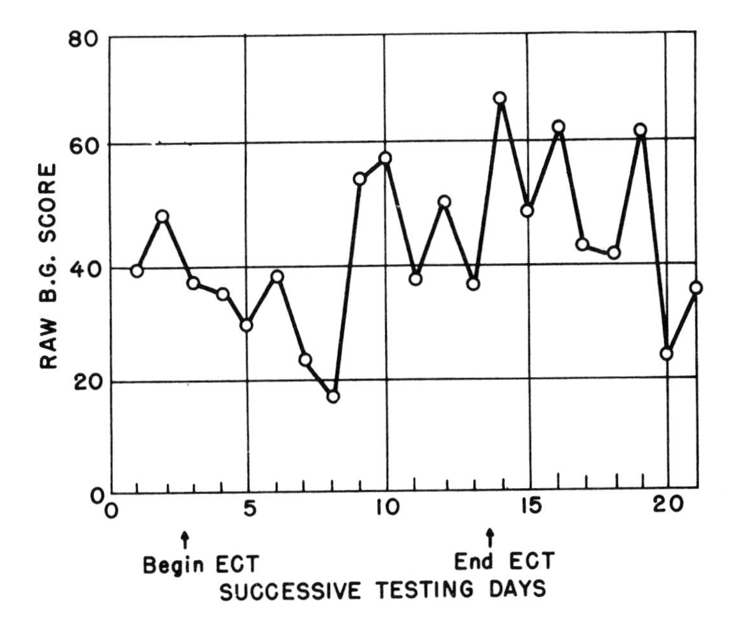

FIG. 8. B-G test scores and ECT (case D).

other hand, none of our nonpatients obtained a Z score over 79. If we select a Z score of 50, the mean of the nonpatient population, as a cutoff score, we can see, from figure 5, that we would have screened out 94 per cent of the total patient population and 96 percent of the psychotics, but also, we would have screened out about 50 per cent of the nonpatients.

One standard deviation above the mean, or a Z score of 60 would seem to be a reasonable cutoff score since theoretically that should include 84 per cent of the nonpatient population, which seems about right in view of what is known about the incidence of psychiatric illness in the so-called normal population. Erecting a vertical from this score on figure 4 we see that it would actually screen out about 20 per cent of the nonpatients instead of the expected 16 per cent. This discrepancy is due to the fact that the distribution of scores on our nonpatients is somewhat skewed. In addition to the 20 per cent of nonpatients a cutoff score of 60 would also have screened out 82 per cent of the total patient population, 86 per cent psychotic and 79 per cent neurotic. In fact, a Z score of 60 is just about the point of crossing for frequency polygons of the patient and nonpatient populations, plotted on the same baseline.

We may look at cutoff scores in terms of theoretical probabilities based on the normal curve. If, for instance, a subject receives a Z score of 80 the chances, based on our data, are about 1 in 1000 that he will be normal. With a Z score of 72 the chances are 1 in 100 that he will be normal. With a Z score of 67 the chances are 5 in 100 that he will be normal. It should be borne in mind, however, that in thus considering cutoff scores the fact of skewness in the distribution of the normative population will reveal discrepancies between theoretical expectancy and our data. The extent of this discrepancy can easily be ascertained from figure 5 or table 5. Thus table 5 shows that, actually, no nonpatient received a Z score of over 79 and that 2.7 per cent of the nonpatients, rather than one per cent, received a Z score of 72 or higher. Even so, based on our data, we would feel fairly safe in betting that a subject with a Z score of 72 or over was in need of psychiatric help. The other side of the picture is that such a high Z score as a cutoff would also admit many subjects in need of psychiatric help. A Z score below 72 does not mean a subject does not need psychiatric help. About 48 per cent of our patients obtained Z scores below 72.

If the purpose is to screen out as many subjects as possible who may be in need of psychiatric help without too much regard for the number of individuals not in need of psychiatric help who are also screened out, then a cutoff score should be found which will screen out the maximum number of patients, and compatible with that, admit the maximum number of nonpatients. A Z score of 50 would be such a cutoff point. It would screen out, for our population, 94 per cent of all patients—96 per cent of psychotics and 91 per cent of neurotics.

Z scores between 50 and 72 would seem, therefore, to be suspect. With Z scores of 50 and below we can be fairly confident that the subject does not need psychiatric help, and with Z scores of 72 and above we can be fairly confident that he does. All this would be beautifully true if we presented a perfectly reliable method of scoring, which we do not. The authors found an average raw score difference of four points between themselves. It is probable that other scorers will vary as much as that, if not more. We suggest, therefore, on very practical grounds, that cutoff scores slide between 60 and 80, with the latter as a limiting score.

PART II:

CLINICAL USE OF THE BENDER-GESTALT TEST

6: INTRODUCTION

Our findings have suggested that the deviations scored by us are not, for our normative population, measuring drawing ability or I.Q. within average limits. Test scores are correlated with whether or not an individual is the patient of a psychiatrist. There is some indication that they correlate with the severity of psychiatric illness. What little data we have been able to present beyond the age norms of our standardizing population suggest a correlation with age below the age of 15 and above the age of 50. Using the test to follow the effects of ECT also suggests that scores are correlated with psychological confusion resulting from ECT. We have a little data, which added to the qualitative findings of Bender, suggest that scores are also correlated with mental deficiency and damage to the cortex.

Clinical use of the test, therefore, becomes extremely complicated. The quantitative score is, we feel, helpful in diagnosis when such things as the possible effects of cortical damage or mental deficiency are ruled out by other means. Even so, the burning question often put to psychological examiners—"Is he psychotic?"—is not very well answered by quantitative score except in extreme cases. When the test is used as an instrument of clinical diagnosis, as distinguished from its mechanical use as a screening device, the examiner is not content with the probabilities based on quantitative score. He needs to make the best prediction possible for the individual case. To do this with the Bender, clinical judgment must be added to quantitative score. It is our purpose, in the sections that follow, to supply knowledge of the test upon which clinical judgment can be based; this judgment, when added to quantitative score will, we hope, increase the accuracy of prediction in the individual case.

Our first approach will be to examine the records of children. At the age of six, children of normal I.Q. begin to make drawings of the designs which look like the stimuli. We have found it possible to score the records of children of this age although we do not feel that the scoring is as reliable as it is for adults. With children below age six, our method of scoring is not feasible. The age six, therefore, will be our baseline of judgment for drawings of individuals beyond that age. Knowledge of the performance of children is, we feel, a necessary basis for intelligent use of the test as a clinical instrument. Psychotics, for instance, are "regressive" on this test in the sense that they reproduce the designs in a manner similar to children. Adults with cortical damage produce drawings similar in some respects to very young children, as do mental defectives. To use these facts one needs to be well grounded in the scorable deviations common to children of various ages. We shall, therefore, devote considerable space to the records of normal children.

A persistent problem facing the psychological examiner is the question of so-called " organicity." "Does the psychological record show signs indicative of damage to the cortex?" is a frequent and reasonable question often asked of the examiner. The answer to such a question involves the difficult and plaguing task of attempting to differentiate between deviations in performance due to psychogenic and histogenic, genogenic or chemogenic factors (14). The B-G test cannot, in the absence of other data, answer that question, except occasionally in extreme cases which are also clinically apparent. There are times, however, when it provides valuable confirmatory evidence to other procedures. In order to understand how it is possible to use the test in this manner it is necessary to know, insofar as possible, what deviations are primarily due to psychogenic factors, and what are due to actual cortical deficit. [Our use of the term "cortical deficit" implies malfunctioning of, and actual damage to, the cortex owing to either genogenic, histogenic or chemogenic factors (12).]

Our data for cortical deficit and the differential diagnosis of psychogenic disorders has not been gathered systematically. Although we shall, within the limits of our data, present quantitative evidence for our discussion, we shall not hesitate to employ qualitative observations where these seem reasonable, and illustrate with the single case where this seems logical.

7: THE RECORDS OF CHILDREN AND THOSE WITH CORTICAL DEFICIT

Bender, in her original monograph, reports findings on 800 children, ages three to eleven, inclusive, and presents normative data for these ages, describing and illustrating representative productions for the different ages. Her data were drawn from nursery schools, public schools, hospital wards and outpatient departments of pediatric and psychiatric services. Presumably, her normative data are based on all of these samples. She writes (9, p. 112): "All of the figures are satisfacorily produced at the age of eleven years. Adults add only a certain motor perfection, or perfection in detail in sizes and distances." What Bender means by satisfactory will be presented in our discussion of the individual designs, at which time we shall present our own findings with a limited population. The fact that children make satisfactory drawings is of first importance in considering the records of adults. Bender's data, therefore, are basic to the discussion which follows. Although we shall summarize and build upon her work in this chapter, we recommend a careful reading of her mongraph for a thorough knowledge of children's performance on this test.

In the chapters on standardization and validity, scores on children's records were reported to illustrate the effect of age and intelligence on B-G scores. We shall report that study in greater detail here, preparatory to our discussion of children's records. These B-G records were obtained from 46 normal children (not patients) who ranged, in age, from 6 years 3 months to 9 years 3 months. The children were first, second, and third grade students in a private school. They were equally divided for sex. With a few unavoidable exceptions owing to illness, etc., 100 per cent samples were obtained from the classes.[1] The children were above average I.Q. with a mean Stanford-

[1] For these records and those of the psychologically disturbed children used in the study of validity, we are indebted to Miss Janet Youngs, interne at the Emma Pendleton Bradley Home and Butler Hospital. Records of disturbed children were also collected for us by Mr. Kennison Bosquet, Psychologist for the Providence Child Guidance Clinic, to whom we wish to express our thanks.

Binet I.Q. (Form L) of 120, ranging from 101 to 142. Mean raw B-G scores for these records, divided into three groups are given below.

Age Range in months	N	B-G Scores Mean Raw
75–82	20	95
87–98	14	70
99–111	12	52

Correlation of age, in months, with raw B-G score yielded a product moment coefficient of –.58, which is significant at the one per cent level of confidence. (P equals .01 when r equals .37.) Our mean scores show a fairly regular progression downward with increasing age. The results, therefore, suggest that, in contradistinction to the scores of adults of the normative population, age is an important determinant of scores for children. This finding is, of course, merely corroborative of what is knwon of the development of drawing ability in children. This topic is reviewed by Bender (9).

The product moment correlation coefficient between I.Q. and age, for this population, is + .12, and between B-G score and I.Q., –.05. For what it is worth we partialled out the effect of age and obtained a partial r of + .03 between B-G score and I.Q. We conclude, therefore, that for this superior population the B-G score is not a function of I.Q. This finding enabled us to group our data by age without regard for I.Q.

Since the significance of our data depends on the validity of the deviations scored by us, an attempt was made to obtain some estimate of the validity of our method of scoring for children. We were able to match 12 of our non-patient children with 12 patients suffering from psychogenic disorders from the Emma Pendleton Bradley Home. This data on the matched groups is summarized below.

	Age in Mos.		Stanford Binet I.Q.		Mean Raw B-G Score
	Mean	*Range*	*Mean*	*Range*	
Normals	100.0	80–111	117	104–137	56.8
Patients	100.0	80–113	114	98–139	90.8

For the mean difference of 34 score points a "t" of 4.29 was obtained, indicating a significant difference between the groups. Although certainly not conclusive, our finding suggests that in addition to measuring maturation, our method of scoring the B-G records is measuring in children something similar to that which it measures for adults. This latter measurement is, however, complicated by the important effect of age and cannot be quantitatively useful without age norms, which are not, at present, available. Our purpose, at this point, however, is not to standardize the test for children, but rather, to use knowledge of the deviations made by children as a basis for qualitative clinical judgment of adult records.

Table 6
Children's Raw B-G Scores by Design
Mean Raw B-G Score by Designs

Age Group in Months	N	1	2	3	4	5	6	7	8
75-86	20	11.6	14.9	11.7	8.7	9.0	12.5	13.2	9.4
87-98	14	7.9	6.4	8.5	8.4	8.7	10.1	10.0	6.5
99-111	12	4.2	5.8	10.3	5.4	4.4	7.5	6.5	4.4

Table 7
Age Norms for Essential Accuracy of Reproduction.*
(After Bender 9, p. 132)

Designs

Age at which design reproduced	1	2	3	4	5	6	7	8
6	x			x	x			
7	x			x	x			x
8	x			x	x	x		x
9	x			x	x	x		x
10	x	x		x	x	x	x	x
11	x	x	x	x	x	x	x	x

*See text for definition of this term.

For the population of 46 normal children mean scores were calculated by designs for each age group. Table 6 shows this data. Table 6 shows a fairly regular decrease in scores on all designs with increasing age, except for design three. We have prepared table 7 based on Bender's findings which shows that design three is the most difficult for children, not being correctly reproduced until the age eleven. Bender's data, table 7, indicated that by the age of seven designs one, four, five, and eight are correctly reproduced. Table 6 based on our population of 46 normal children of superior intelligence shows that these are the same designs receiving the lowest mean scores for the age group 6–7. Except for design 6 similar agreement will be found for the other age groups of our popuation. Bender shows design 6 correctly reproduced at the age of eight, with the criterion that they be simply two wavy lines crossing at right angles. Our scoring system on the other hand demands closer adherence to the stimulus.

Having indicated a good deal of agreement between our findings based on 46 children of superior intelligence with those of Bender based on a much larger population we shall consider each design and the deviations found in children's drawings. We shall then use this knowledge in the appraisal of adult records.

Table 8.
Certain Deviations of Normal Children, Normal Adults, and Psychotics Contrasted

	Children (Ages in yrs. and mos.)				Adults	
	6-3 7-2 N = 20	7-3 8-2 N = 14	8-3 9-2 N = 12	6-3 9-2 N = 46	Psychotics N = 46	Normals N = 46
Distortion (All Designs)	32	7	5	44	7	0
Rotation (All Designs)	40	16	11	67	25	0
Workover (All Designs)	21	15	12	48	88	15
Fig. Missing (All Designs)	3	2	1	6	3	0
Confused Order	5	0	2	7	3	0
Overlapping Designs	7	3	0	10	16	4
Compression	2	2	2	6	5	1
2nd Attempt (All Designs)	2	4	2	8	36	5
Circles for Dots (Designs 1, 3, 5)	4	2	0	6	2	0
Perseveration (Designs 1, 2, 6)	18	6	2	26	1	0
Wavy Line (Designs 1, 2)	35	34	19	88	54	37
Shape Circle (Design 2)	13	3	1	17	12	0
Deviation in Slant (Design 2)	5	6	2	13	18	5
Dashes or Dots (Design 2)	2	0	0	2	8	2
Blunting (Design 3)	1	1	0	2	1	0
No. Dots (Design 3)	14	6	5	25	5	3
Sq. and Curve Not Joined (Design 4)	4	2	0	6	1	0
Angles (Design 6)	16	9	5	30	15	8
Fig. Not Crossed (Designs 6, 7)	1	1	0	2	0	0
Angles Ext. or Miss. (Designs 7, 8)	31	14	12	57	38	15

Design 1.

Table 7 shows that, according to Bender, this design is correctly reproduced by six year olds. She defines an acceptable reproduction as follows (9, p.116): "Very small loops or dots; length of series resembles that of test form." For our population of superior children 6–7 years of age we found a definite tendency for them to perseverate the dots, often going clear across the page with the line of dots. This tendency seems to be rare for children over eight in our population. Another common deviation found in our children was a definitely wavy direction of movement rather than the straight line demanded by the stimulus. Our 6–7 year old children also displayed a tendency to work over dots which resulted in something that looked like a filled circle, or a thickened blob of pencil markings of peculiar shape. The substitution of large circles for dots, although it occurred, was rare even for our 6–7 year olds. All of these deviations seem to show decreasing incidence with age. The incidence of these deviations for our population of children is shown in table 8. For this design, among children of normal I.Q., age 6–7, without psychogenic illness, we should not be surprised to obtain in a given record, a wavy line of large circles running across the entire page. Figure 9 shows several typical reproductions. Above the age of 9 we should look with some suspicion on the presence of large circles, or the perseveration of the line of dots.

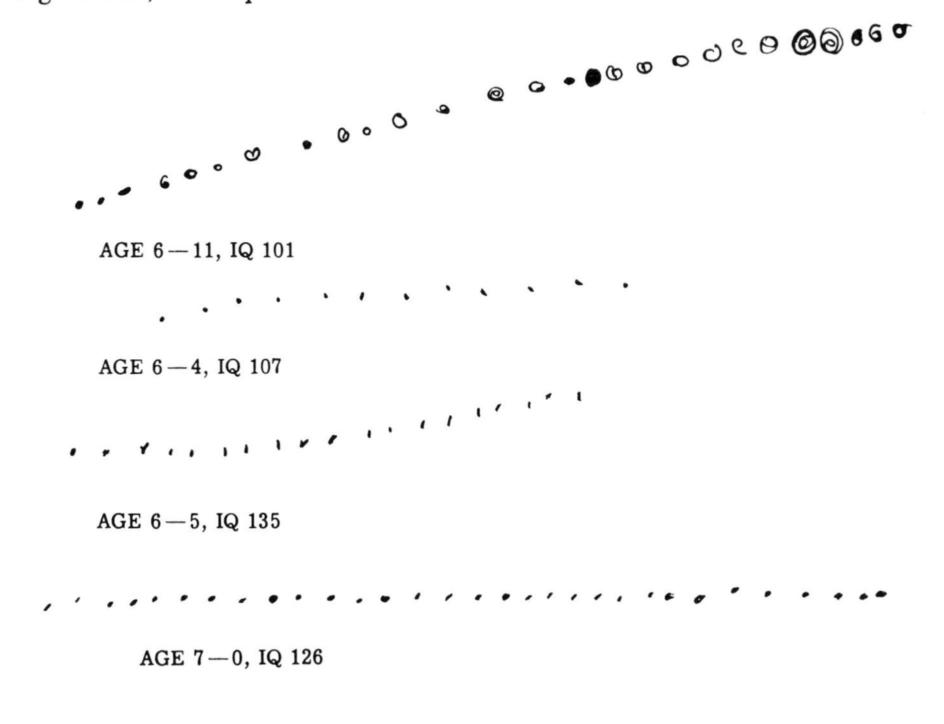

FIG. 9. DESIGN 1. Examples of children's drawings.

Design 2

Table 7 indicates that this design is satisfactorily produced by Bender's population at ten years of age in a manner defined by her as follows (9, p.118): "Small good loops in a horizontal series of vertical rows of three, plus an attempt to slant the first row and add the others so that the whole figure slants." Sixty per cent of her six year olds, however, performed according to the following criterion (p. 118): "Vertical rows of three small loops; the rows are perseverated two or more times in the horizontal direction; figure is likely to be uneven, but there is no attempt to slant the rows."

Table 6 shows that design 2 is the most difficult for our population of 6–7 year olds. The chief deviations making for high scores in this group are:

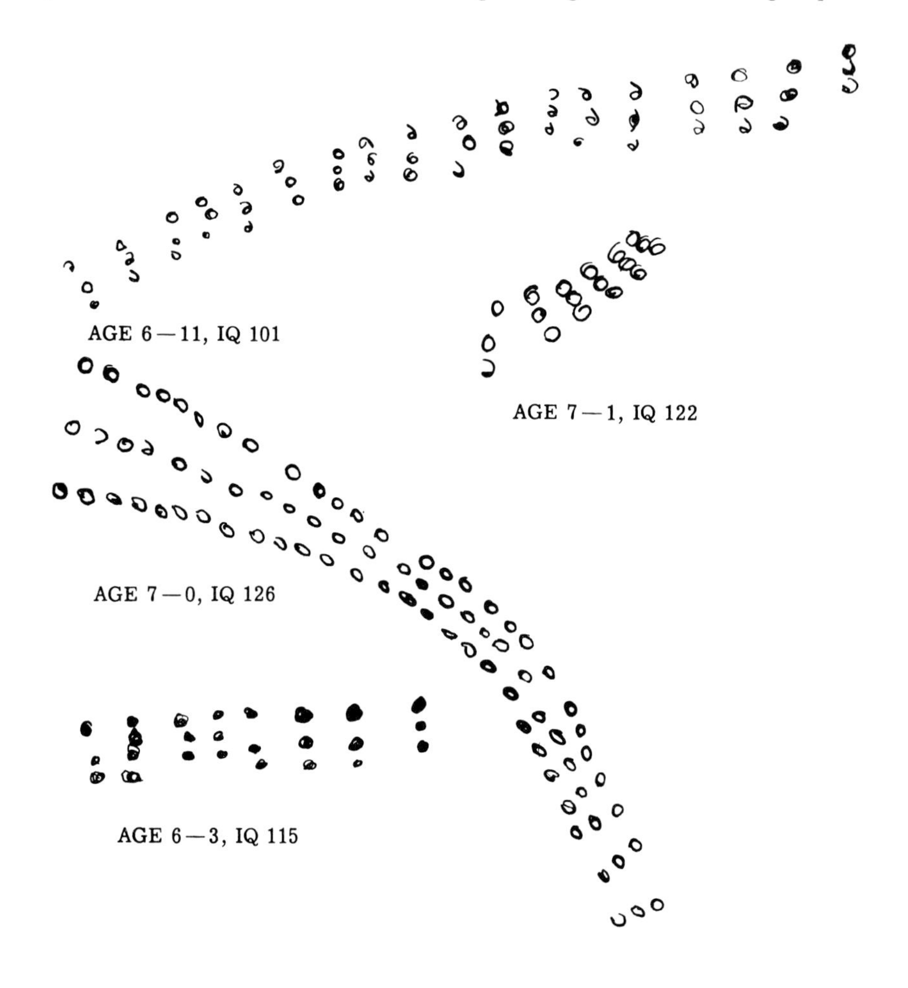

FIG. 10. DESIGN 2. Examples of children's drawings.

1) Wavy rather than straight horizontal line of circles, as in design 1.

2) Perseveration of columns with a tendency to make columns all the way across the page, as in design 1.

3) Deviations in vertical slant. We have not found that a slant differing from that of the stimulus is a discriminating deviation, provided that the slant, whatever it is, is maintained. We have found, however, that variability in slant is discriminating. (See Appendix for item analysis.) Deviation in slant was not uncommon in our population of children. Table 8 shows the incidence of this deviation. It tends to decrease with increasing age.

4) Distorted shape of the circle. Our 6–7 year olds tended to make circles of irregular shapes. There is a marked drop in this tendency with increasing age.

5) Rotation of the design either by turning the stimulus card or by inversion of the reproduction from a properly oriented stimulus card. This deviation is extremely common in our population of 6–7 year olds, and not uncommon with our 8–9 year olds; there is some decrease in incidence at the latter ages.

In summary for this design, we should say that normal expectation for a 6–7 year old would be a reproduction of irregularly shaped circles in columns of threes, with variable slant, in a wavy line across the page, with the likelihood that the entire test design will be rotated, and the possibility, although rare, that dots or dashes will be substituted for circles. Figure 10 shows typical drawings obtained. For individuals above the age of nine we should be suspicious of dots or dashes substituted for circles, the presence of perseveration, irregularly shaped circles, marked deviations in vertical slant, and sharp changes in direction of movement.

Design 3

According to Bender successful reproduction, not attained on this design until the age of 11, is defined as follows (9; p.120): "Single dot with a dextrad series of dotted angles of progressively larger size, with more dots. The last angle may tend to become arc-shaped." In agreement with Bender our data indicated continuing difficulty with this design for all of our normal children. (See table 6.) A recognizable representation of an arrowhead is, however, reproduced by the age of six. Eighty per cent of Bender's population of six year olds produced a drawing defined by her as follows (9, p.120): "Single dot with a dextrad series of dotted arcs of progressively larger size with more dots. The first two arcs in the series contain the correct number of dots, but in the last two the number is only approximated. The last two arcs may tend to become straight lines. (In a very few cases small loops are made instead of dots.) The number of arcs is the same as the test form."

Our data indicate the following deviations primarily responsible for high scores in our 6–7 year olds.

1) Rotation, as in design 2.

2) Number of dots incorrect. There may be more or less dots than in the stimulus. The incidence of this deviation tends to decrease with increasing age.

3) Distortion of stimulus so the reproduction, merely a conglomeration of dots, does not look at all like the stimulus. (See manual for definition of this deviation.) This deviation is rarely encountered in children above the age of eight.

4) Blunting of the arrowhead, i.e., obliteration of point of arrowhead. This deviation, although encountered, is rare even for our 6–7 year olds. It is not found in our population above the age of eight.

5) Substitution of circles for dots, as in design 1.

In summary, normal expectation for this design from a 6–7 year old of average intelligence without psychogenic illness, might be characterized as follows: a rotated reproduction consisting of circles, dashes, or dots, or a combination of all three, in which the point of the arrowhead is blunted, and the number of dots in the reproduction may be more or less than those in the stimulus. There is a rough resemblance to the stimulus; complete distortion is rare after the age of seven. Figure 11 shows typical drawings obtained. For subjects above the age of nine reproductions which include blunting, the substitution of all large circles for dots, or distortions, would deviate seriously from expectancy. Less serious, but probably significant, would be an incorrect number of dots and rotation.

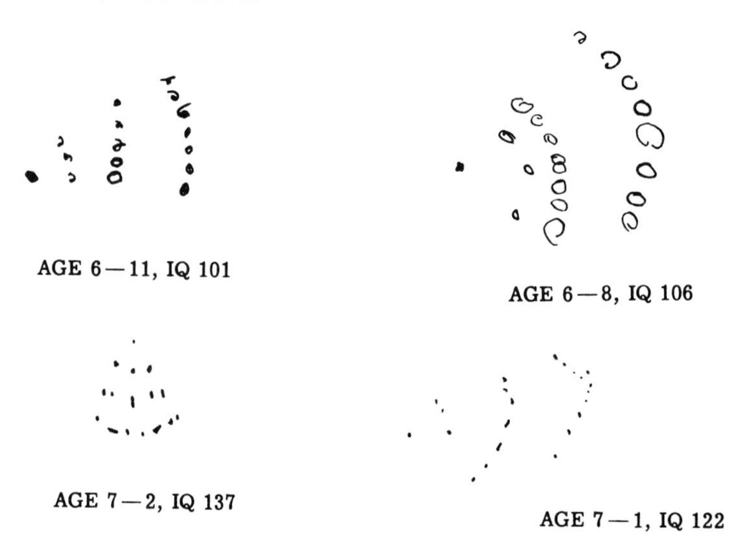

FIG. 11. DESIGN 3. Examples of children's drawings.

Design 4

Successful reproduction of this design, accomplished by 75 per cent of Bender's population of six year olds, is defined by her as follows (9, p. 122): "The first figure is a good open square. There is an indication of an actual oblique relationship." Table 6 indicates that this design is the easiest for our 6–7 year old children. Failure to make a reasonable reproduction of the stimulus was rare. Although asymmetry of the curve was a common deviation, it was not uncommon with normal adults, and we did not feel it worthwhile tabulating. The factors primarily responsible for high scores in our population of 6–7 year old children were the following:

1) Rotation, either of the whole design, or of the curve on the square.

2) Failure to join the square and the circle. This deviation is rare in our seven year old children, and did not occur in the records of eight year olds.

Normal expectation for this design among children 6–7 years old would seem to be an open end square with a curve roughly similar to that of the stimulus, not necessarily joined but oriented approximately to one of the closed ends of the square. The whole design may be correctly reproduced but rotated. (See figure 12.) Marked deviations from expectancy for subjects over nine years of age would be distortion of the stimulus, and failure to join the square and the curve.

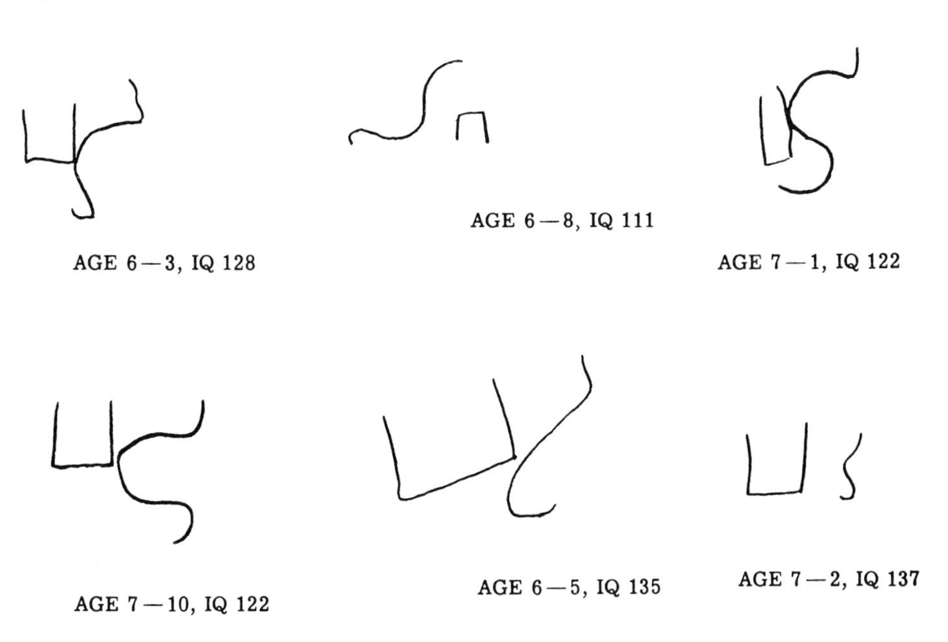

FIG. 12. DESIGN 4. Examples of children's drawings.

Design 5

This design is reproduced by 60 per cent of Bender's population of six year old children in a manner defined by her as follows (9, p. 124): "Dotted arc resembling the test form in size. The dotted dash goes in the right-handed, upward direction. There may be some disorientation in the clock-wise direction." Table 6 indicates that this design was second to design 4 in ease of reproduction for the 6–7 year olds. All of them were able to draw rough approximations of the stimulus. There were no extreme distortions, although solid lines substituted for dots (scored as "distortion") did occur. The deviations chiefly contributing to high scores for our population of 6–7 year olds follow:

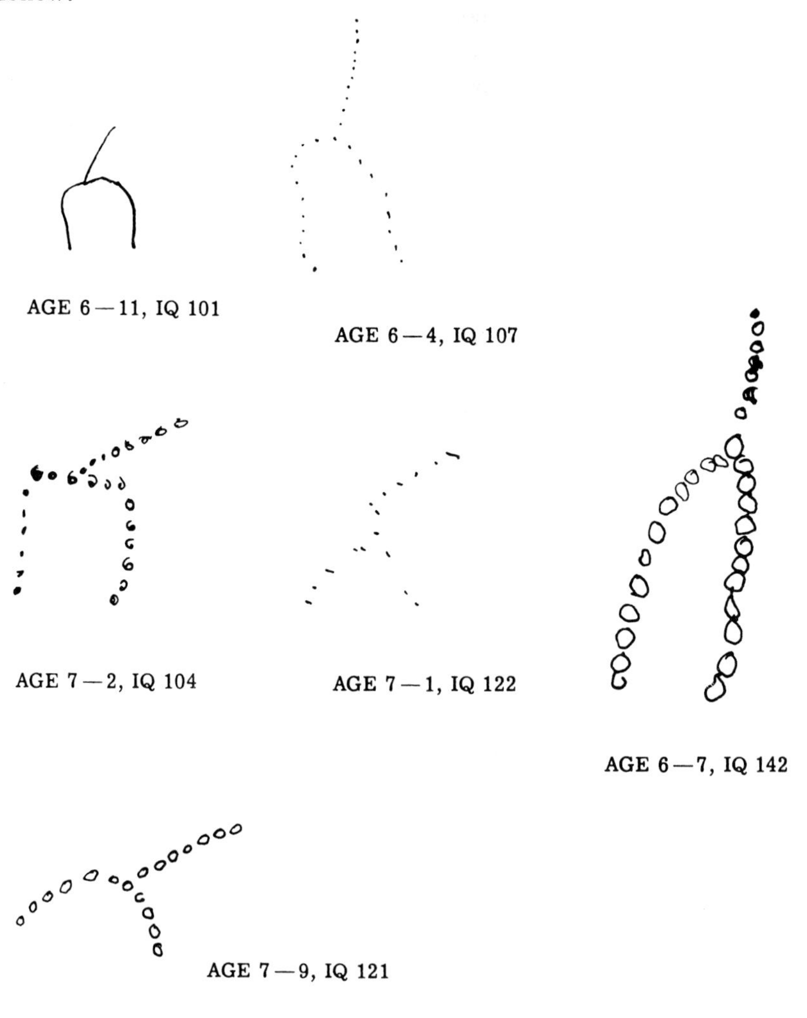

Fig. 13. Design 5. Examples of children's drawings.

1) The substitution of solid lines for dots. This deviation, not uncommon for the 6–7 year olds, was not encountered in the records of children over eight.

2) The substitution of large circles for dots, as in designs 1 and 3.

3) Rotation of the entire design, or the extension, as in design 4.

We should expect, in the records of normal children 6–7 years old, a reproduction similar in shape to the stimulus, made with solid lines, large circles, or a combination of dashes, dots and circles. The whole design may be rotated, or the extension may be rotated on the arc. The number of dots in the design should approximate the number in the stimulus although fewer dots are not an unexpected finding. (See figure 13.) For the records of subjects over nine years of age, we should not expect to find the substitution of solid lines for dots, the substitution of large circles for dots, or fewer than 10 dots in the arc. Rotation of the extension or the entire design is rare in the records of children over nine years of age.

Design 6

According to Bender this design is not produced with any degree of accuracy until the age of eight (see table 7), and it is not until the age of 11 that uniform curves crossing at an oblique angle are produced. Her data show, however, that 60 per cent of her six year olds produced drawings defined by her (9, p. 126) as "two wavy lines crossing at right angles." Table 6 indicates that this design remains a difficult one for our population, being, next to design 3, the most difficult for our 8–9 year olds. By the age of six, however, reproductions roughly similar to that of the stimulus are obtained, with deviations which are on a continuum with older age groups.

The deviations primarily responsible for high scores in our population of 6–7 year olds follow:

1) Extra curves, i.e., five or more curves, or angles, are found in the reproduction rather than the four of the stimulus. This tendency we have called "perseveration," as in designs 1 and 2. It is rare in our children above the age of eight.

2) Rotation of the entire design or of the vertical curve. This deviation is not infrequent in our eight year olds.

3) Angles instead of curves. This tendency is also encountered in eight year olds. The incidence of angles in six year olds derives from the fact that they have a tendency to make a series of arches rather than sinusoidal curves, whereas in the eight year olds an occasional angle may be substituted for a sinusoidal curve.

4) Distortion. This tendency is not common even with the 6–7 year olds. When found it arises from the fact that although two wavy lines crossing each other are reproduced there is little resemblance to the stimulus.

5) Part of the design missing. This deviation is noted when there are less than three curves in a line. Only two of the 6–7 year olds were scored for this deviation.

6) Failure to cross the lines. None of our 6–7 year olds failed to produce crossing curves. We note this deviation here for its significance in later discussion.

In summary of this design, we should expect, from a normal child 6–7 years old, two crossed wavy lines with two or more curves in each line. There may be many more than two curves, e.g., seven or eight. The curves may be roughly sinusoidal or a series of arches. The whole design may be rotated. The vertical curve may cross the horizontal at almost any angle. (See Figure 14.) We should expect, in a subject of over nine years of age that the curves would be roughly sinusoidal, that there would be not more than five or six curves to a line and not less than three, and that there would not be a consistent substitution of angles for curves.

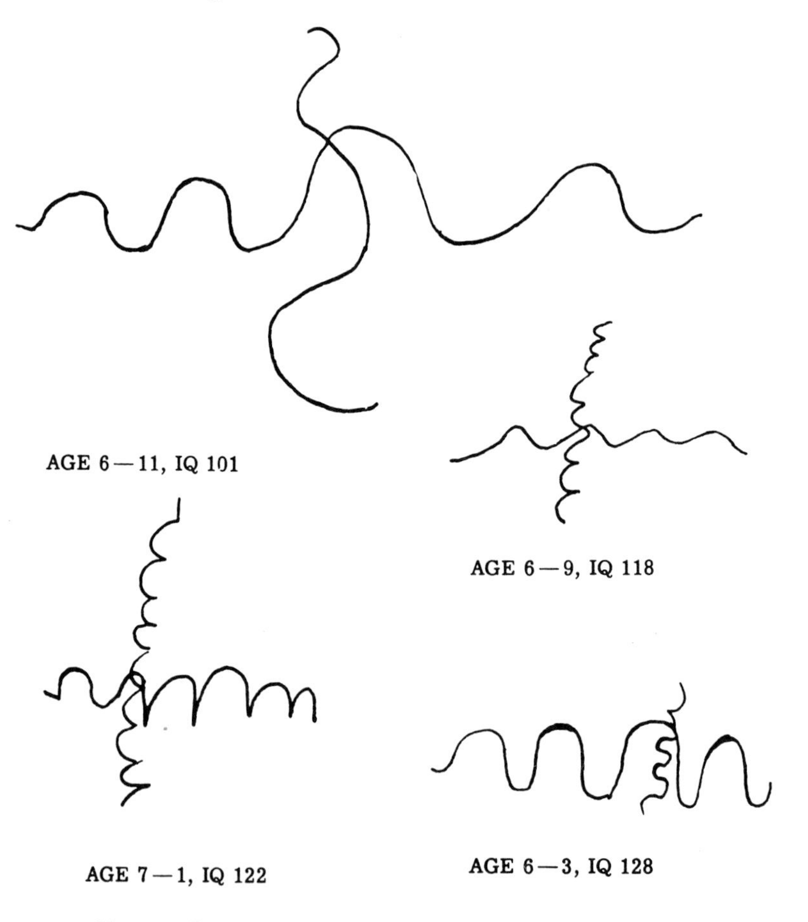

Fig. 14. Design 6. Examples of children's drawings.

Design 7

This design is not satisfactorily produced until the age of 10, according to Bender. Productions at this age are defined by her as follows (9, p. 126): "More or less good hexagonal forms which overlap. One figure is usually larger and differently shaped than the other." Our data (table 7) suggest that this design is a difficult one for our population of children, being one of the most difficult at each age group. We find that even at the age of nine, although there are no gross deviations from the stimulus, there are a sufficient number of minor deviations so that high scores on this design are common.

Chiefly responsible for high scores in our population of 6–7 year olds are the following deviations:

1) Angles extra or missing. This deviation was common. "Angles extra" usually resulted from a straight line with kinks in it, "angles missing," from failure to make a proper hexagon. There is a fairly high incidence of this deviation in our 8–9 year olds.

2) Rotation, either of the entire design, or of one hexagon upon the other. Thus, instead of forming an acute angle between them, the two hexagons may be at right angles to each other, or there may not be any angle at all, one hexagon being simply placed on top of the other.

3) Distortion. This deviation is common in 6–7 year olds, rare in 8–9

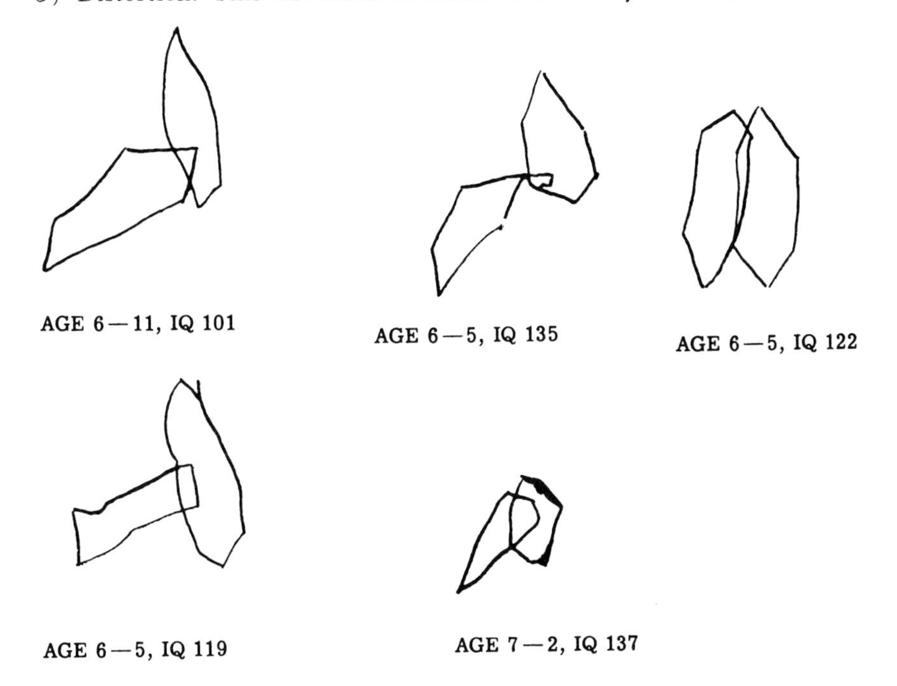

FIG. 15. DESIGN 7. Examples of children's drawings.

year olds. It arises out of the fact that although two overlapping figures are reproduced, one or both of them bear little resemblance to a hexagon.

4) Part of design missing. This deviation is rare in our 6–7 year olds. We list it because of its significance for later discussion.

5) Failure to cross hexagons. This deviation, also, is very rare in 6–7 year olds. Bender's data indicate it to be more common for five year olds.

For this design then, we would expect the reproductions of 6–7 year olds to consist of two overlapping figures which may or may not look very much like hexagons. Angles are, however, present in the reproduction, although, there may be more or less than six angles to a figure. The figures may be joined at almost any angle. (See figure 15.) From subjects over nine years of age we should not expect marked deviations from the stimulus. We should expect overlapping figures resembling hexagons. There may be angles extra or missing, but not to the extent that part of the design is missing.

Design 8

According to Bender this design is satisfactorily produced by the age of seven in a manner defined by her as follows (9, p. 130): "More or less carefully formed hexameter with inside figure a fairly good diamond." Her data indicate that her six year olds do only slightly less well on this design than her seven year olds. Our data suggest this to be one of the easiest figures for our population of children, with deviations similar to that of design 7.

We should expect normal 6–7 year olds to reproduce a design roughly similar to the stimulus, with an outside figure containing angles, more or less than six; and an inside figure, smaller, with more or less than four angles. (See figure 16). The entire design may be rotated. The inside figure may overlap the boundaries of the outside figure, or it may not touch them.

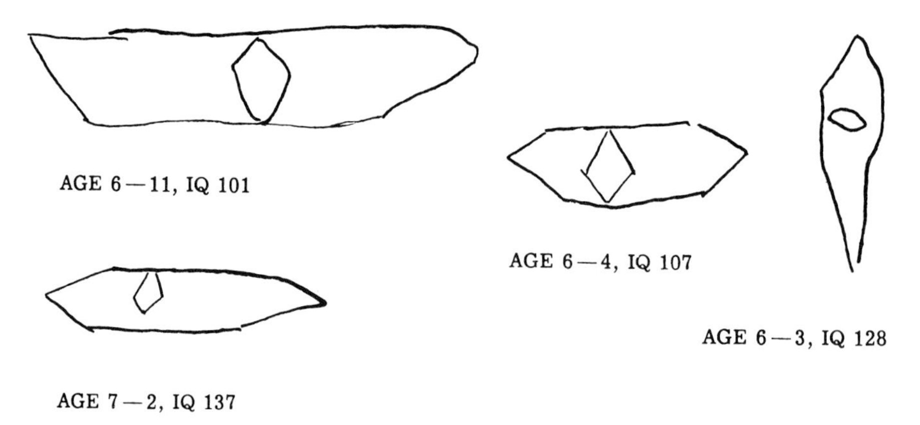

Fig. 16. Design 8. Examples of children's drawings.

Whole Configuration

Certain deviations scored by us have to do with the arrangement of the designs on the paper, called *whole configuration score*. Deviations contributing to high scores for our 6–7 year olds in this aspect of the test follow:

1) Order. Failure to follow a logical order was common, but order so haphazard as to be considered confused was relatively uncommon even for our 6–7 year olds.

2) Overlapping designs, i.e., designs 3 and 4 overlapping. This deviation was not uncommon for 6–7 year olds. We should say it is rare for 8–9 year olds.

3) Compression of all designs into one half of the alloted space. This deviation occurs but is not common in our population of children.

4) Second attempt, i.e., the execution of the designs more than once. Where this occurs more than twice it may take on the character of perseveration. This latter aspect, perseveration, was very rare even for our 6–7 year olds.

With respect to the arrangement of the designs on the page, we should expect for normal children, 6–7 years old, that reproduction might not be placed in a logical order, that designs might overlap, that they might all be compressed into one half of the page, or that a design might be reproduced more than once. For subjects over nine years of age we should not expect confused order. We should not expect second attempt amounting to perseveration. (See Appendix for examples of children's drawings.)

In discussing each design we have taken the ages 6–7 as our base age because at that age we first obtain reproductions in which the majority of deviations scored by us are continuous with the scorable deviations found in the records of adults. We have contrasted these with the age nine because by that age children are able to make reasonable facsimiles of the stimulus. Bender writes (9, p. 133): "The ages over seven add very little more than an improvement of obliquity, and an increase in the numbers of combinations." Thus by taking the age of nine as our contrasting age we feel fairly safe in suggesting that the incidence of deviations common to 6–7 year olds, and not common for ages of nine or above, is indicative of at least failure in normal maturation.

Our data has shown that deviations scored by us are correlated with psychogenic illness. We would postulate, now, that it is possible there are two kinds of deviations, one kind resulting from psychogenic illness and one kind from failure in maturation, or organic causes. We suggest, (*a*) that the deviations common to children below age nine, and not common to psychotic adults, are indicative of damage to the cortex when found in adults of average I.Q., and (*b*) that the deviations common in the records of children below age nine, and also common in the records of psychiatric patients of average I.Q.

without damage to cortex, are indicative of psychogenic disorders when found in the records of adults.

In an attempt to distinguish between these two kinds of deviations we have prepared table 8, which summarizes what we feel to be the important deviations discussed in connection with each design. In order to prepare this table we selected at random from our files, 46 adult normals and 46 adult psychotics, without regard to age or education. We simply counted the deviations shown for each of the groups of children and for the adult normals and psychotics. Table 8 shows that some of the deviations common in children are also common in psychotics, and, in some instances, not uncommon in the records of adult normals. These deviations, obviously, are not indicative of lack of maturation on an organic basis. We have not calculated confidence levels for the difference in occurrence of the deviations because we do not believe that the findings shown in the table represent anything conclusive. We present the table merely to show that it is possible from our data to get results similar to opinions we might have advanced based on clinical experience with the test. We have not made a quantitative study of the records of mental defectives, or of individuals suffering from damage to the cortex. We are now, at this point in our discussion, merely in the process of adding to the clinician's experience with the test so that he may, to the quantitative method of scoring the test, add qualitative observations which may increase the possibility of accurate diagnosis. We should not, therefore, be happy if table 8 be considered a table of "signs."

The interested clinician should, however, examine table 8 carefully. The findings suggested there accord well with what we have found to be true in clinical practice. Take, for instance, perseveration in designs 1, 2, and 6. This deviation occurs 18 times in the 6–7 year olds (90%), 14 times in the 7–8 year olds (43%) and twice in the 8–9 year olds (17%), a total of 26 times for all 46 children. It occurs only once in the records of the 46 adult psychotics and not at all in the records of the norma. adults. This deviation should now be contrasted with wavy lines in designs 1 and 2, which is fairly common in the records of children, psychotics, and normal adults. Wavy line, obviously, is not the kind of deviation we are interested in at this point. We are, however, interested in perseveration, and other deviations with a similar frequency distribution, e.g., square and curve not joined in design 4, figures not crossed in designs 6 and 7, several attempts at the same design amounting to perseveration, circles substituted for dots on designs 1, 3, and 5. Deviations of this sort suggest primitivation of reproduction similar to those found in the drawings of individuals suffering from discernible, structural damage to the cortex. They are also found, to some extent, however, in the reproductions of indivuals suffering from psychogenic illnesses, and cannot, therefore, be applied blindly. In addition, unless some other information is available it is difficult to distinguish between the records of mental defectives and of individuals suffering from organic brain diseases or traumatic injury to the brain.

Bender writes (9, p.75): "It seems that the gestalt function is more involved the nearer the lesion comes to the occipital region." Later, in the same paragraph she writes (p. 75): "Thus, in a general way, we may conclude that the area most probably involved in disturbances of the visual motor gestalt function, as exemplified by these copied test forms, is that between the temporal, parietal and occipital lobes of the dominant hemisphere." The area of the lesion, therefore, is also important in the type of deviation observed. Our experience is in agreement with Bender's observation. Lesions in the occipital lobe are apt to be reflected in the more primitive deviations such as the inability to cross the curves of design 6 or the hexagons of design 7. On the other hand, we have observed very little disturbance in the ability to reproduce the Bender design in individuals with frontal lobotomy or lobectomy. Circumscribed lesions, especially in the nondominant hemisphere, result in less disturbance in the ability to reproduce the design than pervasive lesions and acute, confusional states following trauma to the cortex. It would be difficult indeed to apply "signs" to such complex phenomena!

In general, where the I.Q. is within average limits and indications of primitivation are found in the record, damage to the cortex may be suspected. This criterion should, however, be used with caution. The same type of clinical reasoning needs to be applied to the B-G as to other kinds of psychological tests. Thus, for instance, although some kinds of perseveration are found in the records of psychotics, extreme instances of perseveration are usually found only in the records of individuals suffering from damage to the cortex or mental deficiency. If, for example, we were given the record shown in figure 17, we should with little hesitation categorize it as "organic." It shows perseveration in designs 1 and 2, blunting in design 3, substitution of circles for dots in designs 1, 3, and 5, inability to cross over in designs 6 and 7, and distortion of several designs. We should be right, of course, because it is the record of a mental defective, 18 years of age with a Wechsler-Bellevue I.Q. of 34. It is not the record of an individual suffering from trauma to the cortex or acute organic brain disease. It could be the record of an individual in advanced stages of a vascular disorder like cerebral arteriosclerosis, but his illness would be far advanced. It is our guess that any individual of normal intelligence giving a B-G like that shown in figure 17 would exhibit very prominent indications of acute cerebral disorder.

Figure 18 shows the record of another mental defective, age 14, with a Wechsler-Bellevue I.Q. of 32. In addition to other indications of primitive reproductions this record shows rotation in almost every design. Now, according to table 8, rotation is not uncommon in psychotics, but note, twenty-five rotations for 46 subjects suggests an average of less than one rotation per record.

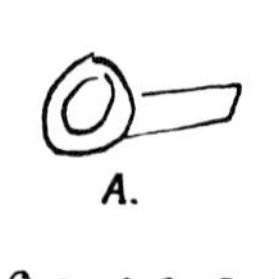

FIG. 17. C.A. 17–10, W-B I.Q. 34. (Design numbered by the authors.)

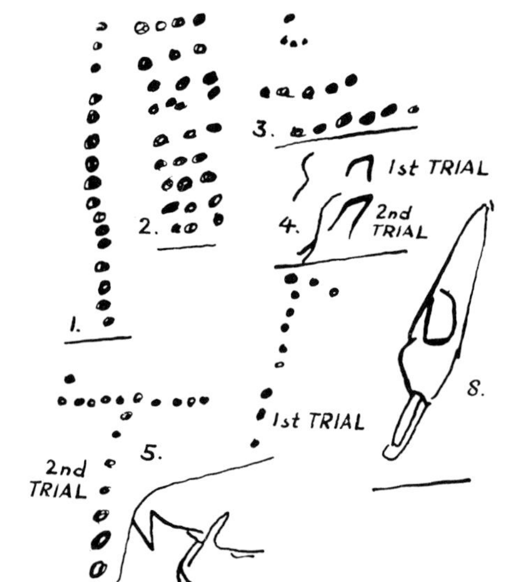

FIG. 18. C.A. 13–11, W-B I.Q. 32, S.B. I.Q. 50, M.A. 4–3. Cornell Coxe M.A. 5–3, I.Q. 61. (Designs numbered and lines drawn by the authors.)

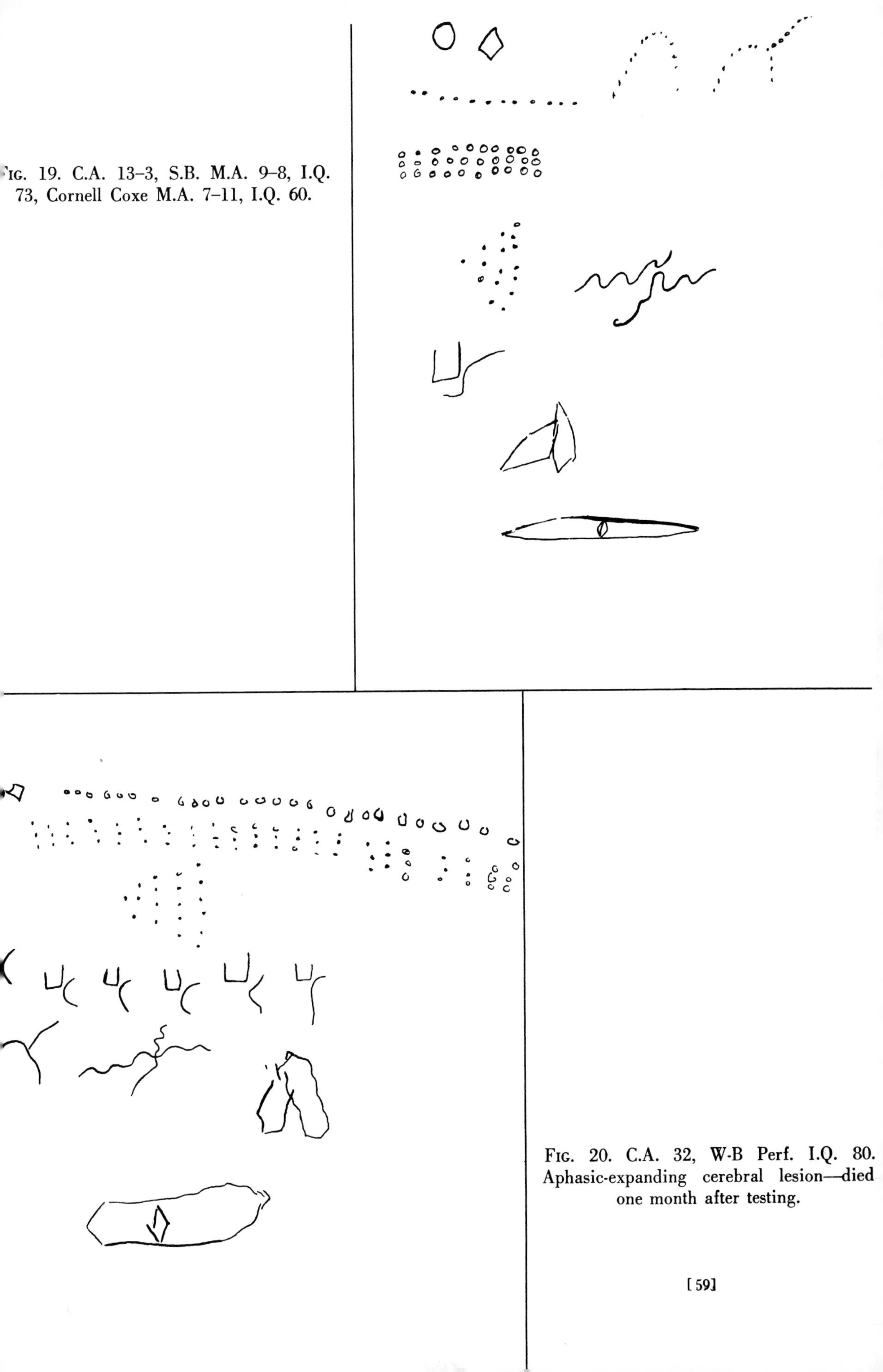

FIG. 19. C.A. 13–3, S.B. M.A. 9–8, I.Q. 73, Cornell Coxe M.A. 7–11, I.Q. 60.

FIG. 20. C.A. 32, W-B Perf. I.Q. 80. Aphasic-expanding cerebral lesion—died one month after testing.

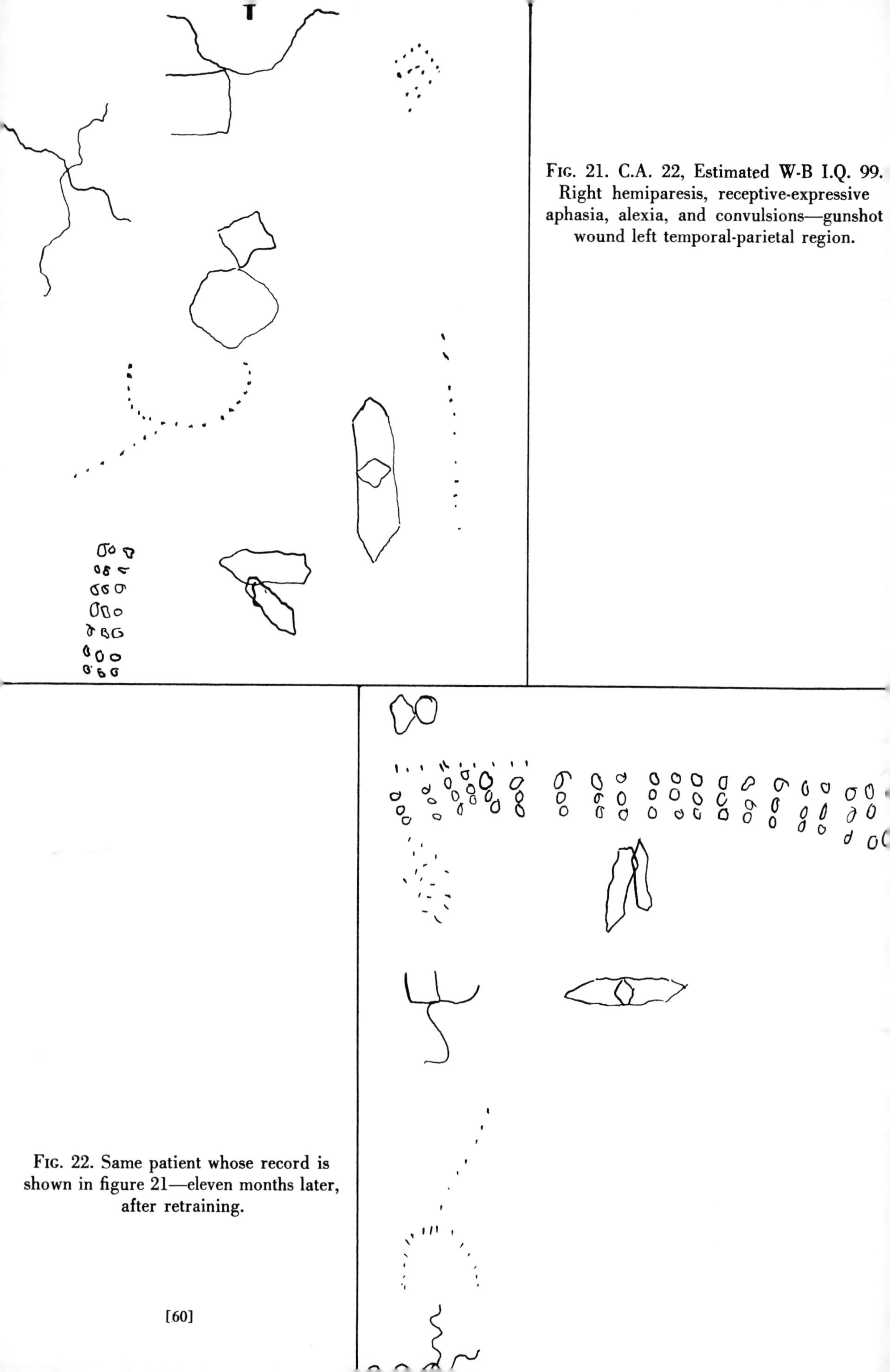

Fig. 21. C.A. 22, Estimated W-B I.Q. 99. Right hemiparesis, receptive-expressive aphasia, alexia, and convulsions—gunshot wound left temporal-parietal region.

Fig. 22. Same patient whose record is shown in figure 21—eleven months later, after retraining.

Fig. 23. C.A. 22, W-B I.Q. 90, encephalopathy left temporal-parietal area.

Fig. 24. Same patient whose record is shown in figure 23, seven months later, after retraining.

All the designs of figure 18 are rotated. Such a finding is far beyond expectancy even for a confused psychotic, it is much more in line with expectancy for very young children.

Figure 19 shows the record of an individual of borderline I.Q., age 13 years 3 months, Stanford Binet I.Q. 73. Note that with increasing I.Q. the number of indications of primitivation of forms is less. The square and curve of design 4, are not joined; and the curves of design 6, not crossed. Less serious deviations are the second attempt of design 5, and the tendency to distortion on designs 7 and 8. Compare these, now, with the record shown in figure 20, which was obtained from an individual of 32 with a Wechsler-Bellevue performance I.Q. of 80. Note the extreme perseveration exhibited in designs 1, 2, 3, and 4, the distortion of design 5, and the inability to overlap the hexagons in design 7. The arrangement of the designs on the page, the size, and the order are good. We should guess that the occipital lobe is involved, but we should also guess that the lesion is not circumscribed, i.e., that other parts of the brain are affected owing to the extent of primitive deviations. This patient died of an expanding lesion one month after being tested.

Figure 21 is that of a 22 year old patient, estimated I.Q. 99. At the time of testing he was suffering from a right hemiparesis, receptive and expressive aphasia, complete agraphia and alexia and convulsions—the result of a gun shot wound in the left temporal-parietal region. The test was executed with the left hand since the patient did not have the use of his right hand, although he had been right-handed prior to injury. All the designs are rotated. The order is confused. There are a number of columns missing in design 2. The execution of the individual designs is in general good, allowing for the fact that the patient had to use an unaccustomed hand in drawing. The square and curve of designs 4 are joined. The curves of design 6 are crossed and the hexagons of design 7 overlap. We should guess that the occipital lobe is not involved. If that be so then the effect of the lesion is not pervasive enough to be generalized in its effect on cortical functioning, and we should consider it a circumscribed lesion. This record should be compared with that of the expanding lesion shown in figure 11. Figure 22 shows the record of the same individual as in figure 21 eleven months later, after retraining in the use of the left hand and in speech. Figure 22 shows good order and absence of rotation, but perseveration in design 2 suggests the continuing effect of damage to the cortex.

Performance on the B-G test can indicate damage to the cortex only when the damage shows its effect by pronounced disturbance of the ability to execute the test. We know that nine year old children can reproduce the designs without marked deviation from the stimuli. When, therefore, an individual is functioning at a maturational level of nine years with respect to his ability

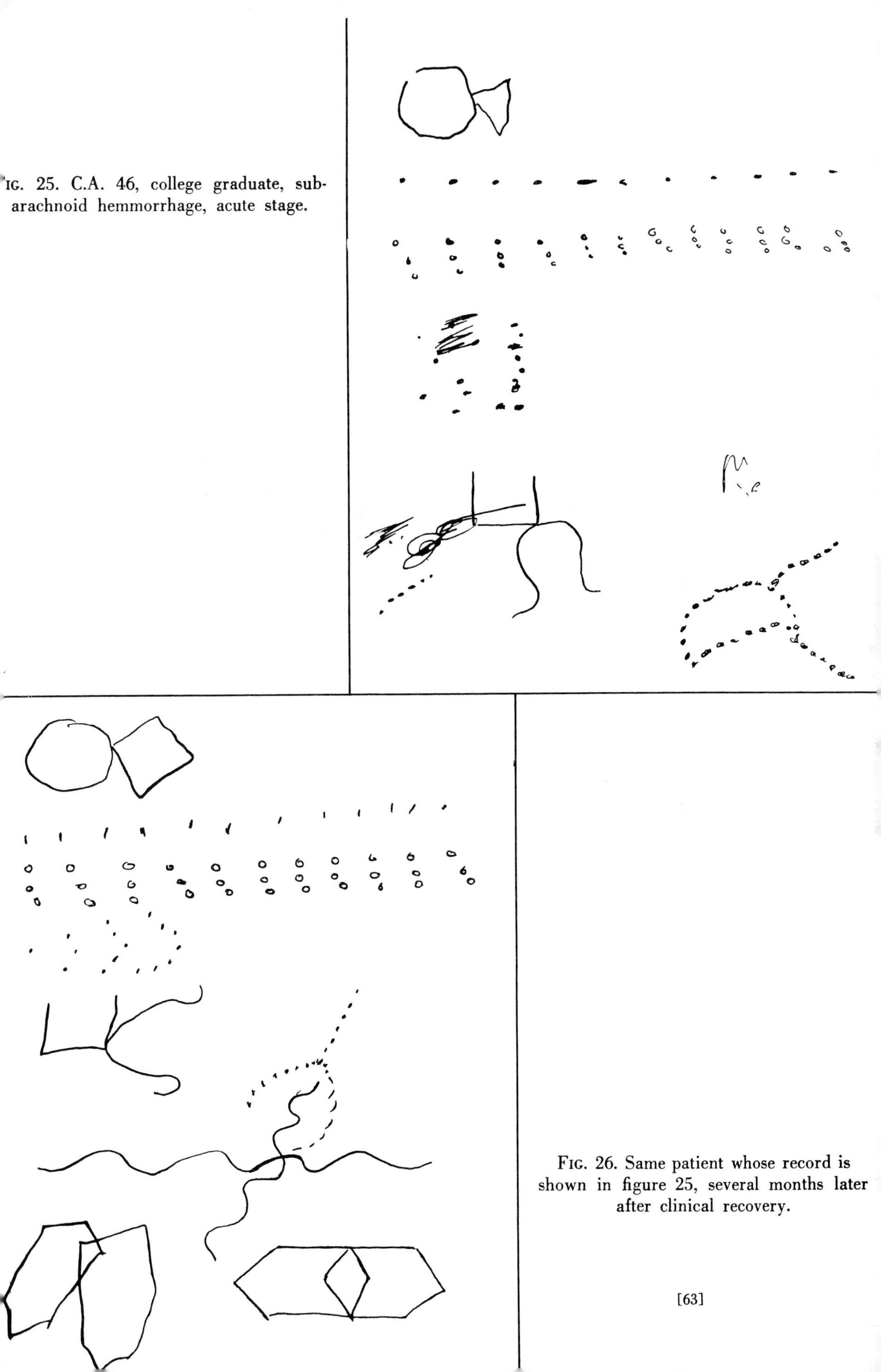

FIG. 25. C.A. 46, college graduate, subarachnoid hemmorrhage, acute stage.

FIG. 26. Same patient whose record is shown in figure 25, several months later after clinical recovery.

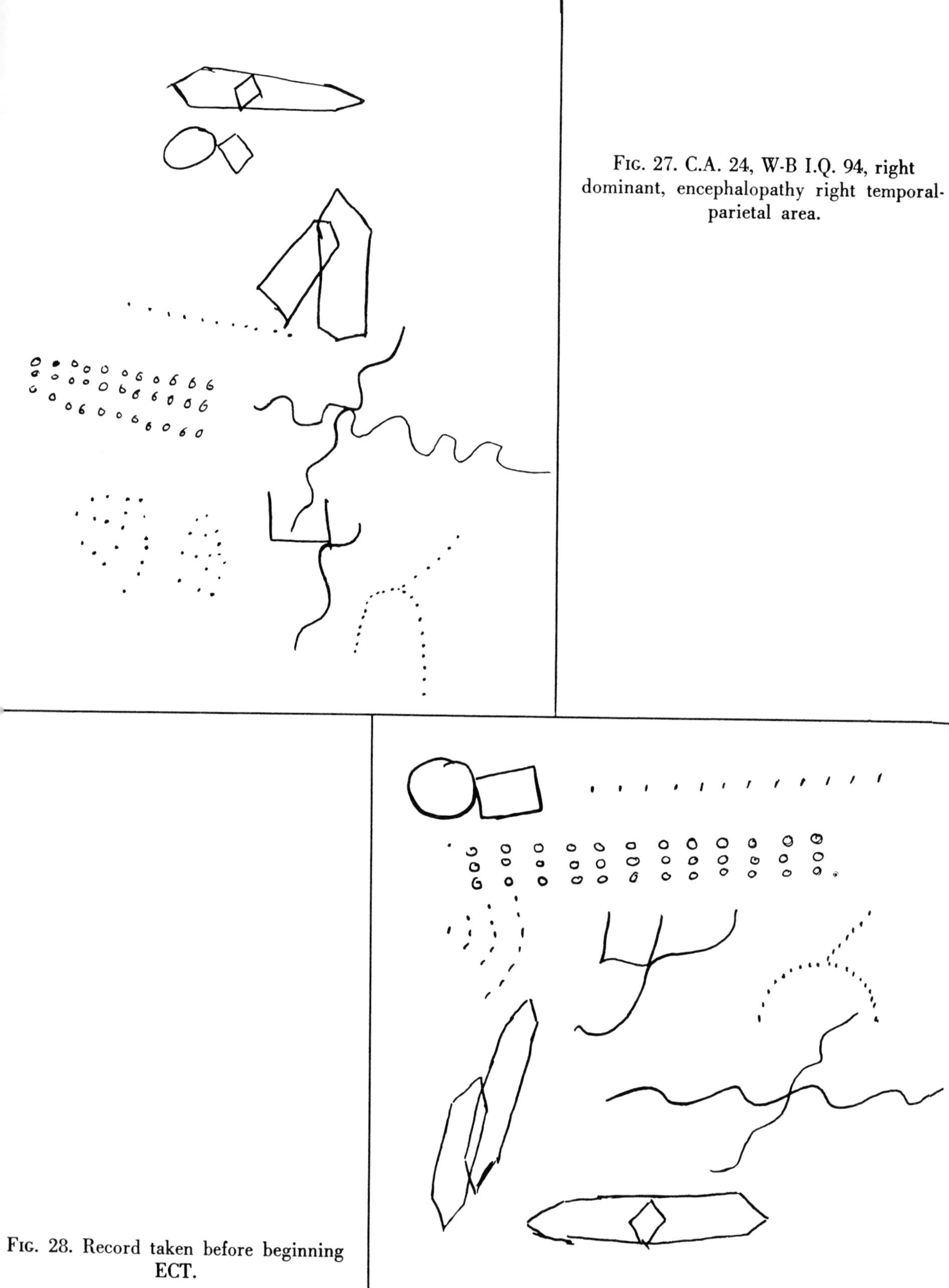

FIG. 27. C.A. 24, W-B I.Q. 94, right dominant, encephalopathy right temporal-parietal area.

FIG. 28. Record taken before beginning ECT.

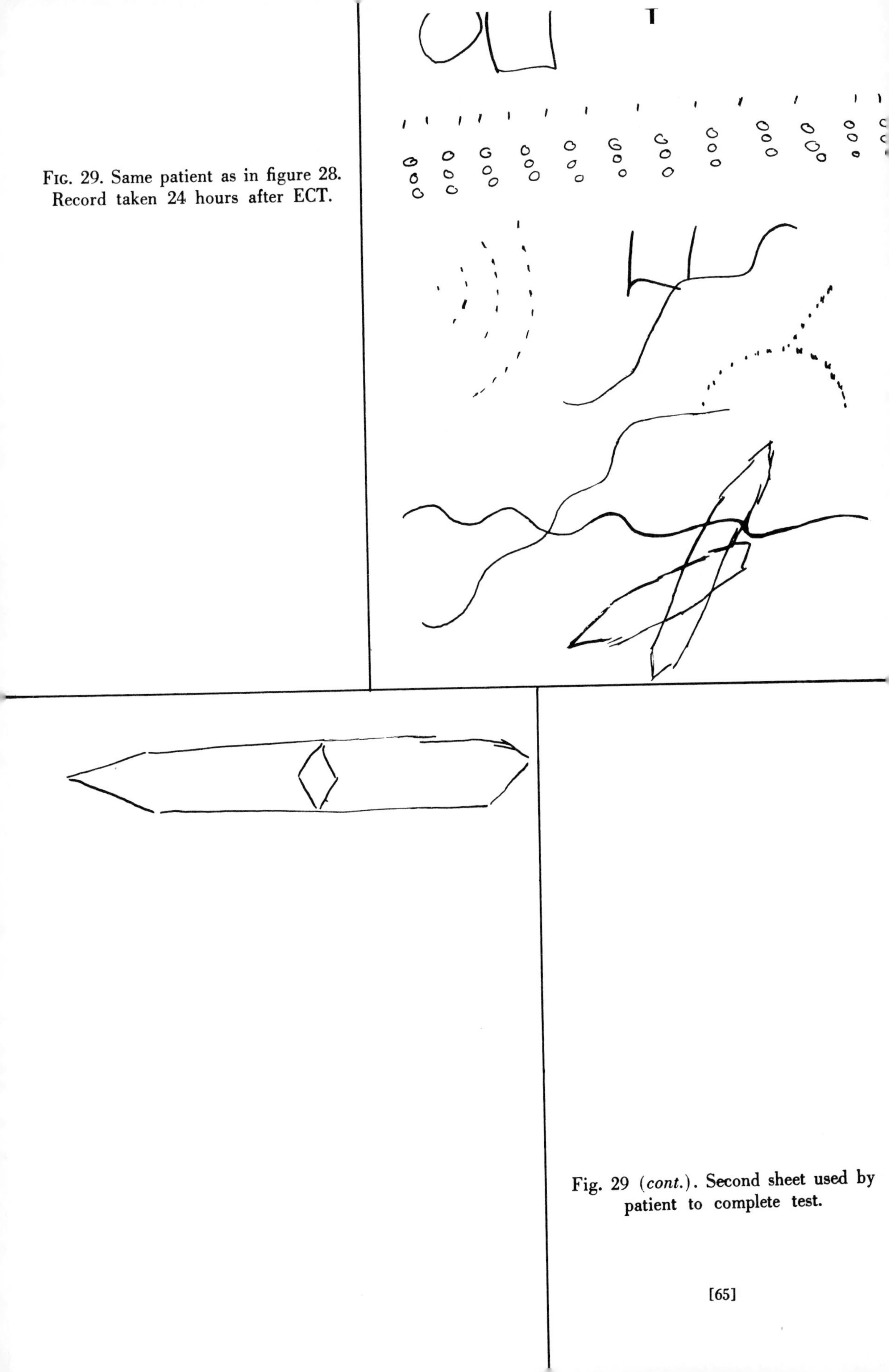

Fig. 29. Same patient as in figure 28. Record taken 24 hours after ECT.

Fig. 29 (*cont.*). Second sheet used by patient to complete test.

to reproduce the designs, so to speak, we cannot distinguish between his deviations and those of individuals suffering from psychogenic disorders. This fact suggests that damage to the cortex has to be rather severe in its effect on the functioning efficiency of an adult of normal I.Q. before it can be detected by means of performance on the B-G test. This fact also suggests that actual lesions may exist which cannot, on the basis of the deviations noted by us, be detected in performance on this test.

Figure 23 shows the record of a 22 year old patient, I.Q. 90, right dominant, with encephalopathy left temporal parietal area. Note the deviations in shapes of the circles in design 2, distortion of the hexagon of design 7, rotation of designs 7 and 8, second attempts on designs 4 and 8, and the tendency to perseverate on design 6. Although the patient had a partial paralysis of the right hand the drawings were excuted with that hand. The patient was also aphasic. After several months of intensive training in the use of the right hand, and in speech, the patient produced the drawings shown in figure 24, which show little in the way of deviations attributable to brain damage according to the deviations noted by us.

Figure 25 shows part of the record of a college graduate 46 years of age in the acute stages following the effects of a subarachnoid hemmorrhage. Figure 26 shows the record of the same individual taken several months later after clinical recovery. It would be difficult to distinguish between the record shown in figure 26 and that of a patient suffering from psychogenic illness without other information.

On the other hand, figure 27 shows the record of a 24 year old patient, I.Q. 94, right dominant, with encephalopthy *right* temporal parietal area. This record shows tendencies toward perseveration in designs 3 and 6, distortion and second attempt in designs 3, and part of design missing in design 7, obviously an "organic" record. Where the lesion is on the same side of the cortex that is dominant, it is usually difficult to detect with the B-G, unless, as in this case, the lesion is rather extensive.

For the sake of completion we present the test records of a patient before and during a series of electroshock treatments. Figure 28 shows the B-G record taken before the onset of ECT; figure 29, 24 hours after the tenth treatment. The patient was a psychotic, depressed. Note that in figure 29, taken 24 hours after ECT, indications of damage to the cortex are found in the record, perseveration and blunting in design 3, and rotation in design 7. Confusion is suggested in the overlapping of designs and distortion in size.

Performance on the B-G test, then, is not always able to suggest damage to the cortex, but when it does, it seems to indicate damage of a serious nature. It may, in some cases, indicate the locus of the lesion and whether it is circumscribed or pervasive.

8: THE BENDER-GESTALT TEST AND PSYCHOGENIC DISORDERS

For adults of normal I.Q., ages 15 to 50, and with one year or more of high school education, scores on the B-G test are not correlated with I.Q. for our population. Within the age range 15 to 50 scores are not correlated with age. They are, however, for these populations, correlated with whether or not a person is the patient of a psychiatrist. In addition, there is some evidence to support the belief that they are correlated with seriousness of psychiatric illness, i.e., psychotics tend to make higher scores than neurotics. These statements are the substance of our research with the B-G test. In discussing the clinical use of the test with psychogenic disorders we can add very little to these fundamental facts. We shall, however, attempt to show how these facts can be of use in clinical practice.

The B-G will, we assume, be a part of other tests and procedures aimed at assisting psychiatric diagnosis, and prognosis for recommended treatment. For the ten minutes it takes to administer the test and for the five minutes it takes to score it, it need not give much to be worthy of a place in a battery, nor should too much be expected of it. But it should not be used at all if it cannot supply a definite piece of information about *every* patient to whom it is administered. Very often we have seen clinicians put the B-G record aside with the remark: "The Bender shows nothing." We assert that the Bender is always of significance as part of a battery of psychological tests.

It is not our purpose, in this section, to discuss the B-G test as a projective technique in the sense that the Rorschach is a projective technique. If patients are asked to free associate to the design, content is sometimes obtained which is diagnostic of the patient's mental illness. Miss Margaret Carter, psychologist for the Veteran's Administration Mental Hygiene Clinic in Providence, in an as yet unpublished study, is using this technique with the B-G test. Her findings suggest that it is possible to categorize responses thus obtained in a manner similar to that in which Rorschach responses are categorized. She found, for instance, that vista responses were not uncommon. With respect to content, her results indicated a tendency for individuals with paranoid ideation to see the dots of design 1 as fence posts. That such results should be forthcoming is not unexpected in the light of previous investigations (52). However theoretically interesting it may be, such an approach needs a great deal more research before it can be of practical use.

Without the method of eliciting associational content to the designs, the B-G test is, nevertheless, a projective technique in another way. We suggest that the subject's feelings about the designs may influence his execution of them. Wolff's work (52) has demonstrated that graphic movement can be influenced in this way. If the subject associates the design with something unpleasant then he may render a poor drawing of it. On the other hand, he also may, because of this fact, be all the more meticulous in his execution of the design. Eyesenck (17) has suggested that subjects may differ in aptitude for ideomotor activity. This factor, too, may participate in performance on a given design.

On our suggestion, Miss Carter, in connection with the study previously mentioned, asked 22 patients and 22 matched nonpatients, adults, to rank order the designs in terms of unpleasantness, collecting records from these same individuals. She then counted the number of deviations made by each subject for each design. This procedure resulted in two sets of ranks for each subject for each design. The results, calculating rho for each design, were generally inconclusive; about half the designs showing some relationship between the rank order of unpleasantness and deviations; and the other half, none. Designs 1, 4, 7, and 8 suggest some relationship, but designs 2, 3. 5, and 6 show none. Table 9 summarizes the data by design. Note that for both patients and nonpatients designs 6 and 7 are the most unpleasant, in that order; but, whereas design 7 shows fairly good agreement between unpleasantness and deviation ranks, design 6 does not. Design 3 is, in terms of number of deviations, the most difficult, which is in agreement

Table 9
Mean Rank Orders of Unpleasantness and Mean Numbers of Deviations

Test Figure	Mean Rank of Unpleasantness*		Rank of Mean No. of Deviations*	
	Pts.	Nonpts.	Pts.	Nonpts.
1	1	4	2	3
2	6	3	1	1
3	2	2	8	8
4	5	5	4.5	4.5
5	4	6	6	7
6	8	8	4.5	4.5
7	7	7	7	6
8	3	1	3	2

*From least unpleasant and least no. of deviations, Rank Order 1, to most unpleasant and most no. of deviations, Rank Order 8.

with what we found to be true for our 8–9 year old children. It is, however, one of the least unpleasant for both normals and patients. This finding suggests that the difficulty of the design is an important, uncontrolled variable in this study of relationship between affective tone of the design and performance. In our method of scoring, the designs are not equated for difficulty. In any case, Miss Carter's study, preliminary in nature, does not preclude the possibility that the affect with which an individual approaches a design may influence his execution of that design. Other studies of a similar nature (7, 13, 40, 52) would lead us to believe that such would be the case.

In addition to the possibility that performance may be a function of the affective tone of the individual design for the subject (which may also be a function of ideomotor aptitude) we need to consider, as a possible factor influencing performance, the subject's attitude to the test as a whole, i.e., as a task, any task, of work under the given circumstances of testing. In this case the effect of attitude, if it influenced behavior on the test, would be general, applying equally to all designs. Obviously, in our method of scoring we do not know to what extent scores are influenced by the effect of the individual design on the subject, and to what extent by the subject's attitude toward the task of taking the test. If both are being measured then the effect on scores must be additive.

In the ordinary administration of the B-G test the subject is asked to copy the designs. He does this with greater or less compliance. He may resent the idea of being asked to do such a silly task, and regardless of the fact of a testing situation, hastily and in ill humor, do a poor job of copying the designs; or, being suspicious he may copy them meticulously, using guide lines and taking a good deal of time to make exact reproductions; or, being superior and good-humored and thinking the whole thing is of not much importance, he may sloppily dash off the test in jig time; or, being fearful and doubtful of his ability to execute the drawings properly, he may make poorly controlled and tremulous movements with many corrections. Attitudes and performance like the above result in high scores by our method of scoring. On the other hand, the subject may approach the task as most of our nonpatients did, without particular comment, keeping his ideas of the test to himself, and execute reasonable reproductions, obtaining a Z score of about 50.

We know that adults of average I.Q., between the ages of 15 and 50, without damage to the cortex, have the *capacity* to execute drawings resulting, on the average, in a Z score of 50. When they reproduce the designs poorly and/or arrange them in a confused manner on the page, resulting in a high score, we have to ask ourselves why they do this. Is it because they are *momentarily* bored, resentful, fearful, superior, or suspicious, and are these attitudes specific to the testing situation? We do not doubt that attitudes of the moment specific to the testing situation may influence performance in certain instances, but we do doubt that this was true for the majority of cases tested by us. We believe that the same sort of factor enters into performance on the B-G test as, say, makes for "functional impairment" on the Wechsler-Bellevue, resulting in "significant scatter." We believe this factor to be attitude towards the task as a whole. Performance on the B-G test seems, however, perhaps because of the abstractness of the stimuli, to be more affected by attitudes than the Wechsler-Bellevue, just as the Rorschach seems to be more affected by them.[1]

If, then, not capacity, but attitudes make for greater deviations from the stimuli, our results suggest the possibility of generalizing from attitudes to the B-G test to attitudes towards other stimuli in the environment. Unfortunately, our research has not revealed in any systematic fashion the particular kinds of attitudes which are behind high scoring records. All we know is that certain attitudes if held over a period of time tend to result in a person becoming the patient of a psychiatrist and that these attitudes as reflected in B-G performance are correlated with above average scores on the test. The suspiciousness of the paranoid, the guilt of the depressed, the resistance and negativism of the catatonic, the ambivalence of the obsessed, these are attitudes toward people, things and the self. To the extent that they affect behavior they contribute to psychiatric illness which, in turn, is related to performance on the B-G. Attitudes, therefore, making for behavior which takes on the nature of psychiatric illness are related to B-G score. Not all attitudes, however, make for consequent behavior. For the extent to which attitudes of the type indicated do affect behavior leading to psychiatric illness, we have previously suggested, for the purposes of this discussion, the term *ego strength*, which we shall use in the practical considerations to follow.

---

[1] We would speculate that deviations on the Bender may, in a sense, be more significant than those on the Rorschach; for when a person in our culture writes down his deviation, as it were, for the whole world to see, we would guess that he is "sticking his neck out farther" than merely saying a deviation, i.e., that the act of writing involves a greater commitment than the act of saying. Freud (18, 19) on the other hand, has characterized this situation as one in which, in the normal individual, unconscious wishes leading to motor behavior are inhibited by ego defenses. He points out, however, that when there is pathological enfeeblement of ego defenses or pathological enforcement of unconscious excitations, "forbidden" unconscious impulses and potential motor expression may coexist. Freud further suggests that the coexistence of unconscious impulse and potential motor expression may be true of psychosis. Presumably this implied tendency to express ideation by gross deviant behavior is on a continuum, some aspect of which is being measured by our method of scoring the B-G test.

High Scoring Records

Ash, in a recent article (6) has reported a study of the reliability of psychiatric diagnoses, which is in essential agreement with previous studies reporting the difficulty of achieving reliable diagnoses in psychogenic illnesses. The various symptoms which form the bases for psychiatric diagnoses are facts, observable by anyone, but unfortunately, they do not exist in a pure state, nor are they always consistent in a given individual. They are, according to psychoanalytic views (1) surface phenomena indicative of more fundamental psychic disturbances. By categorizing patients on the basis of a more reliable though cruder criterion—psychotics (primarily inpatients) and neurotics (primarily outpatients)—we have attempted to avoid the problem of psychiatric diagnoses. Our scores and the deviations on which they are based do not, therefore, indicate particular psychiatric diagnosis. We have suggested they are measuring some aspect of ego strength, a term for which we have no adequate definition except to say that, among other things, it seems to lie along some continuum with the extent to which reality is distorted, as do our scores.

High scores are, therefore, indicative of little ego strength. That there is some truth to this statement is evident when we look at records receiving extremely high scores. Figure 30 shows the record of a confused manic, age 36, high school education, Z score 190. Little difficulty is encountered with such records. They are easily spotted as extremely ill individuals in poor contact. Figure 31 shows the record of a 32 year old college graduate, an excited inpatient, diagnosed manic-depressive, manic, Z score 92. Figure 32 is the record of a 15 year old girl, one year of high school, diagnosed schizophrenic, mixed type, Z score 95. In both of these records, as in the previous one (figure 30), the very high scores and the qualitative aspects of the records are fairly conclusive for severe psychological illness, i.e., with behavior so deviant that the patients need to be confined to a mental hospital under constant supervision.

A Z score of 75 is two and one half standard deviations from the mean of a normal distribution. The chances are about 1 in 100 that a record with such Z score would be normal, i.e., that of a nonpatient. Increasing the probability that a Z score of 75 would be that of a *normal* record are those errors of measurement stemming from the unreliability of the scoring system, the fact of a somewhat skewed distribution in the normative population, and other uncontrolled factors contributing to errors of measurement in the individual case. Thus, even with Z scores as high as 75 clinical judgment is important in estimating the extent of psychological illness in the individual case. We shall, by the use of illustrative cases, attempt to indicate the nature of such judgment.

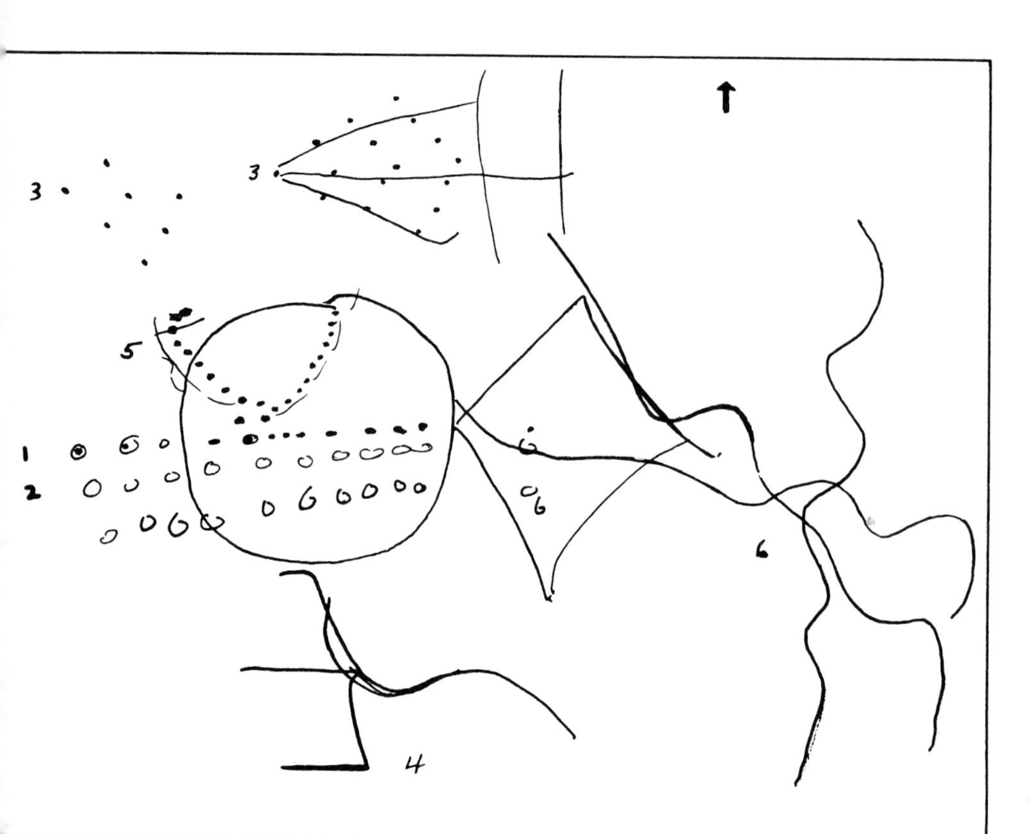

Fig. 30. Manic-depressive (manic), male, age 36, high school education, Z score 190.

(Two sheets used by patient.)

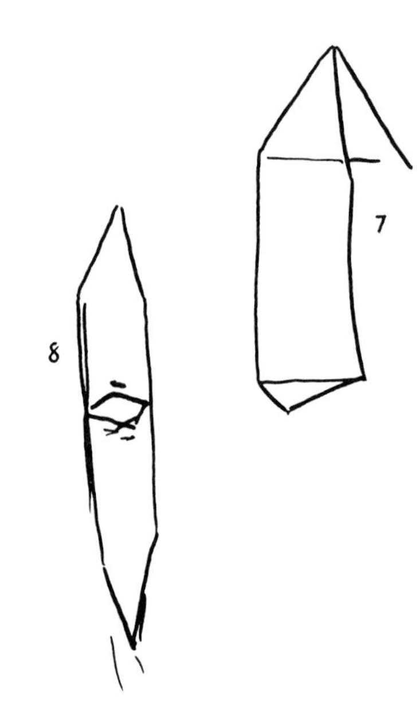

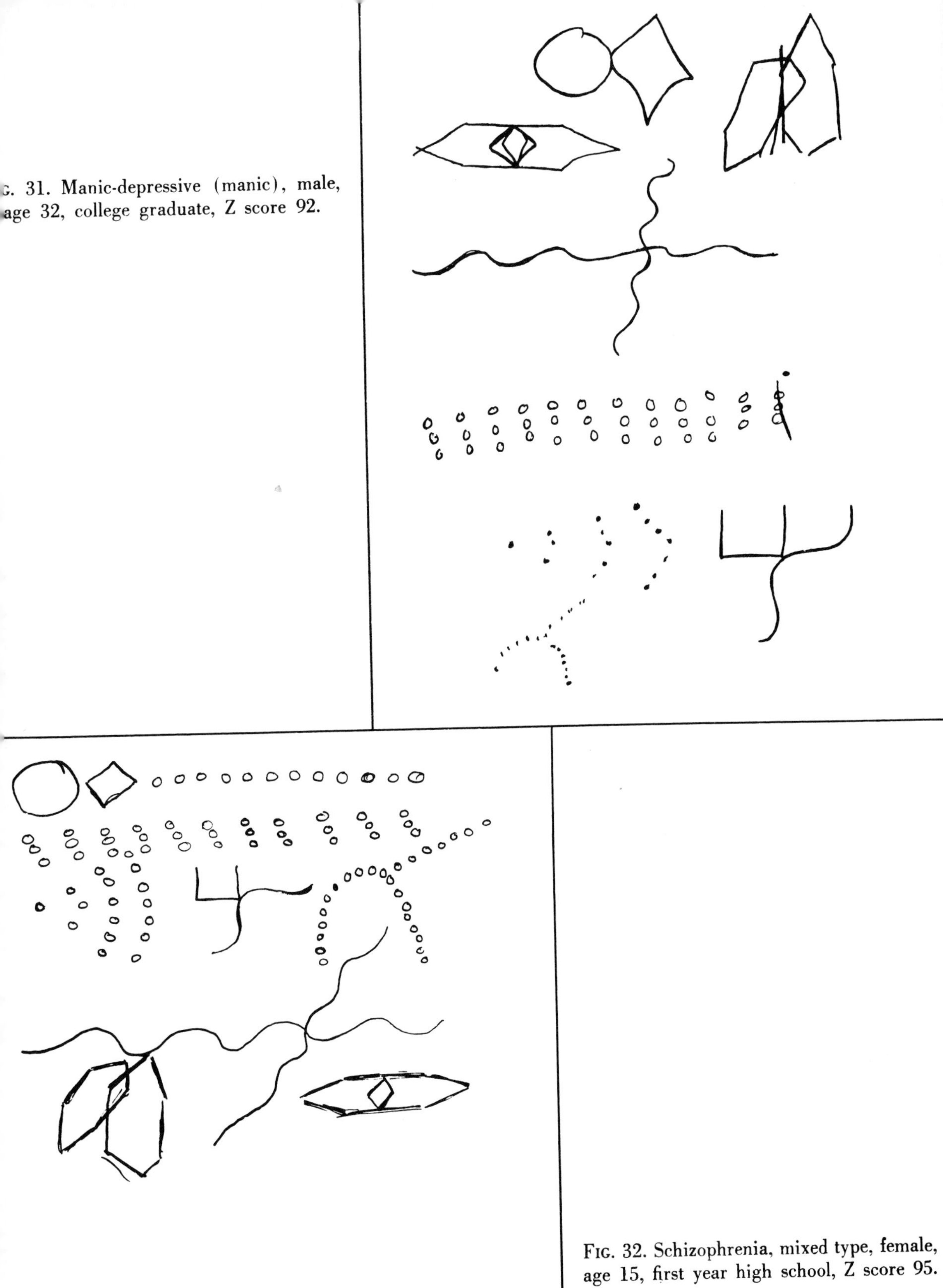

G. 31. Manic-depressive (manic), male, age 32, college graduate, Z score 92.

Fig. 32. Schizophrenia, mixed type, female, age 15, first year high school, Z score 95.

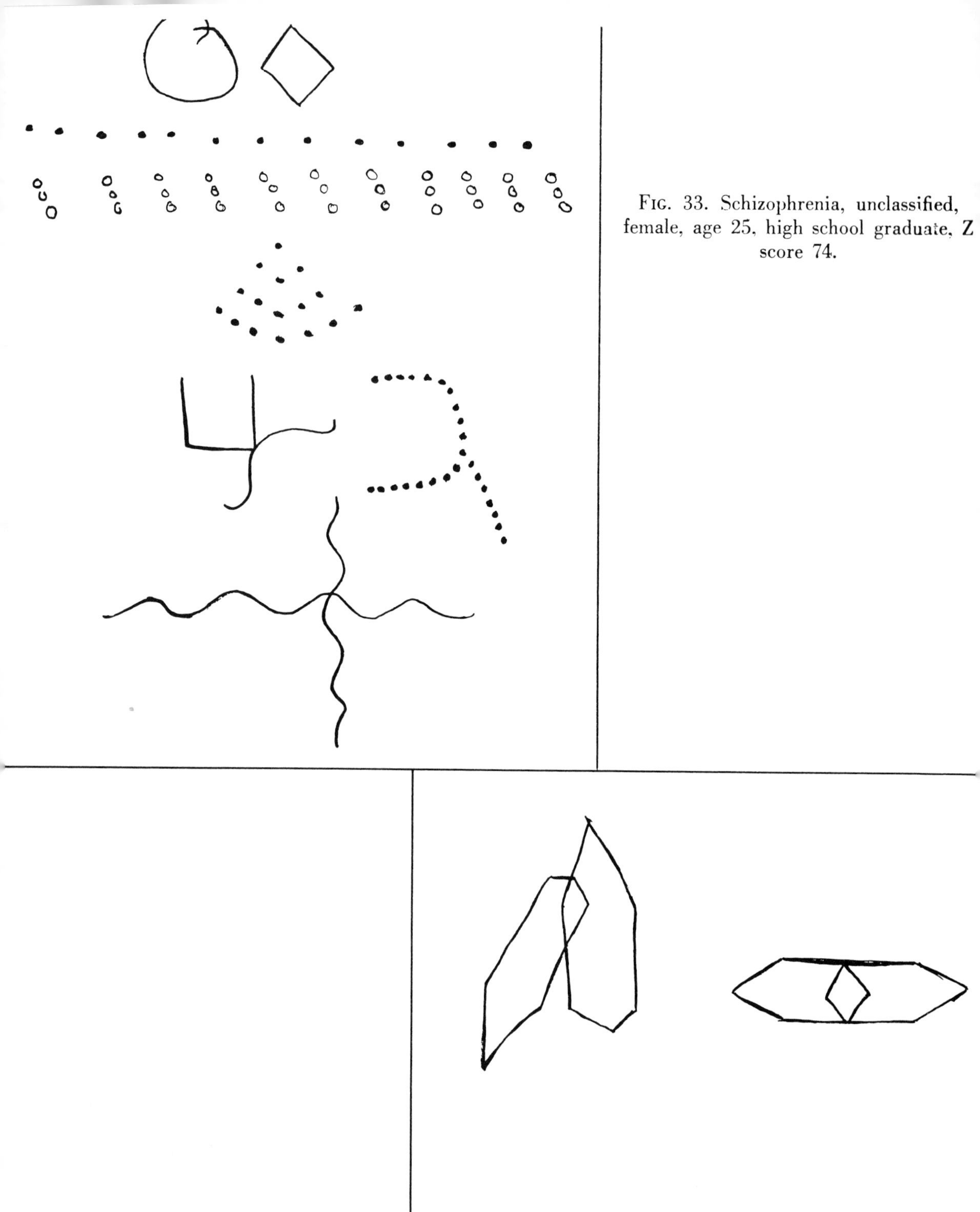

FIG. 33. Schizophrenia, unclassified, female, age 25, high school graduate, Z score 74.

Fig. 33 (*cont.*). Second sheet used by patient to complete test.

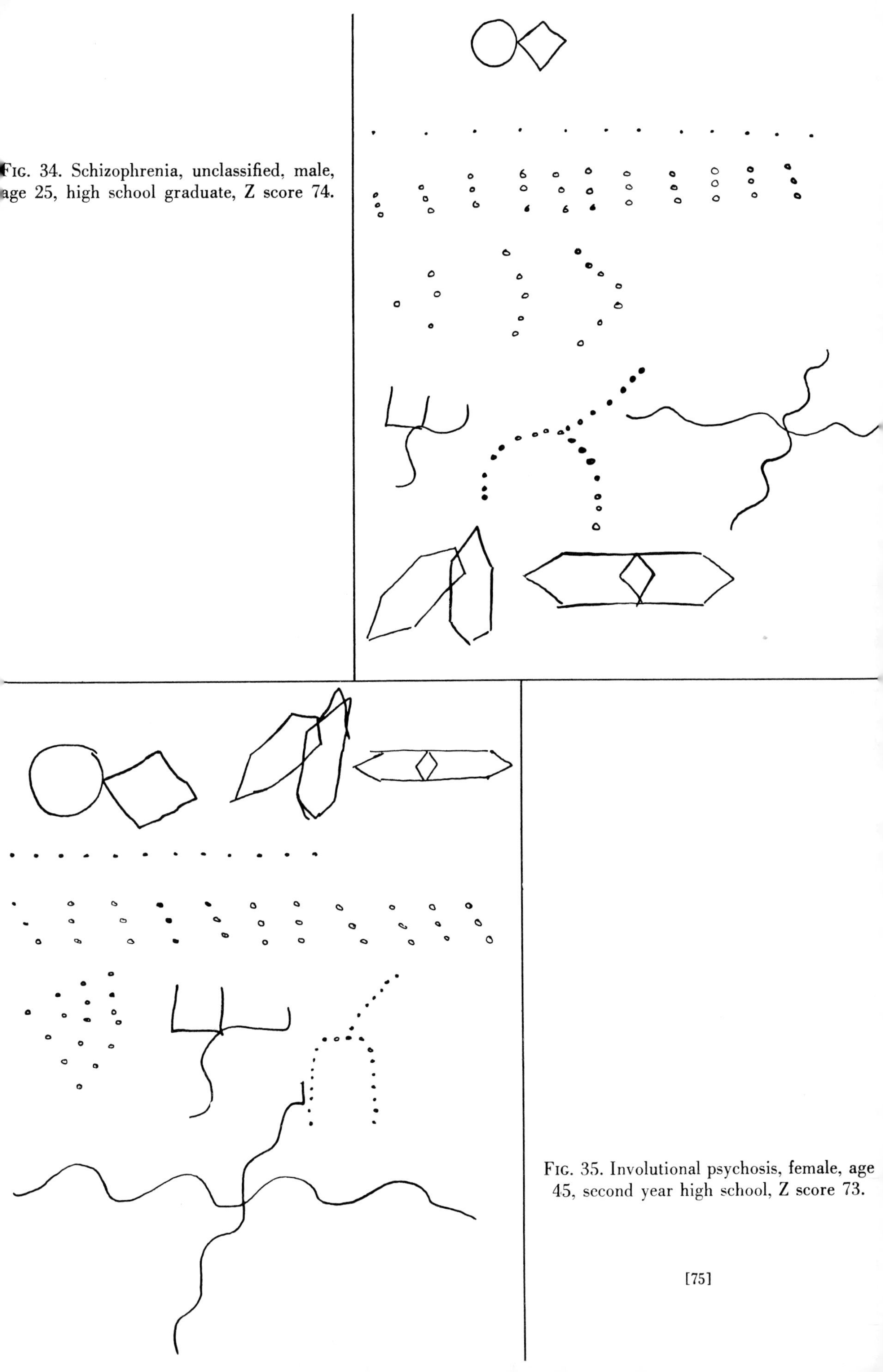

FIG. 34. Schizophrenia, unclassified, male, age 25, high school graduate, Z score 74.

FIG. 35. Involutional psychosis, female, age 45, second year high school, Z score 73.

Figures 33, 34, and 35 show the records of psychotics with Z scores in the seventies. Figure 33 is the record of a 25 year old woman, a high school graduate, an inpatient diagnosed schizophrenic, Z score 74. The designs are fairly well executed, placed in logical order. Note, however, that two major deviations (with score of 8) occur, i.e., designs 3 and 5 rotated. Having noted this fact we may also take cognizance of the formation of the dots in designs 2, 3, and 5. They are so worked over that they become filled circles—a common practice in children.

Major deviations in an otherwise fairly good record constitute a "break," just as an extreme distortion of the stimulus in an otherwise fair record on the Rorschach constitutes a "break." By "break," in clinical jargon, we mean the possibility of a break with reality, i.e., the possibility of behavior which might be characterized as psychotic.

Figure 34 shows the record of a 25 year old high school graduate, male, an inpatient diagnosed schizophrenic, Z score 74. Here, again, although the designs are, on the whole, fairly well copied, the substitution of circles for dots on designs 3 and 5 are breaks indicative of serious psychological illness. On that background we may also note the marked deviation in slant of design 2, and the failure to make the point of design 3. Figure 35 is the record of a 45 year old female, two years high school, an inpatient diagnosed involutional, Z score 73. Note one major deviation, the substitution of circles for dots in design 3, and add to this the marked deviation in slant, design 2, and the unerased first attempt on design 7. Each of these three records shows major deviations of one sort or another, which is typical of high scoring inpatient psychotics.

Figure 36 is the record of an outpatient, a neurotic male, age 22, high school graduate, Z score 81. Here we see that, in spite of the fact that the patient's score is higher than that of the inpatient psychotics just discussed, no major deviations occur. The record is heavily penalized for the presence of tremor in nearly all of the line drawings. The record, however, is that of a seriously incapacitated psychasthenic, according to the psychiatrist. Figure 37 shows the record of another neurotic outpatient, male, age 30, one year of college, Z score 71. Here, again, although the score is about as high as that of the psychotics, no major deviation occurs; a number of minor deviations contribute to the high score.

We present, now, the records of three high scoring normals, (that is, they were not, as far as we know, patients of a psychiatrist), all attending night school, and all gainfully employed. Figure 38 is the record of a 35 year old male, a color matcher in a chemical plant, a high school graduate, Z score 71. Figure 39 shows the record of a 35 year old male, a wash tender in a chemical plant with one year of high school, Z score 70. Figure 40 is the record of a 29 year old male, a dyer in a chemical plant with a high school education, Z score 70. All of the records show poor execution but none show major deviations. One would be hard pressed, of course, to distinguish these records from those of the neurotics but, then, some so-called normals are difficult to distinguish from some neurotic patients by any procedure, objective or subjective. Based on our findings the chances are about 5 in 100 that the three "normal" individuals, whose records we have presented, are not in need of psychiatric assistance.

A good deal of emphasis has been placed on the incidence of major deviations in the records of inpatient psychotics. We selected, at random from our files, the records of 46 inpatients, psychotics, 46 outpatients, neurotics, and 46 nonpatients, and counted the incidence of major deviations. For the nonpatients one major deviation was found (lines not joined on design 7); for the neurotic outpatients, 17; and for the psychotic inpatients, 52.

There are times when high scoring records are obtained under circumstances which make it reasonable to suspect that some factors incidental to the testing situation contribute to high scores. In such cases we have not, in clinical practice, hesitated to retest, either on the same day, other tests intervening, or on the following day. If the test has in the first instance, been properly accepted by the subject there is surprisingly little effect of practice. We have found the greatest difference on retest in the records of high scoring nonpatients. Most patients show little difference between test and retest when the test is repeated the same day. In an attempt to push the effect of retest to an extreme we have urged some patients, on immediate retest, to do their very best. Figures 41 and 42 show two records obtained from a 30 year old female catatonic. Figure 41 shows the record obtained on first testing, Z score 89. Figure 42 shows the record obtained immediately following the first test with instructions to "take your time and do your very best," Z score 83. We suggest that results with retesting on the B-G may be interpreted in a manner similar to that in which results with "testing the limits" on the Rorschach are interpreted.

In summarizing our discussion of high scoring records we should say that high scores would generally be interpreted in terms of the probability of psychiatric illness based on our normative data. In clinical practice we usually have the advantage of knowing that the subject is a patient of a psychiatrist, which helps in considering the individual case, i.e., the need for psychiatric assistance is a "given." In the records of patients we should consider the presence of major deviations as indicating a greater degree of psychiatric illness than where these deviations are absent; providing, of course, we have ruled out the possibility of mental defect or cortical damage.

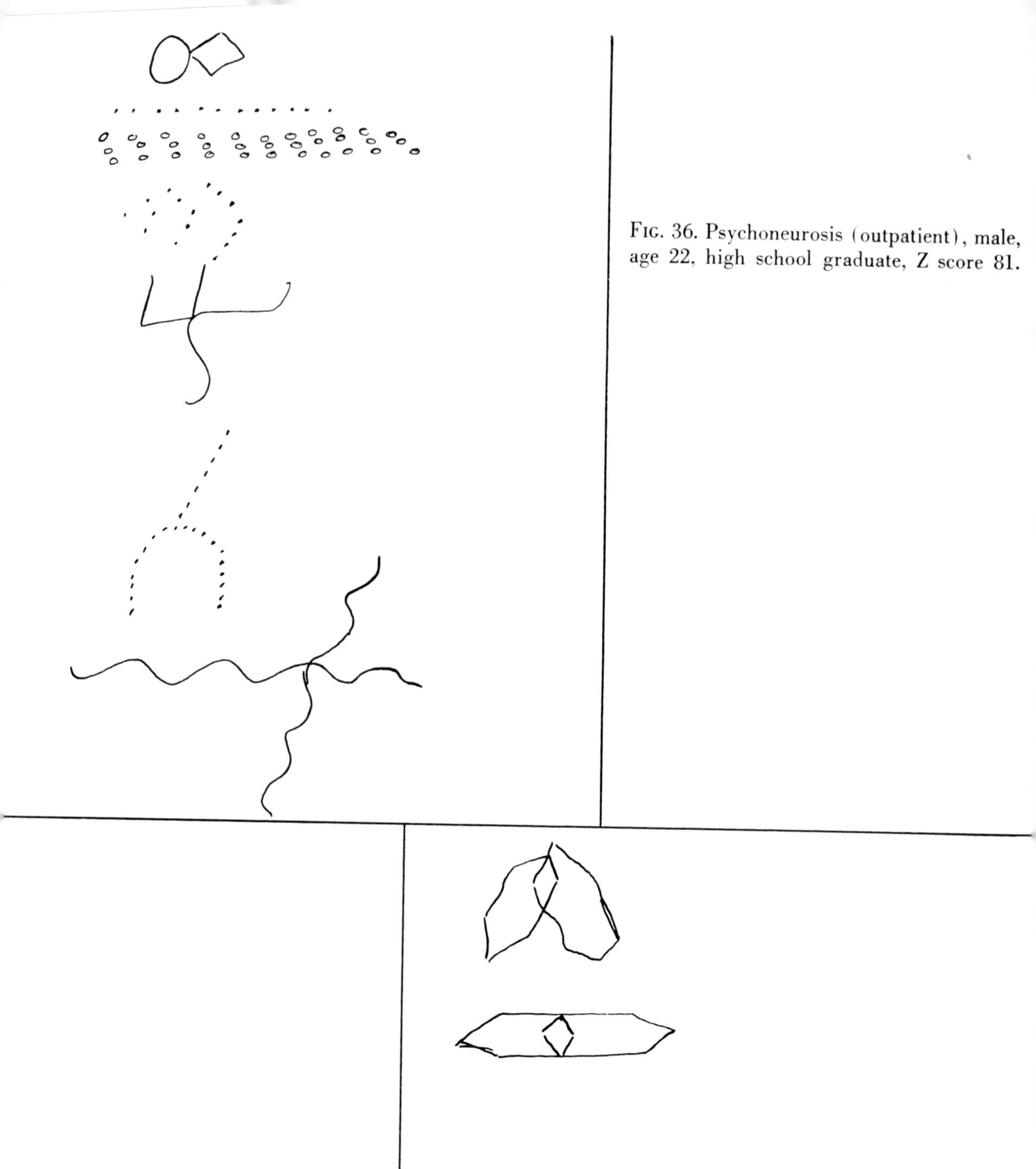

Fig. 36. Psychoneurosis (outpatient), male, age 22, high school graduate, Z score 81.

Fig. 36 (*cont.*). Second sheet used by patient to complete test.

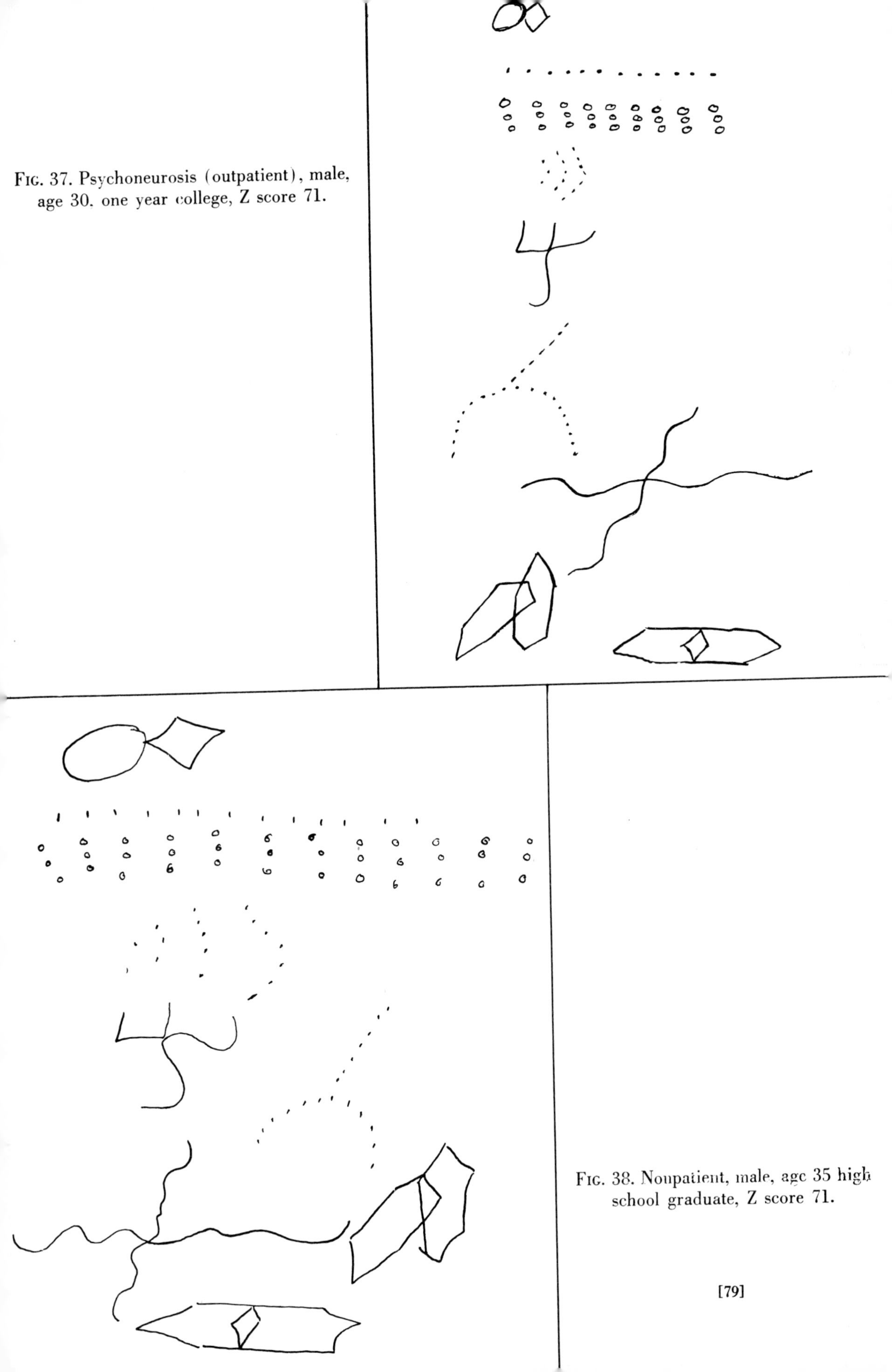

Fig. 37. Psychoneurosis (outpatient), male, age 30, one year college, Z score 71.

Fig. 38. Nonpatient, male, age 35 high school graduate, Z score 71.

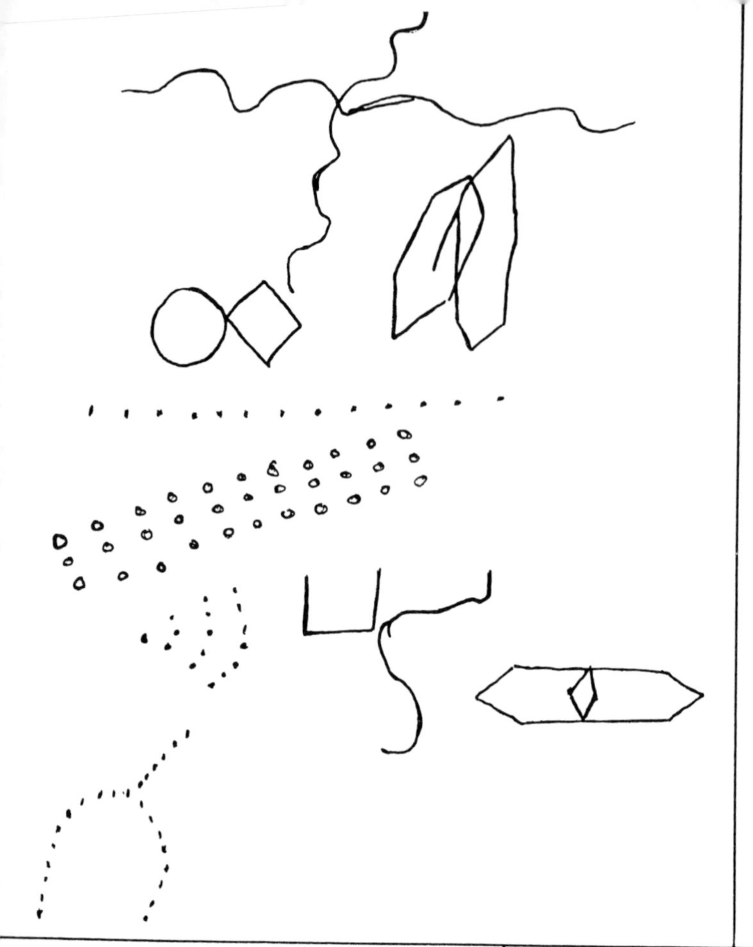

Fig. 39. Nonpatient, male, age 35, one year high school, Z score 70.

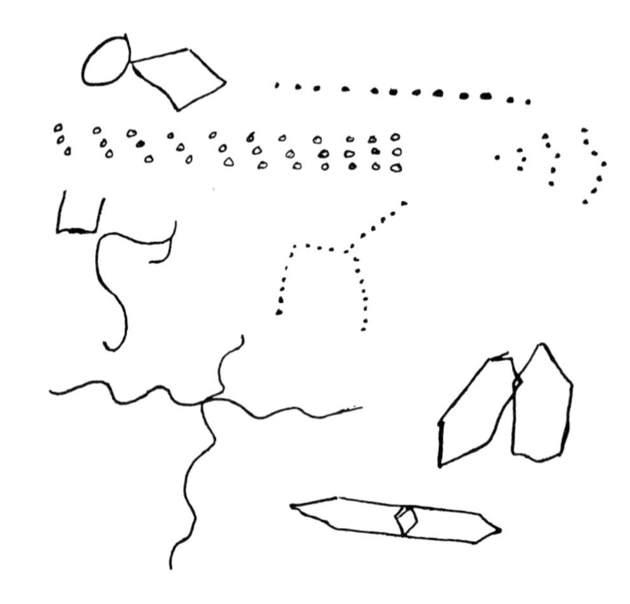

Fig. 40. Nonpatient, male. age 29, high school graduate, Z score 70.

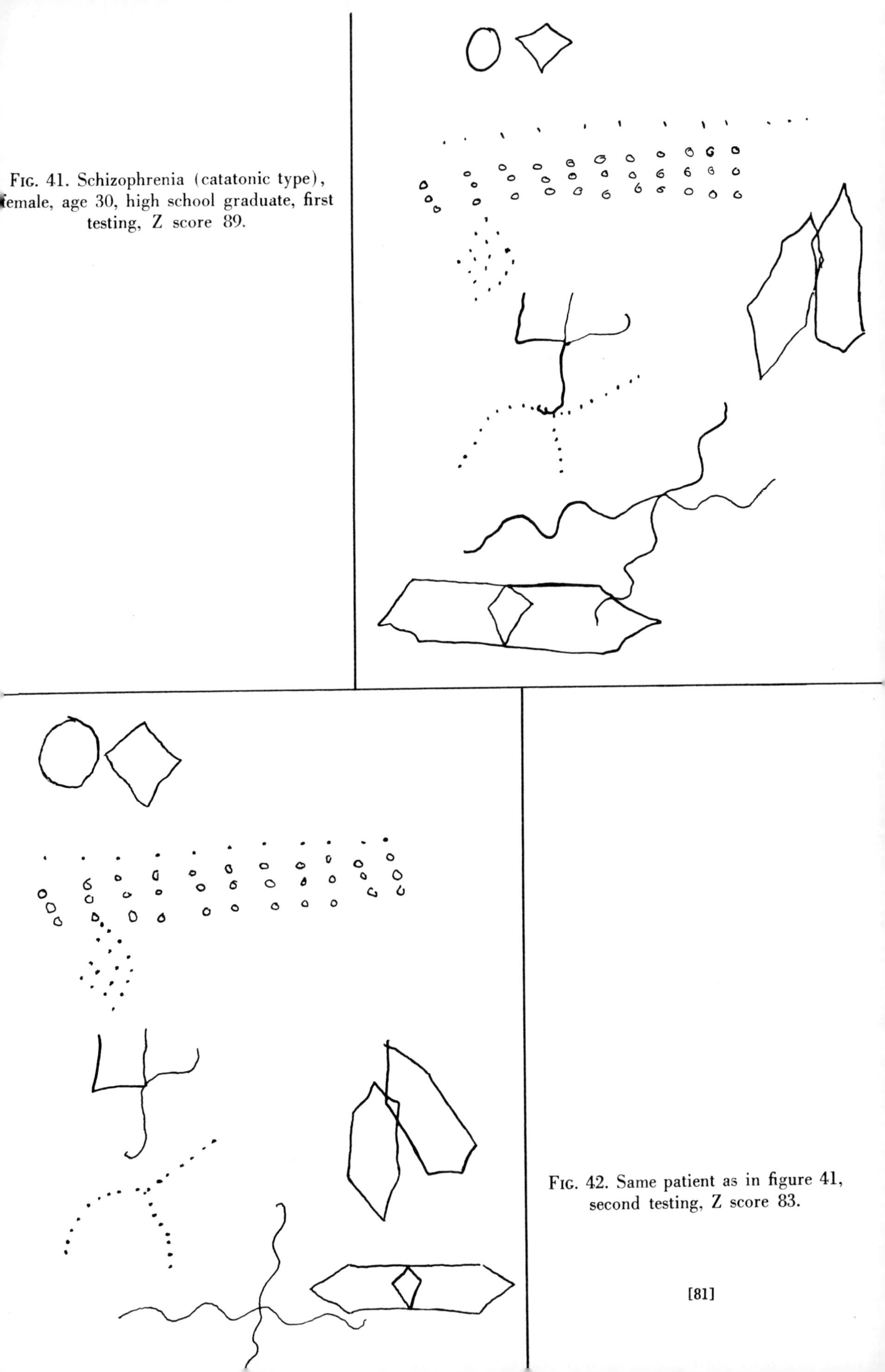

Fig. 41. Schizophrenia (catatonic type), female, age 30, high school graduate, first testing, Z score 89.

Fig. 42. Same patient as in figure 41, second testing, Z score 83.

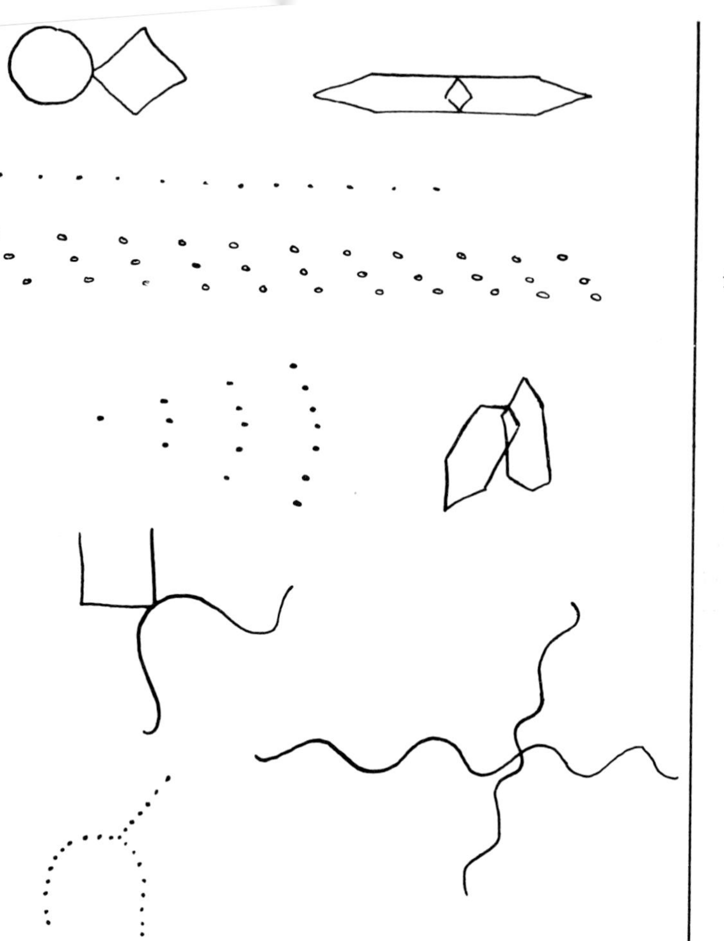

FIG. 43. Schizophrenia (catatonic type), female, age 20, college student, Z score 56, "improved."

Low Scoring Records

If, as we hypothesize, the B-G test is measuring some aspect of ego strength, then it is not surprising that low scoring records should be obtained from some patients. Low B-G scores should, according to our notion, indicate relatively greater ego strength. Is this possible in psychotic patients? A great many psychotics do recover. Our data suggest that low B-G scores in psychotics may be related to tendency to recover.

In the study previously cited (Chapter 5) where the B-G scores of the patients who improved as a result of hospitalization were compared to those unimproved, the mean Z score of the improved (N equals 43) was 61, and the mean Z score of the unimproved (N equals 22) was 82. We should, therefore, say that a Z score of about 60 constituted a low score for an inpatient psychotic. Figures 43, 44, and 45 are records of three of the improved patients. Figure 43 shows the record of a 20 year old female, a college student, diagnosed catatonic schizophrenic, Z score 56. After about four months of hospitalization with psychotherapy she was discharged markedly improved. When seen a year later she was doing well in her studies and was, she said, well and happy. Figure 44 is the record of a female manic-depressive, depressed, college education, age 28, Z score 60; she improved after several months of routine hospital care, with no definitive therapy. Figure 45 is the record of a 46 year old female, high school education, diagnosed involutional psychosis, Z score 66. After a series of ECT and several months hospitalization, she was discharged "improved."

Not all of the improved inpatient psychotics of our study gave low scoring records and not all the unimproved gave high scoring records. Of the 43 patients discharged improved, 11, or 25 per cent, had records scoring over 65. Figure 46 is the record of a low scoring, unimproved female, discharged after several months of hospitalization, with psychotherapy—a college graduate, diagnosed neurotic, Z score 63. The patient was an attempted suicide and displayed compulsive symptoms during her entire stay at the hospital. Nevertheless, when last heard of, 18 months after discharge, she was gainfully employed. Figure 47 is the record of a high scoring improved patient, a college graduate, female, diagnosed schizophrenic, Z score 81. A Wechsler-Bellevue I.Q. indicated severe functional impairment. The B-G record, in spite of its high scores, shows no major deviation other than "ends not joined." Thus, although this patient was extremely disturbed at the time of testing she did not, in performance on the B-G test, show deviations typical of very disturbed inpatients. We should say that, considering the patient's acute condition, the B-G record indicated unexpected strength.

The presence of a low scoring B-G record in a matrix of test results indicating severe disturbance may sometimes serve to season test interpretation. Figure 48 is the record of an inpatient, female, college graduate, age 45, Z score 56. She obtained a Wechsler-Bellevue I.Q. of 121. Her Rorschach showed a tendency to bizarre associations with a great many frank sex responses, the over-all Rorschach picture being similar to that often obtained from paranoid schizophrenics. At medical staff conference she was considered in good contact, free of psychotic manifestations, and diagnosed psychoneurotic, mixed type. When heard from one year later she was "doing well" with occasional visits to a psychiatrist. It turned out that she had been four and one-half years under analysis before coming to the hospital, which perhaps, accounted for the extremely "loose" Rorschach.

Fluctuating Scores

The classical example of the fluctuating record is, of course, that of the manic-depressive. Figure 49 is the record of a 55 year old manic-depressive, male, college graduate, Z score 96, an inpatient of long residence in the hospital. He is well preserved, and actively occupied with intellectual pursuits during the intervals between manic attacks. He may go for months, seemingly perfectly normal, quiet, unobtrusive, pleasant. During these periods he is allowed full privileges. The record shown in figure 49 was taken during one of these periods. Figure 50 shows the record of the same patient at the height of manic excitement.

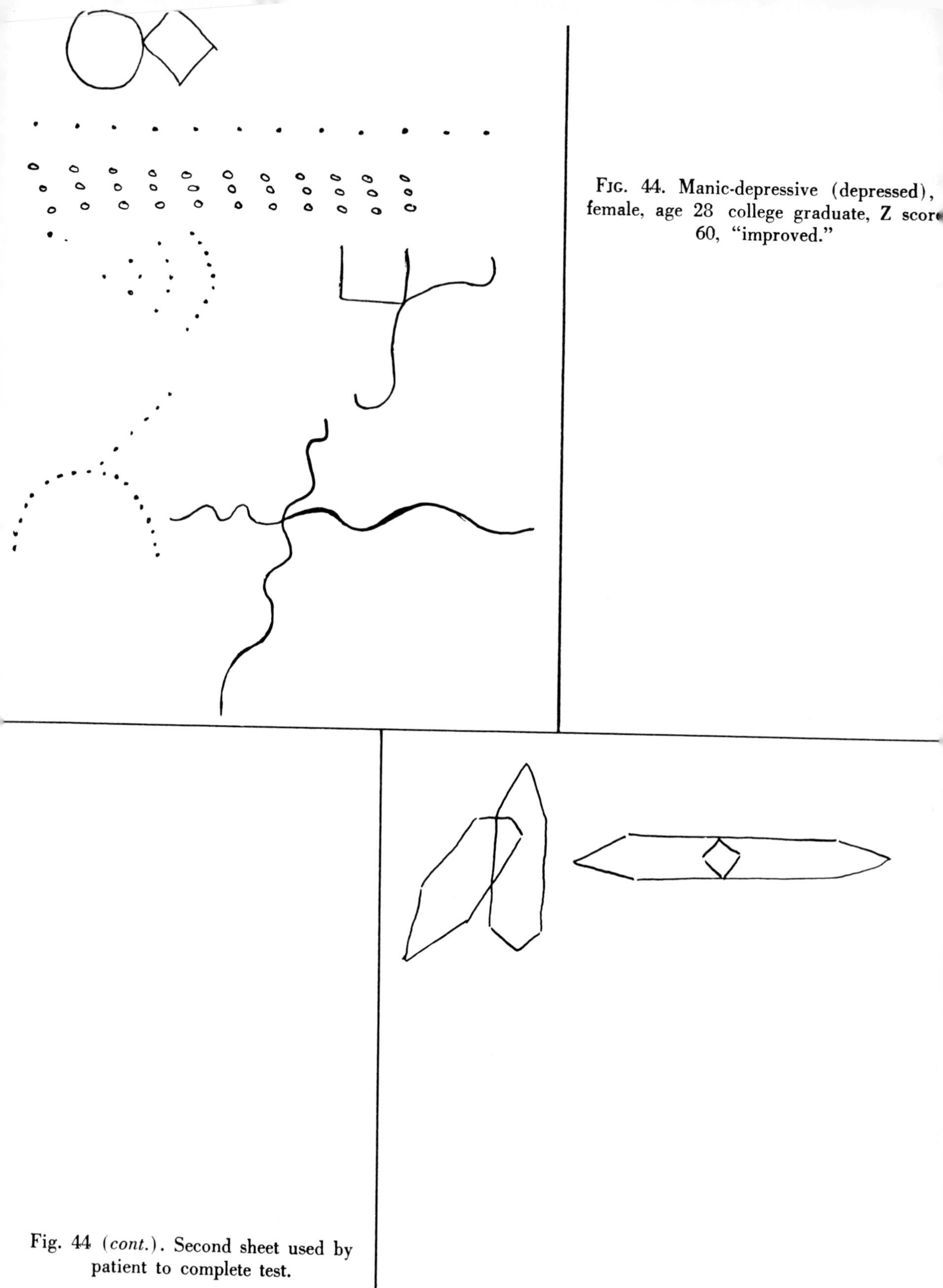

FIG. 44. Manic-depressive (depressed), female, age 28 college graduate, Z score 60, "improved."

Fig. 44 (*cont.*). Second sheet used by patient to complete test.

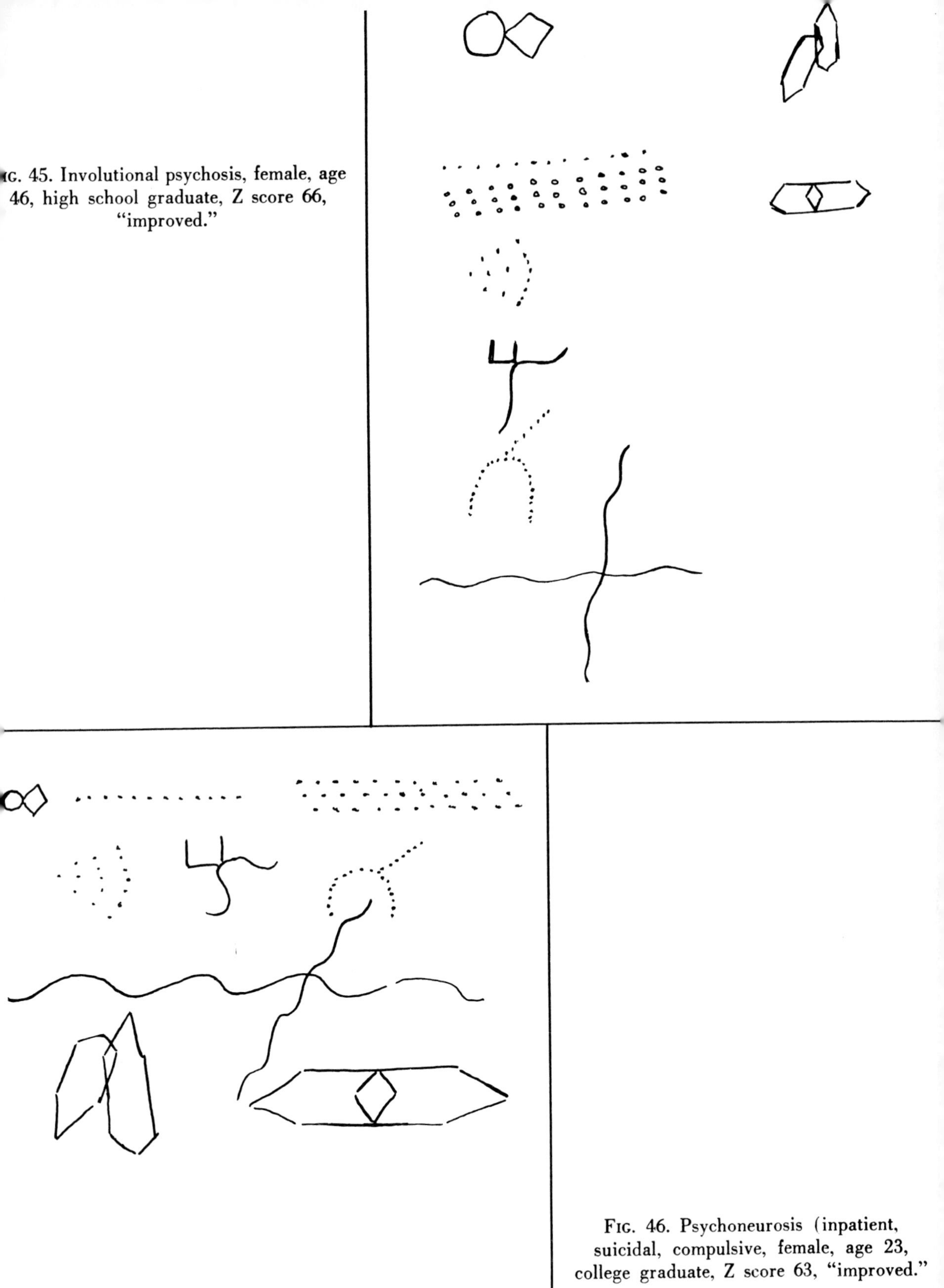

IG. 45. Involutional psychosis, female, age 46, high school graduate, Z score 66, "improved."

FIG. 46. Psychoneurosis (inpatient, suicidal, compulsive, female, age 23, college graduate, Z score 63, "improved."

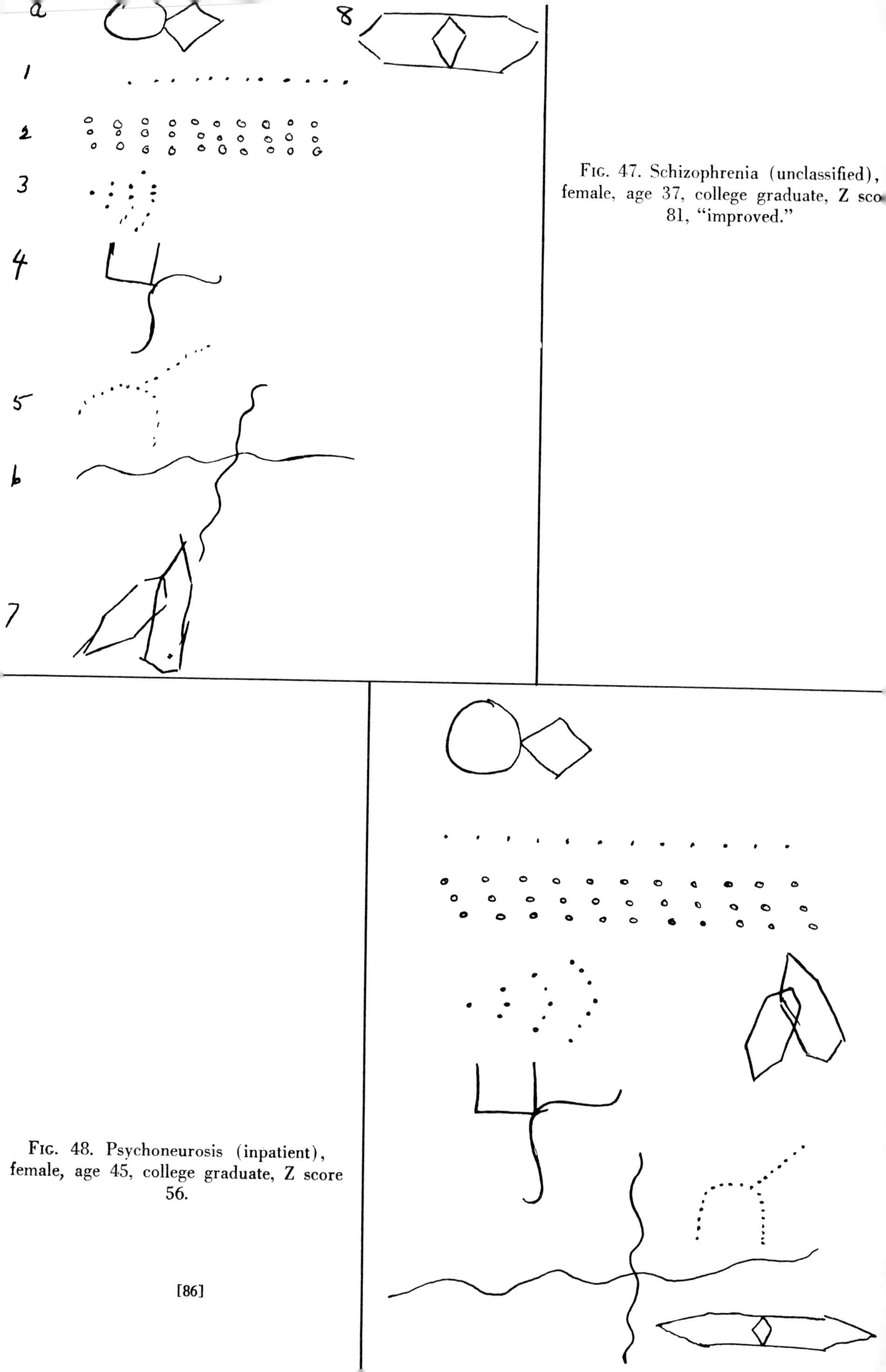

FIG. 47. Schizophrenia (unclassified), female, age 37, college graduate, Z sco 81, "improved."

FIG. 48. Psychoneurosis (inpatient), female, age 45, college graduate, Z score 56.

Fig. 49. Manic-depressive (manic), male, age 55, college graduate, Z score 96.

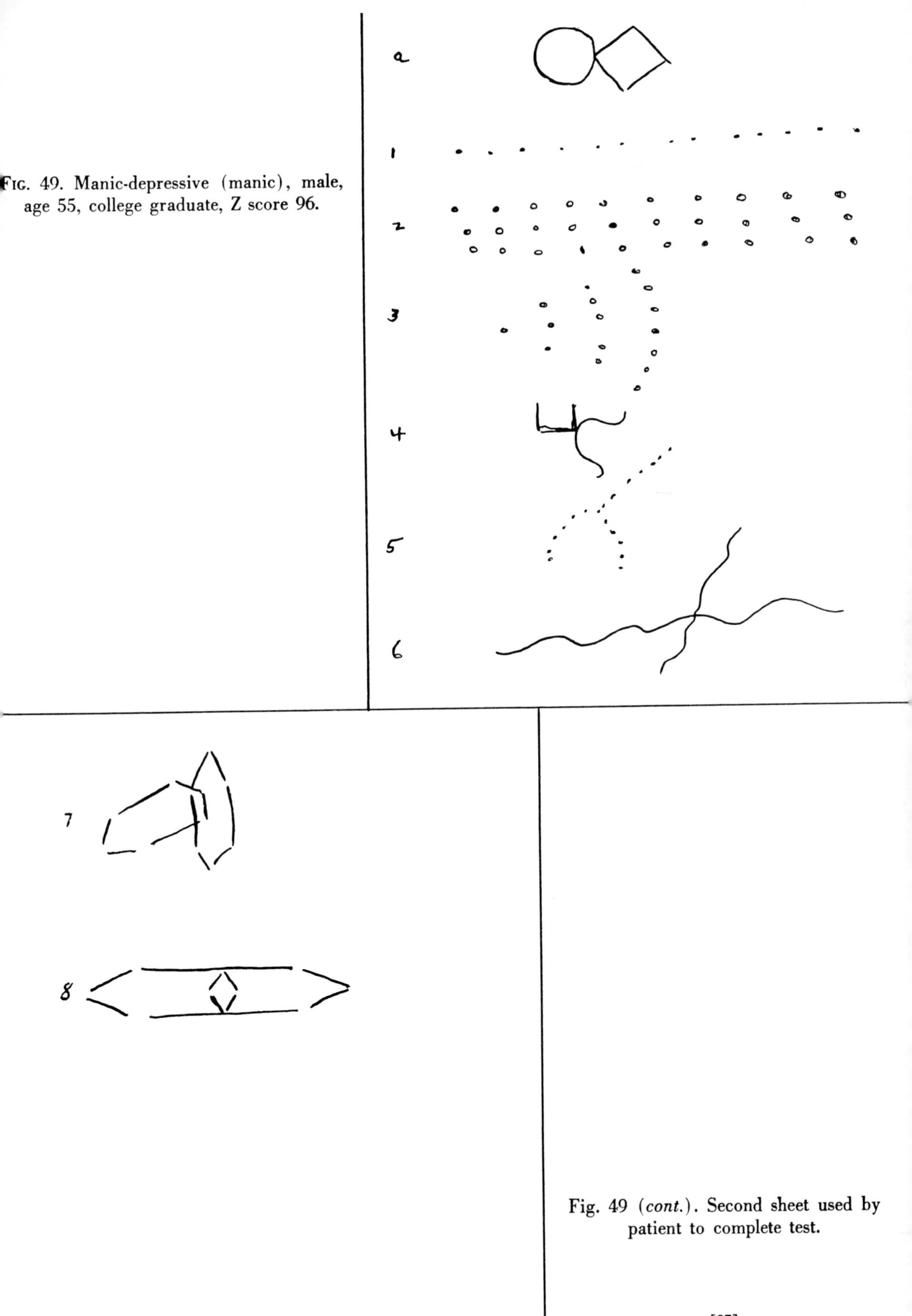

Fig. 49 (*cont.*). Second sheet used by patient to complete test.

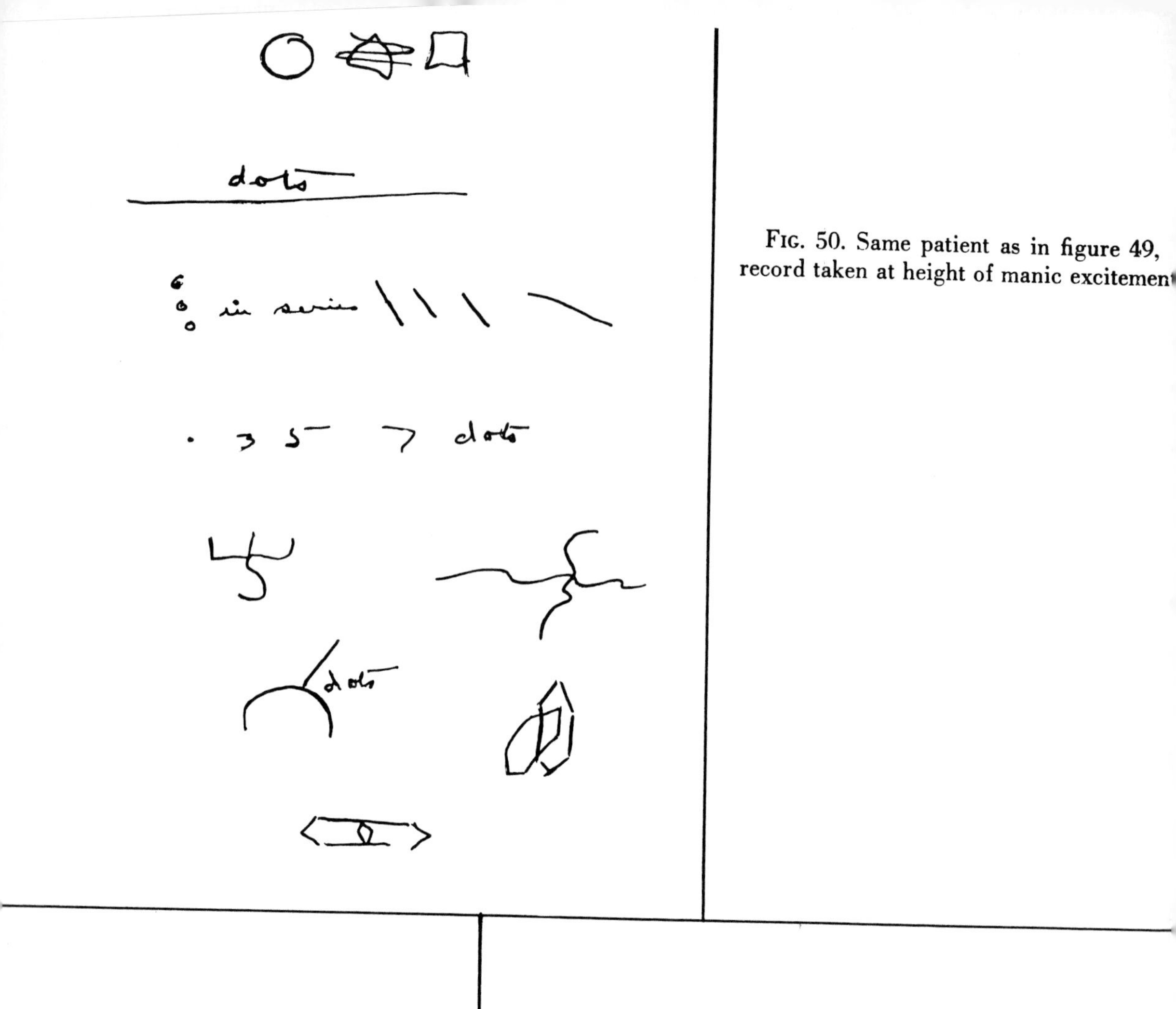

FIG. 50. Same patient as in figure 49, record taken at height of manic excitement

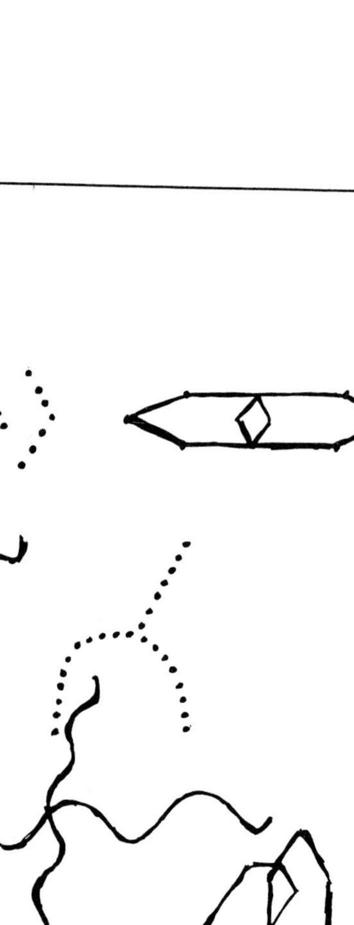

FIG. 51. Part of record of paranoid schizophrenic, male, age 45, college graduate. Note workover of drawings, guide dots and sketching.

Fig. 52. Part of record of paranoid schizophrenic, male, age 49, college graduate. Note guide dots, sketching, extremely light line and arbitrary workover.

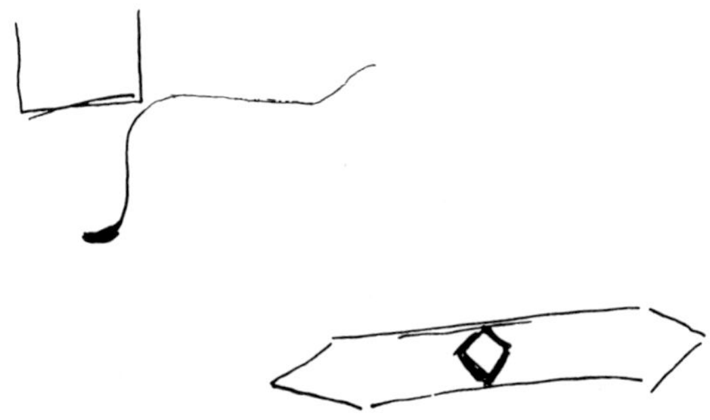

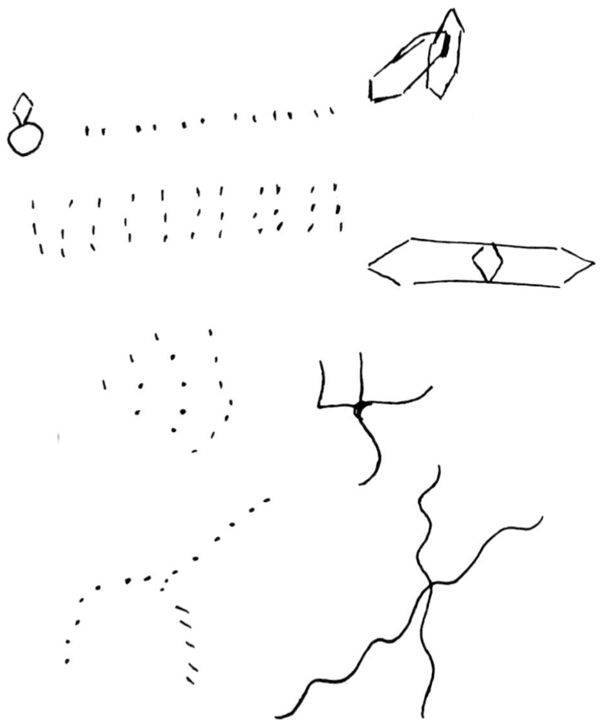

Fig. 53. Outpatient (PN) with pronounced paranoid features, male age 26, grammar school. Note workover in designs 4 and 7.

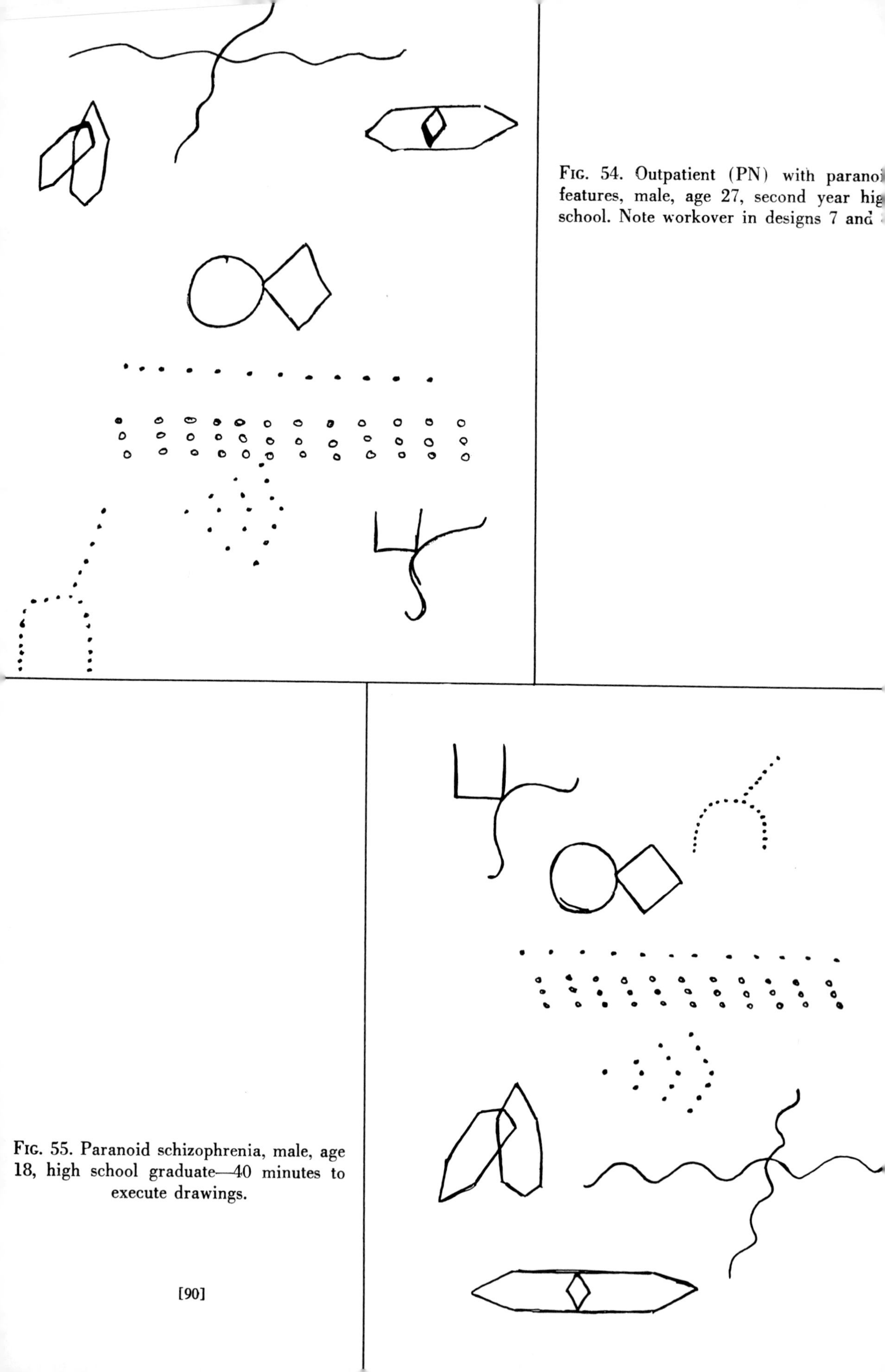

Fig. 54. Outpatient (PN) with paranoi features, male, age 27, second year hig school. Note workover in designs 7 and

Fig. 55. Paranoid schizophrenia, male, age 18, high school graduate—40 minutes to execute drawings.

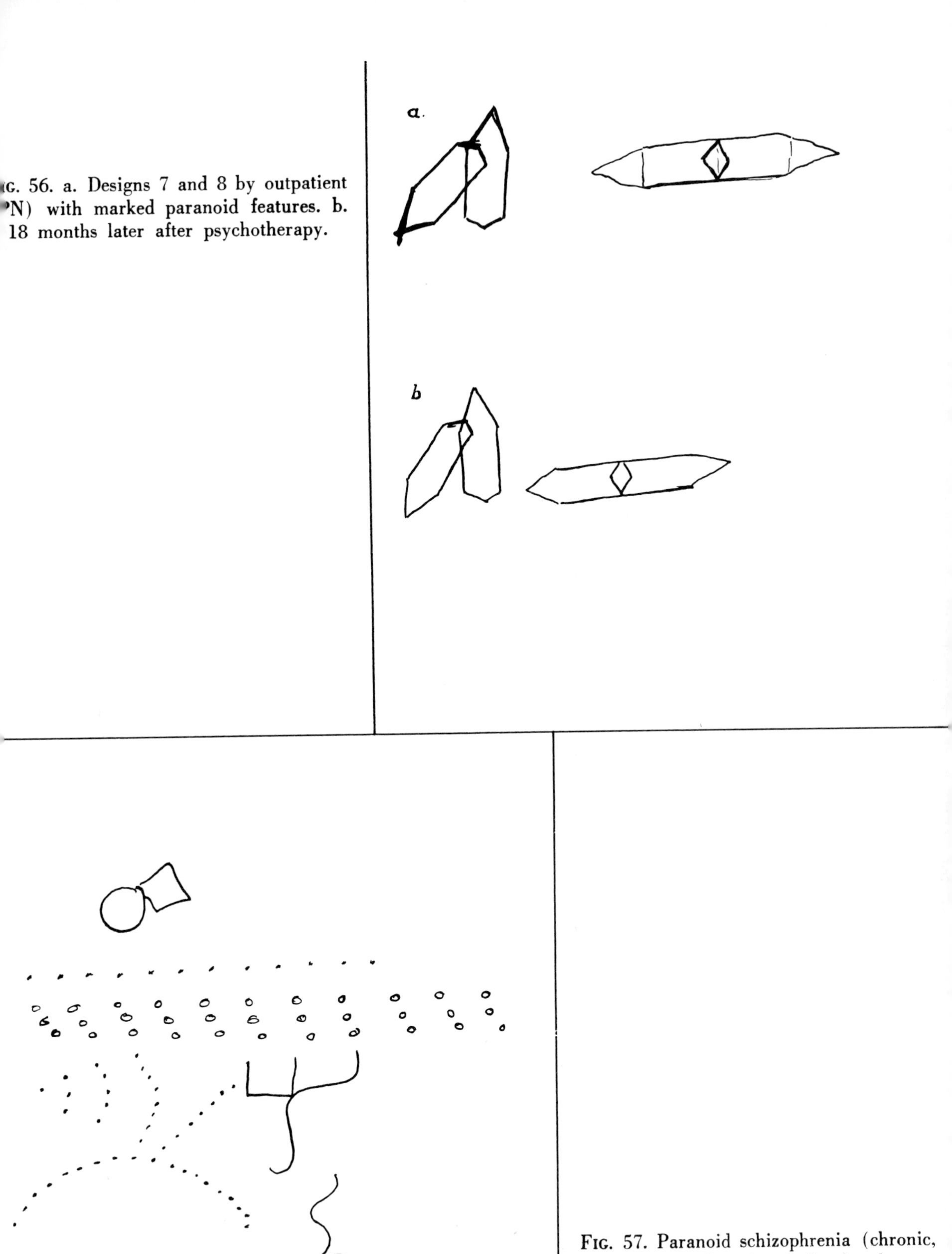

IG. 56. a. Designs 7 and 8 by outpatient
N) with marked paranoid features. b.
18 months later after psychotherapy.

FIG. 57. Paranoid schizophrenia (chronic, "well adjusted" to hospital), female, age 29, college graduate.

If the test is used to follow the course of a patient's progress during hospitalization or as the result of some specific therapy, scores seem to vary with the patient's reaction to treatment. We have already indicated the use of the test to follow the patient's reaction to convulsive therapy. Excited patients tested on admission will generally score higher than if tested when the acute condition has subsided. Thus, one rather excited manic, tested soon after admission, scored 115. Two weeks after admission when the acute excitement had subsided, he scored 89.

Patients who exhibit variable behavior will show fluctuating scores. "Well adjusted" patients will, on the other hand, show a remarkable consistency of scores over several testings. We have not, as previously mentioned, (Chapter 4) been able to show any regular effect of practice, other factors seeming to be of more importance in determining score than the effect of practice. The test, therefore, should prove useful, where repeated measures of psychomotor performances are desired.

Specific Attitudes and Deviations

As we have suggested, the B-G test does not, by our method of scoring, indicate psychiatric diagnoses. We have not, for reasons mentioned previously, attempted, in any systematic fashion, to relate specific deviations to diagnostic categories. In the course of administering several hundred tests we could not, however, fail to note the incidence of certain deviations with certain diagnostic categories and to develop some notions about the relationship.

There seems, for instance, to be a tendency, according to our observations, for paranoid indivuals to work over and "touch-up" their drawings. We shall present parts of the records of several paranoid individuals showing the sort of performance we mean. Figure 51 shows part of the record of a paranoid schizophrenic of long standing, excitable, dangerous, and with poor prognosis, age 45, male, college graduate. The drawings are carefully executed, very heavily pencilled, with line drawings and dots showing considerable thickening due to workover. Figure 52 shows part of the record of another paranoid schizophrenic, an eloper, secretive, who, as a last resort, was subjected to frontal lobotomy. Figure 53 is the record of an outpatient with pronounced paranoid features. Note the workover on designs 4 and 7. Figure 54 is the record of another outpatient with marked paranoid trends. Note designs 7 and 8. Figure 55 is the record of an 18 year old inpatient, a paranoid schizophrenic. He took 40 minutes to copy the designs. Figure 56 shows two executions of designs 7 and 8 by an outpatient with pronounced paranoid features. Figure 56(a) is before psychotherapy; figure 56(b) was taken 18 months later after fairly successful psychotherapy with a marked diminution but not entire absence of paranoid ideation. We have, in our files, the record of one paranoid patient who very carefully sketched each design, one to a page.

Figure 57 is the record of a 29 year old paranoid schizophrenic who has been in the hospital for several years. She is well adjusted to hospital routine and appears content, taking, she says, a great interest in helping new patients to adjust themselves to the hospital. When pressed she will tell of the good she does other patients, intimating she is in the hospital for that reason. Otherwise, she is, for the most part, in good contact and does not feel persecuted. Not all paranoid patients, therefore, work over and touch-up their drawings, and we don't know that all that do are paranoid; but we have observed this type of performance in paranoids with considerable consistency. Our files contain only a few paranoid records that do not show workover and these, as far as we can tell, are the records of chronic and well-adjusted patients. We have observed the presence of workover and touch-up in the records of nonpatients whom we know to be somewhat suspicious of their neighbors and with some tendency to feel persecuted. We should suggest caution in the interpretation of this deviation. Table 8 (Chapter 7) shows that workover is common to psychotics, indicating an average of about two scorable workovers to a record. Nonparanoid patients in common with children are, however, most apt to workover dots, and paranoids the line drawings.

None of the other deviations which we shall mention show the consistency of workover in the records of paranoids, and we do not feel nearly so certain of them. We shall discuss them, briefly, for the possible aid they may be in conjunction with findings from other procedures. Occasionally noted, in the records of hypomanics, is the tendency to leave closed figures open, i.e., the deviation scored is "ends not joined." These same individuals will also tend to make less than the required number of dots or columns for designs 1, 2, and 5 (see figure 50). Tremor, we have noted, is apt to be found in the records of subjects with a great deal of "pentup aggression" providing other factors which may also account for tremor are excluded. Tremor is a very common deviation. It is found in the records of many tense individuals, in some alcoholics, in old age, in various "organic" syndromes. Its interpretation as "pent-up aggression" is, therefore, elusive, and requires considerable corroboration. Compressed drawings, i.e., about one-half the page used for all designs, are sometimes noted in the records of patients with strong feelings of inferiority, and depression (see figure 46). We do not wish to imply that compression is common in all depressed patients, i.e., manic depressives, depressed or involutionals. Most depressed patients observed by us do not compress their drawings. Bender (9, p. 97) writes: "When micrographia occurs it is associated with the poverty of impulses in cases showing lethargy or dullness." In our files micrographia is most often found in compressed drawings. We have noted it, for instance, in the drawings of catatonics in conjunction with otherwise fairly well-executed drawings. (See practice drawings in manual.)

One could, of course, speculate upon the significance of the presence of deviations similar to those found in children, e.g., circles substituted for dots, which are most often found in the records of psychotics. We have not noted, however, that such deviations are specific to any particular diagnosis. Other relationships between deviations and attitudes will be noted by the experienced examiner, e.g., rotation and opposition, but we do not feel that they are of sufficient consistency to be remarked here.

We have attempted, in this section on the clinical use of the test, to show that the B-G record may be economically used as a part of a test battery. Scores on the test give the probability of psychiatric illness. In the records of patients scores are indicative of the extent of the patient's departure from the normative data. We have suggested that low scores may indicate a favorable prognosis for treatment. The presence of major deviations influences judgment as to the seriousness and the nature of the illness. Beyond what information we have been able to impart about the use of the test the discerning reader will have realized that judgment of the individual record requires a good deal of clinical art. The quantification of the Bender-Gestalt test will, it is hoped, assist the clinician; it does not supplant the need for his art.

APPENDIX

Table I.
Item Frequencies, Weights and Phi Coefficients
(260 Nonpatients, 260 patients)

	Frequency Nonpt.	Pt.	Phi	Wt.
Design 1				
Item 1	62	111	.20	2
" 2	1	12	.18*	3
" 3	8	16	.08	2
" 4	2	17		8
" 5	4	7	.18*	2 (each)
" 6	0	1		8
" 7	47	80	.12	2
" 8	2	5	.22*	3 (each)
" 9	0	2	.30*	8
" 10	. . .	. . .		8
Totals	126	251		
Design 2				
Item 1	118	169	.20	2
" 2	6	12	.11	3
" 3	8	35	.20	3
" 4	2	7		5
" 5	1	5		5
" 6	16	51	.22	3
" 7	2	6	.18*	2 (each)
" 8	0	1		8
" 9	1	3	.11*	2
" 10	11	26	.12	2
" 11	0	2	.22*	3
" 12	0	4	.30*	8
" 13	. . .	. . .		8
Totals	165	321		
Design 3				
Item 1	102	129	.22*	3
" 2	10	22	.18*	3
" 3	5	12	.10*	2
" 4	. . .	. . .		8
" 5	32	43	.18	2
" 6	. . .	. . .		8
" 7	6	15		8
" 8	0	2		8
" 9	0	4	.11*	2
" 10	43	81	.12*	2
" 11	0	2	.22*	3
" 12	1	13	.30*	8
" 13	. . .	. . .		8
Totals	199	323		

Table I (continued)

	Frequency Nonpt.	Pt.	Phi	Wt.
Design 4				
Item 1	66	93	.22*	3
" 2	1	14	.12	4
" 3	59	80	.09	1
" 4	5	21	.12	4
" 5	...	...		8
" 6	1	6	.10*	3
" 7	0	6		8
" 8	87	165	.35*	4
" 9	...	...		8
" 10	0	1	.11*	2
" 11	5	18	.22*	3 (each)
" 12	0	5	.30*	8
" 13	0	1		8
Totals	224	410		
Design 5				
Item 1	62	120	.22*	3
" 2	16	28	.18*	3
" 3	6	14	.10*	2
" 4	...	...		8
" 5	100	139	.13*	2
" 6	4	12	.10*	3
" 7	1	3	.18*	2
" 8	0	1		8
" 9	7	20	.11*	2
" 10	41	66	.12*	2
" 11	0	4	.22*	3
" 12	0	6	.30*	8
" 13	0	1		8
Totals	237	414		
Design 6				
Item 1	29	74	.22*	3
" 2	39	69	.12	2
" 3	2	5		2
" 4	0	4		8
" 5	36	61	.18*	1 (each)
" 6	0	3		8
" 7	80	176	.35*	4
" 8	0	1		8
" 9	0	1	.11*	2
" 10	2	9	.12*	2
" 11	1	14	.22*	3
" 12	0	3	.30*	8
" 13	0	4		8
Totals	189	424		

Table I (continued)

	Frequency Nonpt.	Pt.	Phi	Wt.
Design 7				
Item 1	. . .	. . .		8
" 2	20	56	.18	3
" 3	20	27	.09*	3
" 4	16	59	.22*	3
" 5	91	139	.18*	1 (each)
" 6	56	157	.35*	4
" 7	4	11		8
" 8	6	7	.11*	2
" 9	5	11	.22*	3 (each)
" 10	1	15	.30*	8
" 11	0	3		8
Totals	219	485		
Design 8				
Item 1	. . .	. . .		8
" 2	18	49	.20	3
" 3	5	14	.09	3
" 4	10	35	.22*	3
" 5	70	93	.18*	1 (each)
" 6	65	138	.35*	4
" 7	2	10		8
" 8	10	12	.11*	2
" 9	10	31	.12*	2
" 10	5	14	.22*	3 (each)
" 11	0	5	.30*	8
" 12	0	3		8
Totals	195	404		
Configuration				
Item 1	18	33	.11	2
" 2	17	38	.13	2 (each)
" 3	4	14		3
" 4	0	4		8
" 5	20	34	.09	2
" 6	4	13		8
" 7	. . .	. . .		8
Totals	63	136		
Totals—all items	1617	3168		
Mean No. Deviations per Subject	6.2	12.2		

*Combined with same deviation in other designs. Phi coefficient is for combined frequencies.

Table II

Z Scores for Subjects of One Year or More of High School

Ages 15–50 $Z = 1.06\ (x - 18.0) + 50.$

Raw Score	Z Score	Raw Score	Z Score	Raw Score	Z Score
1	32	51	85	101	138
2	33	52	86	102	139
3	34	53	87	103	140
4	35	54	88	104	141
5	36	55	89	105	142
6	37	56	90	106	143
7	38	57	91	107	144
8	39	58	92	108	145
9	40	59	93	109	146
10	41	60	95	110	148
11	43	61	96	111	149
12	44	62	97	112	150
13	45	63	98	113	151
14	46	64	99	114	152
15	47	65	100	115	153
16	48	66	101	116	154
17	49	67	102	117	155
18	50	68	103	118	156
19	51	69	104	119	157
20	52	70	105	120	158
21	53	71	106	121	159
22	54	72	107	122	160
23	55	73	108	123	161
24	56	74	109	124	162
25	57	75	110	125	163
26	59	76	111	126	165
27	60	77	113	127	166
28	61	78	114	128	167
29	62	79	115	129	168
30	63	80	116	130	169
31	64	81	117	131	170
32	65	82	118	132	171
33	66	83	119	133	172
34	67	84	120	134	173
35	68	85	121	135	174
36	69	86	122	136	175
37	70	87	123	137	176
38	71	88	124	138	177
39	72	89	125	139	178
40	73	90	126	140	179
41	74	91	127	141	180
42	75	92	128	142	182
43	77	93	130	143	183
44	78	94	131	144	184
45	79	95	132	145	185
46	80	96	133	146	186
47	81	97	134	147	187
48	82	98	135	148	188
49	83	99	136	149	189
50	84	100	137	150	190

Table III

Z Scores for Subjects of One Year or More of College

Ages 15–50 $Z = 1.10\ (x - 12.7) + 50.$

Raw Score	Z Score	Raw Score	Z Score	Raw Score	Z Score
1	37	51	92	101	147
2	38	52	93	102	148
3	39	53	94	103	149
4	40	54	95	104	150
5	41	55	97	105	151
6	42	56	98	106	152
7	43	57	99	107	153
8	45	58	100	108	154
9	46	59	101	109	155
10	47	60	102	110	156
11	48	61	103	111	157
12	49	62	104	112	159
13	50	63	105	113	160
14	51	64	106	114	161
15	52	65	107	115	162
16	53	66	108	116	163
17	54	67	110	117	164
18	55	68	111	118	165
19	56	69	112	119	166
20	58	70	113	120	167
21	59	71	114	121	168
22	60	72	115	122	169
23	61	73	116	123	170
24	62	74	117	124	171
25	63	75	118	125	172
26	64	76	119	126	173
27	65	77	120	127	176
28	66	78	121	128	177
29	68	79	122	129	178
30	69	80	123	130	179
31	70	81	124	131	180
32	71	82	125	132	181
33	72	83	126	133	182
34	73	84	128	134	183
35	74	85	129	135	184
36	75	86	130	136	185
37	76	87	131	137	186
38	77	88	132	138	187
39	79	89	133	139	189
40	80	90	134	140	190
41	81	91	135	141	191
42	82	92	136	142	192
43	83	93	137	143	193
44	84	94	138	144	194
45	85	95	139	145	195
46	86	96	140	146	196
47	87	97	143	147	197
48	88	98	144	148	198
49	90	99	145	149	200
50	91	100	146	150	201

REFERENCES

1. ALEXANDER, F.: Fundamentals of Psychoanalysis. New York, W.W. Norton, 1948.
2. ANASTASI, A., and FOLEY, J. P., JR.: A survey of the literature on artistic behavior in the abnormal: 1. Historical and theoretical background. J. Gen. Psychol., *25*: 111—142, 1941.
3. ——, ——: An experimental study of the drawing behavior of adult psychotics in comparison with that of a normal control group. J. Exper. Psychol., *34*: 169—194, 1944.
4. ANONYMOUS: A guide to the use of the Bender-Gestalt drawings. Neuropsychiatric Service, Psychology and Social Work Section, Mason General Hospital, Brentwood, L.I., New York, 1945.
5. Army Air Force Aviation Psychology Program Research Report No. 15: The Psychological Program in Army Air Force Convalescent Hospitals (Restricted).
6. ASH, PHILIP: The reliability of psychiatric diagnosis. J. Abnorm. & Social Psychol., *44*: 272—276, 1949.
7. BARTLETT, F. C.: Remembering: a Study in Experimental and Social Psychology. New York, Macmillan, 1932.
8. BENDER, L.: Principles of Gestalt in copied form in mentally defective and schizophrenic persons. Arch. Neurol & Psychiat., *28*: 661—673, 1932.
9. ——: A visual motor Gestalt test and its clinical use. Amer. Orthopsychiat. Assoc., Res. Monog. no. 3, 1938, 176 pp.
10. ——: Instructions for the use of visual motor Gestalt test. New York, Am. Orthopsychiat. Assoc., 1946.
11. ——, CURRAN, F. J., and SCHILDER, P.: Organization of memory traces in the Korsakoff syndrome. Arch. Neurol. & Psychiat., *39*: 452—487, 1938.
12. BILLINGSLEA, F.: The Bender-Gestalt test: An objective scoring method and validating data. J. Clin. Psychol., *4*: 1—28, 1948.
13. BRUNNER, J. and GOODMAN, C.: Need and value as organizing factors in perception. J. Abnorm. and Social Psychol., *42*: 33—44, 1947.
14. COBB, S.: Personality as affected by lesions of the brain. In Hunt, J. McV.: Personality and the Behavior Disorders, v. 1. New York, The Ronald Press, 1944.
15. CORNELL, E., and COXE, W.: A Performance Ability Scale: Examination Manual. Yonkers, World Book Co., 1934.
16. EDWARDS, A.: Statistical Analysis for Students in Psychology and Education. New York, Rinehart, 1946.

17. EYESENCK, H.: Dimensions of Personality. London, Kegan Paul, Trench, Trubner, and Co., Ltd., 1947.
18. FREUD, S.: Interpretation of Dreams. New York, Macmillan, 1933.
19. ——: Metapsychological Supplement to Theory of Dreams, Collected Papers, v. 4. London, Hogarth Press, 1924.
20. GELLHORN, E.: Autonomic Regulations: Their significance for Physiology, Psychology, and Neuropsychiatry. New York, Interscience Publishers, 1943.
21. GLUECK, G.: Psicopatalogia della percezione della forma. Principi della forma nei disequi copiati di malati mentali. Arch. psicol., neurol. e psichiat., *1*: 603—664, 1940.
22. GOLDWORTH, SAMUEL,: A comparative study of the drawings of a man and a woman done by normal, neurotic, schizophrenic and brain damaged individuals. Unpublished doctoral thesis, Department of Psychology, University of Pittsburgh, 1949.
23. GUILFORD, J.: Fundamental Statistics in Psychology and Education. New York, McGraw-Hill Book Co., 1942.
24. HARROWER, M.: Changes in figure-ground perception in patients with cortical lesions. Brit. J. M. Psychol., *30*: 47—51, 1939.
25. HOAGLAND, H., ELMADJIAN, F., and PINCUS, G.: Stressful psychomotor performance and adrenal cortical function as indicated by the lymphocyte response. J. Clin. Endocrinol., *6*: 301—311, 1946.
26. HOSKINS, R.: The Biology of Schizophrenia. New York, W.W. Norton, 1946.
27. HUNT, J. McV., and COFER, C.N.: Psychological deficit. Chapter 32 in Hunt, J. McV.: Personality and the Behavior Disorders, New York, The Ronald Press, 1944.
28. HUSTON, P. E.: The reflex time of the patellar tendon reflex in normal and schizophrenic subjects. J. Gen. Psychol., *13*: 3—41, 1935.
29. ——, SHAKOW, D., and RIGGS, L. A.: Studies of motor functions in schizophrenia: II. Reaction Time. J. Gen. Psychol., *16*: 39—82, 1937.
30. HUTT, M.: A Tentative Guide for the Administration and Interpretation of the Bender-Gestalt Test. U. S. Army, Adjutant General's School, 1945 (Restricted).
31. ——: The use of projective methods in personality measurement in Army medical installations. J. Clin. Psychol., *1*: 134—140, 1945.
32. McCLELLAND, D., and ATKINSON, J.: The projective expression of needs. I. The effect of different intensities of the hunger drive on perception. J. Psychol., *25*: 205--232, 1948..
33. ——, ——, and CLARK, R.: The projective expression of needs. III. The effect of ego-involvement, success, and failure on perception. J. Psychol., *27*: 311—330, 1949.
34. McNEMAR, Q.: Psychological Statistics. New York, Wiley & Sons, 1949.
35. ORENSTEIN, L., and SCHILDER, P.: Psychological consideration of insulin treatment in schizophrenia. J. Nerv. & Ment. Dis., *88*: 397—416. 644—660, 1939.
36. OTIS, A.: Otis Self-Administering Test of Mental Ability. Yonkers, World Book Co., 1922.
37. PASCAL, G.: Quantification of the Bender-Gestalt test: A preliminary report. Am. J. Orthopsychiat. *20*: 418—423, 1950.

38. ——, and ZEAMAN, J.: A note on the validity of Wechsler-Bellevue Scatter. Am. J. Psychiat., *105*: 840—842, 1949.
39. ——, ——: Simple methods for the objective determination of some effects of electroconvulsive therapy on the individual patient. J. Abnorm. and Social Psychol. (In press)
40. POSTMAN, L., BRUNNER, J., and MCGINNIES, E.: Personal values as selective factors in perception. J. Abnorm. and Social Psychol., *43*: 142—154, 1948.
41. RABIN, A.: The Use of the Wechsler-Bellevue scales with normal and abnormal persons. Psychol. Bull., *42*: 410—422, 1945.
42. RAPAPORT, D., GILL, M., and SCHAFER, R.: Diagnostic Psychological Testing. Menninger Clinic Monograph Series, nos. 3 and 4. Chicago, Yearbook Publishers, 1945.
43. RICHARDSON, M., and KUDER, G.: The calculation of test reliability coefficients based upon the method of rational equivalence. J. Educ. Psychol., *30*: 681—687, 1939.
44. SCHILDER, P.: Notes on the psychology of Metrazol treatment of schizophrenia. J. Nerv. & Ment. Dis., *89*: 133, 1939.
45. STAINBROOK, E.: Shock Therapy: Psychologic theory and research. Psychol. Bull., *43*: 21—60, 1946.
46. ——, and LOWENBACH, H.: Writing and drawing of psychotic individuals after electrically induced convulsions. J. Nerv. & Ment. Dis., *99*: 382—388, 1944.
47. TERMAN, L., and MERRILL, M.: Measuring Intelligence. Boston, Houghton Mifflin, 1937.
48. THORNDIKE, E.: The Measurement of Intelligence. New York, Bureau of Publications, Teacher's College, Columbia U., 1927.
49. WATSON, R.: The Use of the Wechsler-Bellevue Scales: A Supplement. Psychol. Bull., *43*: 61—68, 1946.
50. WECHSLER, D.: The Measurement of Adult Intelligence (3rd ed.). Baltimore, Williams and Wilkins, 1944.
51. WERTHEIMER, M.: Studies in the Theory of Gestalt Psychology. Psychol. Forsch., *4*: 301—350, 1923.
52. WOLFF, W.: Diagrams of the Unconscious. New York, Grune & Stratton, 1948.

SCORING MANUAL

THE BENDER-GESTALT TEST

INTRODUCTION

Each test figure, of which there are nine, is called by us a *design*. Thus, the first test figure, the square and circle, is called *design A*. Thereafter, designs are numbered. Each scorable deviation, called an *item*, is numbered, named, and described in this manual. Item numbers are consecutive by designs, the first item in each design being numbered *one*.

Item definitions are supported by examples, except where scoring is obvious. The illustrations accompanying each item are part of the definition of that item. In some cases examples give the meaning of the item so clearly that verbal definition is kept to a minimum. In other cases the examples illustrate when to score and when not to score and help to sharpen judgment for doubtful deviations. It is clear, therefore, that careful scrutiny of item examples and an understanding of the "score" and "no score" examples is important in order to achieve reliable scoring.

A word needs to be said concerning the examples used to illustrate item definitions. These examples are taken from actual records and are apt to show deviations other than the one under consideration. In order to avoid confusion, therefore, the examples used to illustrate an item are *scored only for the item defined*. Such a procedure does not mean that the examples may not have other scorable deviations.

In addition to examples illustrating each item, several examples are given illustrating the total scoring for each design. These examples, taken from actual records, attempt to illustrate difficult scoring and are scored for all scorable deviations. In these examples each scorable deviations is numbered and its location on the drawing is indicated. Careful study of these examples, illustrating the scoring for each design, is also important if reliability in scoring is to be obtained.

Assuming the beginning scorer has read through the manual once, having studied each scorable deviation, he has some understanding of the nature of the scoring system. Before discussing actual scoring we should like to present, briefly, two items of equipment which we have found to be important in scoring. The first of these is the score sheet. It shows the numbers, names, and weights of all scorable deviations, providing a systematic method of accumulating scores by items, design totals, and total for the test. It serves as a check list which not only speeds up scoring but is also indispensable for reliability in scoring, for without some such reminder it is easy to overlook scorable deviations. A sample score sheet is on page 209; on it are entered the name of the subject, his age, education and, after the accumulation of raw scores, his Z score. The other item of equipment which we have found to be important in scoring is a transparent combination ruler and protractor. Although scoring is, in general, by inspection, there are doubtful cases which need to be measured. Beginning scorers may, at first, feel more confident of their judgments if these are confirmed by actual measurement.

Armed with the score sheet, a transparent combination ruler and protractor, the examiner is ready to begin scoring. *Design A is not scored.* Beginning with design 1 the reproduction is examined to ascertain whether or not a scorable deviation occurs. Thus, design 1, item 1, wavy line of dots. If the deviation occurs, the record is scored two and this is tabulated in the appropriate space on the score sheet. Each item for each design and for configuration is checked, and a total raw score obtained. Where no scorable deviation occurs the record is automatically scored one. Two tables are provided in the Appendix for the conversion of raw scores to standard scores. If the subject is between the ages of 15 and 50 and has one year or more of high school, and no college education, the table for subjects of high school education, table II, is used and the standard score found opposite the raw score. If the subject has one year or more of college, table III is used.

Opportunity is provided for practice, and for the beginning scorer to check his own reliability and validity. Forty-five actual records accompany this manual. These are so arranged that 25 of them are for practice and 20 for a check on reliability and validity. The completed score sheets are included with the manual and immediately follow the description of scorable deviations. These score sheets show the number of the record, the age, education, I.Q., diagnosis, item scores, total raw scores, and Z scores, when applicable, for all except the first three drawings.

Records 1 to 25, inclusive, are the reproductions of individuals of various nosological groups. The first three records, of feeble minded subjects, are not scored. These records are included as obvious examples of the reproductions of the feeble minded, typically not scored by us. All of the other records are scored. Some of the records, being reproductions of individuals outside of the normative population, are scored but the raw score is not converted to a standard score. We have included such records because they afford examples of difficult scoring, and to indicate that, although no norms are available, the method of scoring may be used, for purposes of comparison, with individuals outside the normalizing population. Records 1 to 25, then, are intended for practice in scoring. The beginning scorer should attempt to score the reproductions without reference to the completed score sheets. After scoring each record he should check his score against that of the authors, referring to the manual in cases of discrepancy. With reasonable care the beginning scorer should, by the time he has scored 20 records in this manner, be scoring within four or five points of the authors' scores. Users of this manual have reported that by the twenty-fifth record they are scoring at the rate of about five minutes per record.

Records 26 to 45, inclusive, are to be scored by the beginning scorer without reference to the completed score sheets. The beginning scorer should score all 20 records and then, as an estimate of his reliability, compare his scores with those given by the authors. He can, if he wishes, calculate his reliability coefficient. It should be close to .90. Mean scores should not differ more than five points from those given. There is, however, a relationship between the size of the score and the discrepancy between two scorers, i.e., the higher the score the greater the discrepancy. But with high scores a few score points one way or another make relatively little difference—whether a record receives a score of 101 or 109 is of little practical significance. Discrepancies of over five for high scoring records should not, then, worry the beginning scorer unduly.

Ten records of patients and ten records of nonpatients are included in this last batch of reproductions (nos. 26-45). Mean score for the nonpatients (as scored by the authors) is 45.1 and for the patients 80.3. These are not representative records, as the mean scores indicate. We have attempted, insofar as the small sample would permit, to cover the age and education range of the nonpatient population, and to cover a range of diagnostic categories in the patient sample. Within these limits, selection was unbiased. Reliable scoring in this sample of twenty records will lead to perfect validity in differentiating between patients and nonpatients on the basis of Z scores when the 20 records are divided into two groups.

A final word of caution to the beginning scorer. The utility of the data provided in this book depends on the extent of agreement with the authors *in scoring.* The examiner can make no inferences based on the data of this book unless he is fairly certain that his scoring is in agreement with the authors. Experience has shown that reliable scoring can be achieved by careful study of this manual and practice on the records provided, in the manner indicated.

DESIGN 1

(12 Dots)

1. *Wavy line of dots. Score 2.* For this deviation to be scored, the dots should form a distinctly wavy line. Only gross deviations from a straight line of dots are scored (as in examples 1 and 2). In this, as well as in all other deviations, subjective certainty, based on a study of the examples provided, is what is required to score. Thus, a glance at examples 1 and 2 show them to be decidedly "wavy." In cases of doubt, as in example 4, the item is not scored.

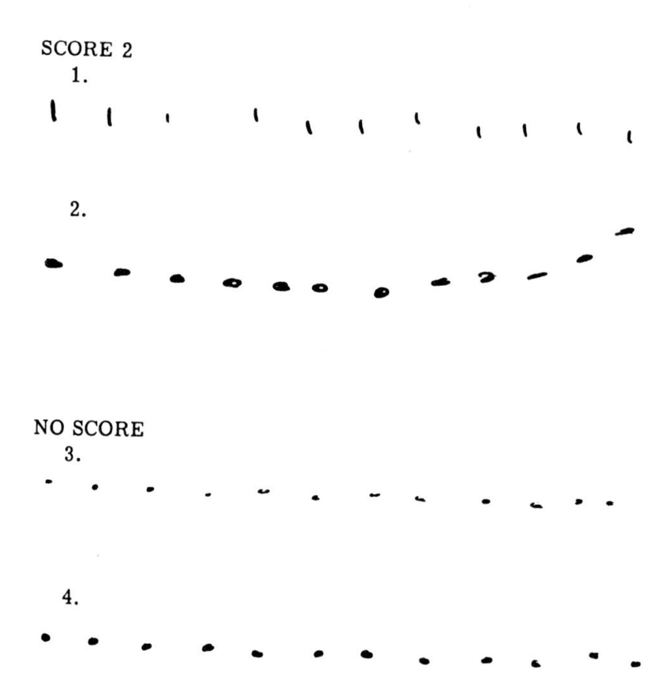

2. *Dots, dashes, and circles. Score 3.* This deviation is scored when there is variability in the reproduction of the stimulus, i.e., when dots and dashes, dots and circles, dashes and circles, or all three, are used in the reproduction. The item is scored when two or more dots are converted to dashes or circles. It is not scored when all the dots, or all except one dot, are converted to dashes or circles (see example 5).

A dash is defined as a line of at least $^{1}/_{16}$ inch; a circle should be clear and unfilled. Enlarged dots and partially filled circles are not considered circles for the scoring of this item (see example 6). Again, in cases of doubt, the item is not scored.

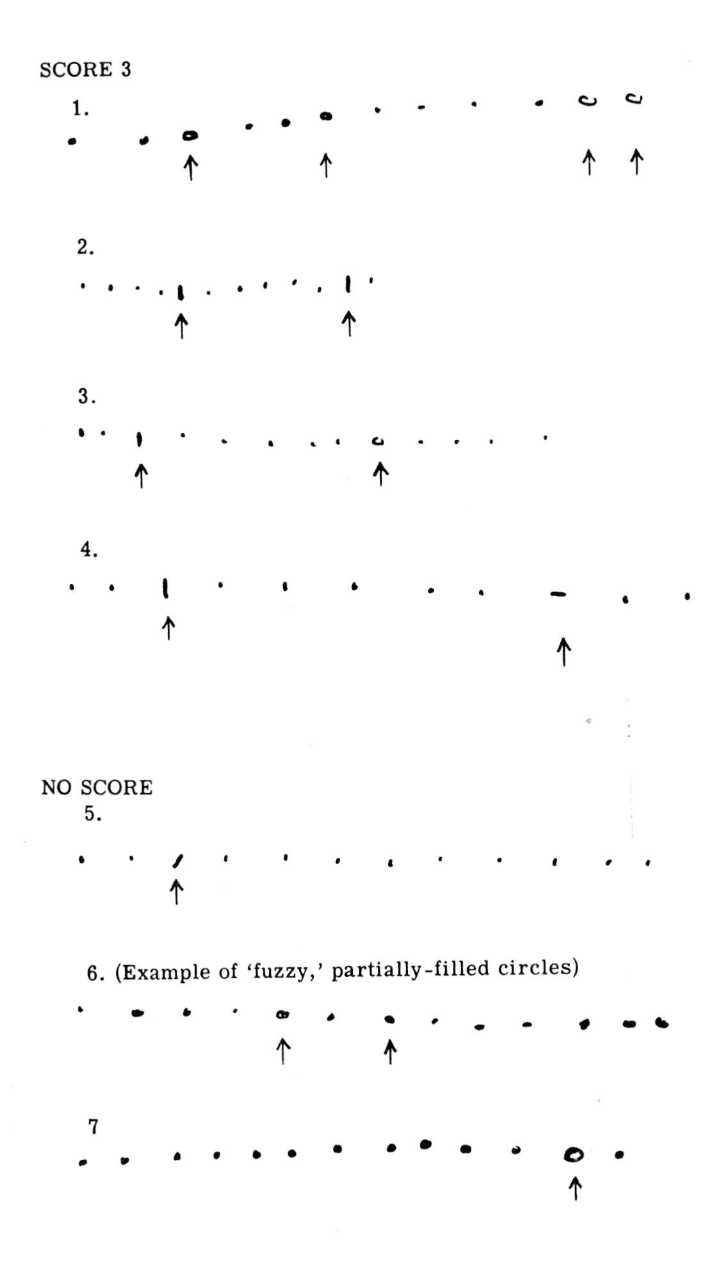

3. *Dashes. Score 2.* For this deviation to be scored all the dots, or all except one dot, must be converted to dashes, i.e., lines of at least $^1/_{16}$ inch, either horizontal or vertical. If, in a line of dashes, two or more of the elements

remain dots as in the stimulus, the reproduction is scored for variability, item 2.

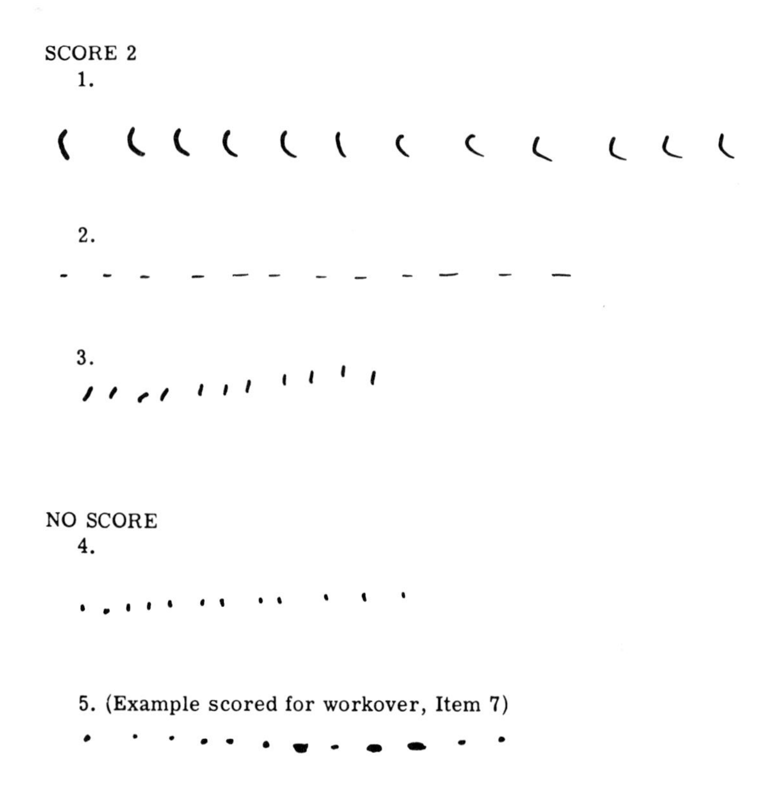

4. *Circles. Score 8.* For this deviation to be scored all the dots, or all except one dot, must be converted to clear, unfilled circles. If, in a line of such circles, two or more of the elements remain dots, the reproduction is scored for variability, item 2.

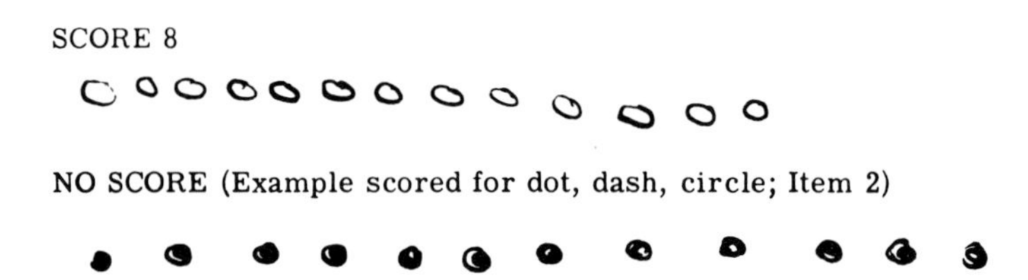

5. *Number of dots. Score 2 for each.* The stimulus for design 1 consists of 12 dots. If, in the reproduction, the number of dots is less than 10, or more than 14 (and the dots are yet a part of the design, not "extra-scattered" dots) the item is scored. For each dot lacking or in excess of this tolerance, the score is 2; e.g., if the reproduction consists of 8 dots, the score for the item would be 4 (example 1).

N. B. If there are 6 or less dots, the reproduction is scored for "part of design missing," item 10.

SCORE 4

SCORE 14

6. *Double row. Score 8.* This item is scored when the design is reproduced on two lines instead of one. The deviation occurs when the subject, lacking in judgment, begins the design in spite of insufficient space, and, when unable to complete the design on one line, continues on the next. The double row deviation differs from that scored under item 8, second attempt, in the number of dots present. (See examples following.)

SCORE 8

NO SCORE (Examples scored for second attempt, Item 8)

1.

2.

7. *Workover. Score 2.* Most normal subjects reproduce the stimulus by single dots, or by slightly thickened dots, i.e., small, filled circles (example 4). Some subjects, however, so belabor the dots that they become large, and appear to result from the expenditure of a great deal of effort. Such elaborations are scored as "workover."

Scorable workover occurs in three instances, as illustrated in the examples: 1) when a single dot is so excessively belabored that it stands out from the line of dots (example 1), 2) when several dots (three or more) are so worked-over that they differ from the remaining dots, although not quite to the extent of the first instance (example 2), and 3) when all the dots appear to result from a great deal of elaboration (example 3).

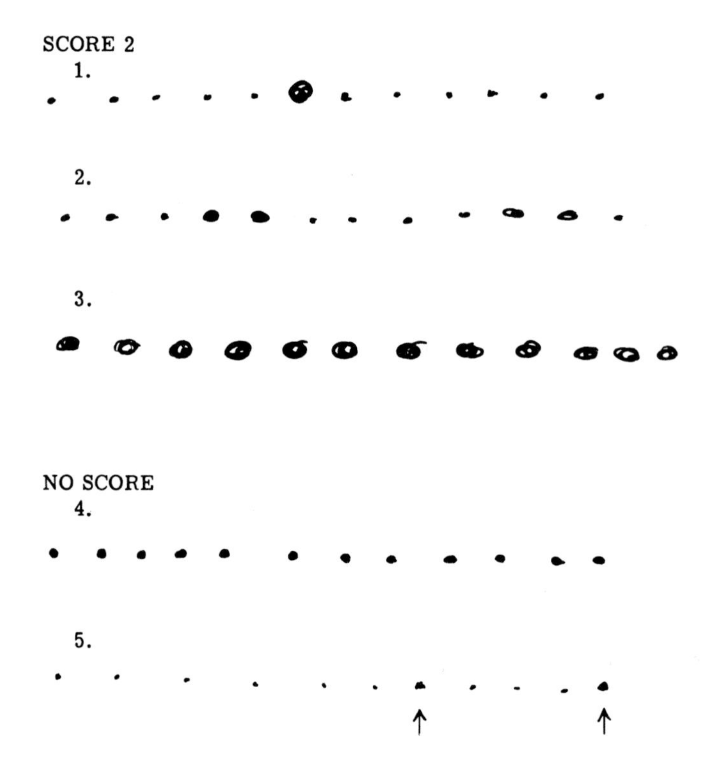

8. *Second attempt. Score 3 for each.* When the subject makes, and fails to erase, more than one attempt to reproduce the design, the item is scored. Attempts crossed out, or incompletely erased, are scored; the score is 3 for *each* such attempt.

9. *Rotation. Score 8.* This item is scored if the design is reproduced vertically rather than horizontally, or if the reproduction is rotated from the horizontal 45° or more. Scorable rotations may come about 1) by inversion of the reproduction from a properly oriented stimulus card, or 2) by a turning of the stimulus card by the subject. *Nonscorable* rotations may result from turning the paper, e.g., when the subject, in order to make the most economical use of the paper turns it to fit in the drawing.

SCORE 8

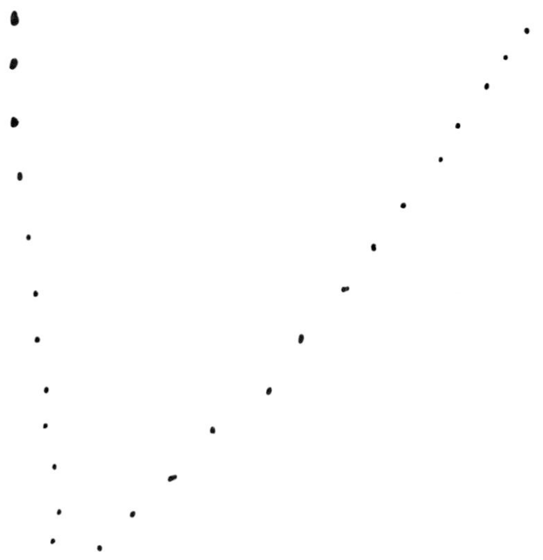

NO SCORE

10. *Part of the design missing. Score 8.* If the design is reproduced with six or fewer dots, the item is scored.

Examples of scoring for Design 1. Items scored are indicated by numbers; location of deviation, by arrows. The total score for the design is below each reproduction.

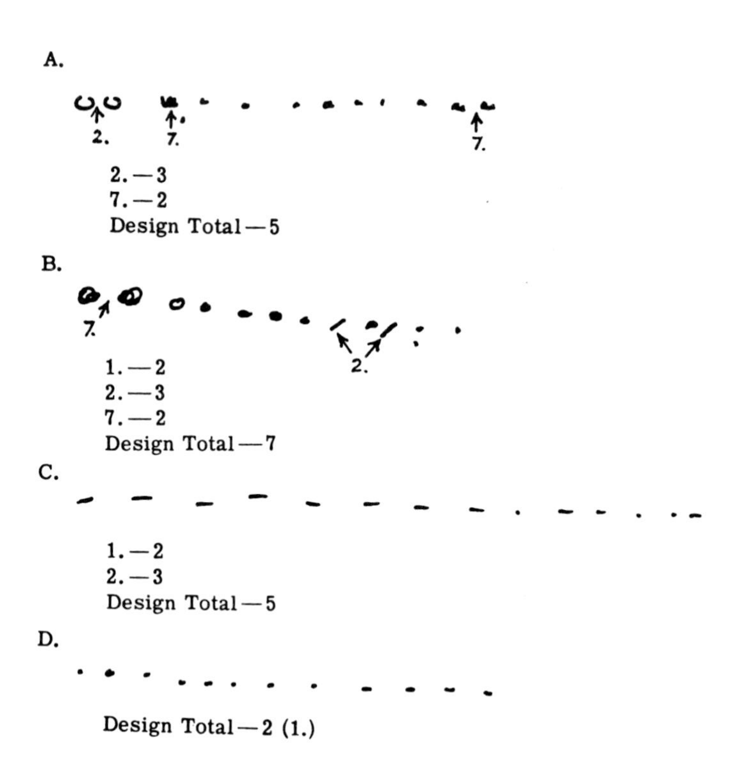

DESIGN 2

(11 Columns of Circles)

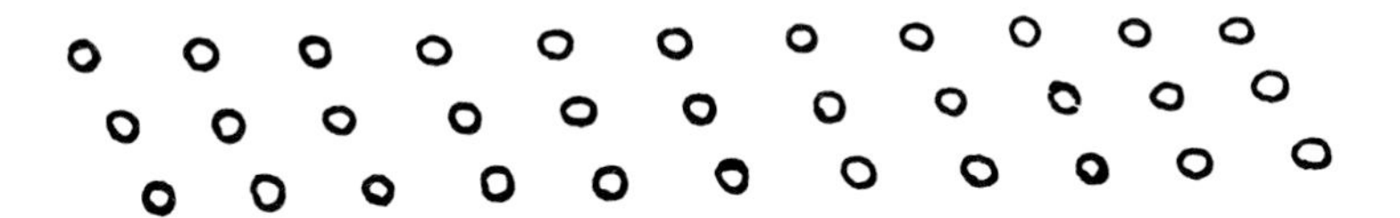

1. *Wavy line. Score 2.* For this deviation to be scored, the bottom row of circles should form a distinctly wavy line. Rotating the paper 90^{0} facilitates observation of this deviation. As in design 1, the scoring is not rigid; in cases of doubt, the item is not scored. Example 3 illustrates a borderline case, not scored.

SCORE 2

1.

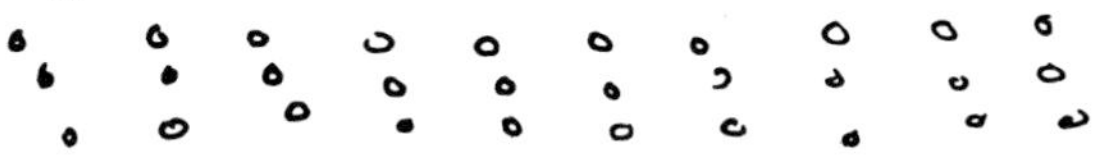

2.

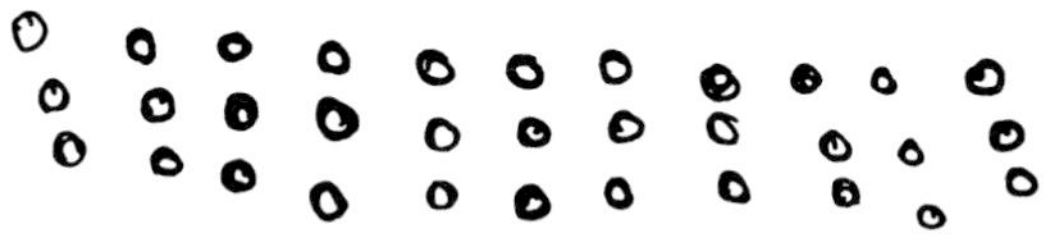

NO SCORE

3.

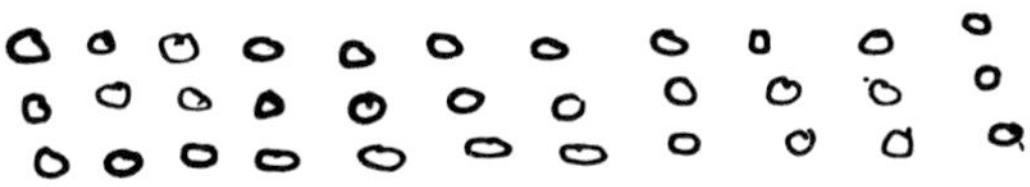

2. *Dashes or dots instead of circles. Score 3.* Where dashes and/or dots are consistently (more than half) substituted for circles, the item is scored.

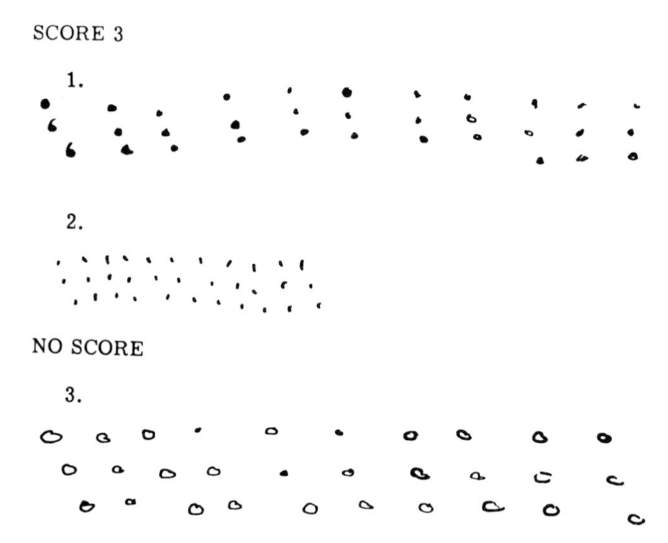

3. *Circles showing tremor or other deviations in shape. Score 3.* Three or more of the circles should show tremor or deviate markedly from the circular, for the item to be scored. Tremor, as it is found in this design, is easily observable as small, irregular changes in the direction of the line. Marked deviations from the circular occur in several ways: the resulting reproduction may appear heart-shaped, diamond-shaped, tear-drop–shaped, and the like (see examples following). In cases of doubt, the item is *not* scored.

SCORE 3

1. (Example scored for tremor)

2. (Example scored for tremor, and deviations in shape)

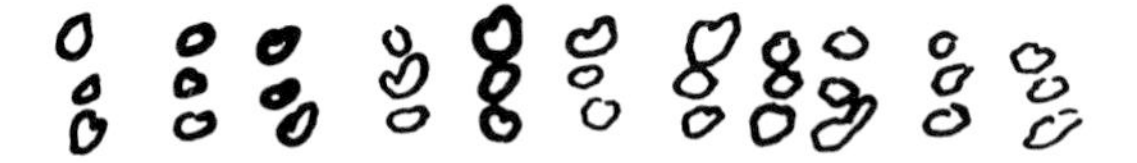

3. (Example scored for deviations in shape)

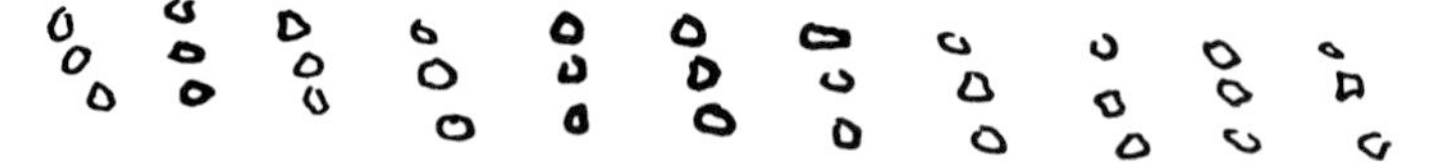

4. (Examples scored for deviations in shape)

NO SCORE

5.

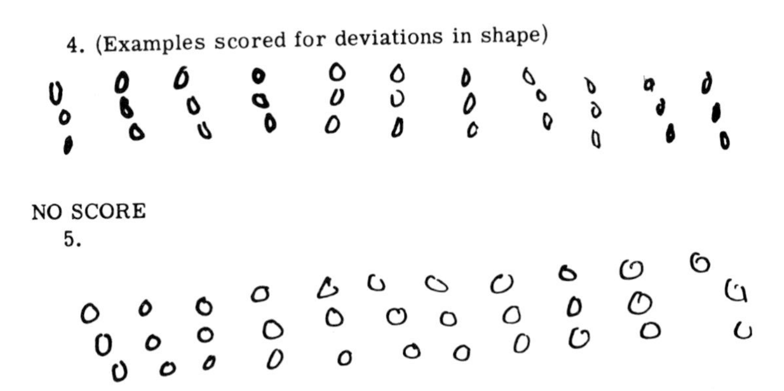

4. *Circles missing or extra in the column. Score 5.* Extra circles may appear in any of three ways: 1) as additions to the individual columns, 2) as overlapping circles in a single column, or 3) as a result of the design being reproduced by rows rather than by columns. These deviations are illustrated in the following examples.

N. B. Example 4 illustrates the difference between the deviations scored "workover," and those scored "circles extra."

SCORE 5

1. (Example of addition to individual columns)

2.

3. (Example of reproduction by rows, resulting in an extra circle

4. (Example of overlapping circles)

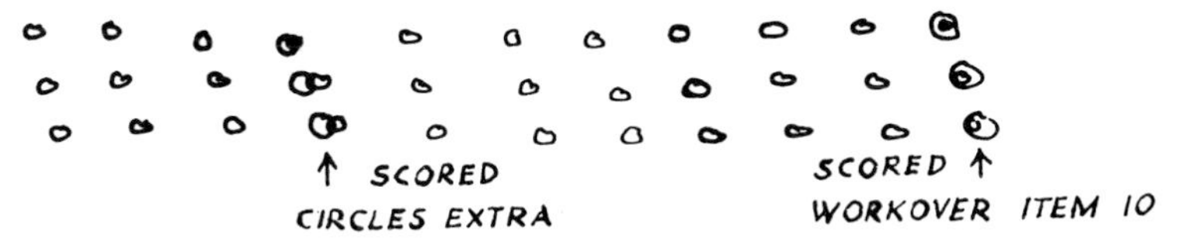

5. *Circles touching. Score 5.* For the item to be scored, the circles must be so placed that they touch or overlap more than once.

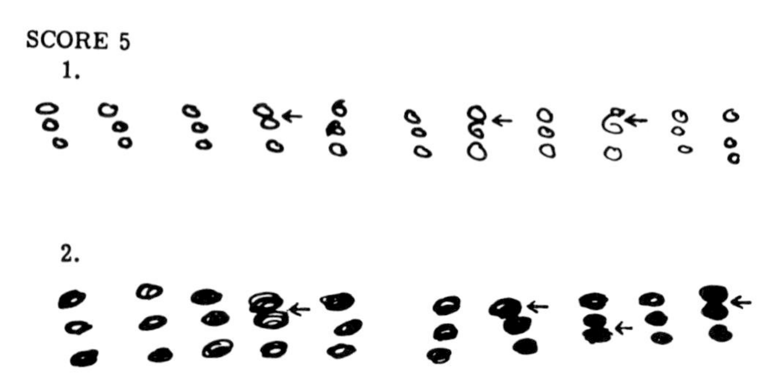

6. *Deviation in slant. Score 3.* There should be two or more abrupt *changes* in the slant of the columns and/or alignment to score here. So long as successive columns are roughly parallel, the item is not scored (example 4). Gradual change in the direction of slant (example 5) is not scored, nor are minor deviations (example 6). Scored deviations occur in two ways: 1) as pronounced change in the direction of slant, and 2) as deviations in alignment (see examples following).

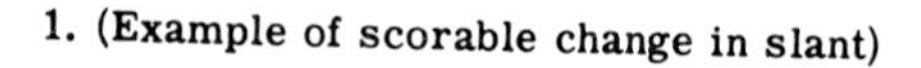

1. (Example of scorable change in slant)

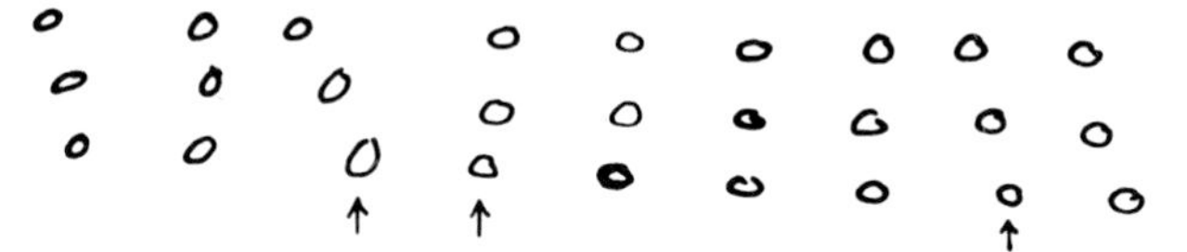

2. (Example of deviations in alignment)

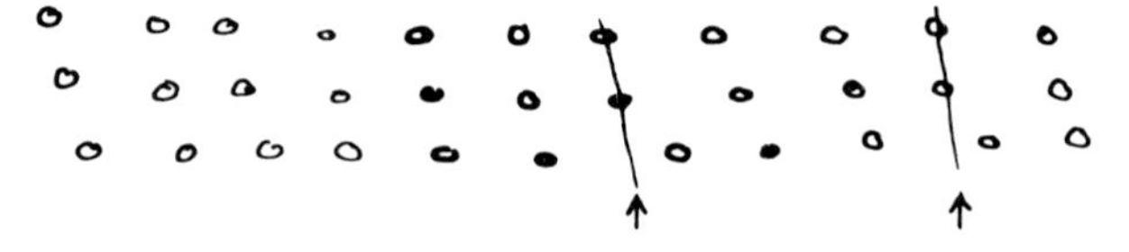

3.

DEVIATION IN SLANT

IN ALIGNMENT

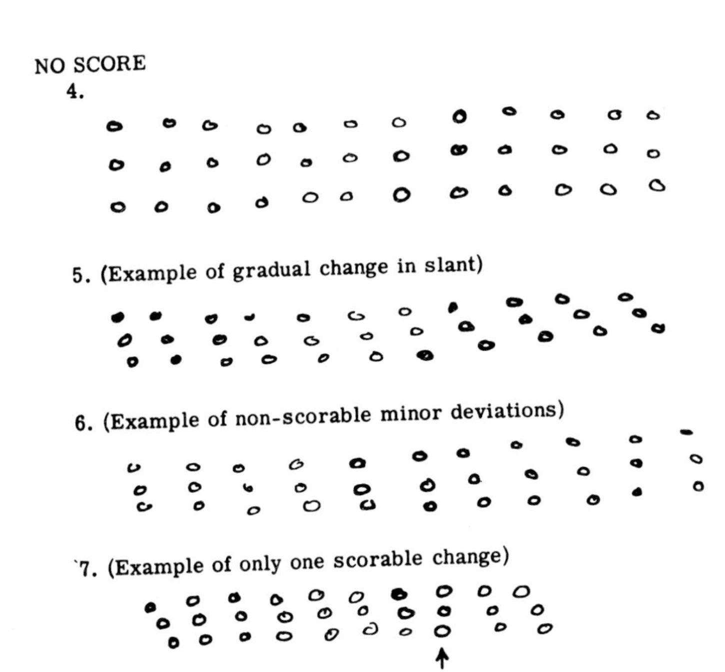

7. *Number of columns. Score 2 for each.* The stimulus for design 2 consists of 11 columns of circles. If, in the reproduction, the number of columns is less than nine, or more than 13, the item is scored. For each column lacking or in excess of this tolerance, the score is 2. The deviation is also scored when one of the columns, usually the last, is crossed out (example 2).

N.B. If there are 6 or less columns, the reproduction is scored for "part of the design missing," item 13.

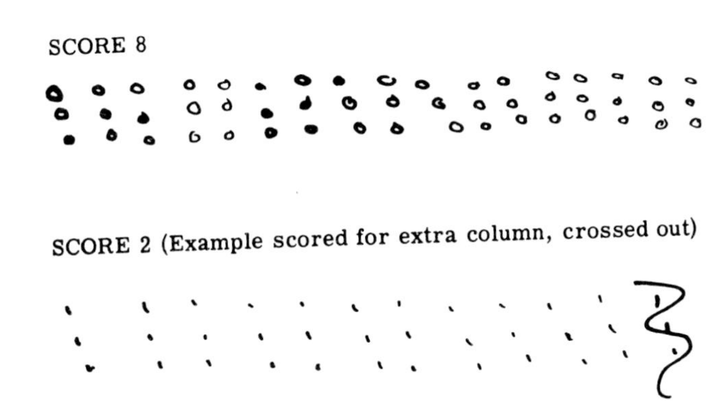

8. *Design on two lines. Score 8.* This deviation has to do with the tendency of some subjects to reproduce this design on several levels as in example 1. This deviation may occur in several ways: 1) as in design 1, the reproduction may be begun on one line and continued on another; 2) the columns may be divided into several series, each with its base on a different level; or 3) one column may be "dropped" decidedly below the level of the remaining columns. The middle circle of the "dropped" column should be at, or below, the base level of the reproduction for the item to be scored.

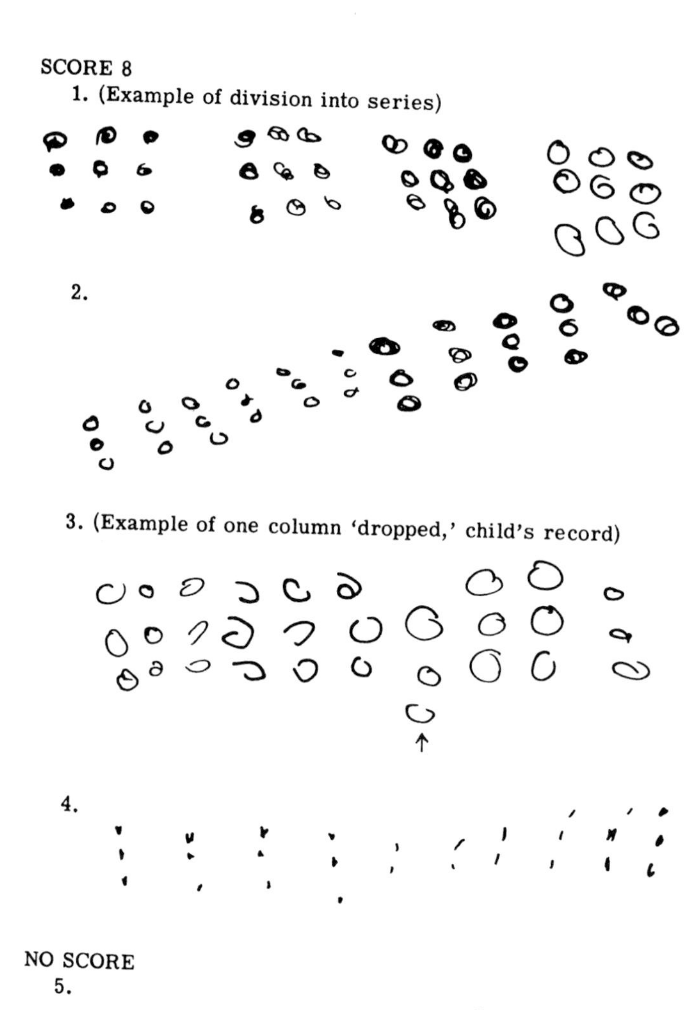

9. *Guide lines. Score 2.* Where lines are made to guide the placement of the circles, the item is scored.

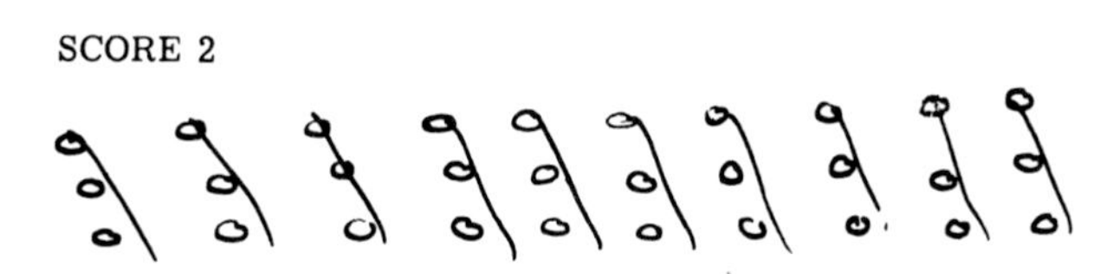

10. *Workover. Score 2.* The stimulus for design 2 is usually reproduced with clear, single-line circles, or with slightly but consistently thickened circles (example 7). When the circles are so belabored that they become large thick masses, workover is scored.

Workover is scored for design 2 in four instances as illustrated in the following examples: 1) when a single circle is excessively belabored so as to stand out in a context of clear single-line circles (example 1), 2) when several circles (three or more) are belabored so that they differ from the remaining circles (example 2), 3) when three or more of the circles contain a dot, dash, or smaller circle, indicating the subject began with a dash or dot and then superimposed a larger circle (example 3), and 4) when all the circles appear to result from a great deal of elaboration (example 4). When the design is reproduced as dots or dashes instead of circles and these are worked over, the item is also scored for item 2 (example 5).

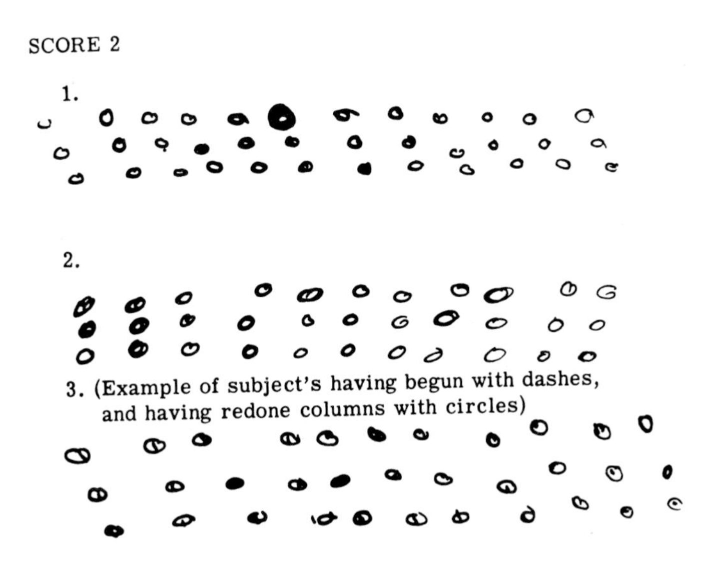

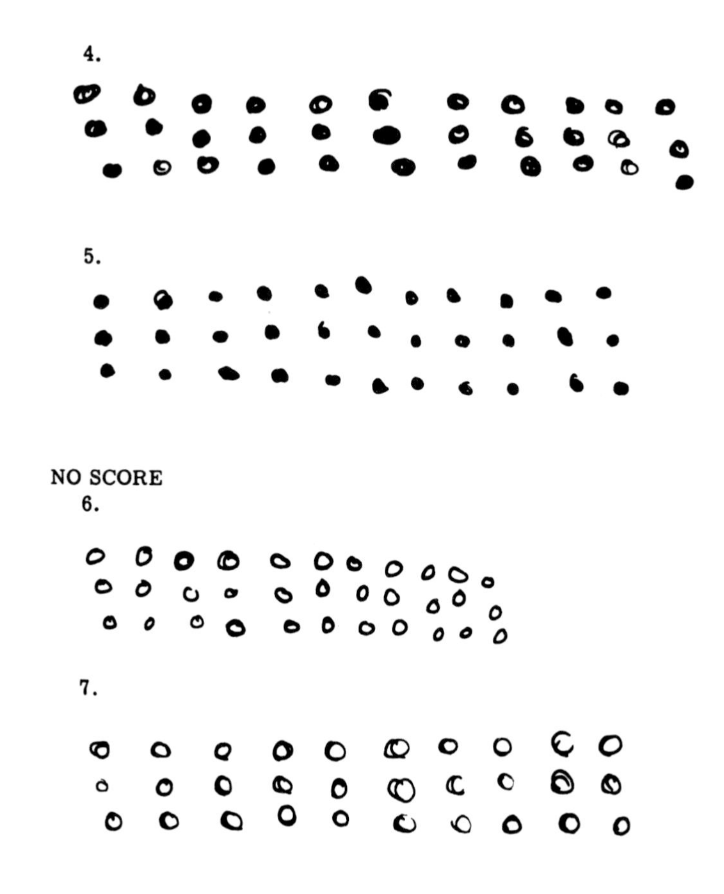

11. *Second attempt. Score 3 for each.* The item is scored as item 8, design 1.
12. *Rotation. Score 8.* The item is scored as item 9, design 1.
13. *Part of the design missing. Score 8.* If the design is reproduced with six or fewer columns, or with two instead of three rows, the item is scored.

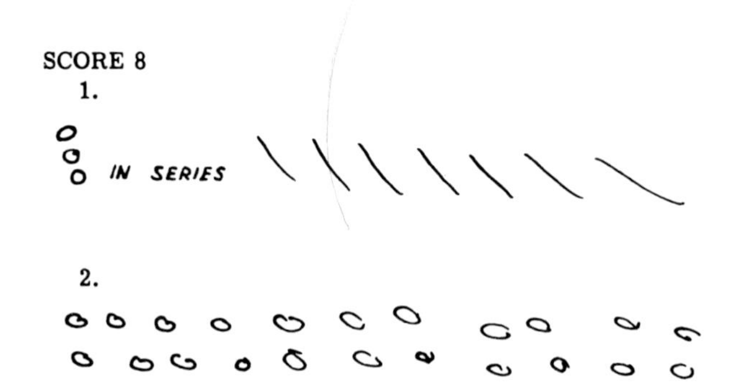

Examples of scoring for design 2. Items scored are indicated by numbers.

A.

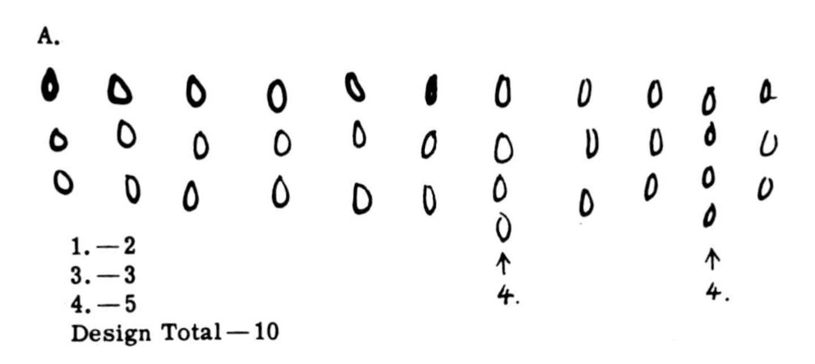

1.—2
3.—3
4.—5
Design Total—10

B. (Example with unscorable minor deviations in slant; unscorable workover)

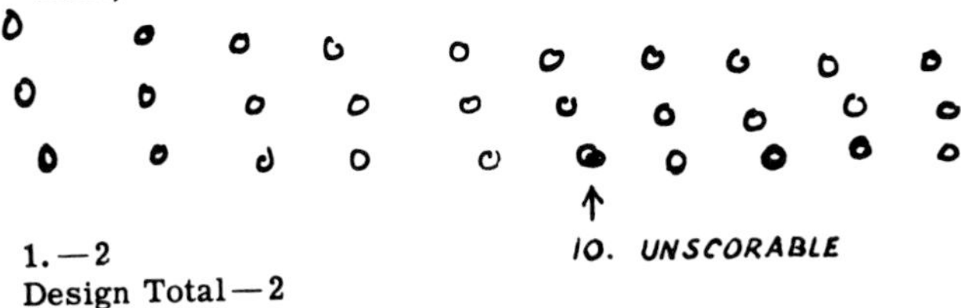

1.—2
Design Total—2

C. (Example with unscorable deviations in shape; unscorable workover)

1.—2
4.—5
Design Total—7

DESIGN 3

(Arrowhead — 16 dots)

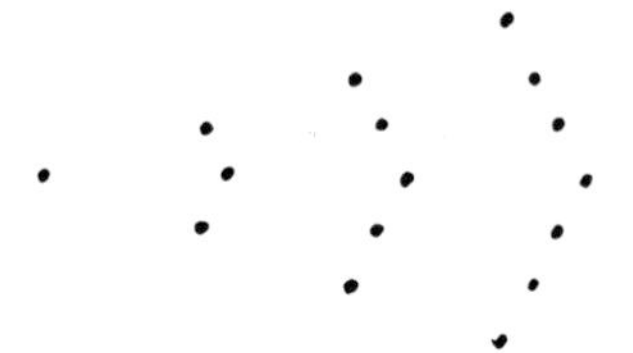

1. *Asymmetry. Score 3.* For the item to be scored, asymmetry should be pronounced. Three types of asymmetry are scored: 1) spacing asymmetry, in which the space between dots varies markedly, 2) angle asymmetry, in which there is great disparity in the angles from the axis (examples 3 and 4), and 3) dot asymmetry, in which there is an uneven number of dots on either side of the axis (examples 5 and 6). The dots of the arrowhead should be approximately equidistant from the axis, and should make approximately equal angles with it. Scorable and nonscorable deviations are illustrated in the examples following; in cases of doubt, the item is *not* scored.

N.B. Asymmetry is not scored when the design is scored for distortion, item 8.

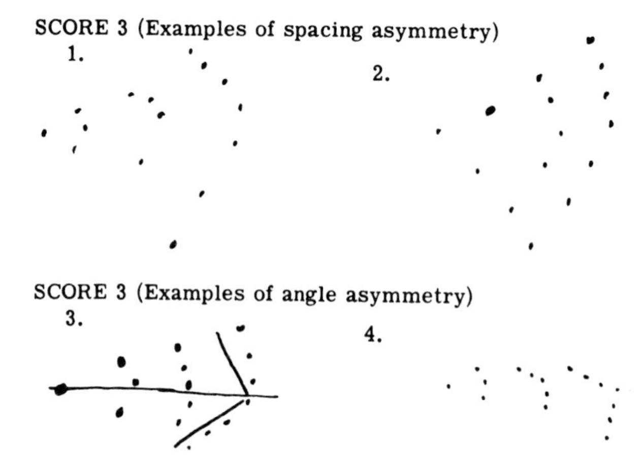

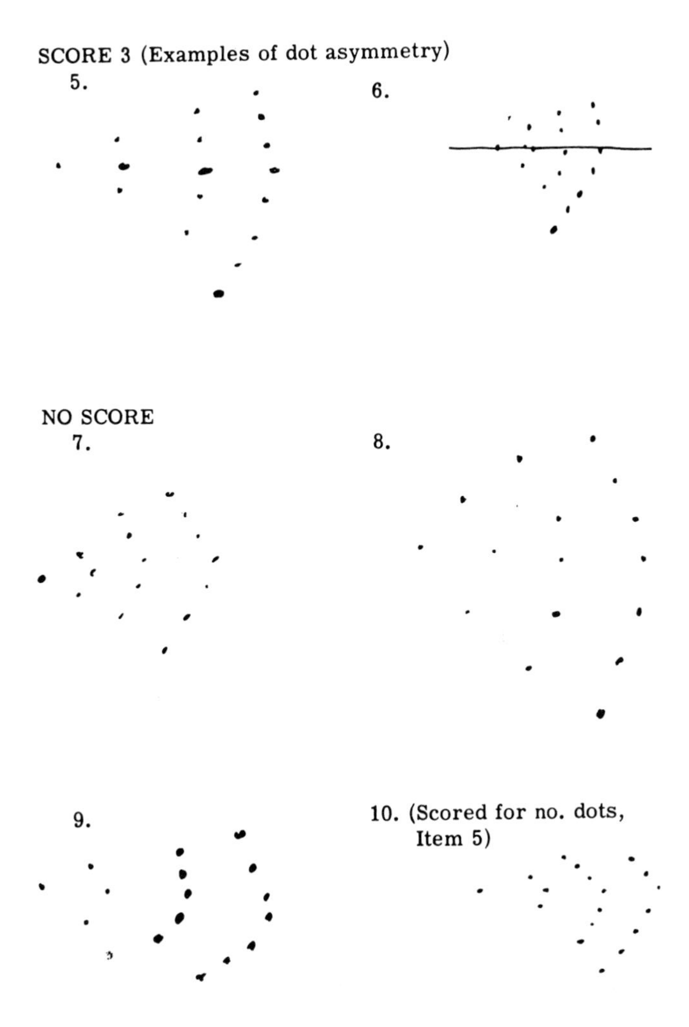

2. *Dots, dashes, and circles. Score 3.* The item is scored as item 2, design 1.

SCORE 3 (Example of 3 clear circles among dots)

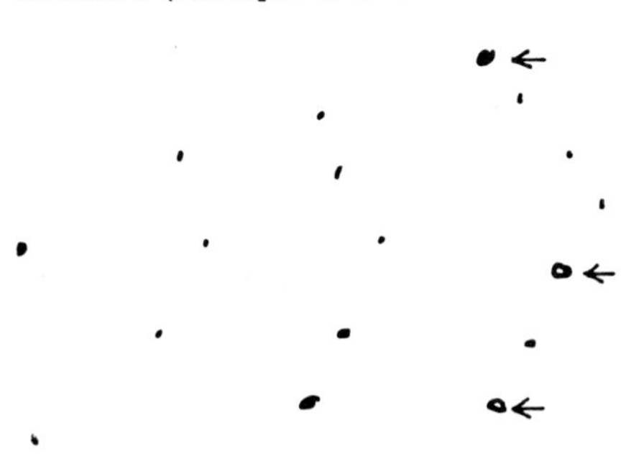

SCORE 3 (Example of 3 dots among circles)

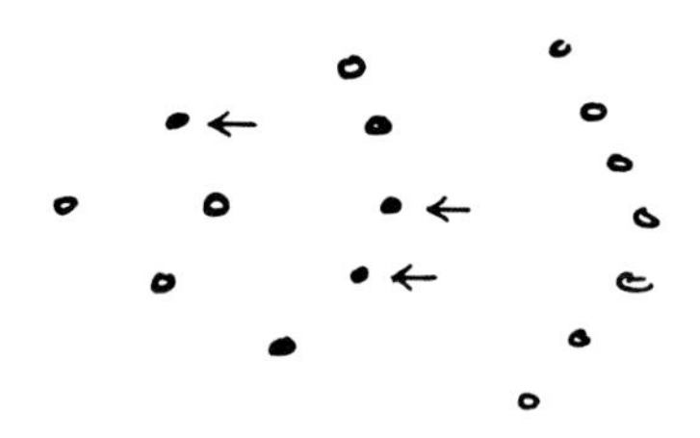

NO SCORE

3. (Scored for workover Item 10)

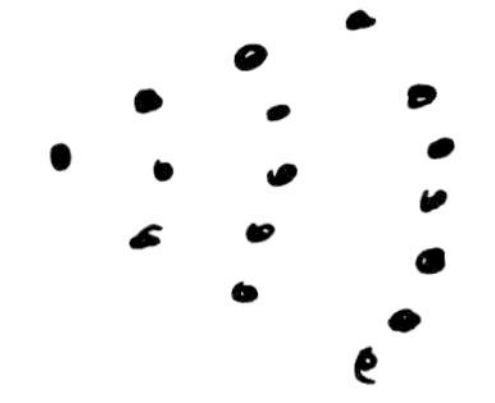

4. (Example with only one circle; scored for dashes, Item 3)

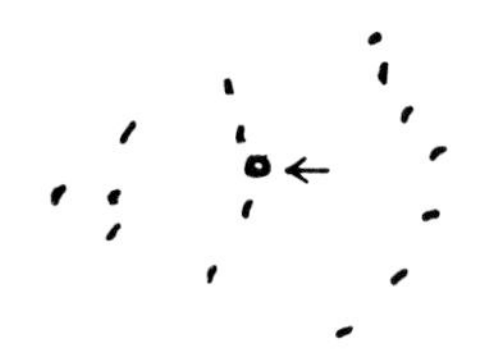

3. *Dashes. Score 2.* The item is scored when all the dots, or all except one dot, are converted to dashes.

SCORE 2

4. *Circles. Score 8.* The item is scored when all the dots, or all except one dot, are converted to clear, single-line circles.

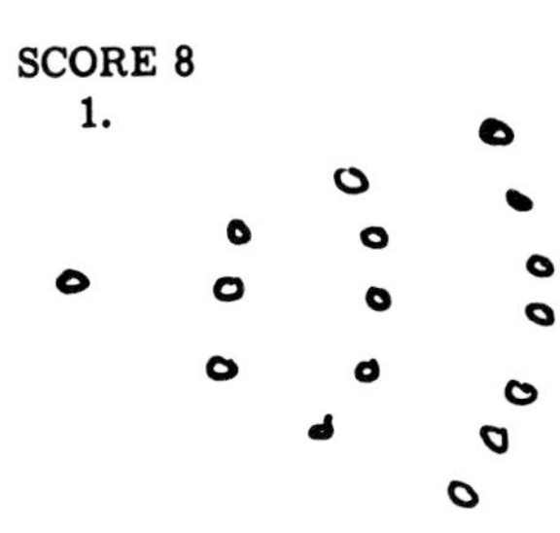

NO SCORE
2. (Scored for dot, dash, circle: Item 2)

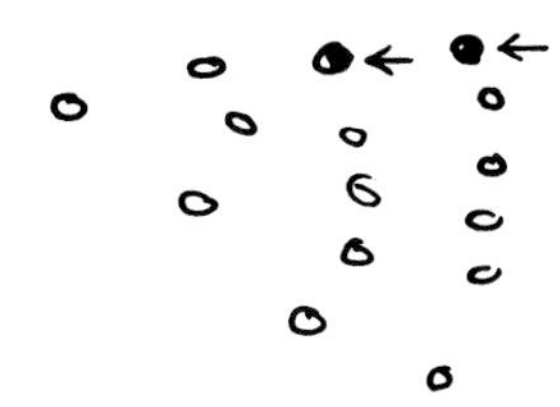

5. *Number of dots. Score 2.* The item is scored when there are more or less than 16 dots, dashes, or circles in the reproduction. The total score for this deviation is 2.

N.B. The item may be scored when the design is scored for distortion, item 8.

6. *Extra row. Score 8.* This deviation is rarely encountered. The item is scored when there is an extra row of dots in the reproduction.

7. *Blunting. Score 8.* The point of the arrow should be obliterated to score this item. Rounding of the arrow, with the middle dot of the first row at

the center of the curve, is *not* scored. Compare example 3, not scored, to example 1, scored. In cases of doubt, the item is *not* scored.

N.B. Blunting is not scored when the design is scored for distortion, item 8.

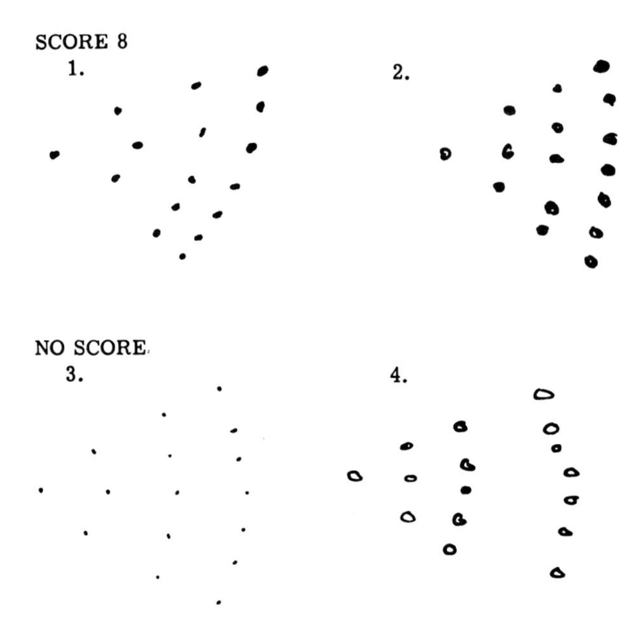

8. *Distortion. Score 8.* To score, there should be destruction of the gestalt, resulting in a loose conglomeration of dots or in an extreme departure from the stimulus. If an arrowhead, using all the dots roughly patterned after the stimulus, is at all discernable, the item is not scored.

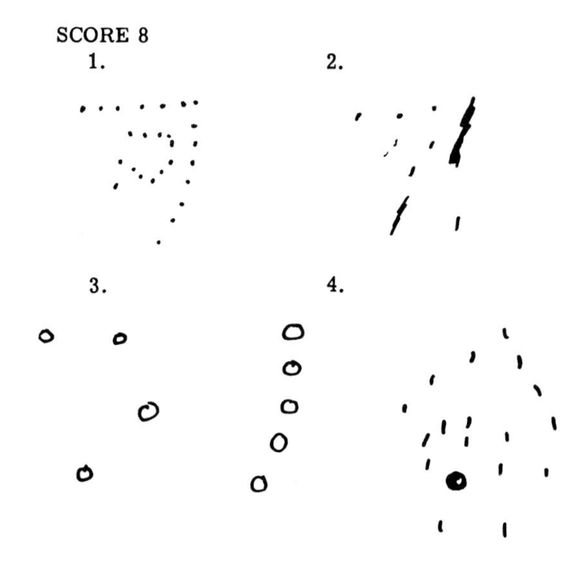

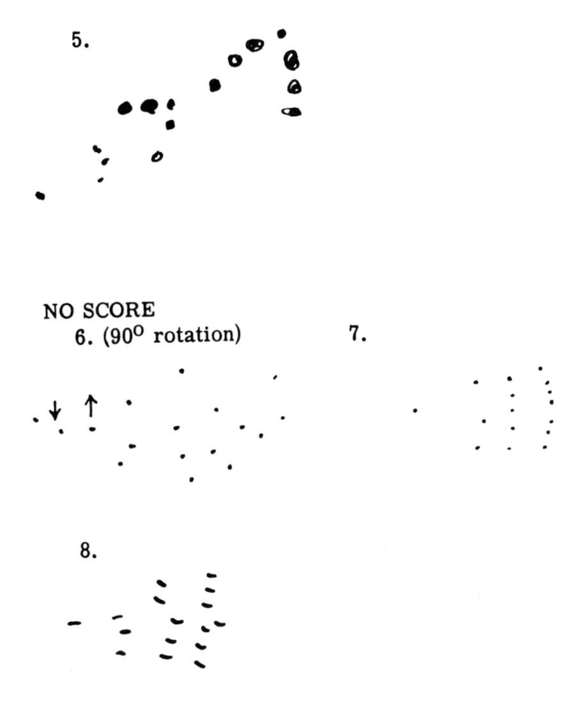

9. *Guide lines. Score 2.* The item is scored as item 2, design 2.

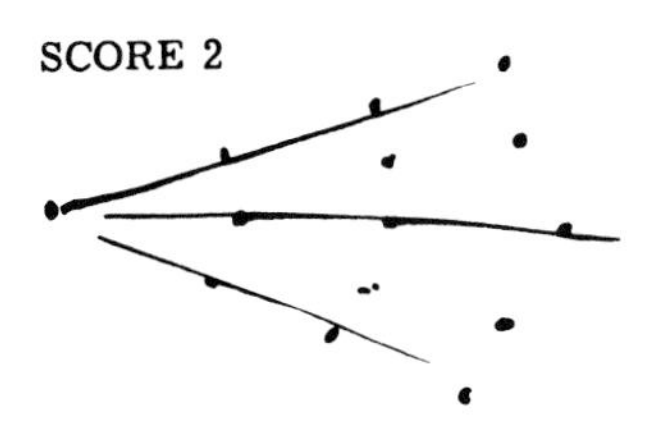

10. *Workover. Score 2.* The item is scored as item 7, design 1.

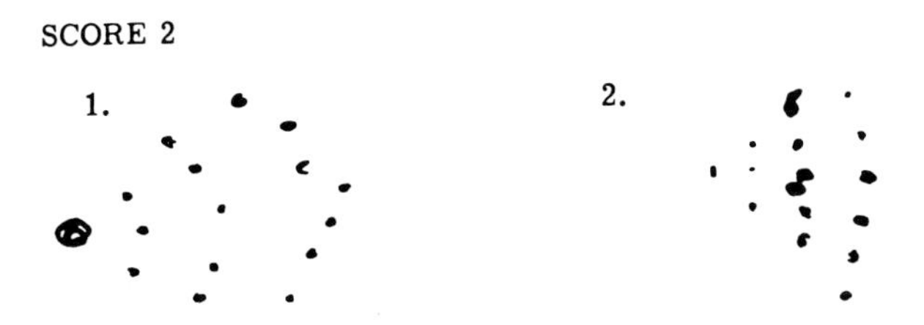

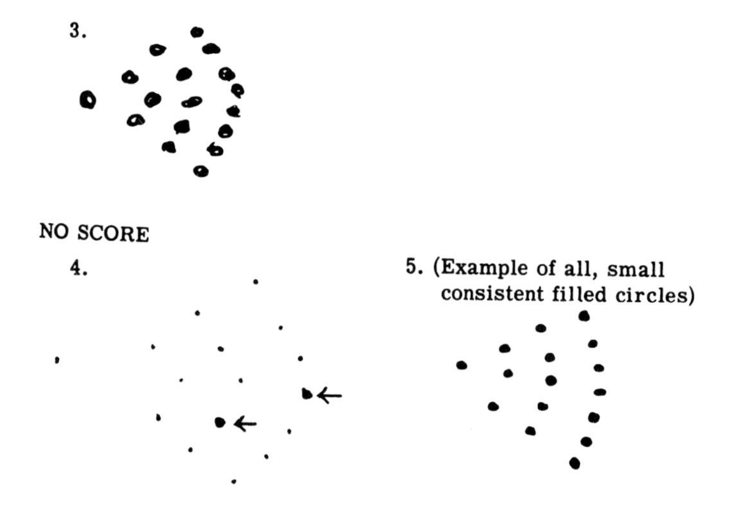

11. *Second attempt. Score 3 for each.* The item is scored. as item 8, design 1.
12. *Rotation. Score 8.* Rotation is scored for design 3 when the design is rotated 45°, 90° or 180° from its proper horizontal axis, whether the deviation occurs in the actual reproduction or in previous turning of the card. Rotation of the paper is *not* scored.

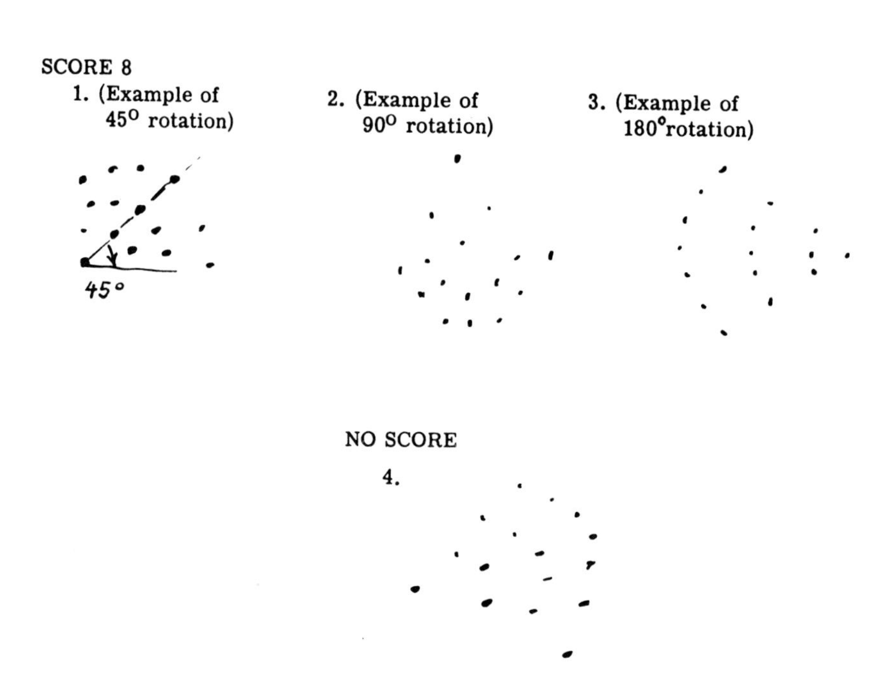

13. *Part of the design missing. Score 8.* The item is scored when one of the rows is completely missing in the reproduction. In such a case, number of dots, item 5, is not scored, unless there is deviation in the number of dots in one of the remaining rows, i.e., an uneven number of dots on either side of the axis, as in example 2.

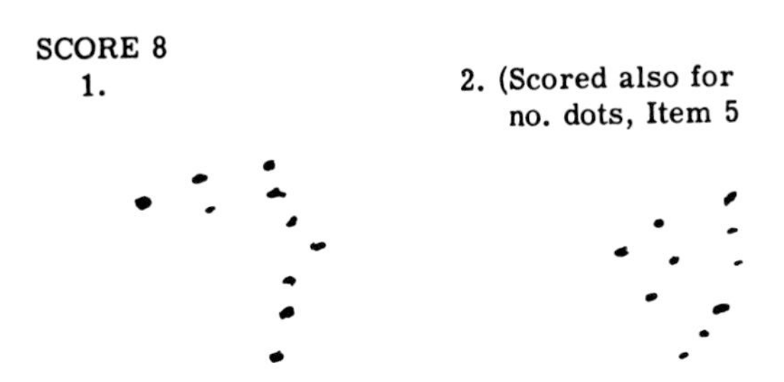

Examples of scoring for Design 3. Items scored are indicated by numbers.

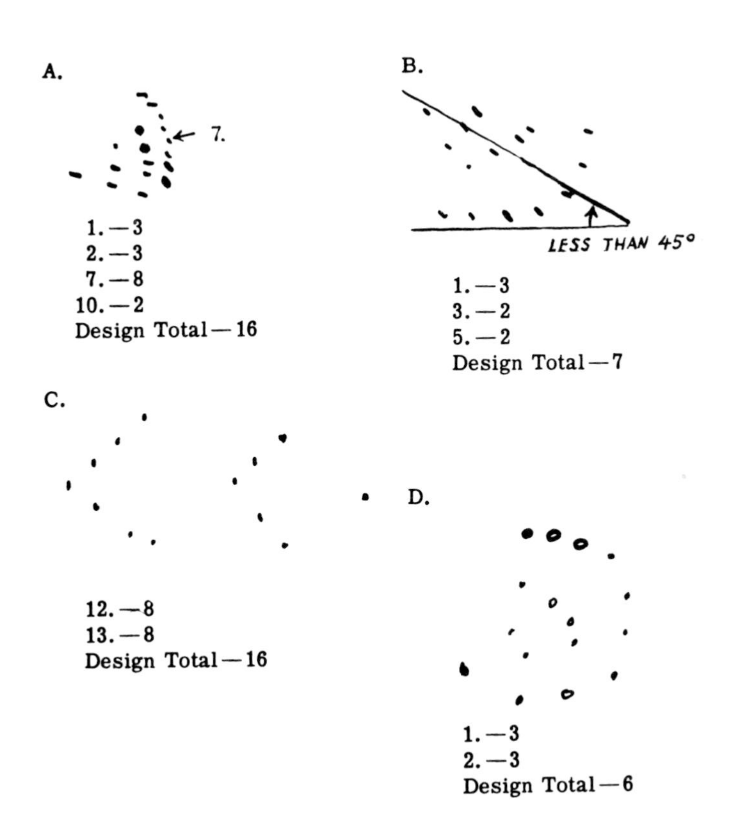

DESIGN 4

(Square and Curve)

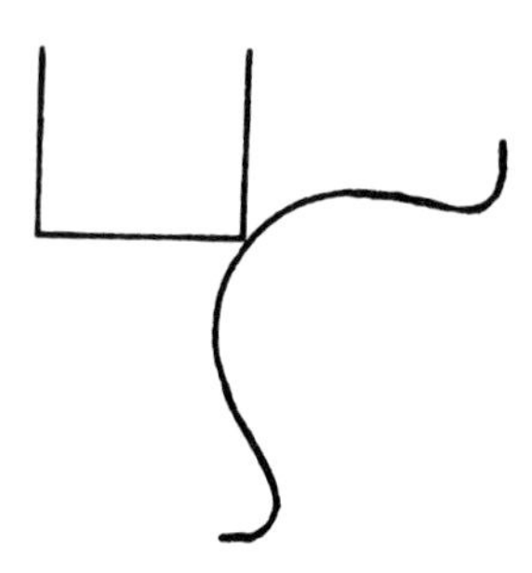

1. *Asymmetry of the curve. Score 3.* For the item to be scored, the halves of the curve should be markedly asymmetrical. Asymmetry may be in terms of contour, or of differences between the two ends of the curve, e.g., one end may be squared-off, curled, frayed, or worked over (see examples following.) The scoring is not rigid; reasonable similarity of the halves is *not* scored; in cases of doubt the item is *not* scored.

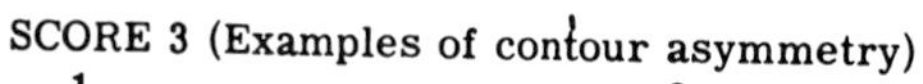

SCORE 3 (Examples of contour asymmetry)

1.

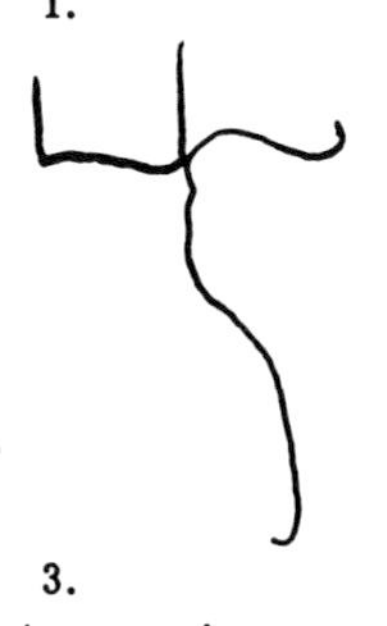

2.

3.

4.

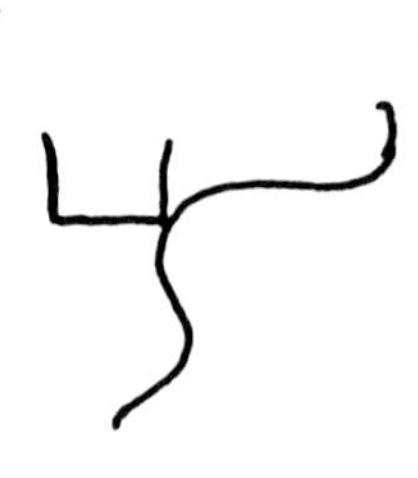

SCORE 3 (Examples of differences between the two ends)

5. (One end 'squared-off')

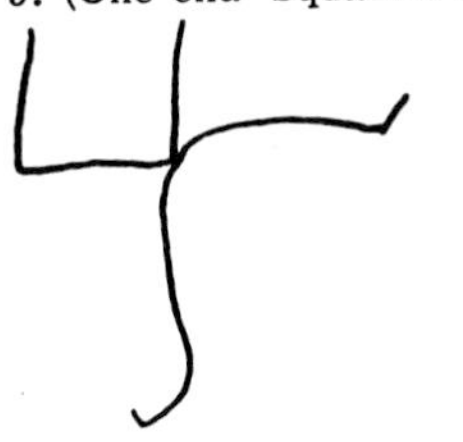

6. (one end 'curled')

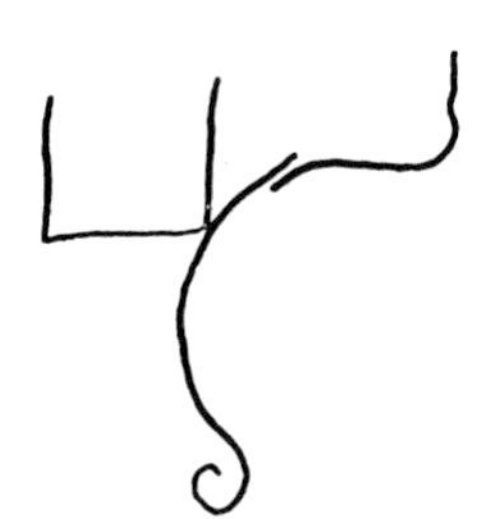

7. (One end 'frayed')

8. (One end 'worked-over')

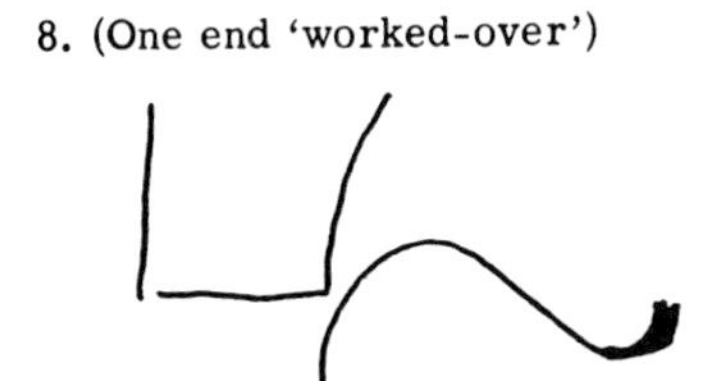

SCORE 3 (Examples of contour and difference asymmetry)

9.

10.

11.

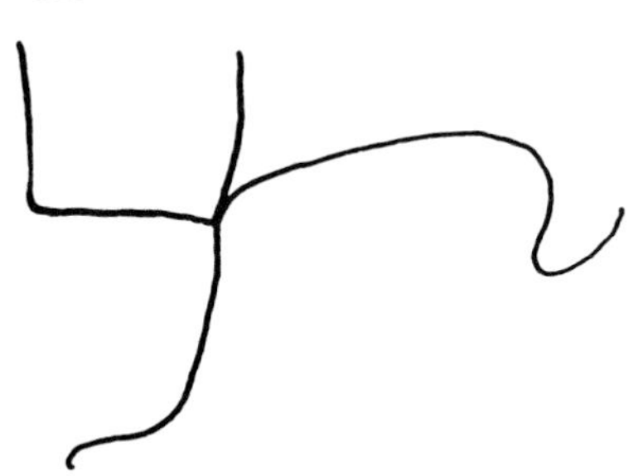

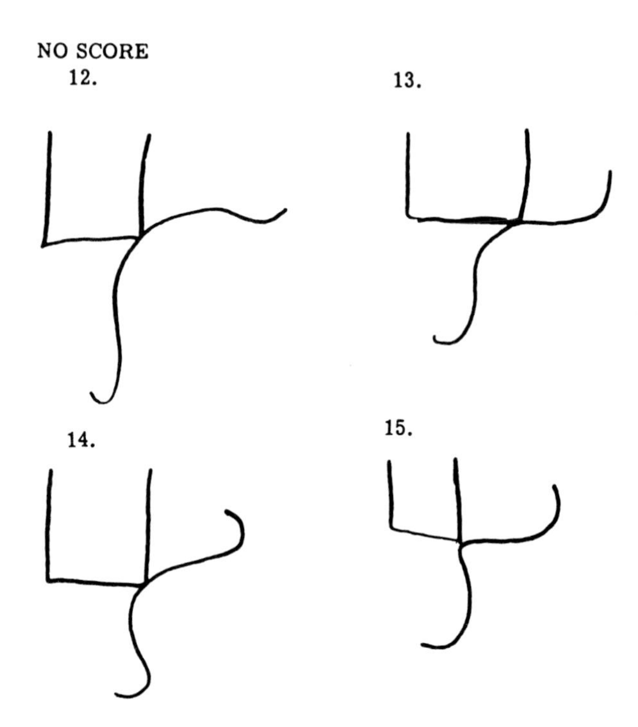

2. *More than one break in the curve. Score 4.* To score, more than one break in the curve must occur. When the design is sketched, the item is not scored, unless there occurs more than one open space in the line of sketching.

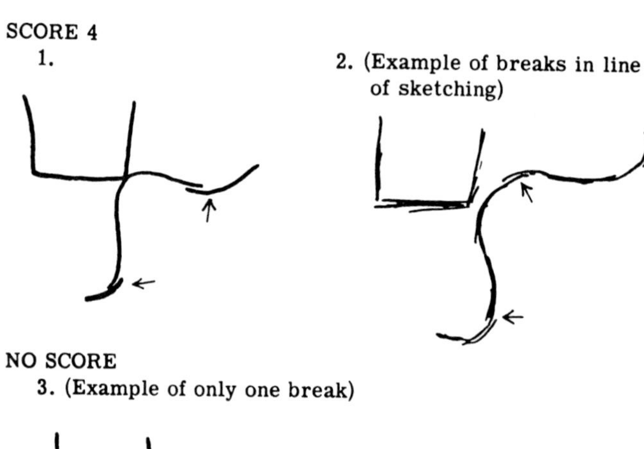

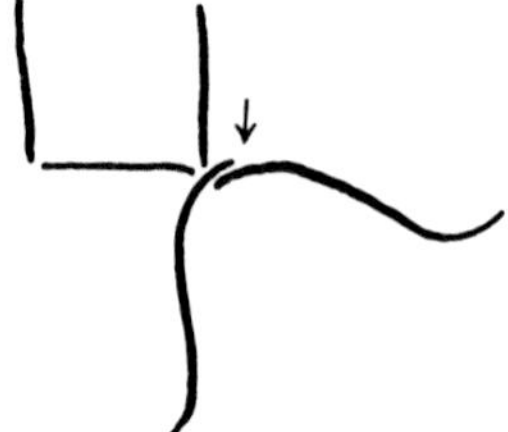

3. *Curve not centered on square. Score 1.* For this item to be scored, the curve should be distinctly "off-center," i.e., when the center of the curve and the lower right corner of the square do not coincide. In cases of doubt, a bisection line may be drawn; the line should be at least ⅛ inch from the adjacent corner of the square for the deviation to be scored (example 1).

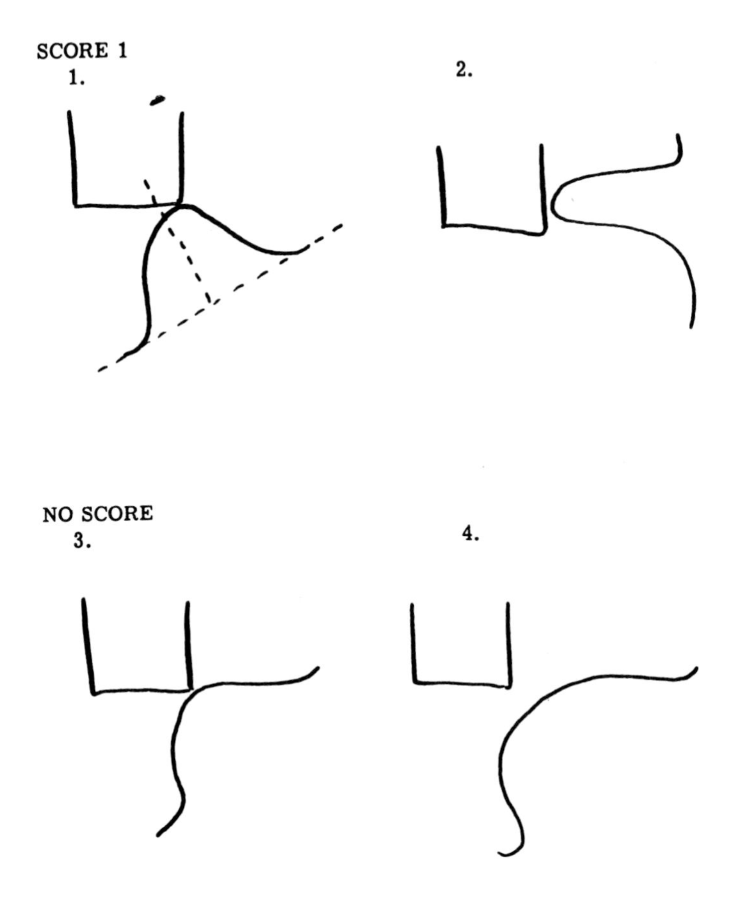

4. *Curls added to extension(s) of the curve. Score 4.* The end(s) of the curve must be extended in a distinctly circular motion for the item to be scored. The curl should turn back on itself, so that, if extended, it would cross the adjacent side of the curve. In cases of doubt, the item is *not* scored.

N.B. If only one of the ends is curled, the reproduction is also scored for asymmetry, item 1.

SCORE 4

1. (Example of one distinct curl)

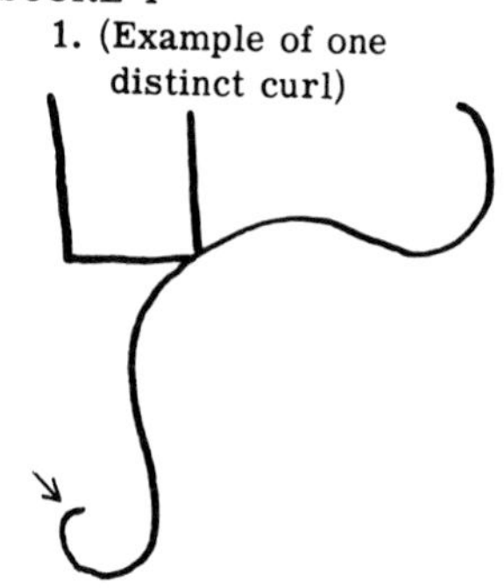

2. (Example illustrating 'turning back' on self)

NO SCORE (Examples not 'turning back' on selves)

4.

5.

5. *Curve and square overlapping or not joined. Score 8.* Where the peak of the curve is separated by ¼ inch or more, from the adjacent corner of the square, or where the curve overlaps the adjacent corner by ⅛ inch or more, the item is scored.

SCORE 8

1. 2.

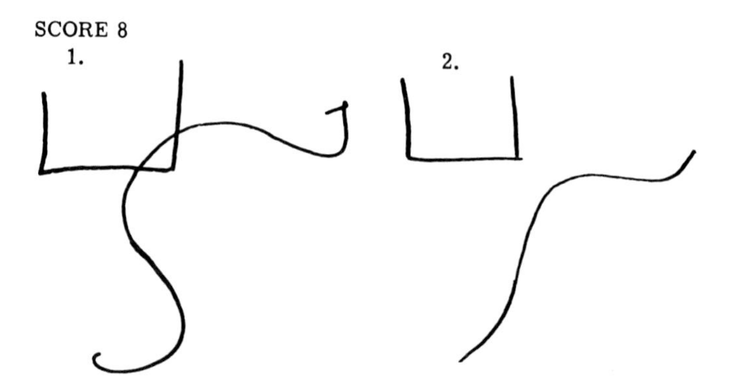

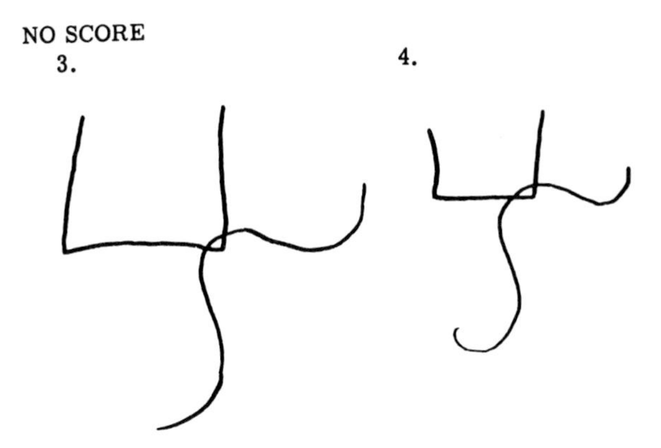

6. *Curve rotation. Score 3.* For perfect reproduction of design 4 one line should bisect the curve and the adjacent angle of the square as shown in the drawing below. The line bisecting the curve should form an angle of 135° with the adjacent side of the square. When this angle is reduced to 90° or less, the deviation is scored. Scoring is, in general, by inspection; although, in cases of doubt, a bisection line may be drawn and the angle measured.

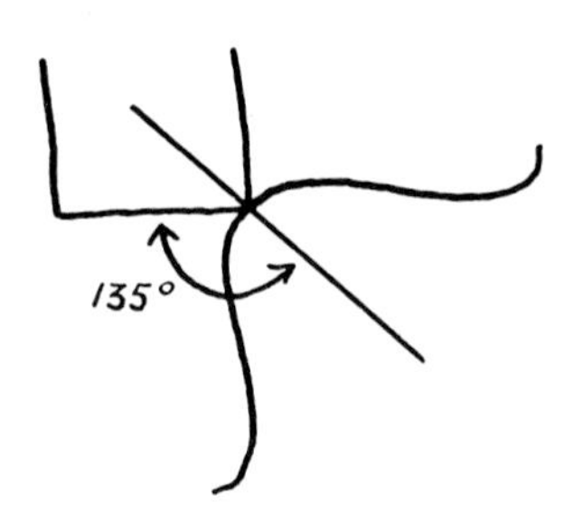

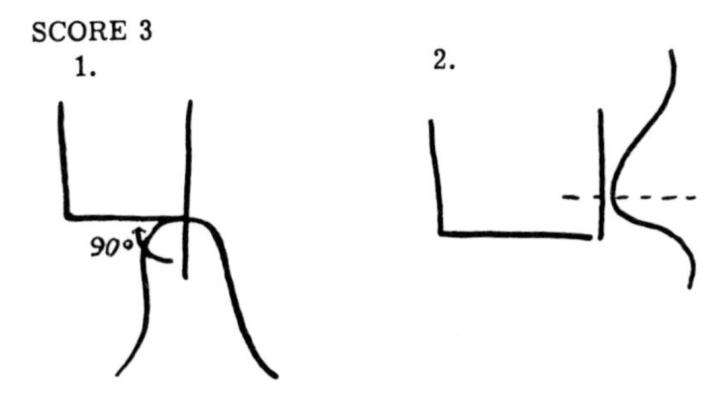

3.

4. (Example also scored for design rotation, Item 12)

NO SCORE

5. (Scored for design rotation, Item 12)

6. (Scored only for 'curve not centered,' Item 3)

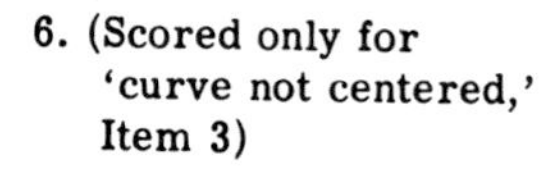

7.

7. *Touch-up to the curve. Score 8.* To score, an extra meaningless line must be attached *after* the curve has been completed. In most cases, the deviation is obvious; in cases of doubt, a decision can be made by considering whether the line is integrated into the curve proper; usually they are in an entirely opposite direction. When there is doubt, the item is *not* scored.

N.B. Asymmetry is not scored unless the contour of the curve itself is asymmetrical.

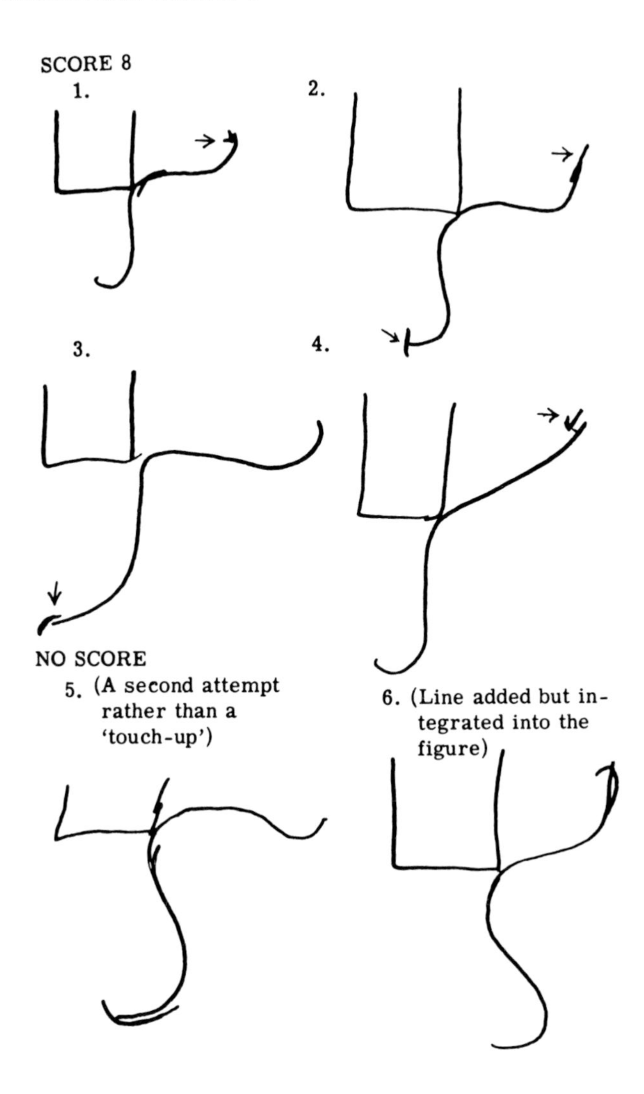

8. *Tremor. Score 4.* Tremor, although a good discriminating item, is one of the most difficult to describe and to illustrate. In general, tremulous lines represent varying degrees of departure from clean, firmly-drawn lines. Tremor may be either of two types: fine, almost imperceptible, or gross, i.e., a generally unsteady line with large deviations from the untended direction of the line.

Tremor should be easily observable without the aid of a magnifying glass to be scorable. In cases of doubt, the item is not scored.

N.B. Use of a magnifying glass has been found necessary in some instances where the question arises whether the tremulous-appearing lines were caused by an uneven writing surface. If, however, the precautions in the directions for test administration are observed, such need should not arise.

SCORE 4 (Examples of fine tremor)

1.

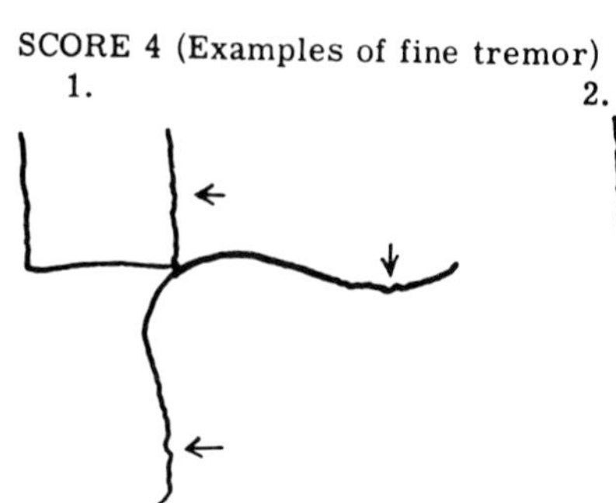

2.

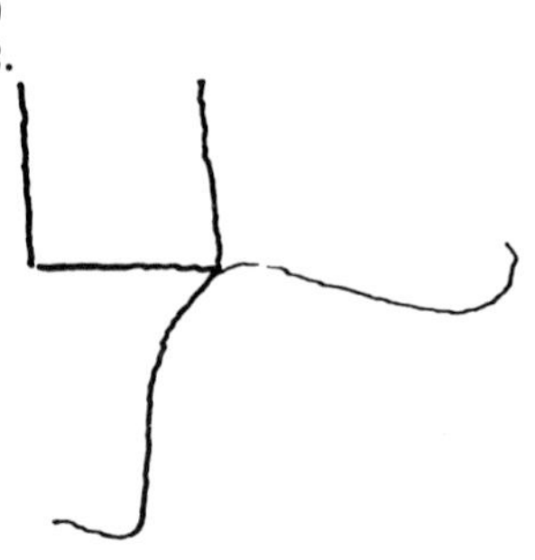

3.

4.

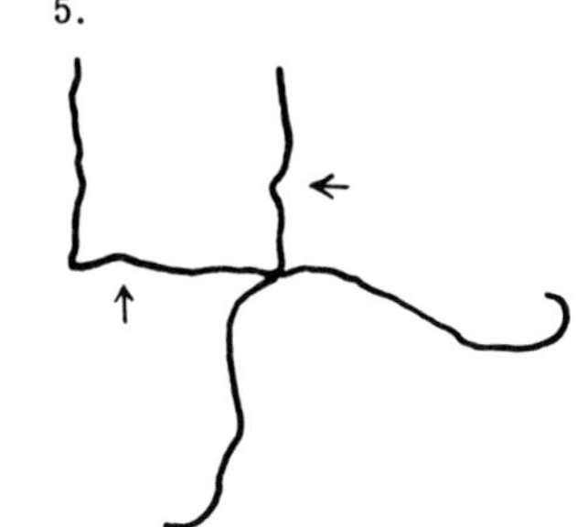

SCORE 4 (Examples of gross tremor)

5.

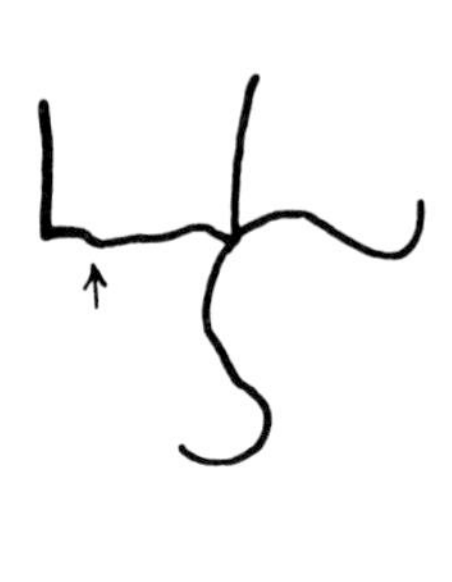

6.

7.

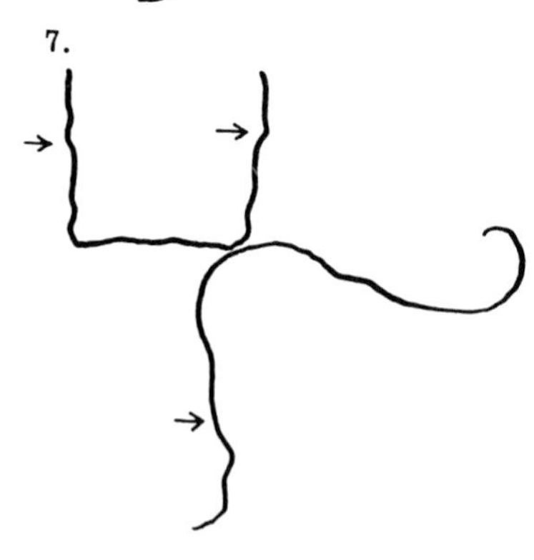

SCORE 4 (Examples of both kinds of tremor in same reproduction)

8. 9.

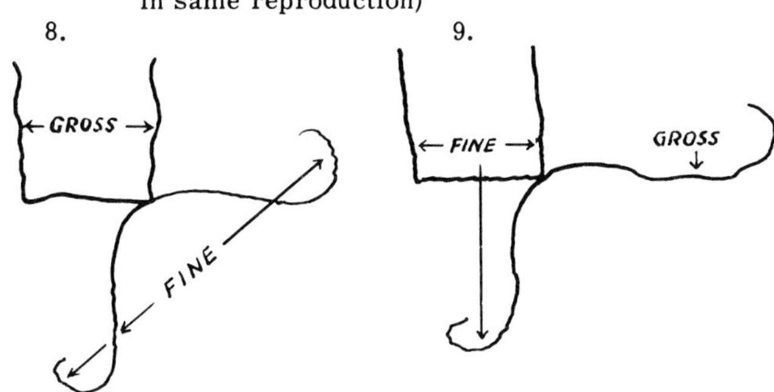

9. *Distortion. Score 8.* This deviation is rarely encountered; to score the item the reproduction should be a marked distortion of the stimulus.

SCORE 8

1. 2.

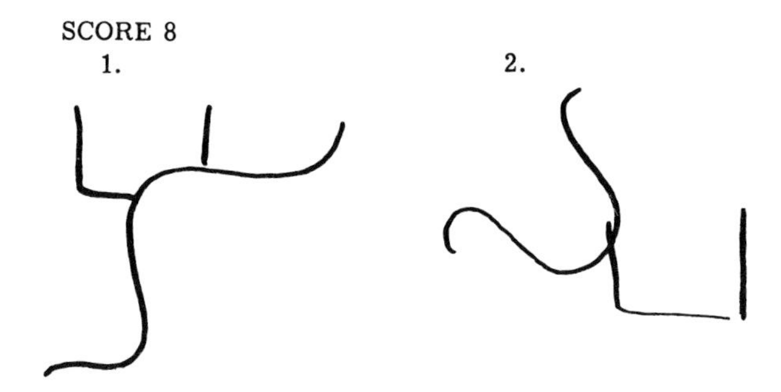

10. *Guide lines. Score 2.* The item is scored, as item 9, design 2, where lines or dots are made to control the placement of the design (example 1). It is also scored where consistent sketching occurs.

N.B. Sketching is a scorable deviation, as it is expressedly prohibited in the instructions given to the subject.

SCORE 2

1. 2. (Example of consistent sketching)

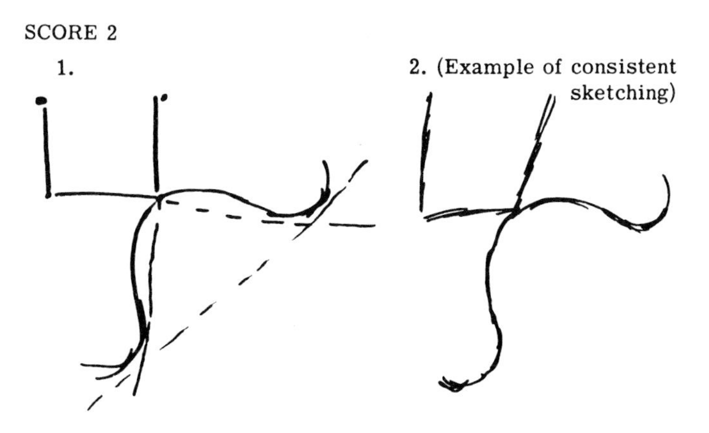

11. *Second attempt. Score 3 for each.* The item is scored, as item 8, design 1, when the subject makes more than one attempt to reproduce the design, and fails to erase his first attempt(s). Second attempts may occur with design 4 in either of two ways: 1) the subject may, as with designs 1 and 2, start a reproduction, give up and start afresh a second reproduction, or 2) the subject may superimpose the second attempt on the first. The score is 3 for *each* attempt.

N.B. This item must not be confused with "double lines" which are *not* scored for design 4. A double line involves usually only one side, or less, of the square, or only a short distance on the curve, whereas a second attempt is usually a redoing of at least half of the square or of the curve. Thus, scoring "second attempt" becomes a matter of judgment: the question for decision being whether the reproduction appears to result from an actual second attempt at reproducing the design (example 6) or from an adjustment or correction line (example 10) made on the one reproduction (termed here "double line").

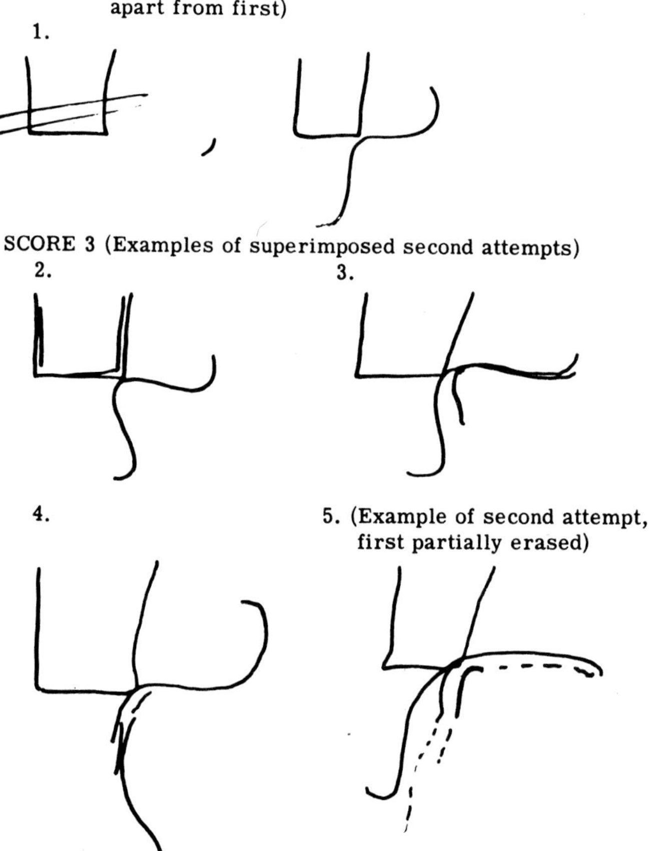

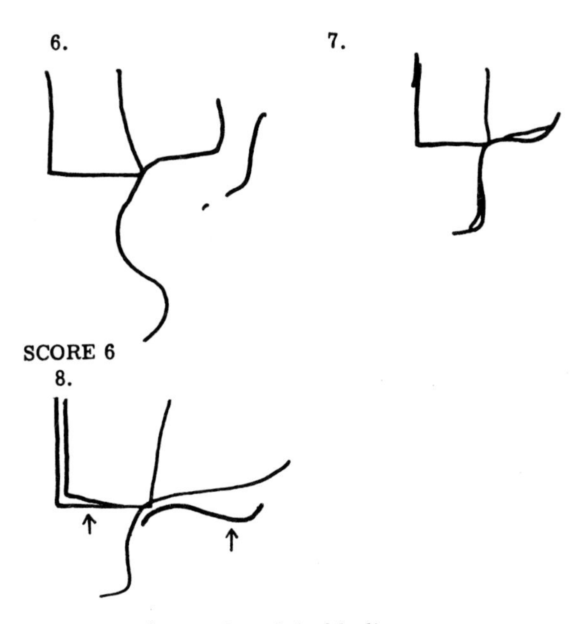

NO SCORE (Examples of double lines—corrections made on first reproduction)

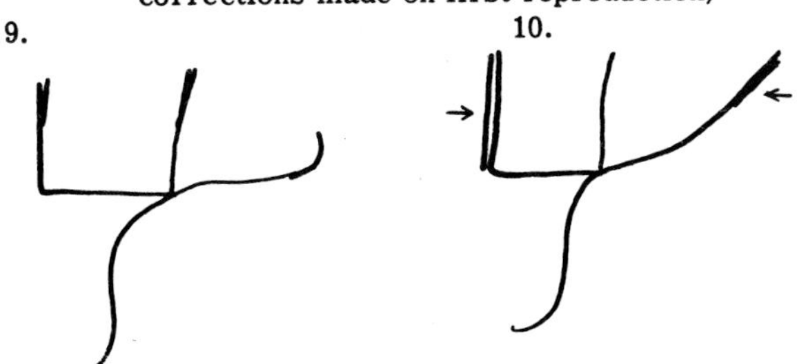

12. *Design rotation. Score 8.* Design 4 is scored for design rotation as well as for curve rotation, item 6. Two types of design rotation occur: 1) when the base of the square is rotated 45° or more from the horizontal (examples 1, 2, and 3), and 2) when the curve is attached to the square more than one third of the distance along that particular side of the square, from its proper point of attachment, i.e., the lower right corner of the square. Double rotation, too, may occur and is scored twice, i.e., score 16 (examples 6 and 7). The item is scored when the rotation results from the copying of the design in a rotated manner, or from the turning of the stimulus card; the item is *not* scored when the paper is rotated.

N.B. Curve rotation, item 6, may also be scored with either type of rotation, or with double rotation; "curve not centered" may be scored only with the first type. The examples following will clarify the scoring.

SCORE 8 (Examples of rotation of entire design)

1. (45° rotation)

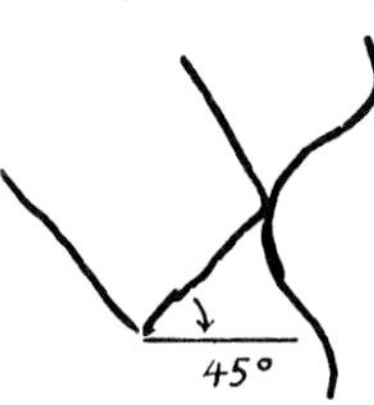

2. (90° rotation)

3. (180° rotation)

SCORE 8 (Examples scored for point of curve attachment)

4. (Point of attachment more than 1/3 distance along base of square

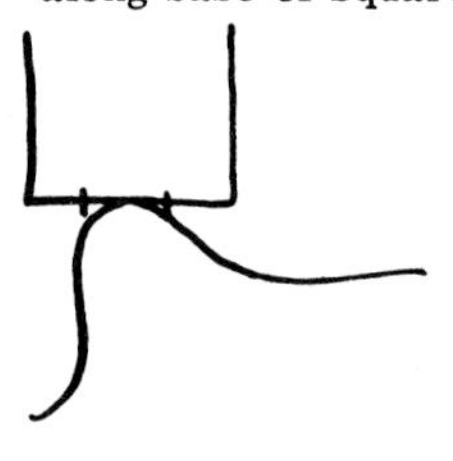

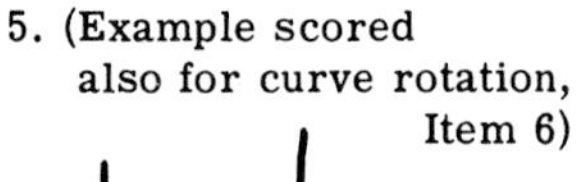

5. (Example scored also for curve rotation, Item 6)

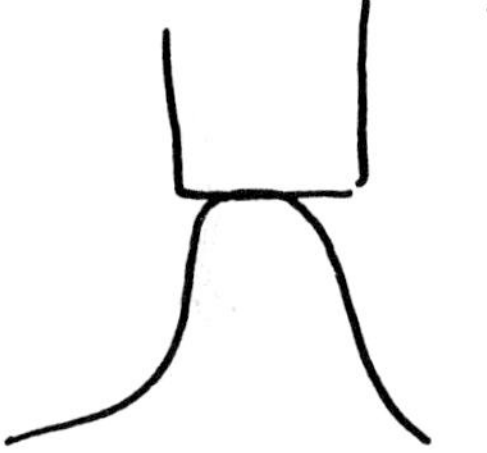

SCORE 16 (Examples of double rotation)

6. (Example scored also for curve rotation, Item 6)

7.

NO SCORE

8. (Scored for curve not centered, Item 3)

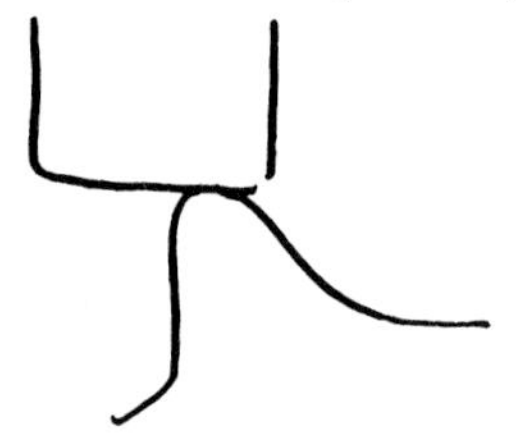

9. (Scored for curve not centered, Item 3; and curve rotation, Item 6)

13. *Part of the design missing. Score 8.* The item is scored when more than one third of either the square or the curve is missing.

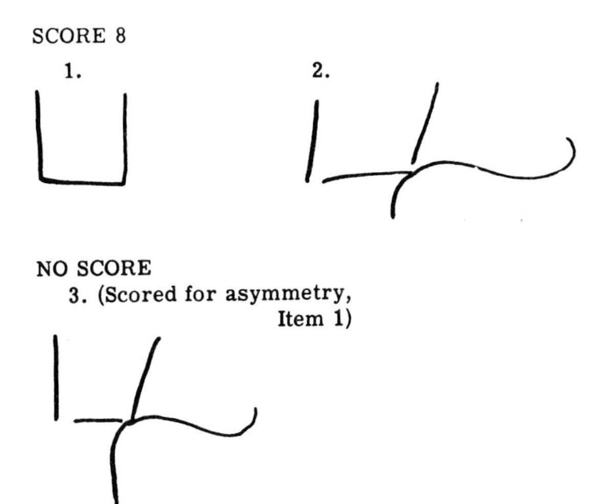

Examples of scoring for design 4. Items scored are indicated by numbers.

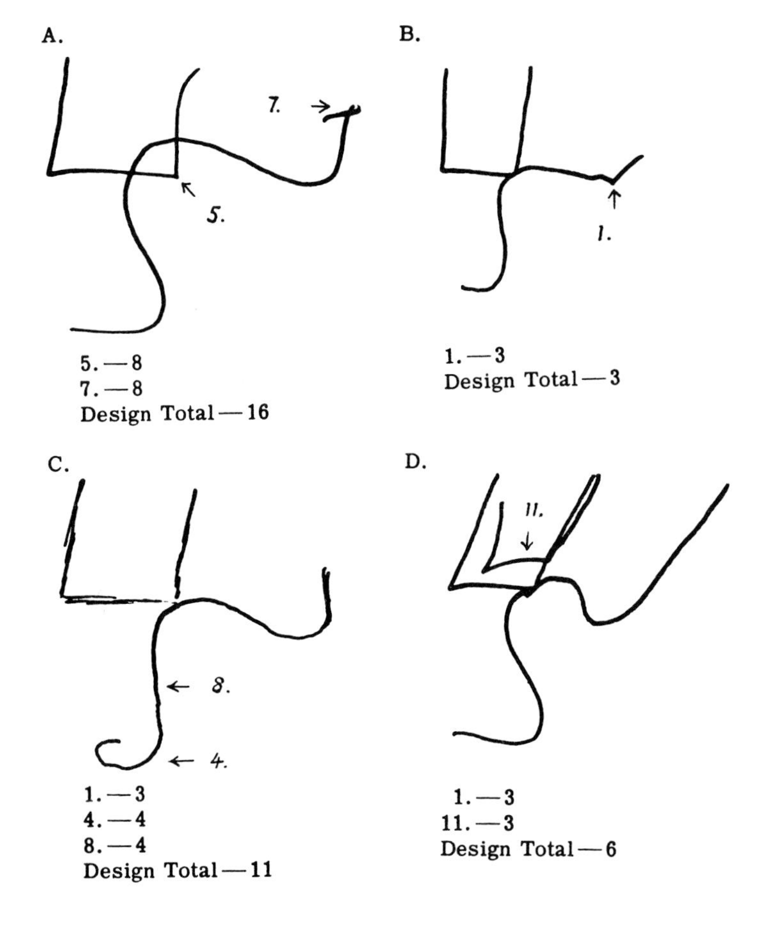

DESIGN 5

(19 Dots in Curve; 7 Dots in Extension)

1. *Asymmetry of the curve. Score 3.* For this item to be scored, the two halves of the curve should differ markedly as in item 1, design 4. Asymmetry may be in terms of contour, difference in the length of the two sides, or other differences in treatment of the two halves of the curve. Reasonable similarity is *not* scored; in cases of doubt, the item is not scored.

SCORE 3 (Examples of obviously asymmetrical treatment of the two sides)

1. (Example of dots doubled and excessively 'worked-over' on one side) 
2. (Example of asymmetrical work-over)

SCORE 3 (Examples of contour asymmetry)

3.

4.

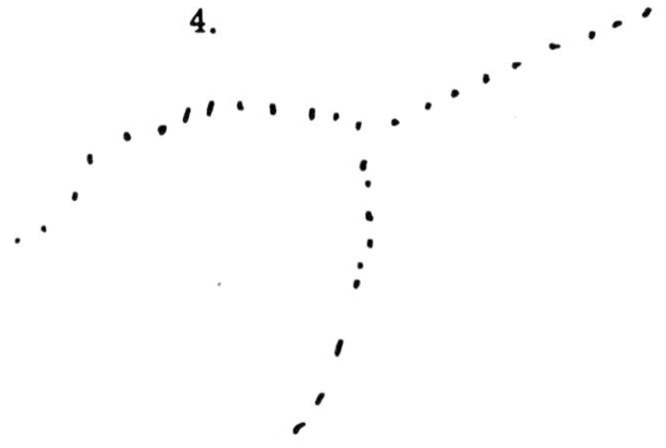

5.

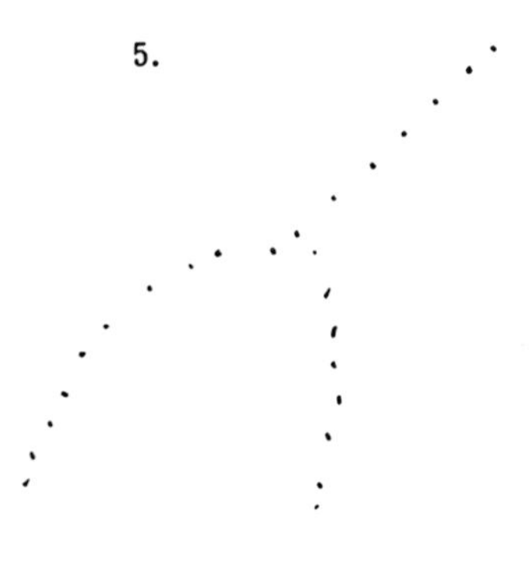

SCORE 3 (Examples of difference in length of the two sides)

6. 7.

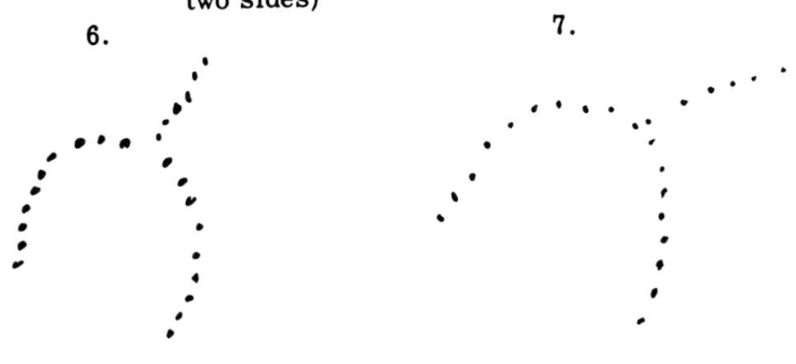

8.

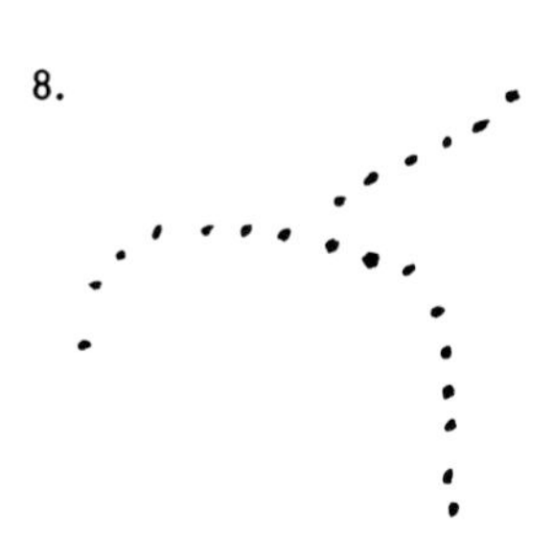

NO SCORE (Examples of reasonable similarity of the two sides)

9. 10.

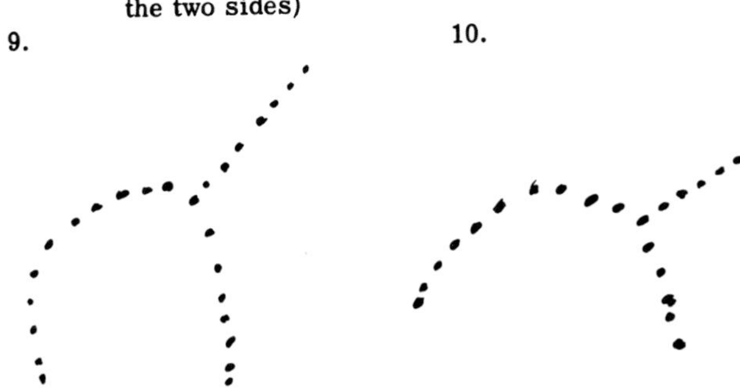

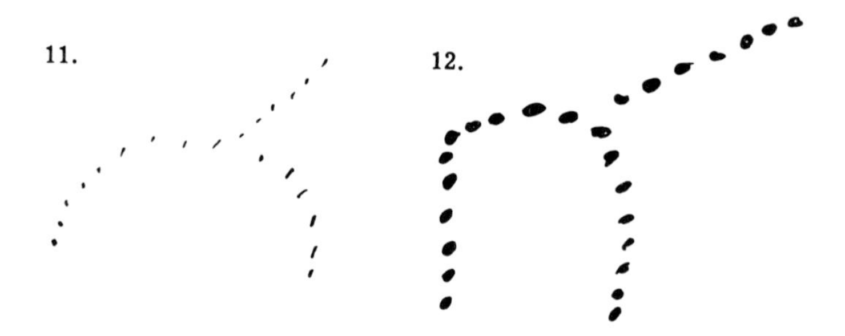

2. *Dots, dashes, and circles. Score 3.* The item is scored for the presence of combinations of dots, dashes, and circles, as defined in design 1, item 2.

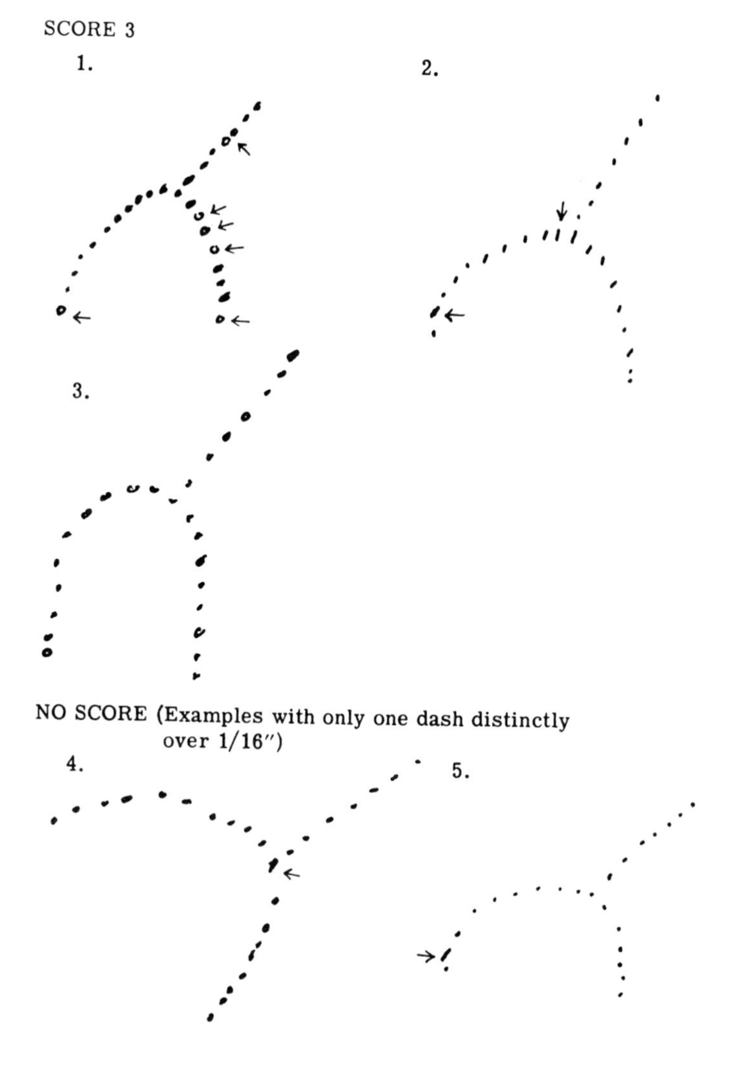

3. *Dashes. Score 2.* The item is scored for the conversion of dots to dashes, as defined in design 1, item 3.

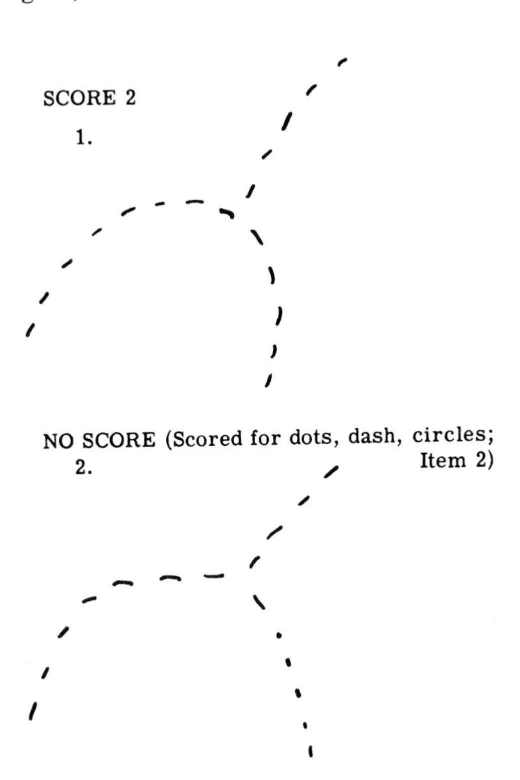

4. *Circles. Score 8.* The item is scored for the conversion of dots to clear circles, as defined in design 1, item 4.

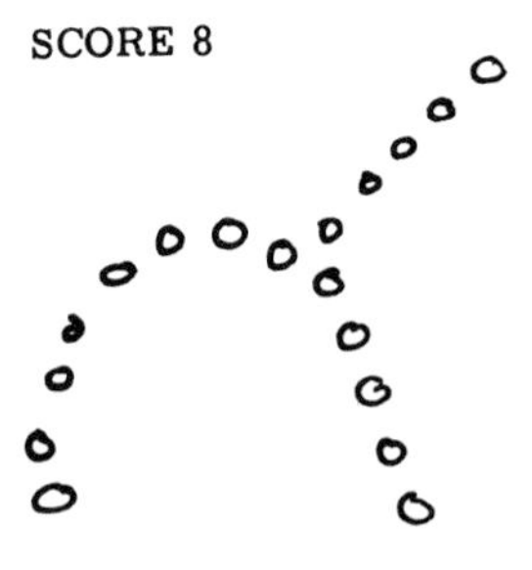

5. *Extension joined to curve at dot. Score 2.* The item is scored when the extension is joined to the curve at a dot, rather than between two dots as in the stimulus. In cases of doubt, a line may be drawn through the dots of the extension to the curve; the item is scored *only* when this line *passes* through a dot.

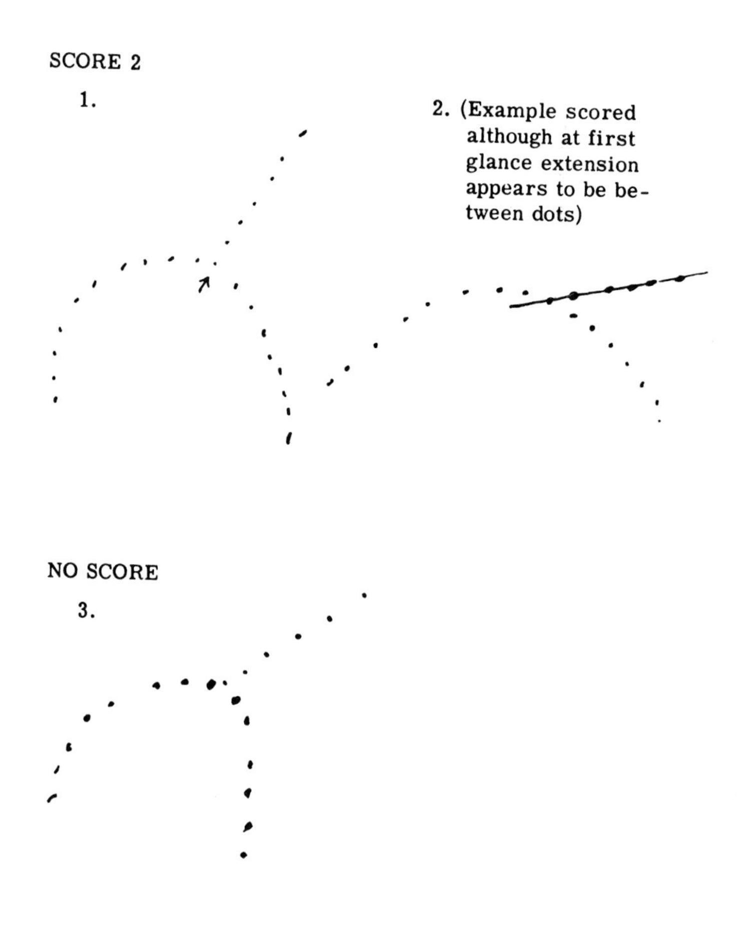

6. *Rotation of the extension. Score 3.* The stimulus for design 5 shows the extension beginning between the eighth and ninth dots from the right end of the curve. Rotation of the extension is scored: 1) when the extension begins at or below the approximate mid-dot of the right side, 2) when the direction of the extension is reversed, to the left rather than to the right, and 3) when the extension begins to the left of center.

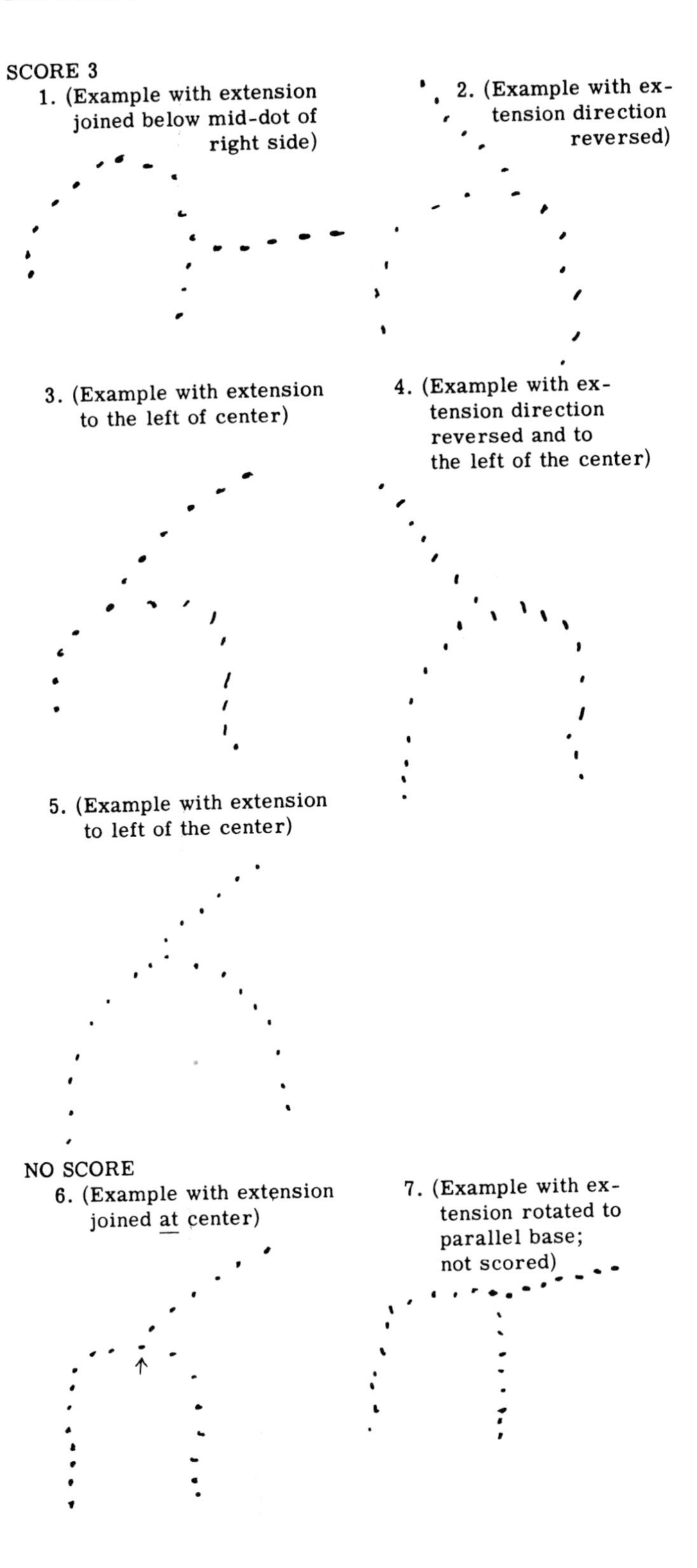
SCORE 3
1. (Example with extension joined below mid-dot of right side)
2. (Example with extension direction reversed)
3. (Example with extension to the left of center)
4. (Example with extension direction reversed and to the left of the center)
5. (Example with extension to left of the center)
NO SCORE
6. (Example with extension joined at center)
7. (Example with extension rotated to parallel base; not scored)

7. *Number of dots. Score 2.* The item is scored when there are fewer than 10, but more than five dots in the curve, and when there are fewer than four dots in the extension.

N.B. When there are five or fewer dots in the curve, distortion, item 8, is scored.

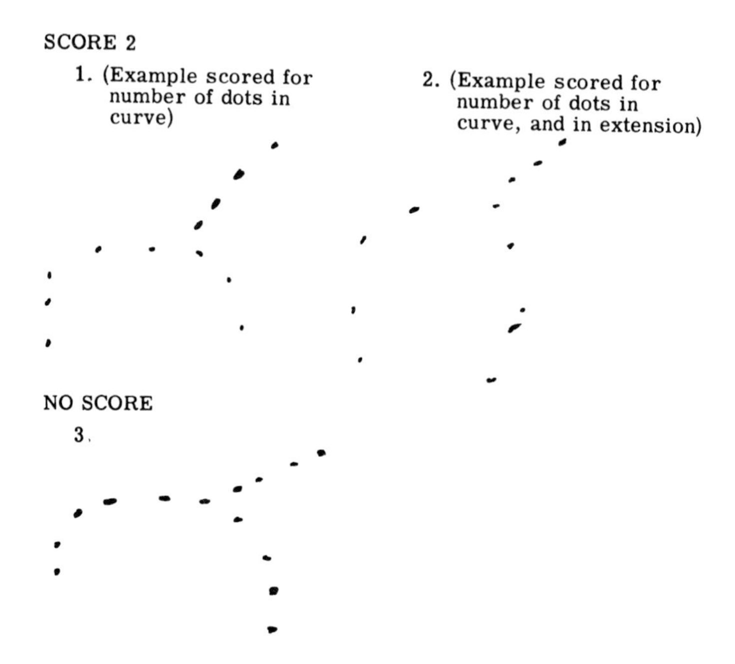

8. *Distortion. Score 8.* The item is scored: 1) when there are five or fewer dots in the curve, 2) when the design is reproduced with lines rather than with dots, 3) when the design tends to a closed circle of dots, or 4) when there is marked distortion of the gestalt, resulting in either a loose conglomeration of dots or an extreme departure from the stimulus.

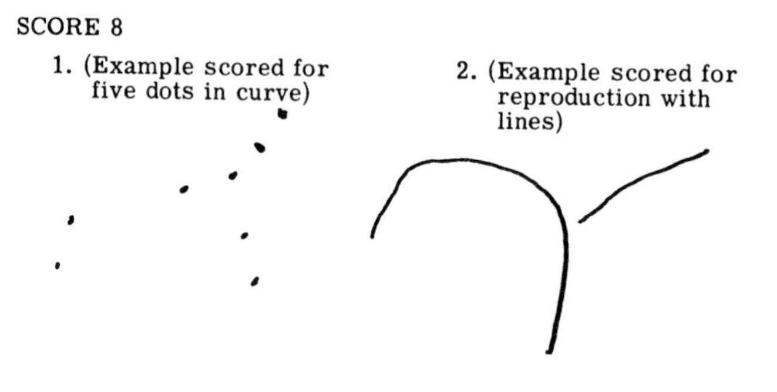

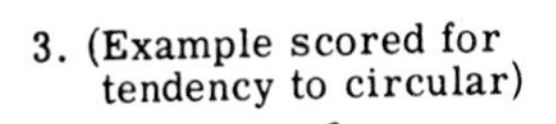
3. (Example scored for tendency to circular)

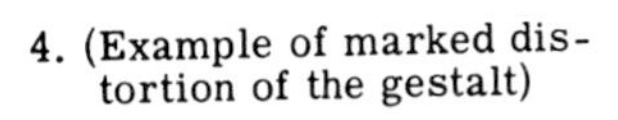
4. (Example of marked distortion of the gestalt)

NO SCORE

5. (Example with tendency to circular on only one side)

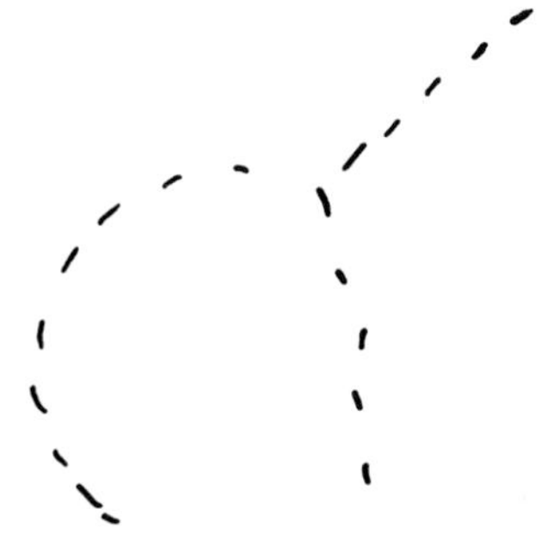

9. *Guide lines. Score 2.* The item is scored as item 9, design 2.

SCORE 2

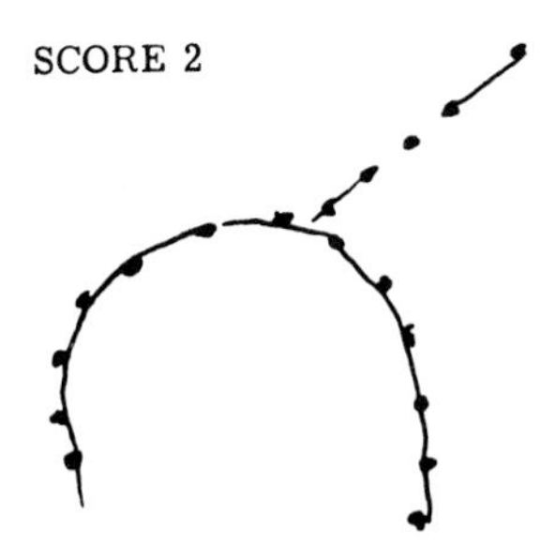

10. *Workover. Score 2.* The item is scored as item 7, design 1.

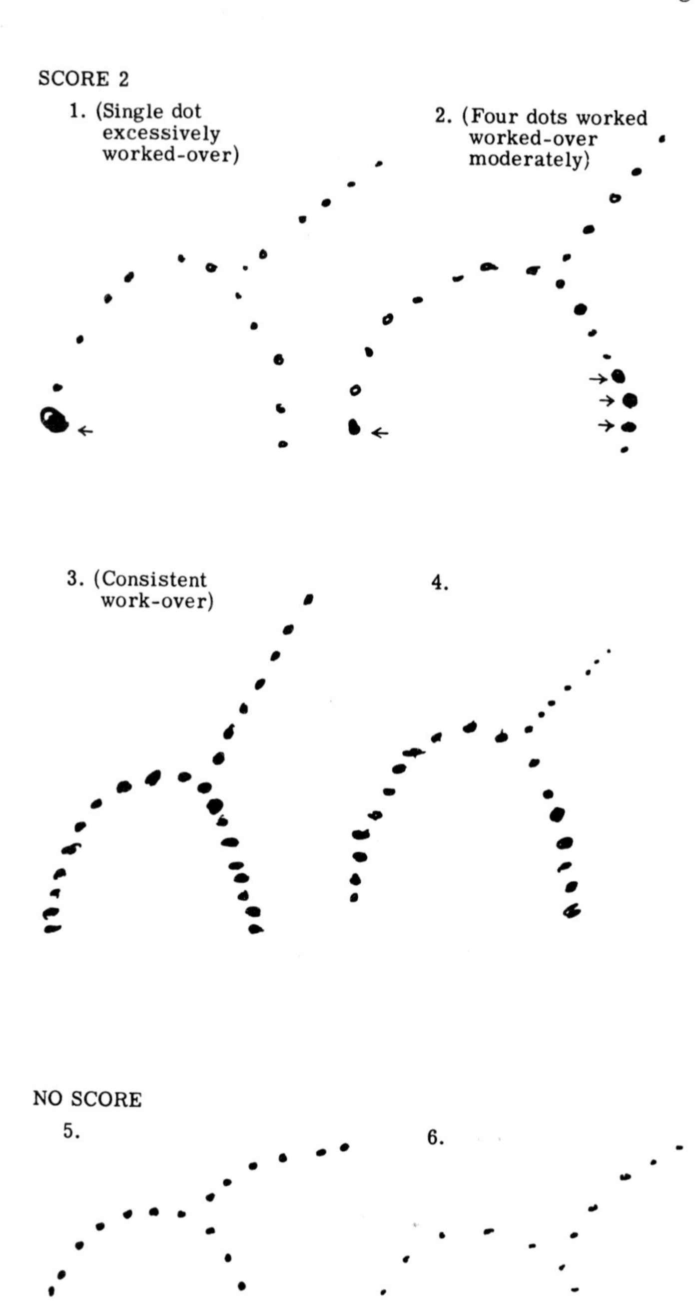

11. *Second attempt. Score 3 for each.* The item is scored as item 11, design 4.
12. *Rotation. Score 8.* The item is scored when the design is rotated 45° or more from the horizontal. The example below will clarify the scoring.

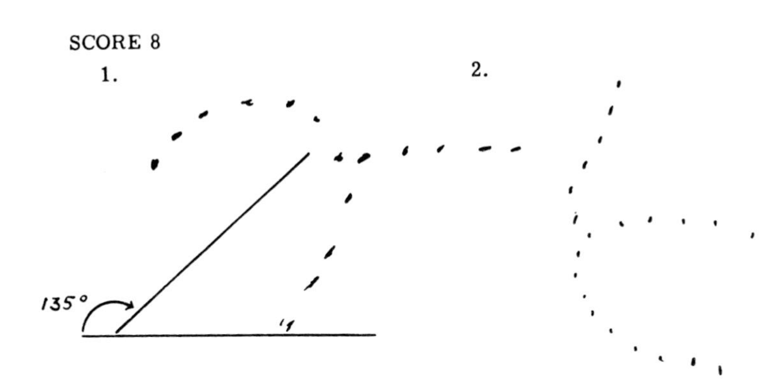

13. *Part of the design missing. Score 8.* The item is scored when the extension or at least half of the curve is missing.

NO SCORE

3. (Scored for asymmetry of length, Item 1)

Examples of scoring for design 5. Items scored are indicated by numbers.

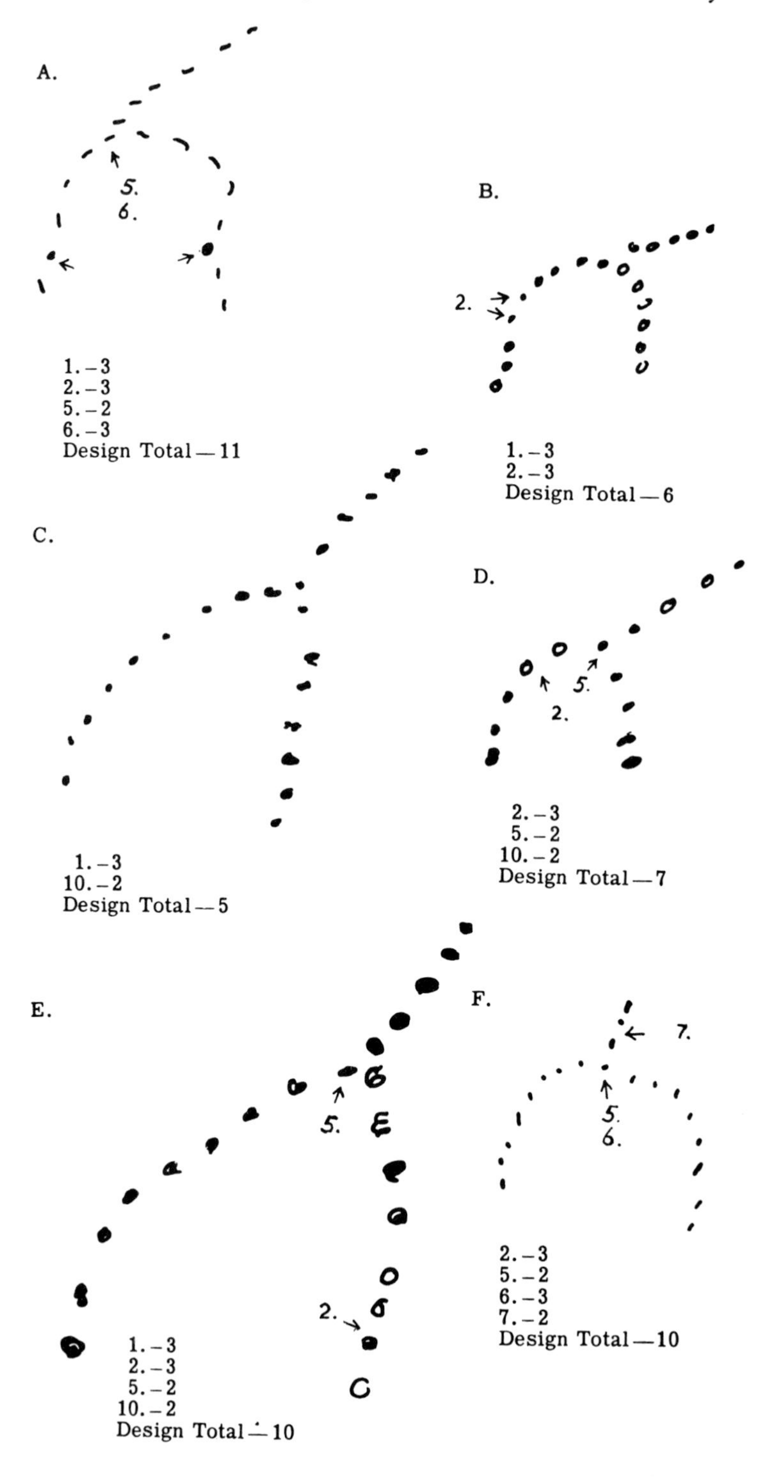

DESIGN 6

(Intersecting Sinusoidal Curves)

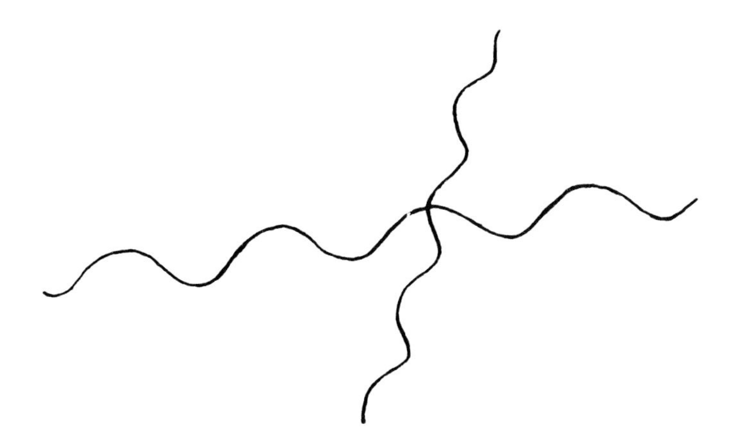

1. *Asymmetry. Score 3.* Asymmetry may be in terms of contour, or of differences between the two ends of either line: e.g., one end may be squared-off, curled, frayed, or worked-over. The examples will clarify the scoring. A reproduction showing reasonably similar sinusoidal curves is *not* scored.

SCORE 3 (Examples of contour asymmetry)

1. (Example scored for asymmetry in both lines)

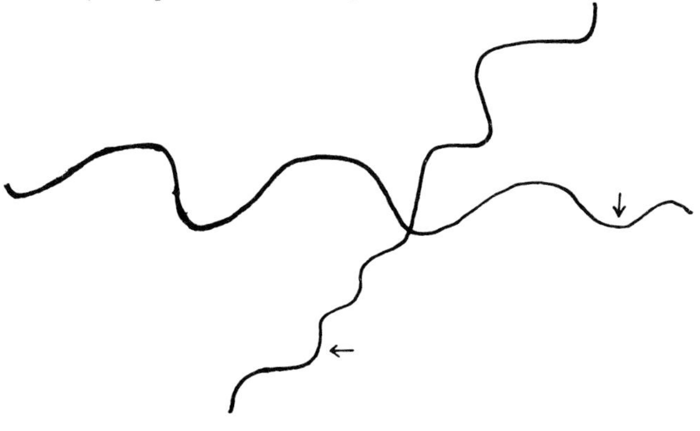

2. (Example scored for horizontal line asymmetry)

3. (Example scored for vertical line asymmetry)

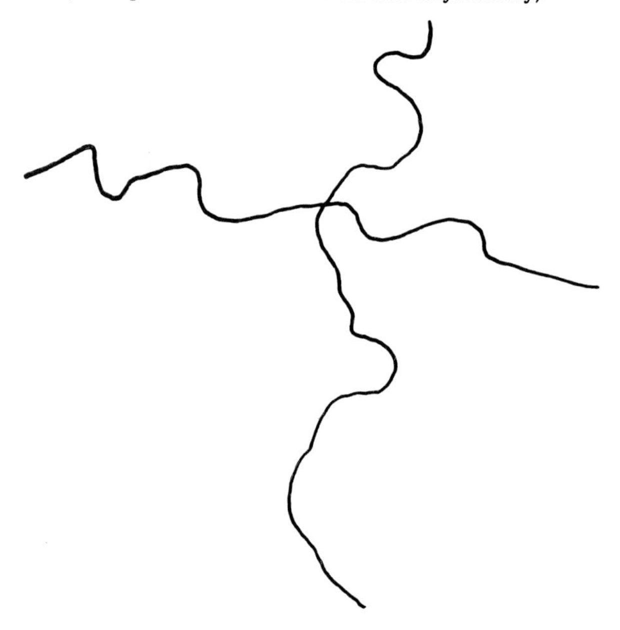

SCORE 3 (Examples of asymmetry in terms of difference between the two ends)

4. (Example scored for one end 'curled')

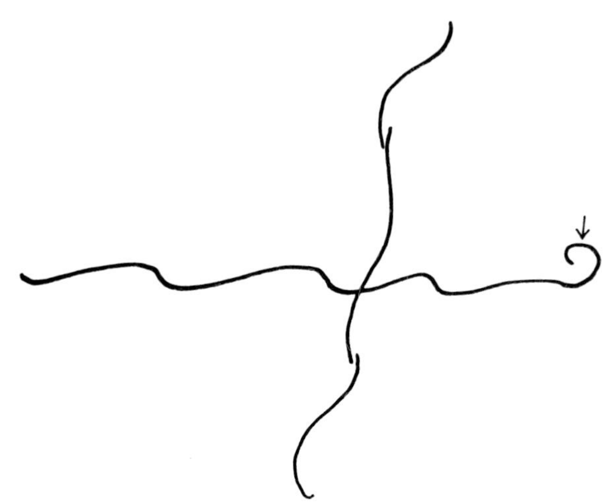

5. (Example scored for one end of each line 'worked-over')

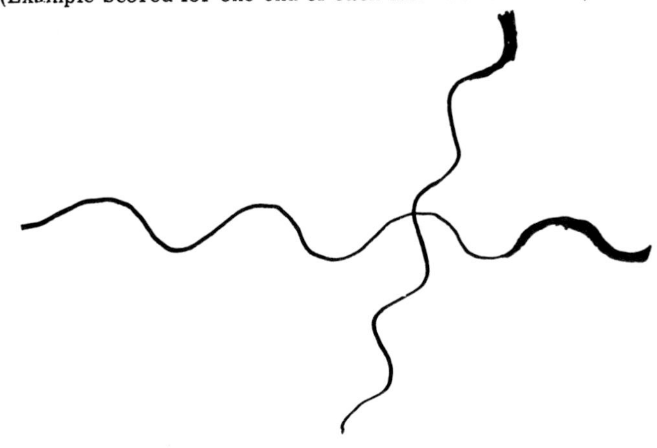

SCORE 3

6. (Example scored for both contour and difference asymmetry)

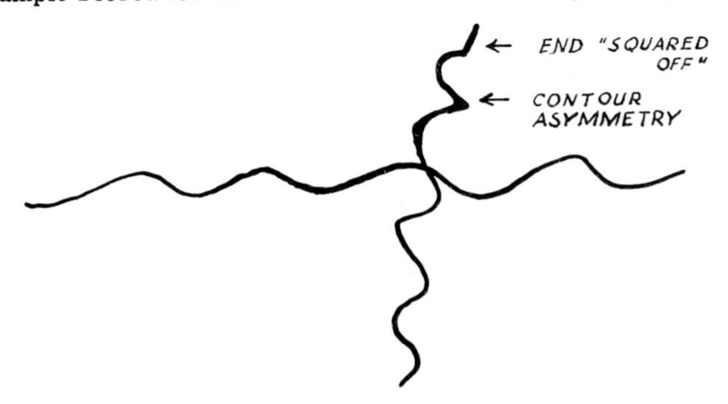

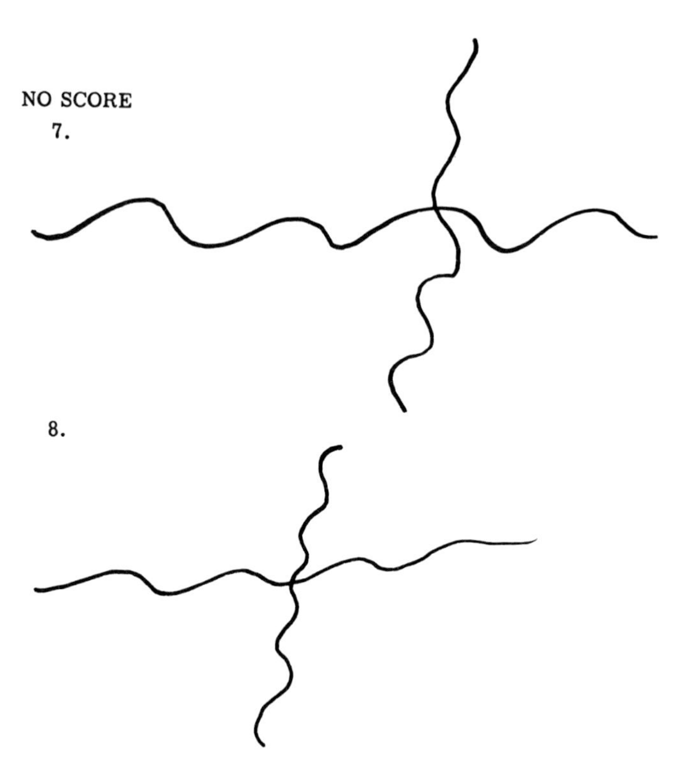

2. *Angles in the curve. Score 2.* For this item to be scored, there should be abrupt, distinctly angular change(s) in direction, i.e., a distinct angle should be substituted for a curve. In cases of doubt, the item is not scored.

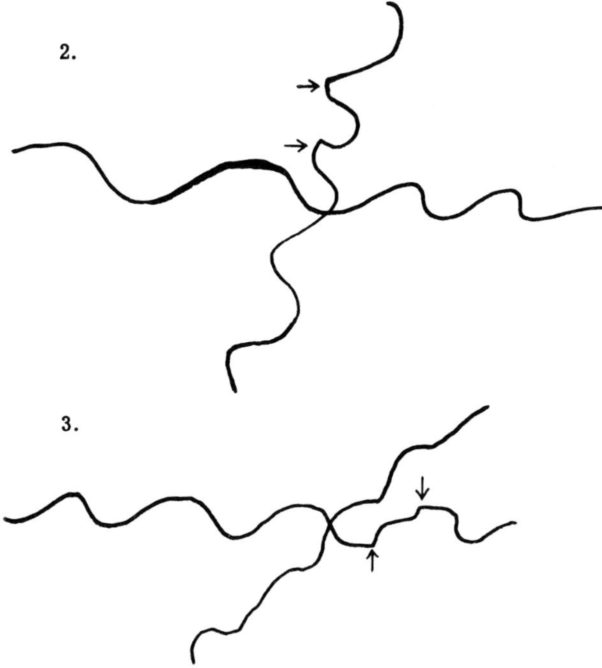

NO SCORE (Examples of changes in direction not sharp enough to be scorable)

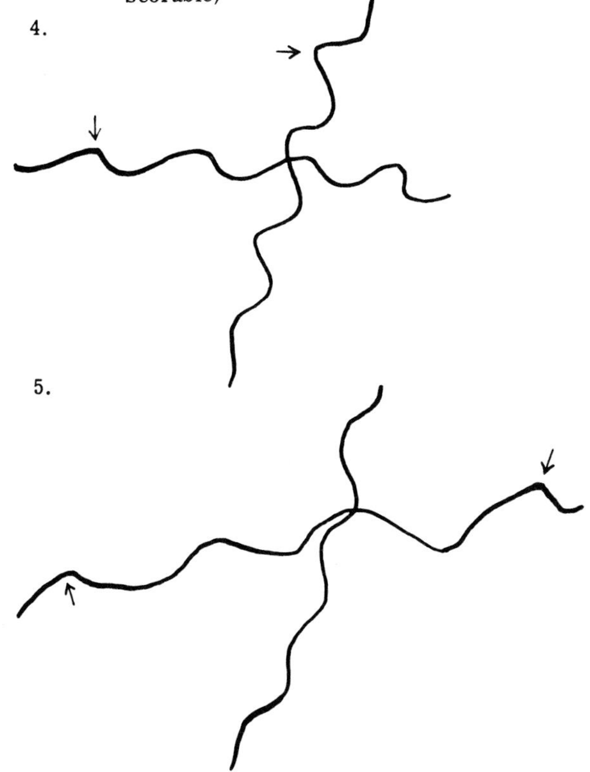

3. *Point of crossing. Score 2 for each.* The stimulus for design 6 shows the vertical line crossing the horizontal at the third curve from the left, and the horizontal crossing the vertical slightly above the middle. For "point of crossing" to be scored: 1) the vertical line should cross the horizontal to the left of center, or 2) the horizontal line should cross the vertical in the lower third. A reproduction may be scored for either, score 2; or for both, score 4. The examples will clarify the scoring.

SCORE 2 (Examples of left crossing of the vertical line)

1.

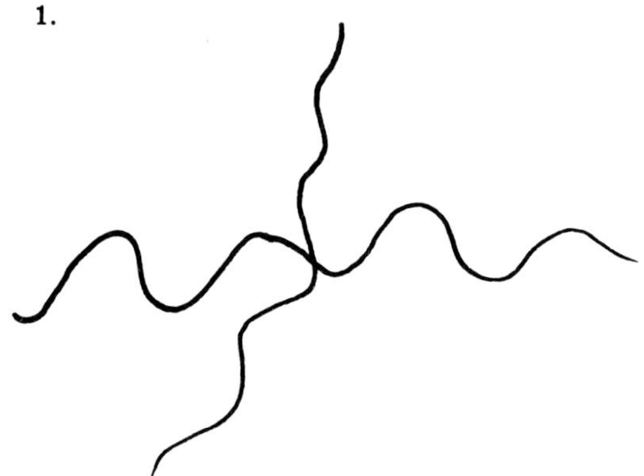

2. (Vertical crosses horizontal left of center, scored: a borderline case)

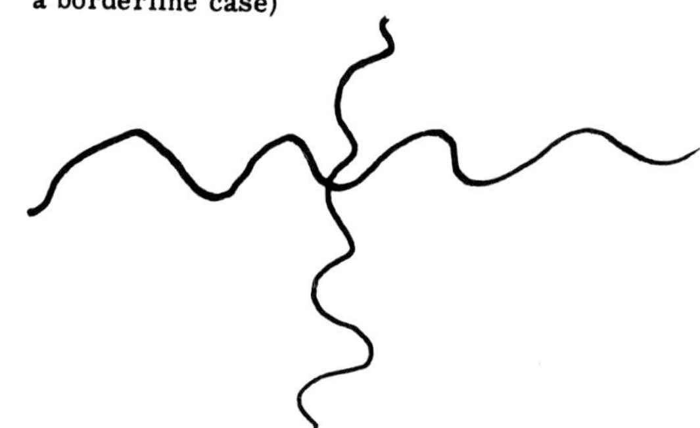

SCORE 2 (Examples of lower crossing of the horizontal line)

3.

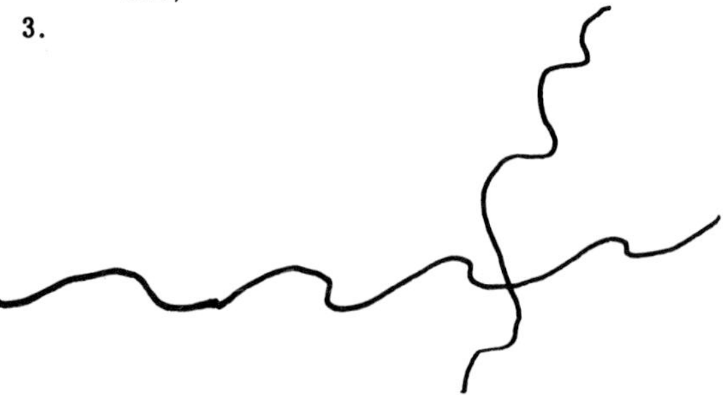

4.

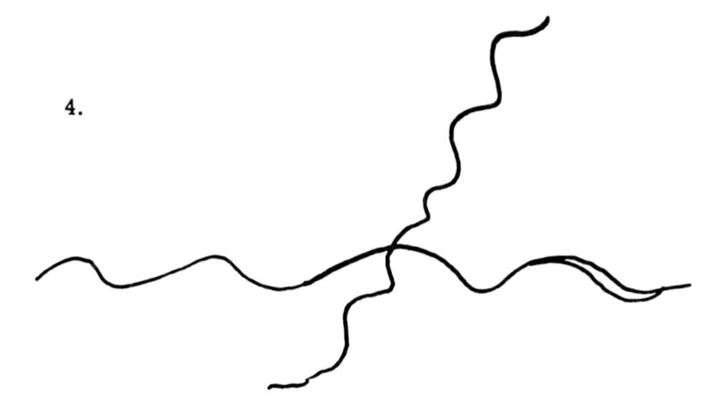

SCORE 4 (Example of double 'point of crossing')

5.

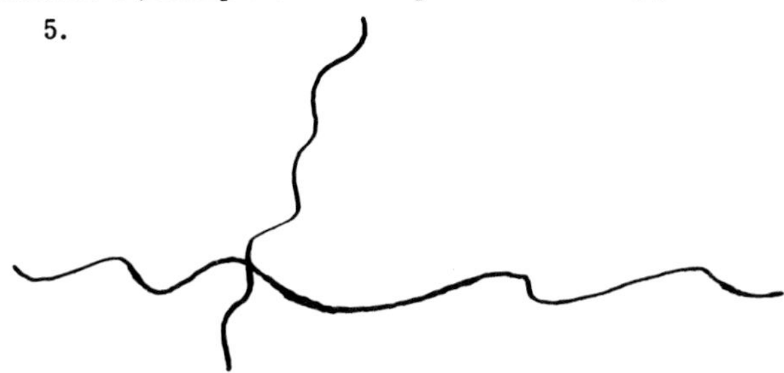

NO SCORE

6. (Example of crossing at center, not scored)

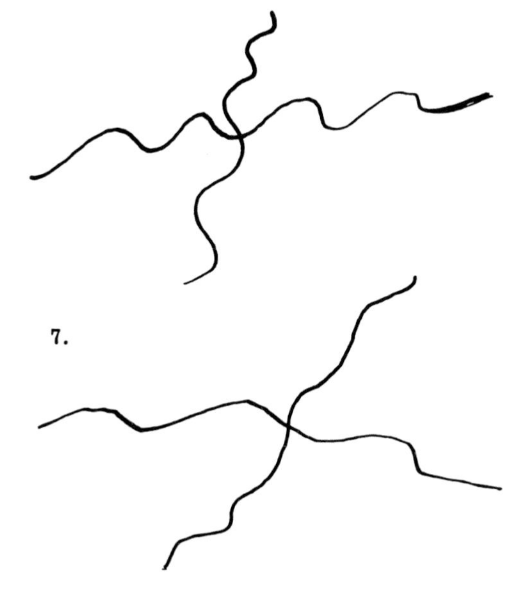

7.

8. (Example not scored for point of crossing, scored for asymmetry, Item 1: although vertical crosses horizontal left of center, point of crossing is at third curve from the left in the horizontal, as in the stimulus)

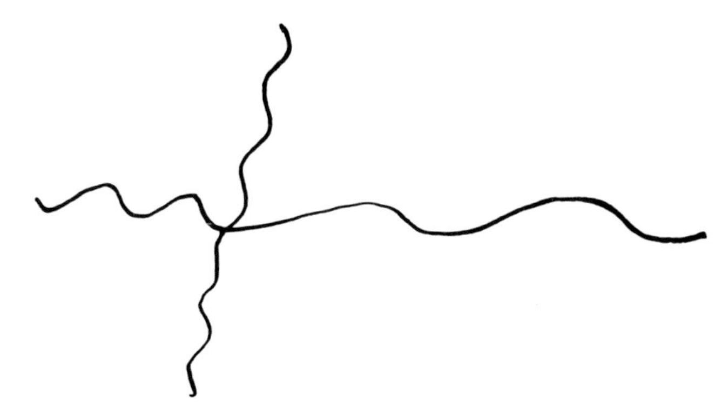

4. *Curve extra. Score 8.* When there are more than five sinusoidal curves in either the horizontal or the vertical line, the item is scored.

SCORE 8

1.

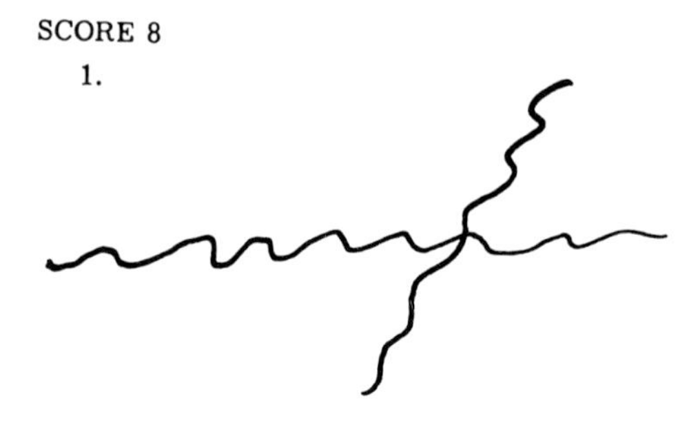

2.

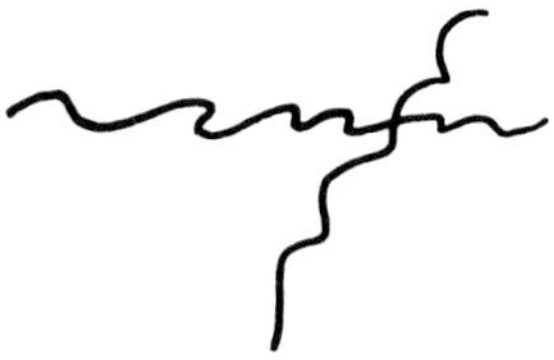

5. *Double line. Score 1 for each.* Each time a distinct double line appears in the reproduction, the score is 1. Double line is *not* scored when there is consistent sketching, unless, as in example 3, such a line is distinctly outside the line of sketching. Double line is *not* scored when the double line actually constitutes a second attempt superimposed on the first. Decision as to which item

to score, double line or second attempt, is a matter for judgment; usually a second attempt is obvious and consists of a redoing of at least one full sinusoidal curve. The examples following will clarify the scoring.

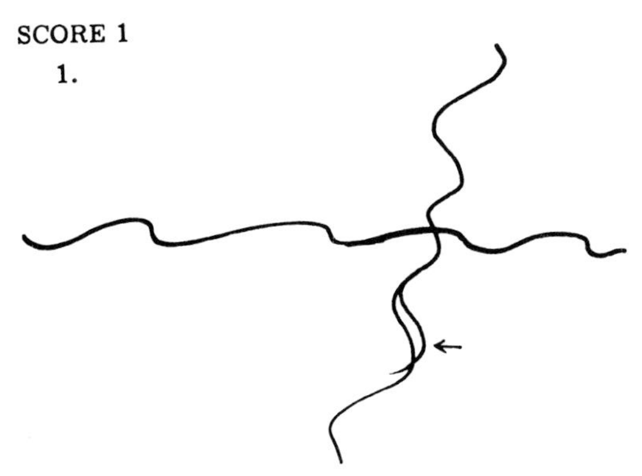

SCORE 4 (Example scored also for second attempt, Item 11)

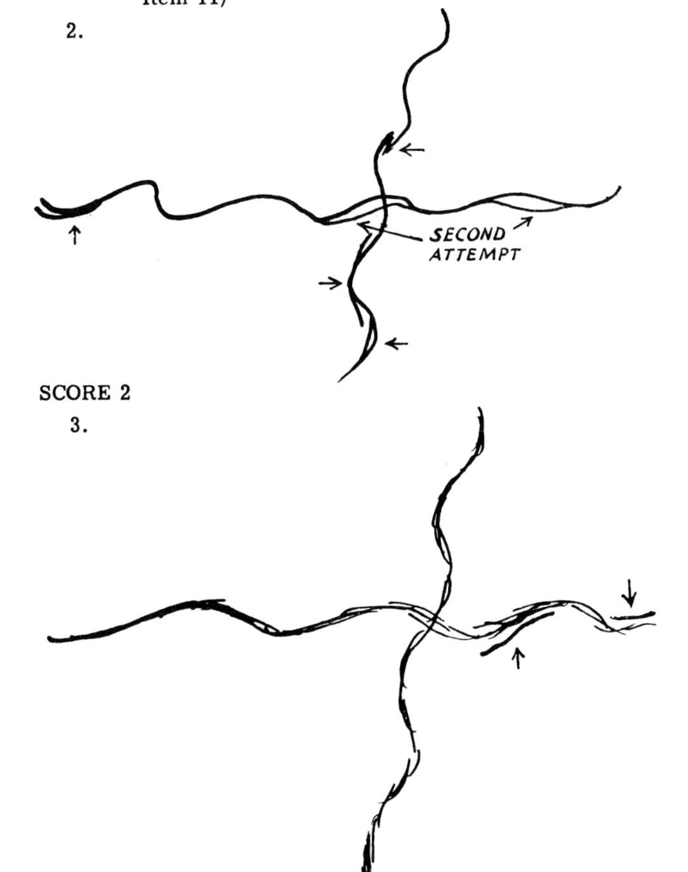

SCORE 2

4. (Example with questionable second attempt, not long enough to be scored)

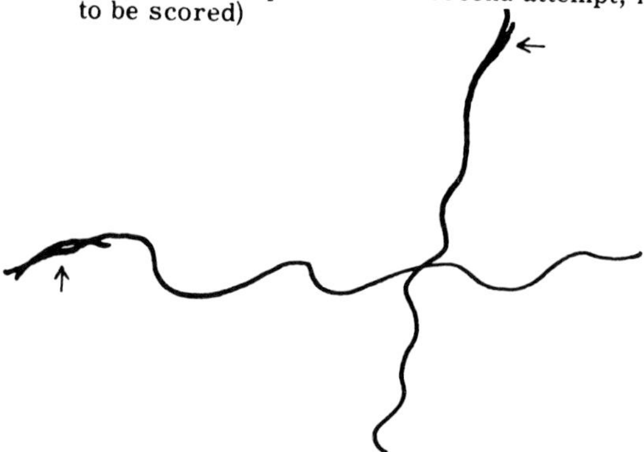

SCORE 2

5. (Example scored also for second attempt, Item 11)

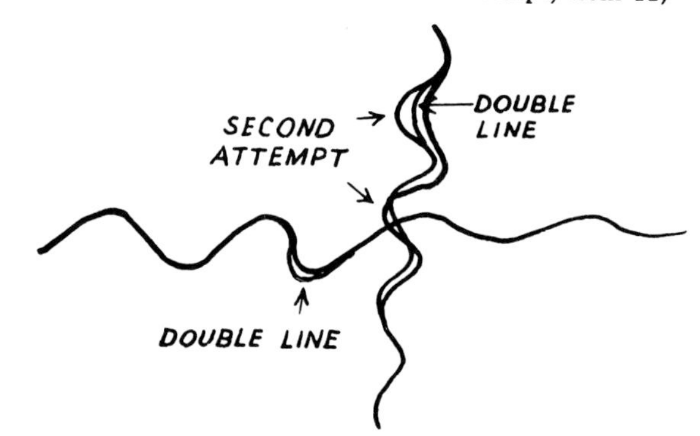

6. *Touch-up. Score 8.* Scoring is the same as that described for design 4, item 7.

N.B. Asymmetry, item 1, i.e., for differences in the ends of the curves, is not scored when touch-up occurs. Asymmetry for contour of the lines, however, may be scored.

SCORE 8

1.

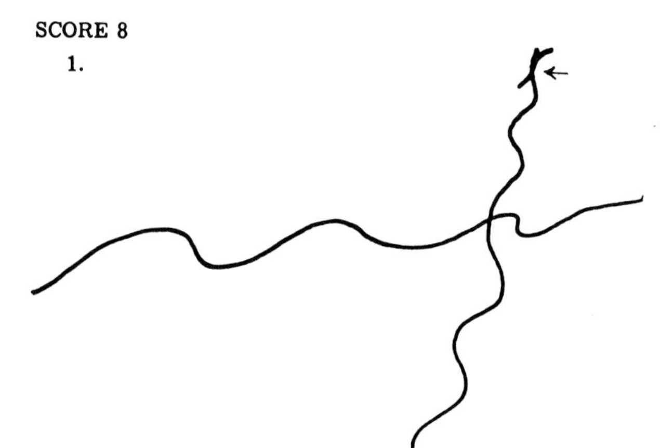

2. (Example with a scorable and a non-scorable 'touch-up': the non-scorable being more or less integrated into the figure: scored too for asymmetry, Item 1)

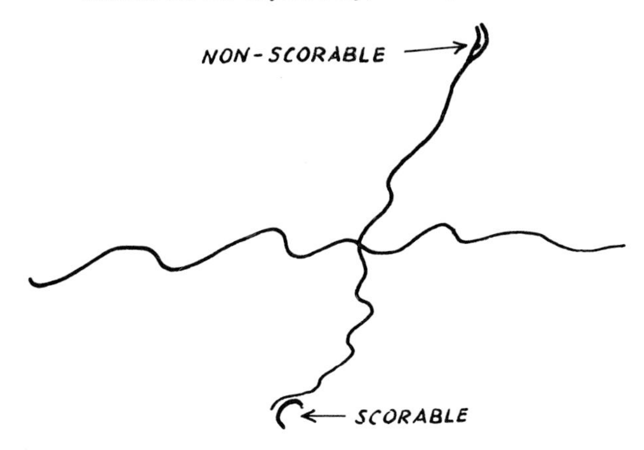

NO SCORE

3.

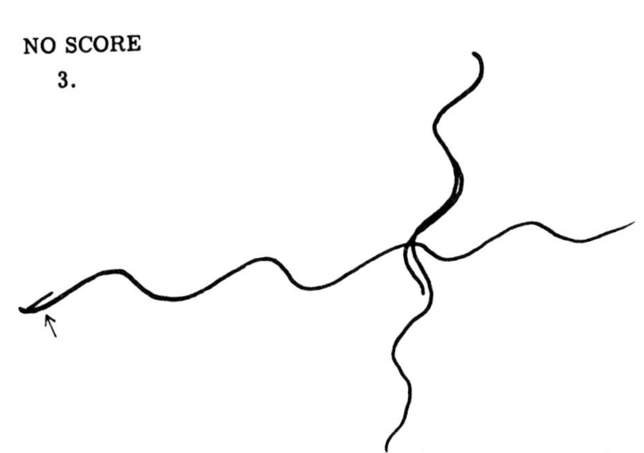

4. (Example of 'frayed' end, scored for asymmetry, Item 1)

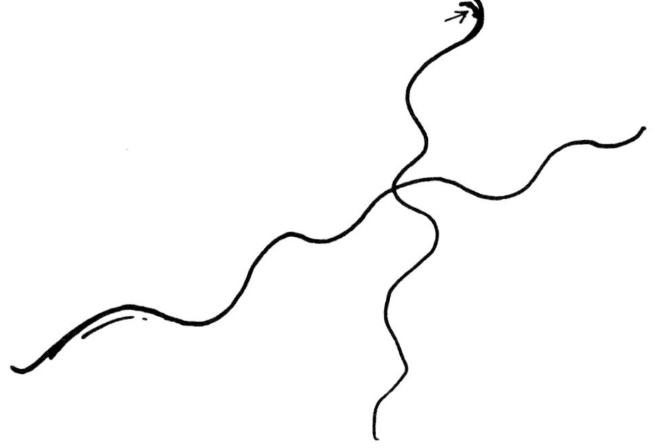

7. *Tremor. Score 4.* The item is scored as item 8, design 4.

SCORE 4 (Examples of fine tremor)

1.

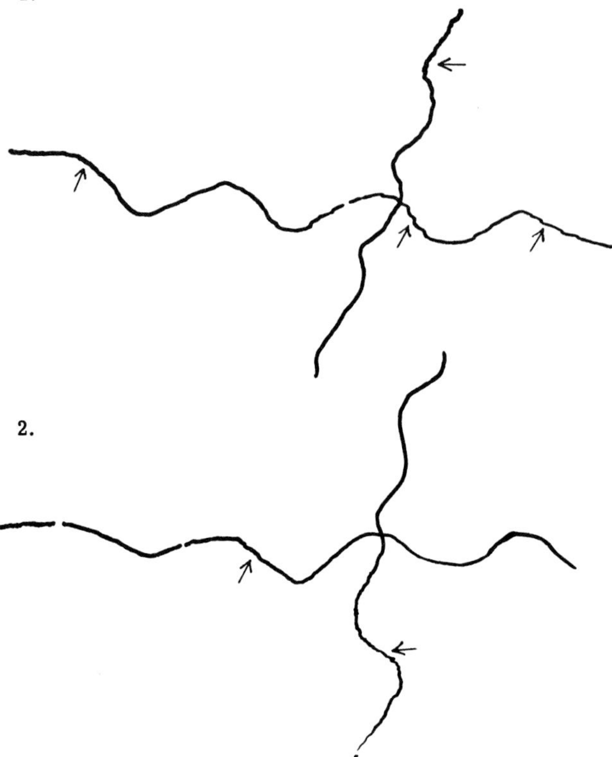

SCORE 4 (Examples with both fine and gross tremor)

3.

FINE

GROSS

FINE

4.

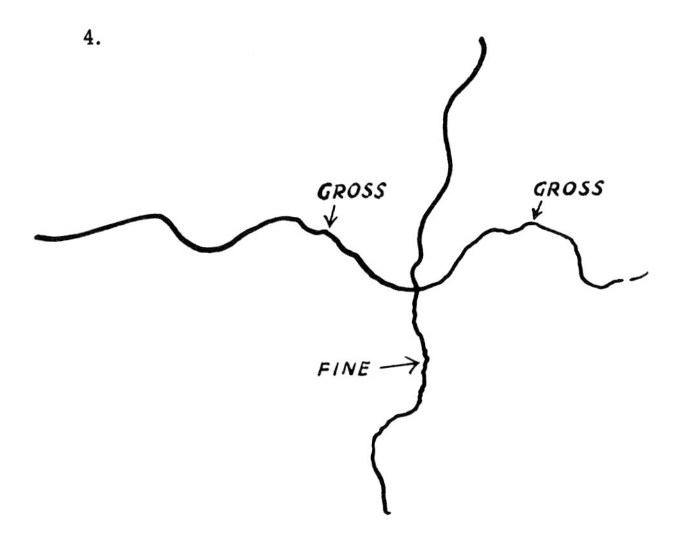

8. *Distortion. Score 8.* Distortion of design 6 is rarely encountered; it occurs most often in the records of children. The item is scored when the essential gestalt is destroyed, e.g., when the sinusoidal curves of one line differ markedly from those of the other (example 1), or when the two lines do not intersect (example 2).

SCORE 8

1. (Example of marked difference in the vertical and horizontal lines)

2. (Example of the vertical and horizontal lines turning perpendicular to themselves, and not intersecting)

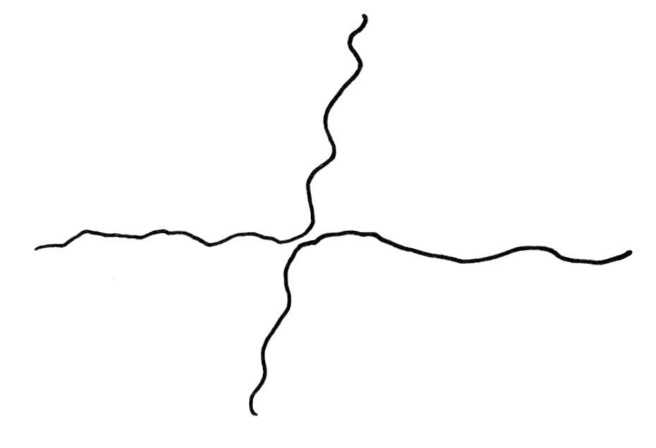

3.

NO SCORE

4. (Example in which the essential gestalt is not destroyed)

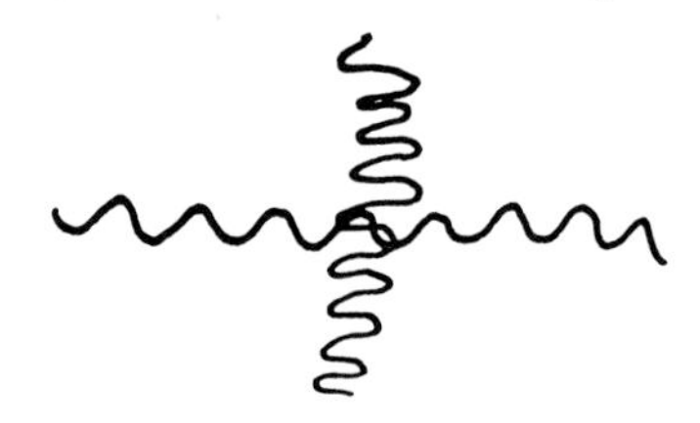

9. *Guide lines. Score 2.* The item is scored as item 10, design 4.

SCORE 2

1.

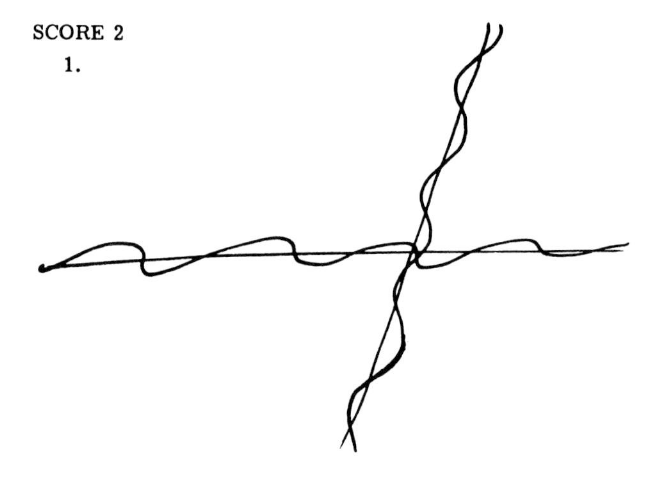

2. (Example of sketching, scored as guide lines)

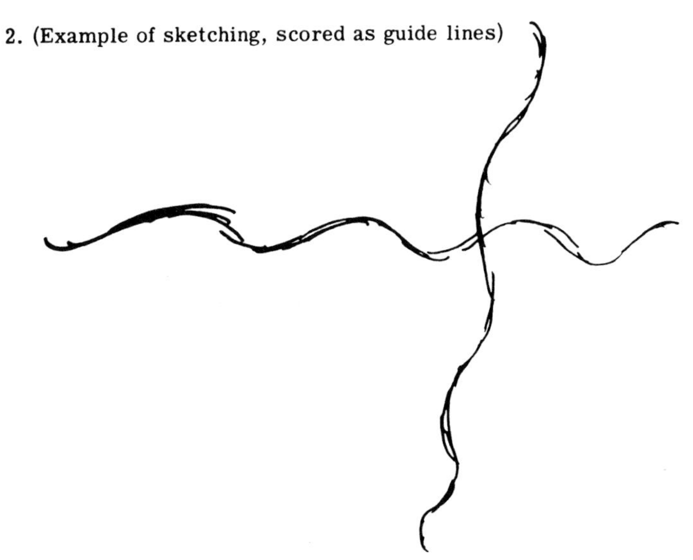

10. *Workover. Score 2.* Most normal subjects reproduce the stimulus by single lines. Some subjects, however, superimpose several lines on the single lines. When such elaboration results in a solid line of at least $^1/_{16}$ inch, workover is scored. The workover may be either of the entire line(s) or of only a portion of the line(s). (Where only one end of a line is worked over, asymmetry, item 1, is also scored.)

Some subjects may, in spite of the test instructions, reproduce the design by sketched lines. In differentiating a worked-over line from one thickly sketched, the matter of contrast is important. Sketched lines, short light lines used to delineate the drawing, may become at some points $^1/_{16}$ inch or more; unless such a widening of the sketched line is *solid*, and contrasted in darkness with the rest of the line, workover is *not* scored. (Sketched lines are scored for guide lines, item 9)

SCORE 2

1.

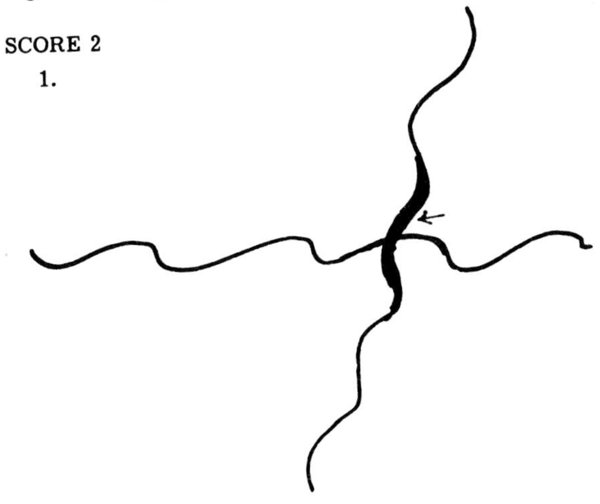

2.

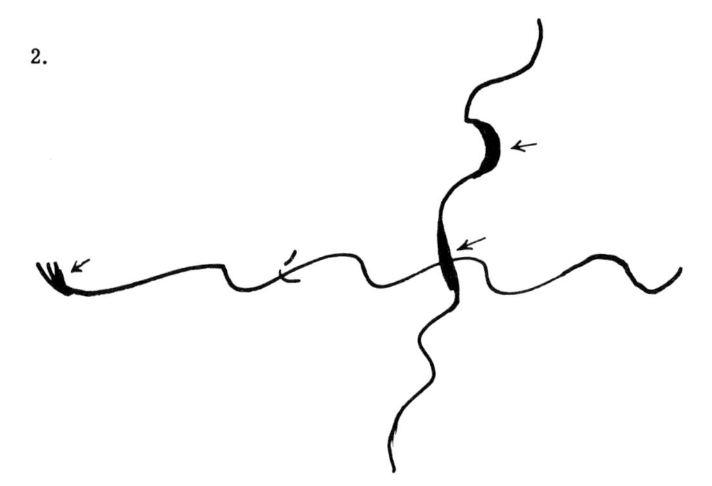

3. (Example of one end worked-over, scored also for asymmetry, Item 1)

4.

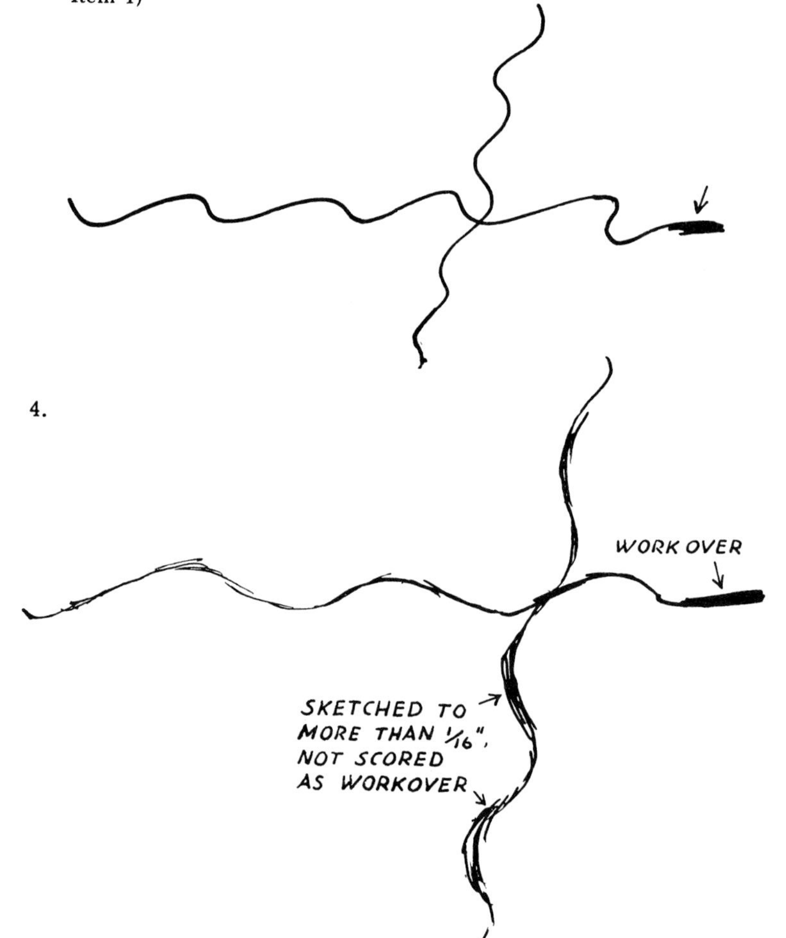

11. *Second attempt. Score 3 for each.* The item is scored as item 11, design 4. The differentiation between double line and second attempt is similar for design 6; i.e., a second attempt is usually a redoing of more than one of the sinusoidal curves whereas a double line is an adjustment for only a short distance along the line. (See examples for item 10, double line.)

12. *Rotation. Score 8.* The item is scored: 1) when the vertical line is rotated to the left, more than 10^0 from the perpendicular, (see examples following), and 2) when the horizontal line is rotated 45^0 or more. Design rotation of 90^0 is rarely encountered and difficult to distinguish from a lengthening of the vertical curve, hence the importance of noting rotations during the actual test administration. Rotation is *not* scored when the paper is rotated. Double rotation may occur, and is scored 16.

SCORE 8

1. (Example of rotation of the vertical)

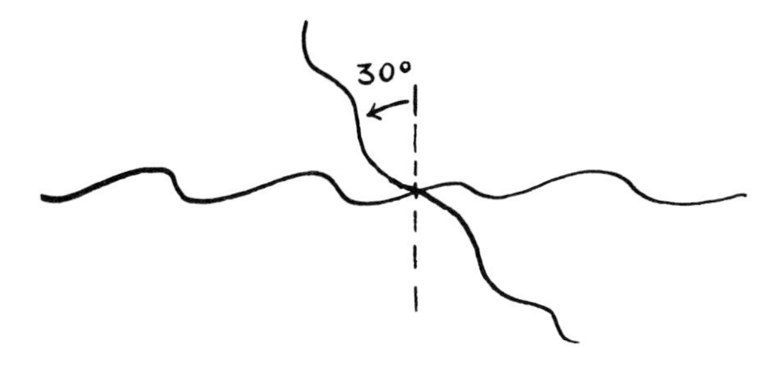

2.

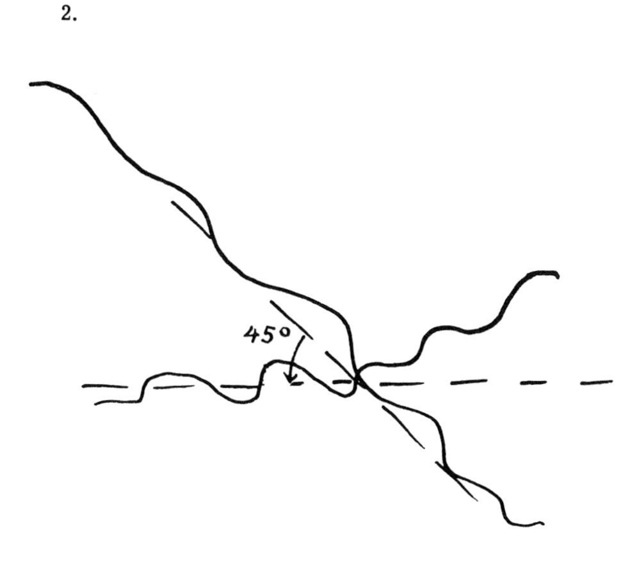

NO SCORE

3.

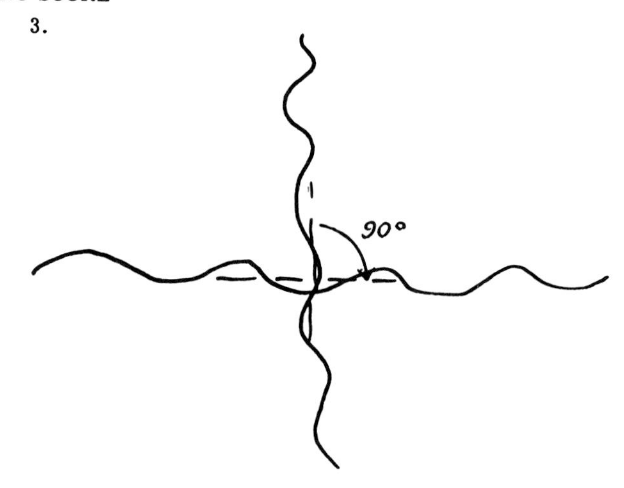

13. *Part of the design missing. Score 8.* One of the lines, or at least one-half of one of the lines, should be entirely missing for the item to be scored. (One-half of a line is defined as two of the sinusoidal curves, regardless of the point of crossing (example 2).

SCORE 8

1. (Example scored for one entire line missing)

2. (Example scored for one-half — two sinusoidal curves — of one line missing)

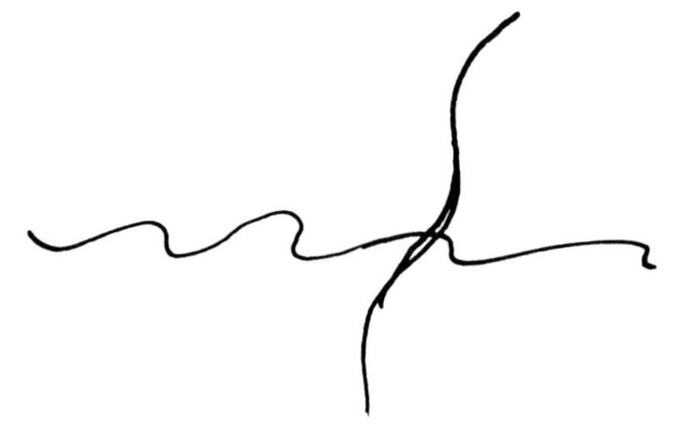

NO SCORE

3.

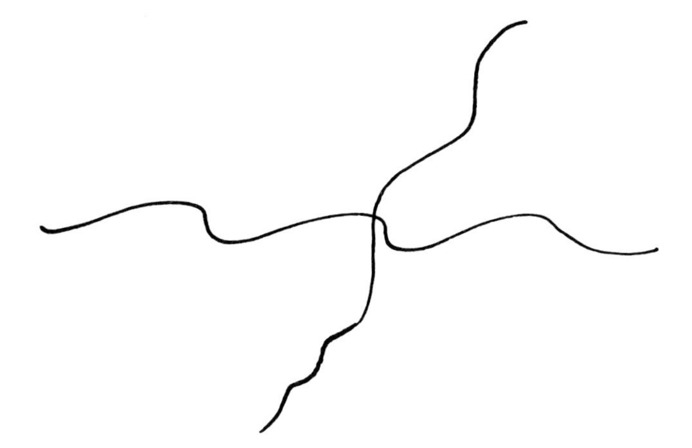

Examples of scoring for design 6. Items scored are indicated by **numbers.**

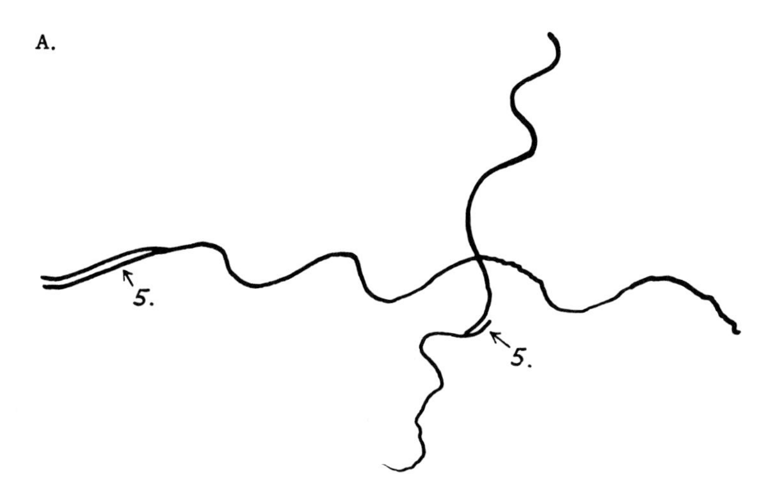

1.—3
5.—2
7.—4
Design Total—9

B. (Arrows indicate scoring for double line, Item 5)

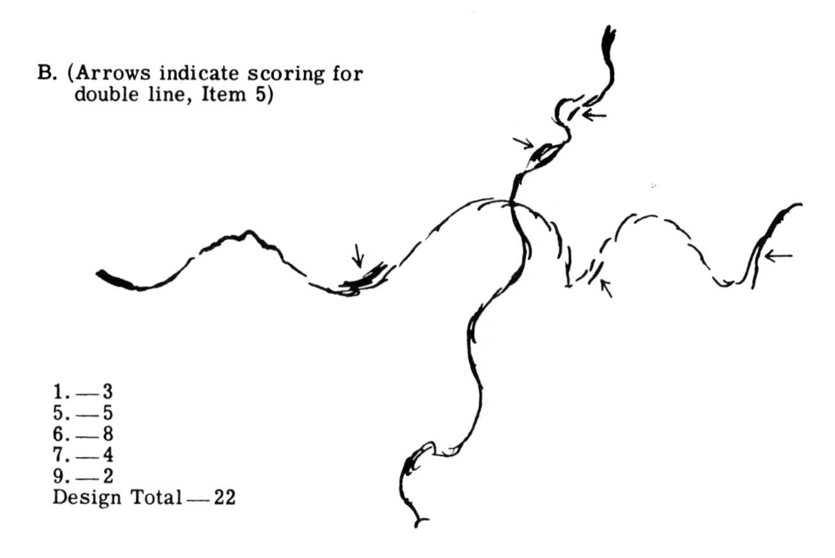

1.—3
5.—5
6.—8
7.—4
9.—2
Design Total—22

C. (Example of questionable reproduction <u>not</u> scored for point of crossing; <u>not</u> scored for rotation of the vertical line)

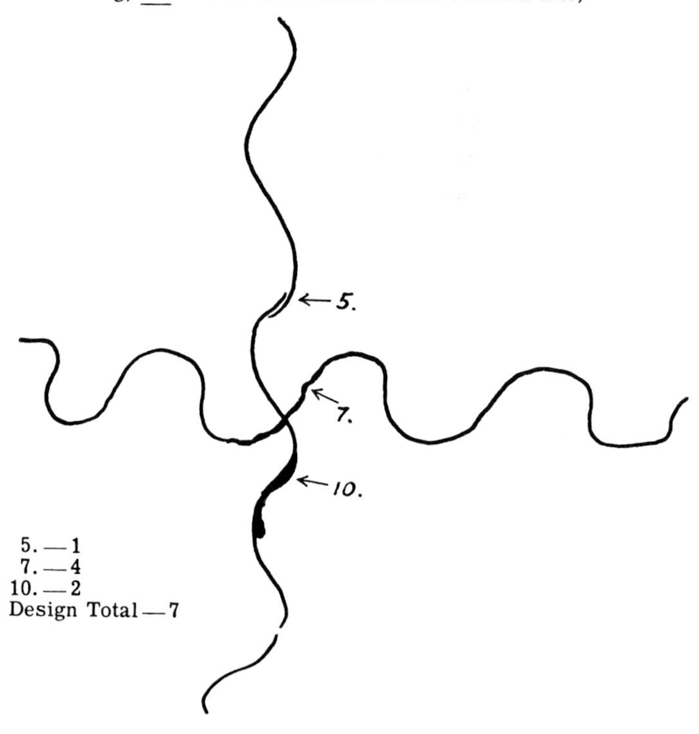

5.—1
7.—4
10.—2
Design Total—7

DESIGN 7
(Overlapping Hexagons)

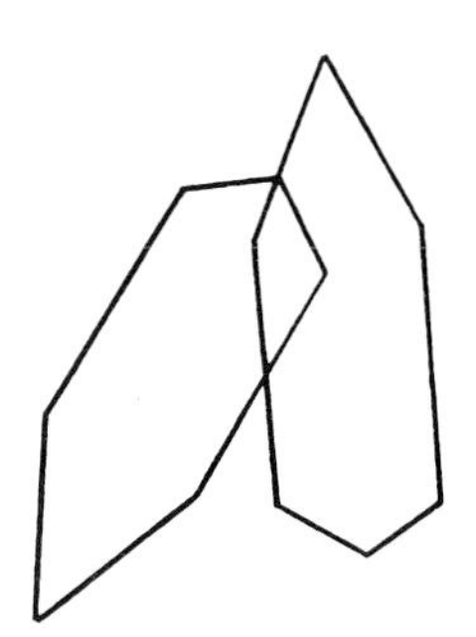

1. *Ends of lines not joined. Score 8.* In reproducing design 7, the subject may fail to join the ends of the lines forming the hexagons. The deviation is scored: 1) when three or more gaps of 1/16 inch occur in either or both hexagons, and 2) when two gaps occur, one of which is approximately 1/8 inch. The scoring is, in general, a matter for judgment, and not rigid (see examples following).

SCORE 8

1. (Example scored for 4 gaps of more than 1/16″)

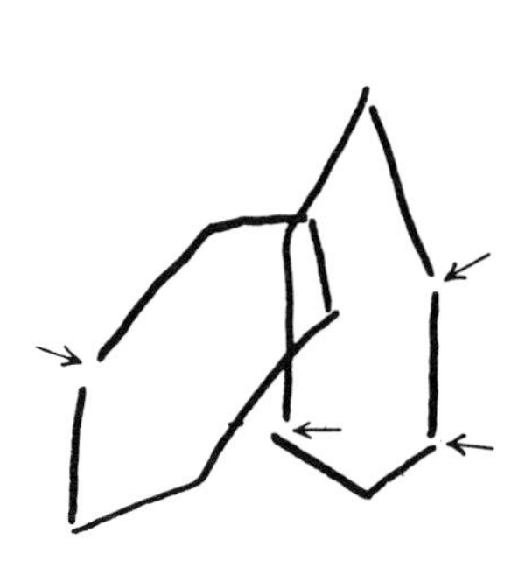

2. (Example scored for 3 gaps, one of approximately 1/8″)

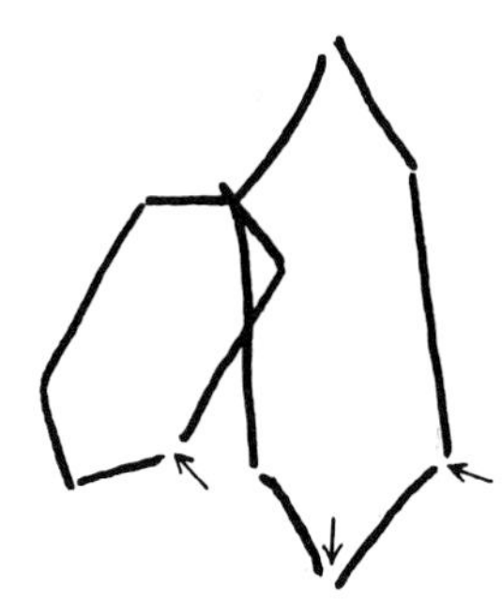

3. (Example scored for 2 gaps of approximately 1/8″)

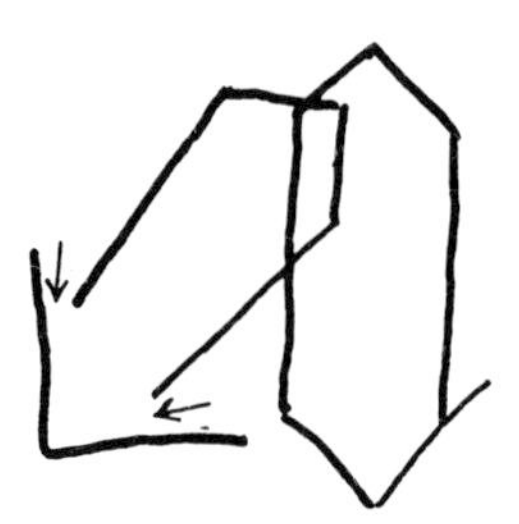

NO SCORE

4. (Example of gaps less than 1/16″)

5. (Example of only one gap of 1/8″)

2. *Angles extra. Score 3.* The item is scored when there occurs in the reproduction more than six angles in either hexagon. The deviation may occur in either of two ways: 1) when there is arbitrary addition of an extra angle, as in example 1, or 2) when there occur abrupt changes in the direction of the straight lines. An abrupt change in direction may constitute a well-defined extra angle as in example 3, or may be a sharp curve as in examples 2 and 4. A curved change in direction should be pronounced. In cases of doubt, a ruler may be held tangent to the curved line; the angle thus formed should be approximately 20°, or more, for scorable deviation (example 4).

SCORE 3

1. (Example scored for extra line to join two ends)

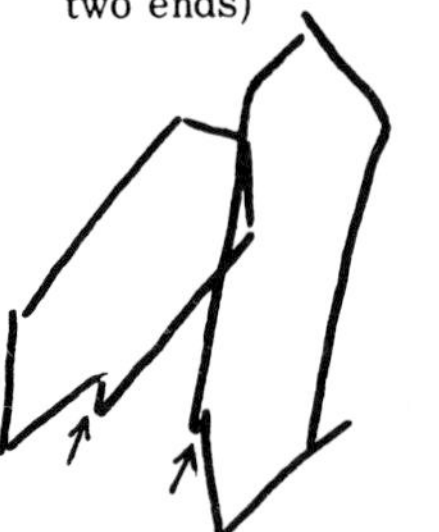

2. (Example scored for both angular and curved changes in direction)

3. (Example scored also for angle missing, Item 3)

4. (Example with scorable curved change in direction, making approximately 30° angle with tangent)

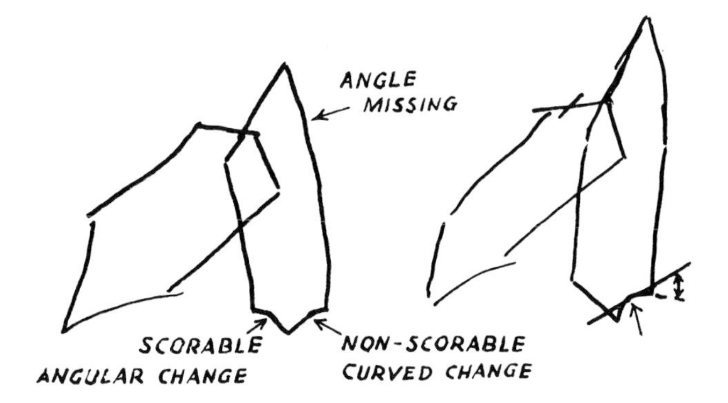

NO SCORE

5.

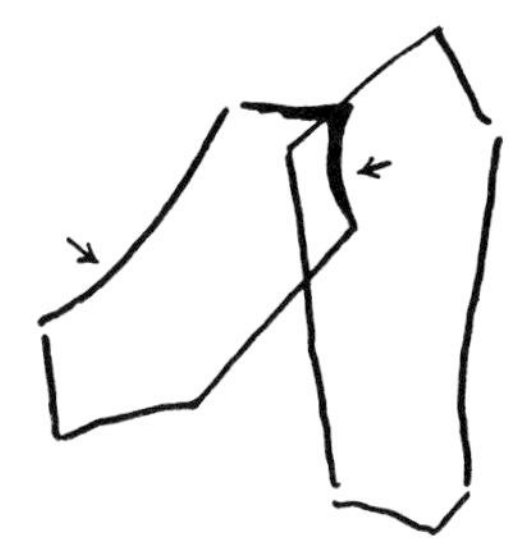

6. (Example with non-scorable curved change in direction, angle approximately 10°)

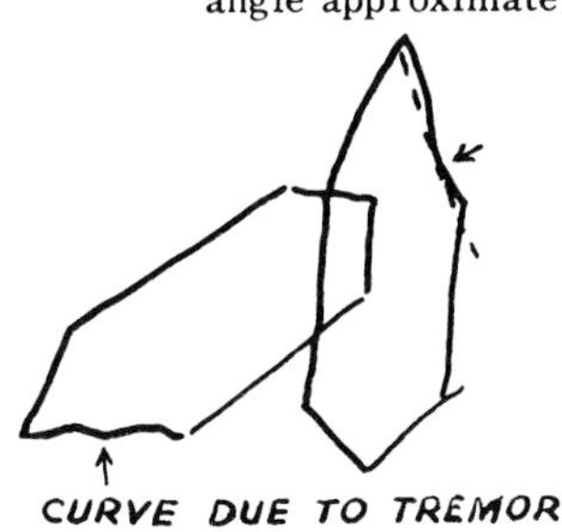

3. *Angles missing. Score 3.* The item is scored when in either hexagon an angle is entirely missing, i.e., when there are five or less angles. The item is not scored when a curve constituting a pronounced change in the direction of the line (defined as in item 2) is substituted for an angle. The examples following will clarify the scoring. In cases of doubt the item is not scored. When there is any attempt to make an angle, although the attempt may not be entirely successful, as in example 5, the item is not scored.

N.B. This item is not scored when a hexagon is scored for "part of the design missing," item 11, unless, of course, the other hexagon—the one not scored for item 11—has an angle missing.

SCORE 3

1. (Example in which there are five angles in right hexagon)

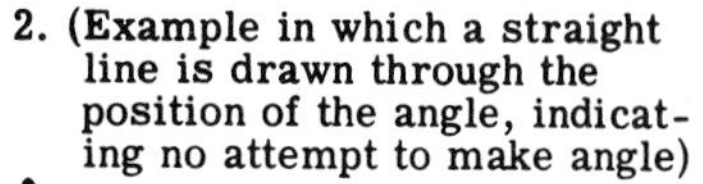
2. (Example in which a straight line is drawn through the position of the angle, indicating no attempt to make angle)

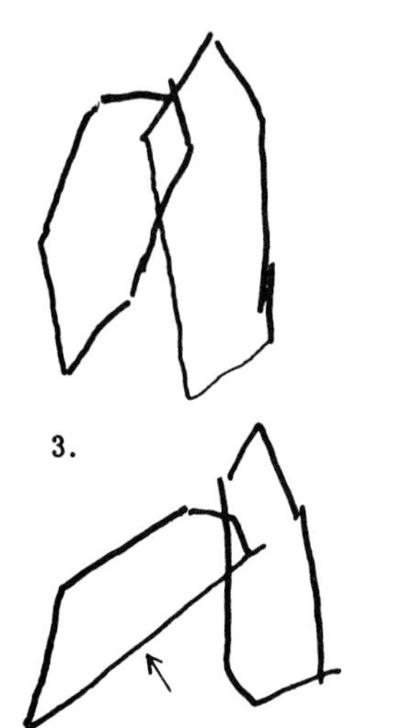

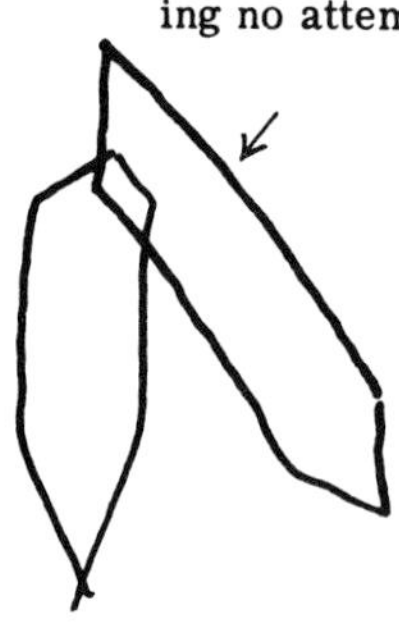

3.

NO SCORE

4.

5. (Clear break indicates attempt to make angle)

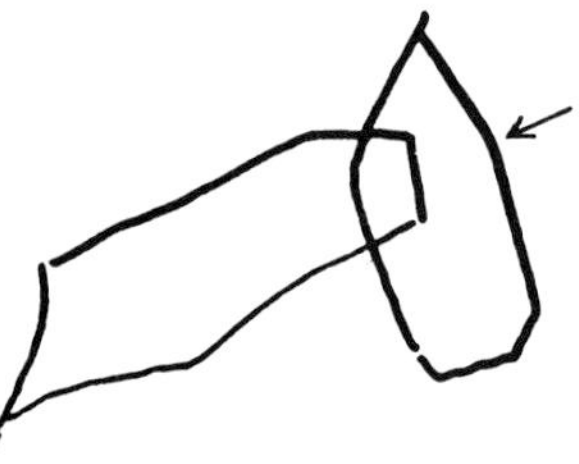

6.

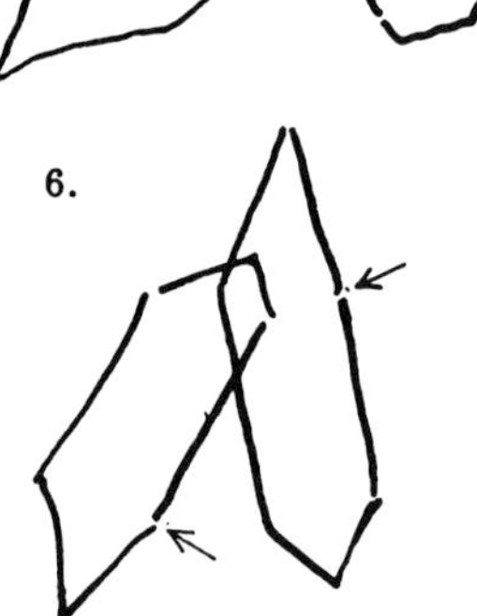

4. *Extra scattered dots and/or dashes. Score 3.* To score, there must occur in the reproduction at least two dots and/or dashes which are not integrated into the design. These meaningless additions may result from touching-up the reproduction, or from some sort of peculiar "doodling" on the side.

N.B. The dots and dashes should be distinct to be scored, and not be confused with imperfections in the paper, or with dots and dashes which may occur as a result of dropping a pencil.

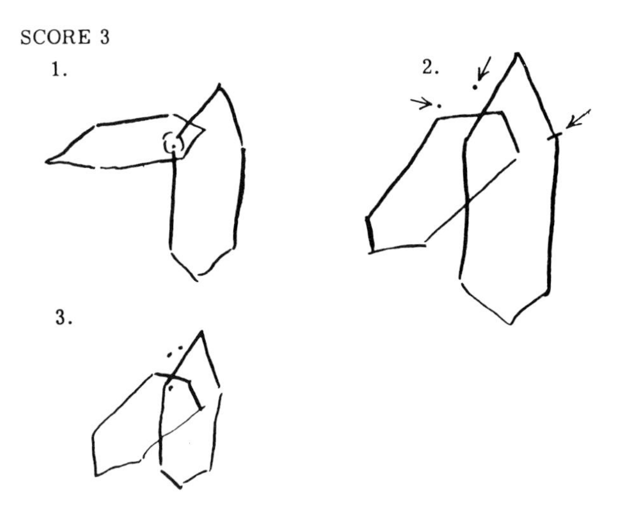

5. *Double line. Score 1 for each.* The item is scored as item 5, design 6. The examples differentiate double line and second attempt.

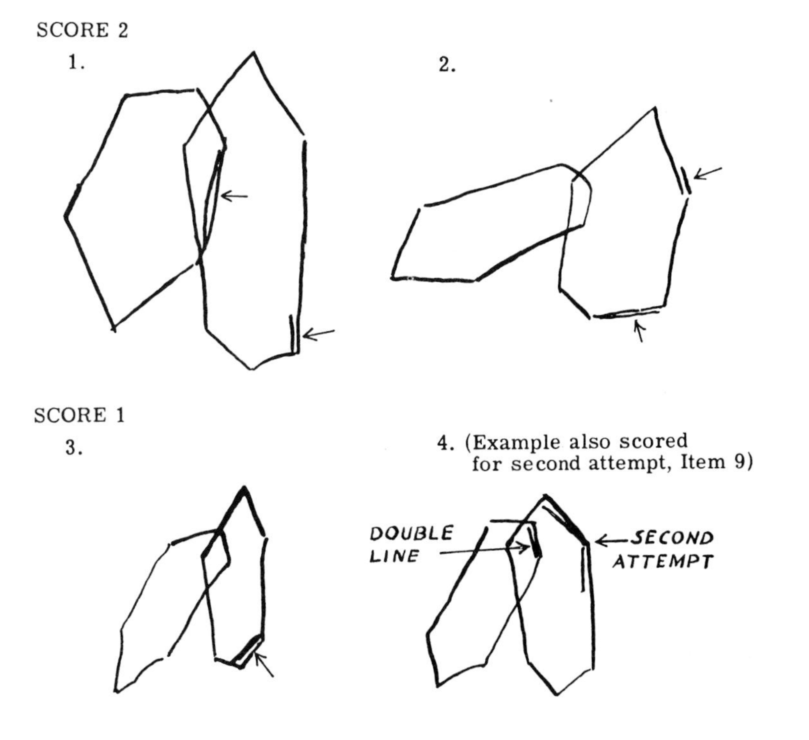

NO SCORE

5. (Scored for sketching, guide lines, Item 8)

6. *Tremor. Score 4.* The item is scored as item 8, design 4.

SCORE 4 (Examples of fine tremor)

1. 2.

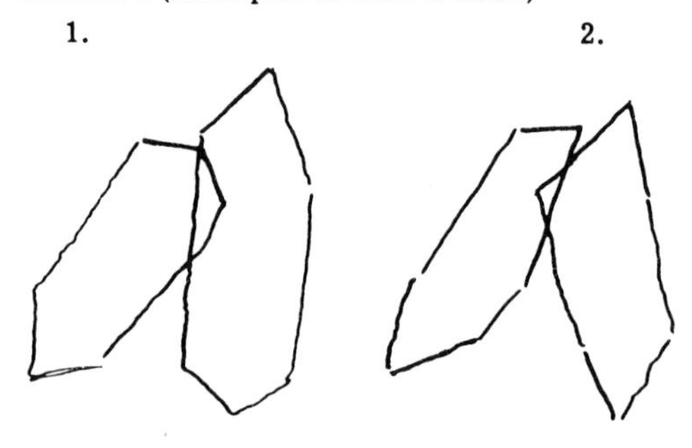

SCORE 4 (Examples of gross tremor)

3. 4.

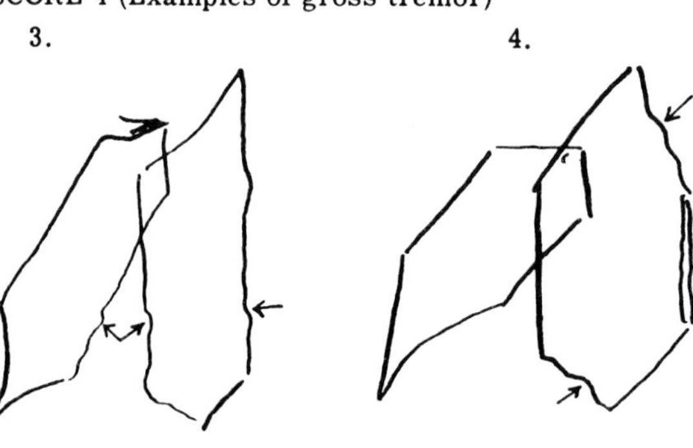

7. *Distortion. Score 8.* Distortion may occur in three ways: 1) when there is disproportion between the sizes of the two hexagons—for scorable deviation one must be approximately twice the size of the other, 2) when the two hexagons do not overlap or when they overlap excessively, as in example 5,

and 3) when the design is otherwise reproduced in a markedly distorted manner. (What is meant by a "markedly distorted manner" will be clarified in the examples following.)

The reproduction may be scored for one, two, or all three types of distortion, although more than one rarely occurs; the scores accordingly are 8, 16, and 24, for the item. In general, the scoring is a matter for judgment; in cases of doubt, the item is *not* scored.

SCORE 8 (Examples of size distortion)

1.

2.

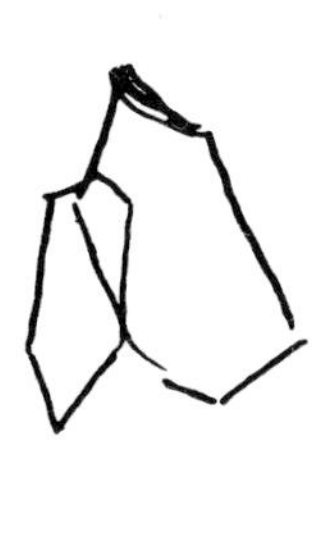

SCORE 8 (Examples of overlap distortion)

3. (Failure to overlap)

4.

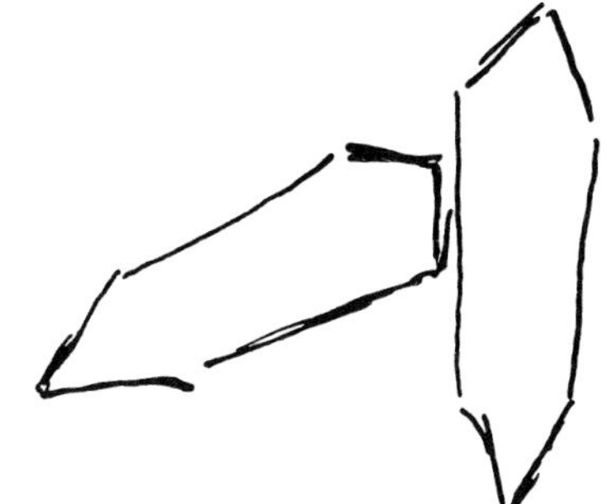

5. (Excessive overlap, left hexagon projects to right of right hexagon)

SCORE 8 (Examples of reproductions in 'markedly' distorted manner)

6.

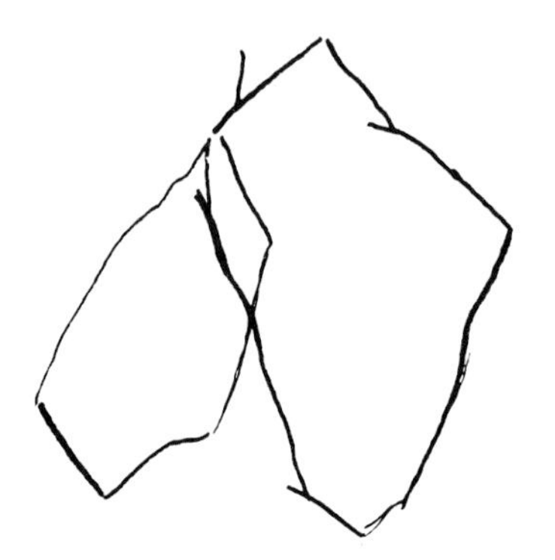

7.

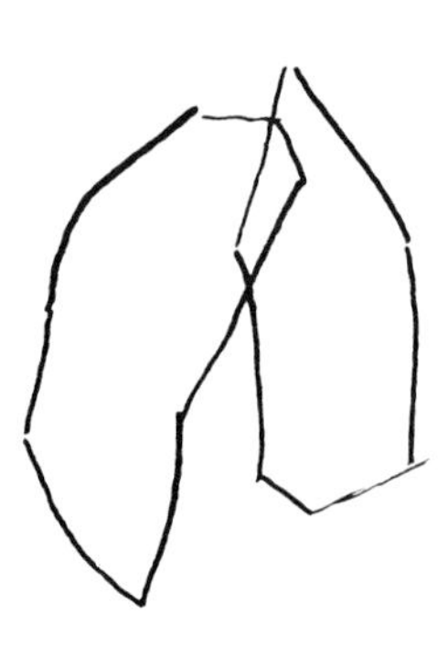

8. (Markedly distorted in placement of left hexagon — more than 1/2 down side of right hexagon)

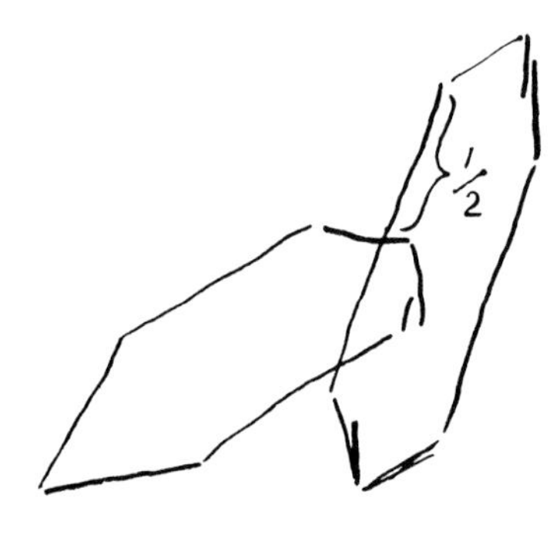

9.

10. (Markedly distorted in placement of opposing angles — angles a and b should be approximately opposed — more than 30° displacement)

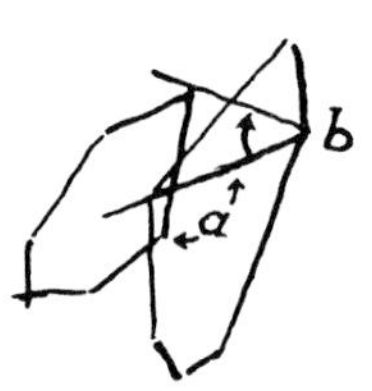

SCORE 16 (Example scored for shape distortion, and placement of left hexagon)

11.

NO SCORE

12.

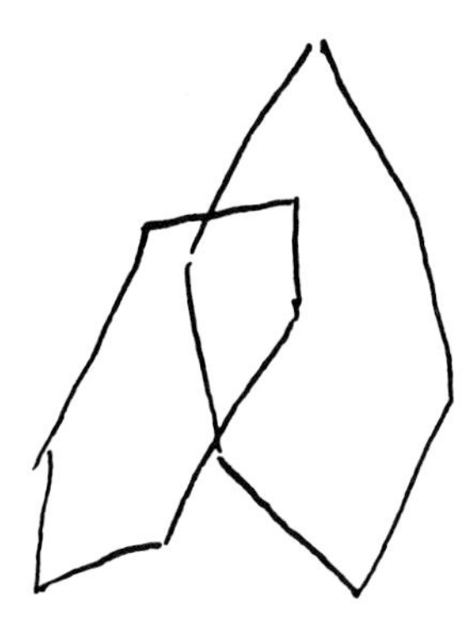

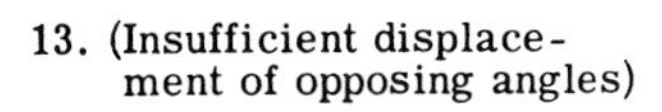

13. (Insufficient displacement of opposing angles)

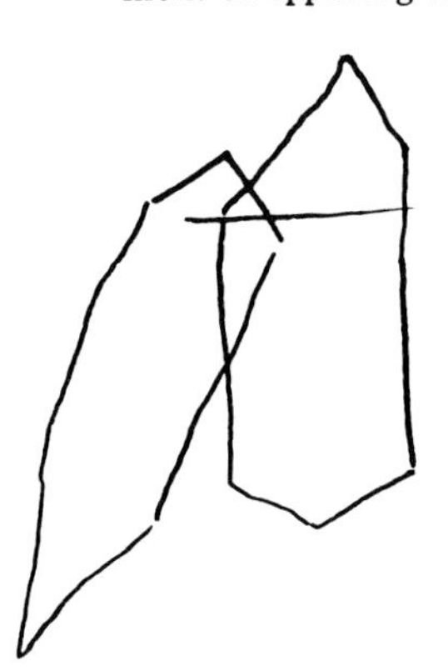

14.

15.

8. *Guide lines. Score 2.* The item is scored as item 9, design 4.

SCORE 2

1. 2.

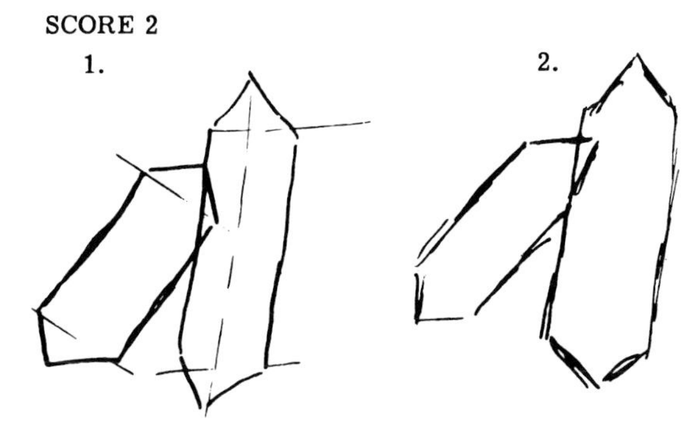

3.

9. *Second attempt. Score 3 for each.* The item is scored as item 11, design 4.

SCORE 3

1.

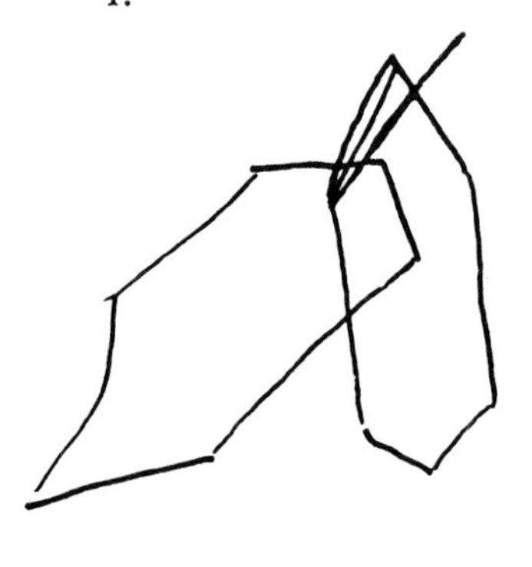

2.

3.

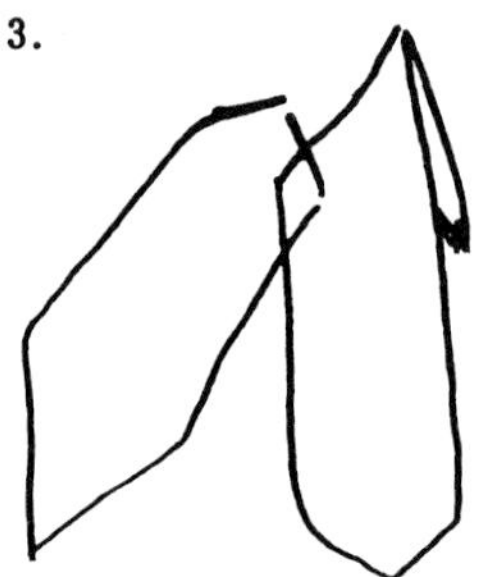

4.

5.

SCORE 6

6.

NO SCORE

7.

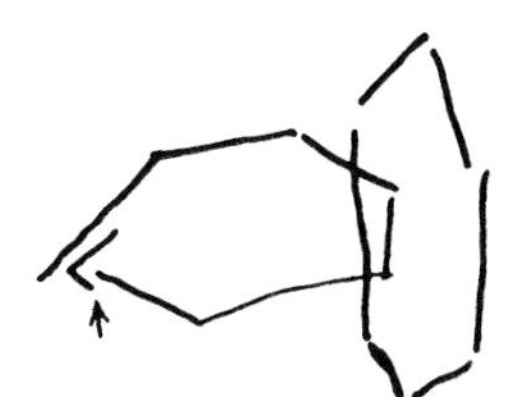

8.

10. *Rotation. Score 8.* Rotation of design 7 is scored: 1) when the lateral hexagon is rotated so that the 30^0 angle of the stimulus design is increased to 90^0 or decreased to 0^0, and 2) when the entire reproduction is rotated. Double rotation may occur, and is scored 16. Rotation is not scored when it results from the turning of the paper. In cases of doubt, the item is *not* scored.

SCORE 8 (Examples scored for rotation of one hexagon on the other, zero angle, lines 1 and 2 do not intersect)

1.

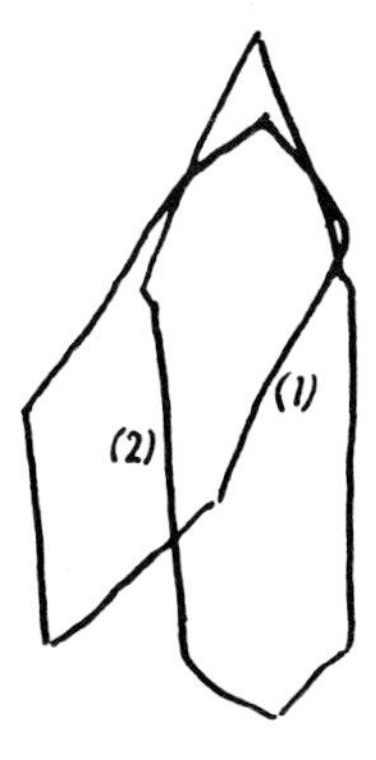

2.

SCORE 8 (Example scored for 90^0 rotation of one hexagon on the other)

3.

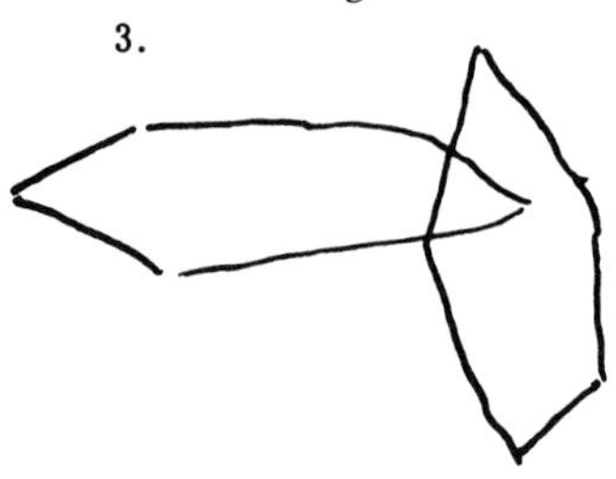

SCORE 8 (Examples score for design rotation)

4.

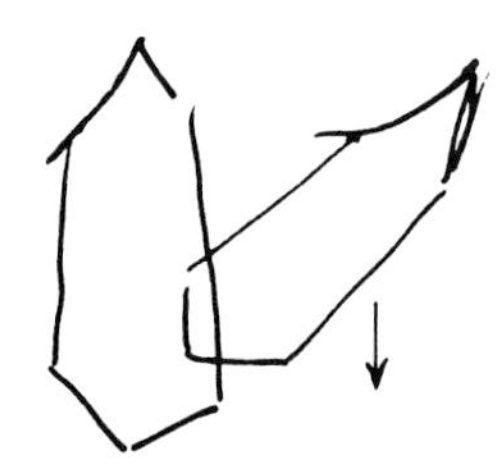

5.

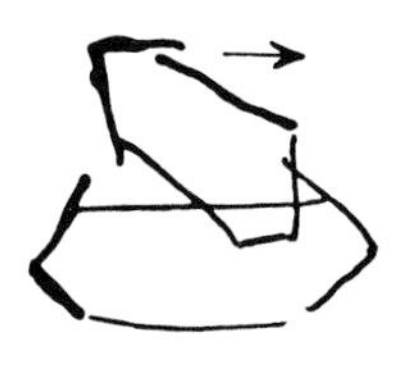

SCORE 8 (Examples scored also for distortion, Item 7)

6.

7

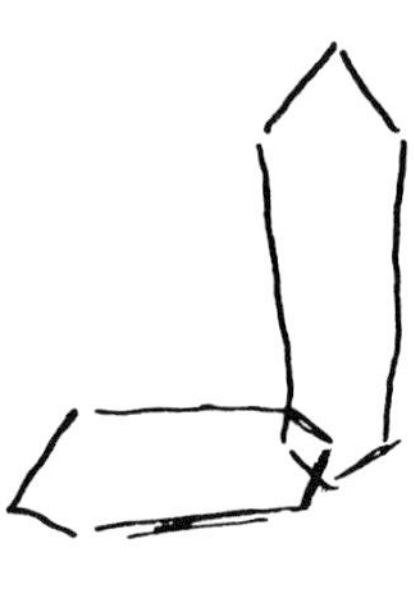

8.

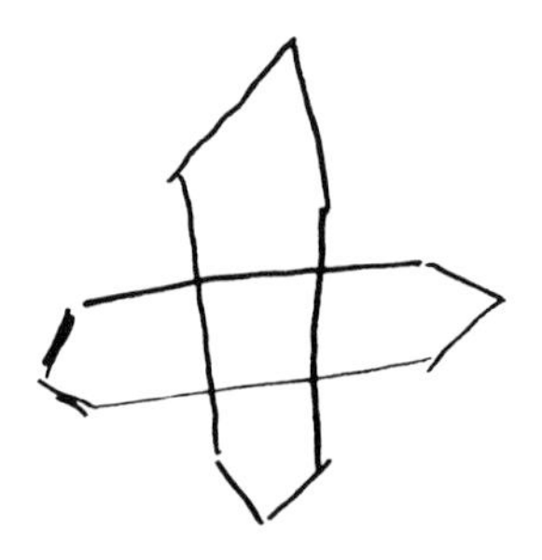

SCORE 16 (Example scored for double rotation)

9.

11. *Part of the design missing. Score 8.* The item is scored when the subject omits a major portion of one of the hexagons.

SCORE 8

1.

2.

NO SCORE

3. (Arrow indicates attempted point of hexagon)

Examples of scoring for design 7. Items scored are indicated by numbers.

A.

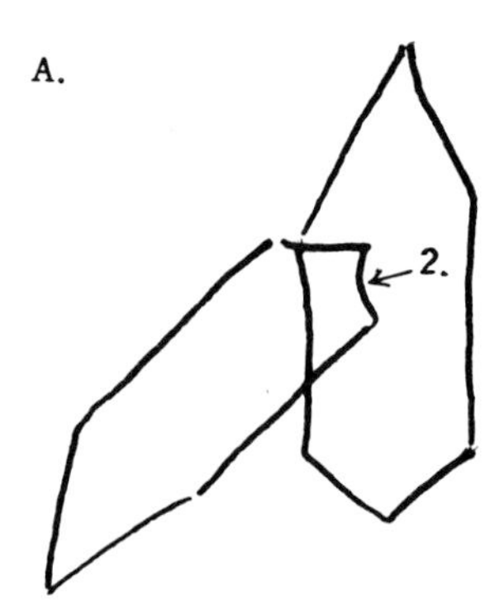

2.—3
Design Total—3

B.

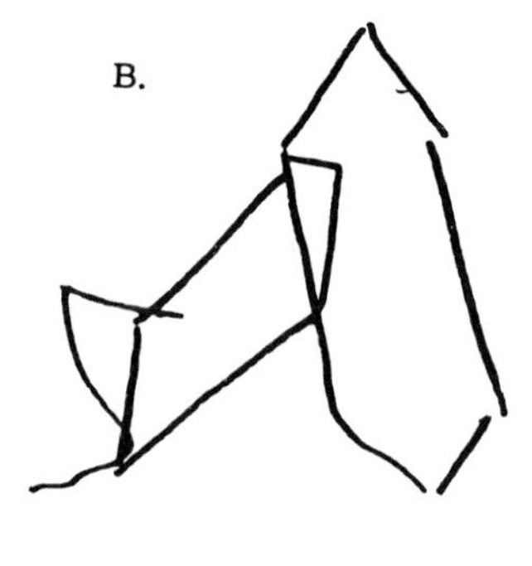

7.—8
9.—3
Design Total—11

C.

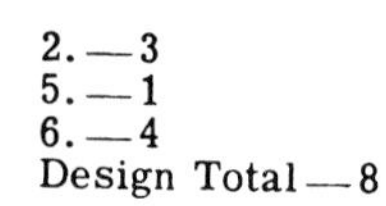

2.—3
5.—1
6.—4
Design Total—8

D.

1.—8
5.—1
7.—16
Design Total—25

E.

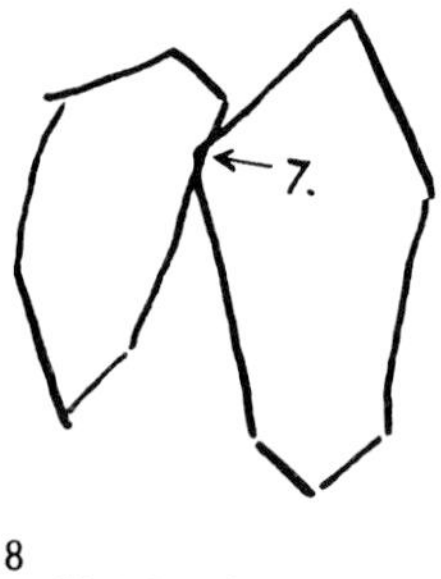

7.—8
Design Total—8

F.

1.—8
Design Total—8

DESIGN 8
(Hexagon and Diamond)

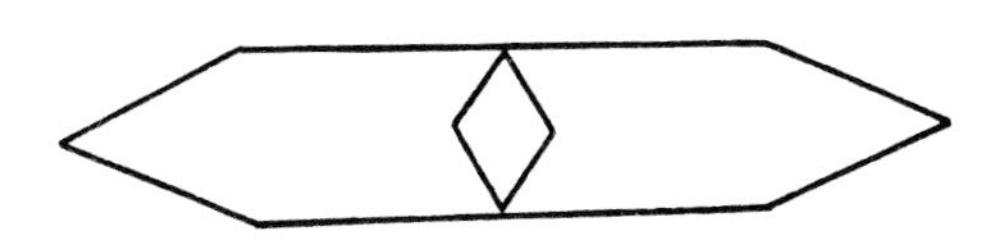

1. *Ends of the lines not joined. Score 8.* The item is scored as item 1, design 7.

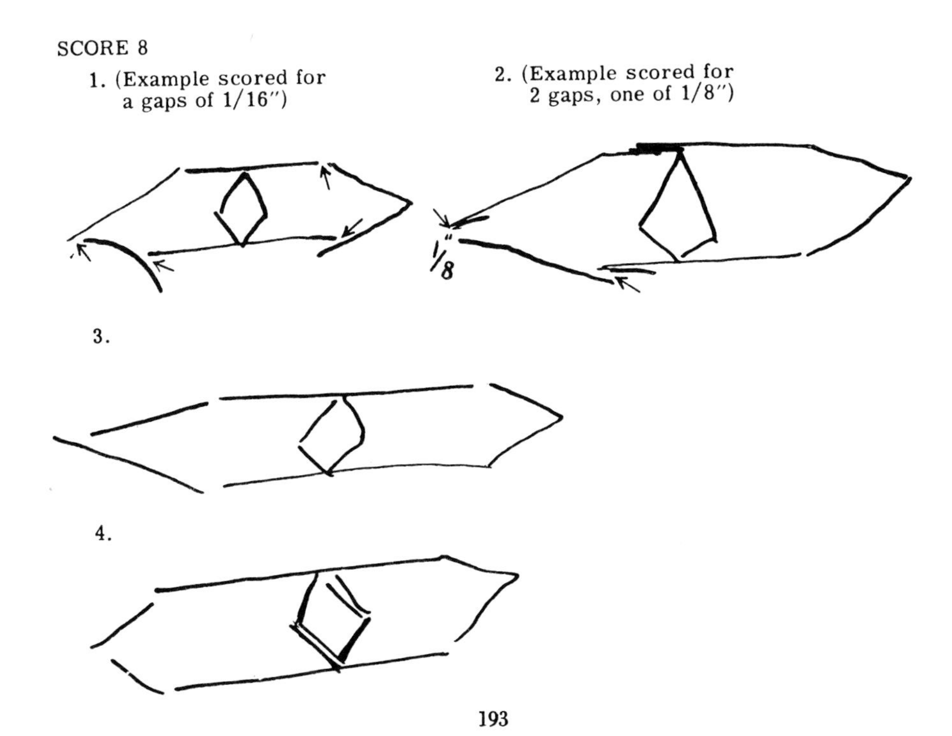

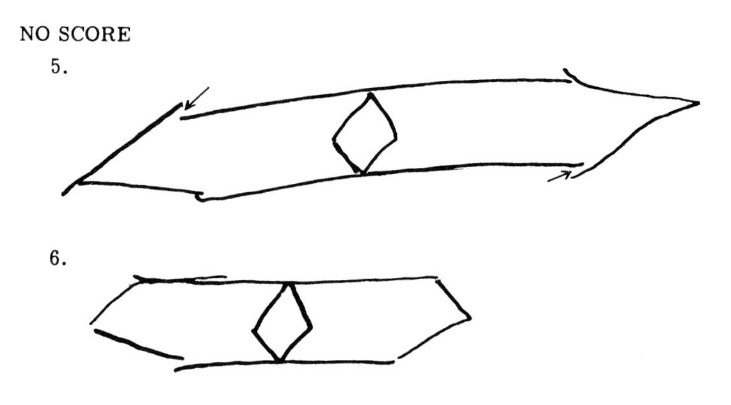

2. *Angles extra. Score 3.* The item is scored when an extra angle occurs in either the hexagon or the diamond, as defined in item 2, design 7.

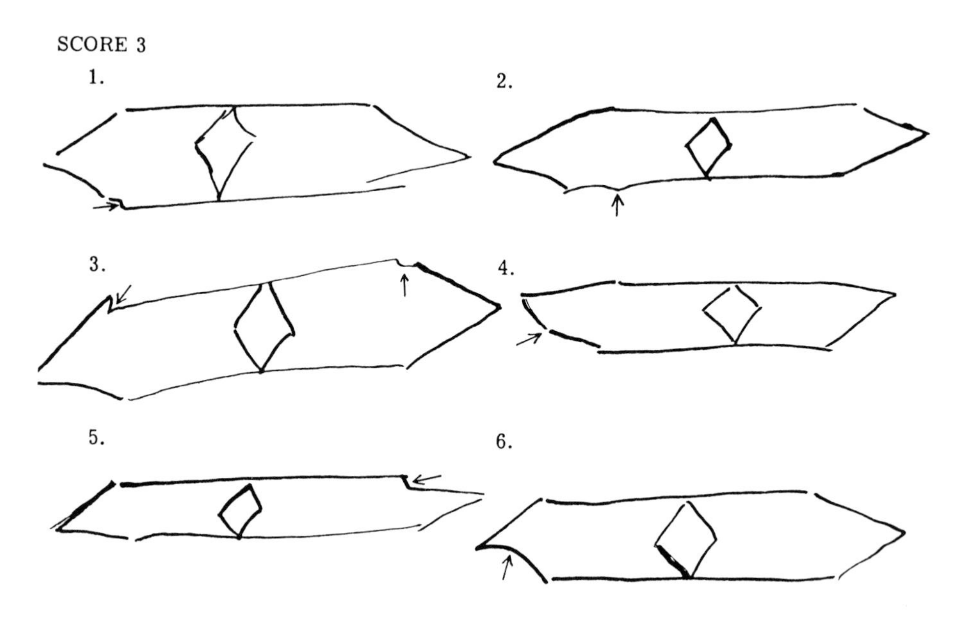

NO SCORE
7.

3. *Angles missing. Score 3.* The item is scored when an angle is missing in either the hexagon or the diamond, as defined in item 3, design 7.

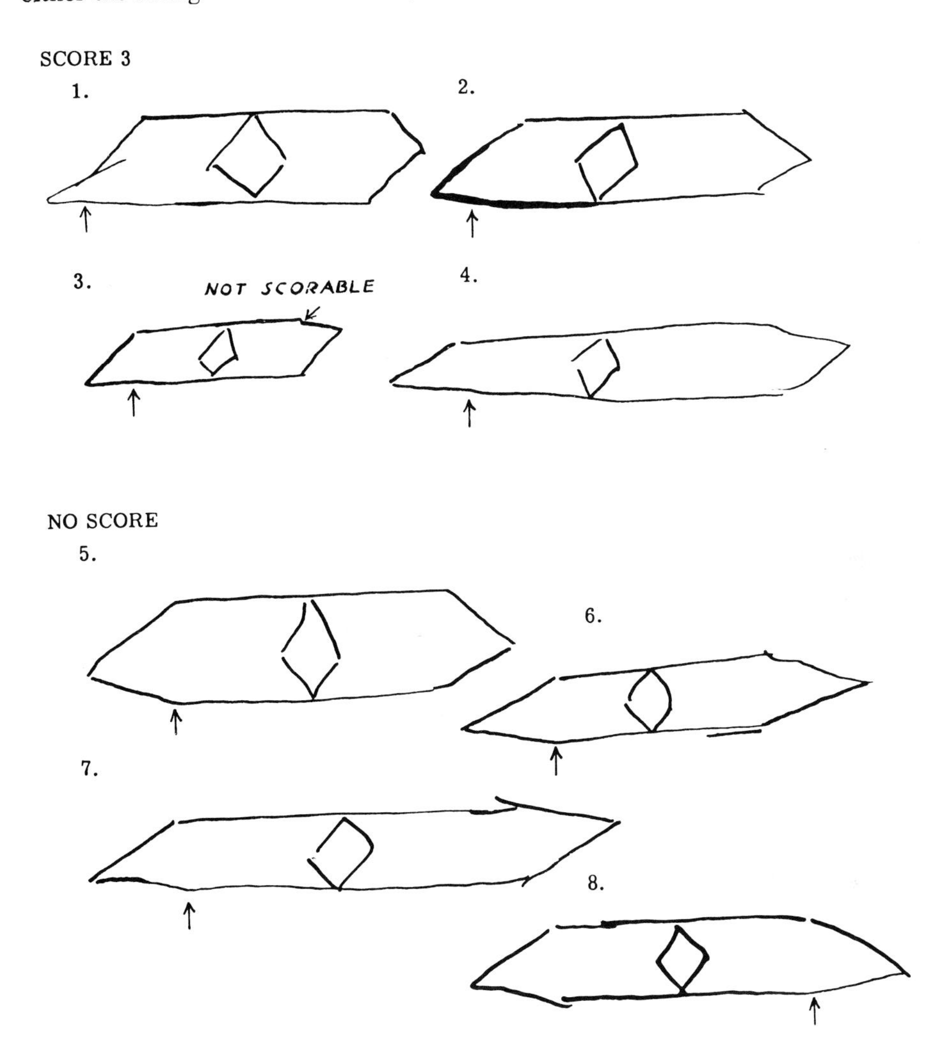

4. *Extra scattered dots and/or dashes. Score 3.* The item is scored for dots and dashes not integrated into the design, as defined in item 4, design 7.

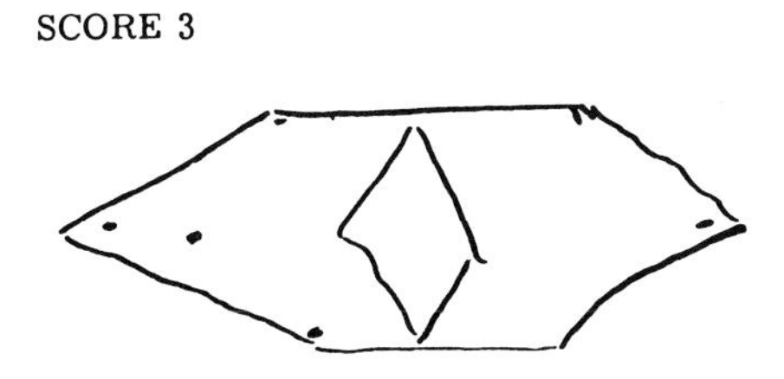

5. *Double line. Score 1 for each.* The item is scored as **item 5, design 6.**

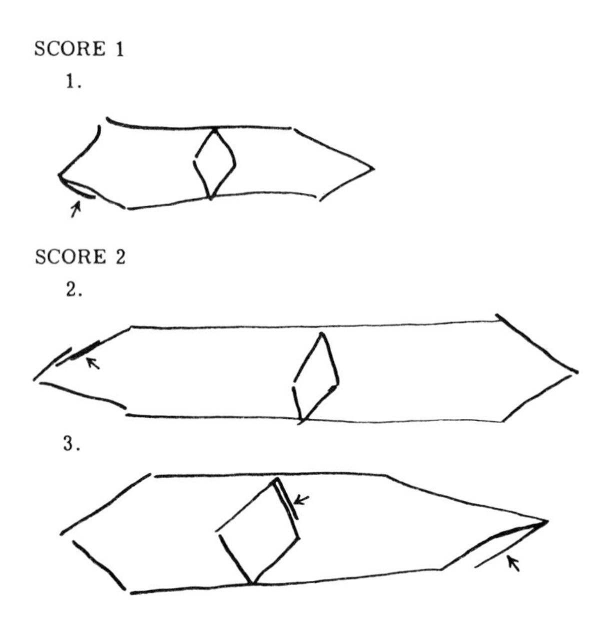

6. *Tremor. Score 4.* The item is scored as item 8, design 4.

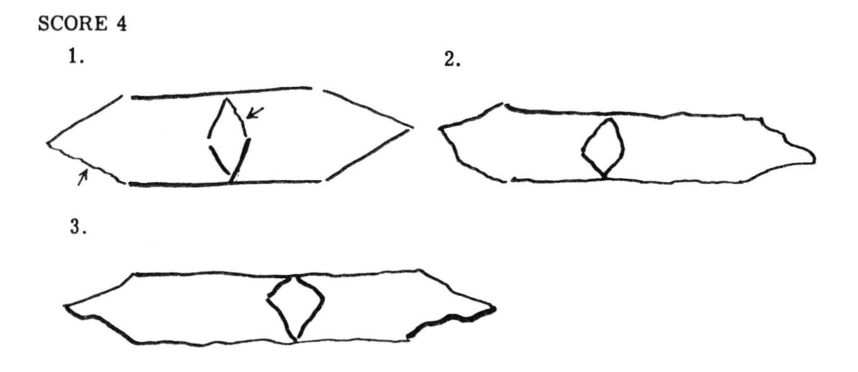

7. *Distortion. Score 8.* Distortion may occur in three ways: 1) when the design is extremely disproportionate in its length–width ratio, 2) when the diamond overlaps the hexagon by more than one-third of its area, when the diamond is so small as to cover only two-thirds of the distance between the sides of the hexagon, or when the diamond is placed in one of the extreme thirds of the hexagon, and 3) when the figure is reproduced in an otherwise markedly distorted manner. (What is meant by 'markedly distorted manner' will be clarified in the examples following.)

The reproduction may be scored for one, two, or all three types of distortion, though more than one rarely occurs; the scores are accordingly 8, 16, and 24, for this item. In general, the scoring is a matter for judgment; in cases of doubt, the item is *not* scored.

SCORE 8 (Examples scored for disproportion in length-width ratio)

1.

2.

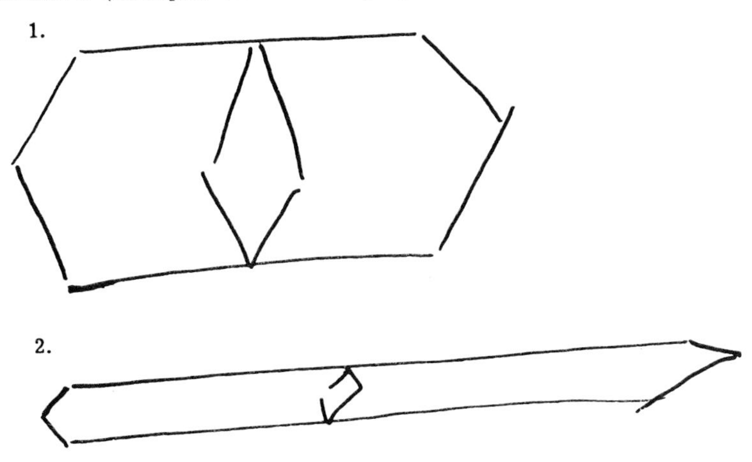

SCORE 8 (Examples scored for 'diamond distortion')

3. (Overlap of more than 1/3 area)

4. (Extension 2/3 or less of distance a to b)

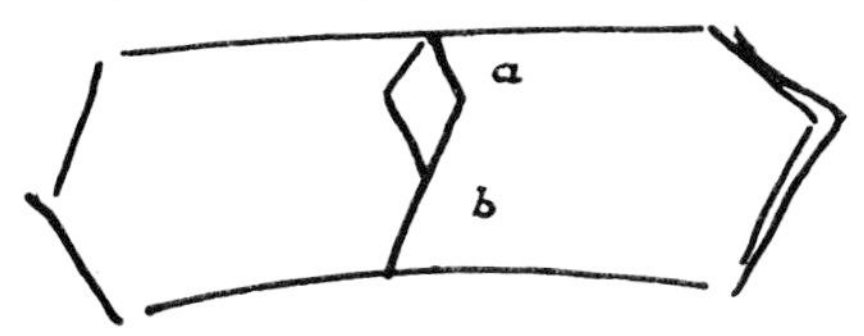

5. (Placement in one of extreme thirds of hexagon)

SCORE 8 (Examples of reproductions in 'markedly distorted manner')

6. (Extreme disproportion in two ends)

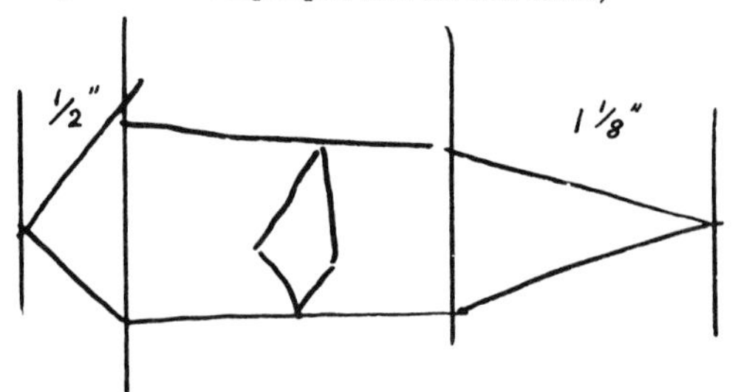

7. (Displacement of opposing angles — more than 30° — see Item 7, Design 7)

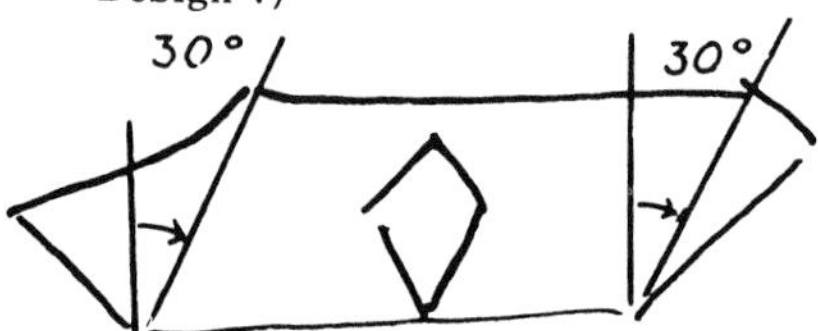

8.

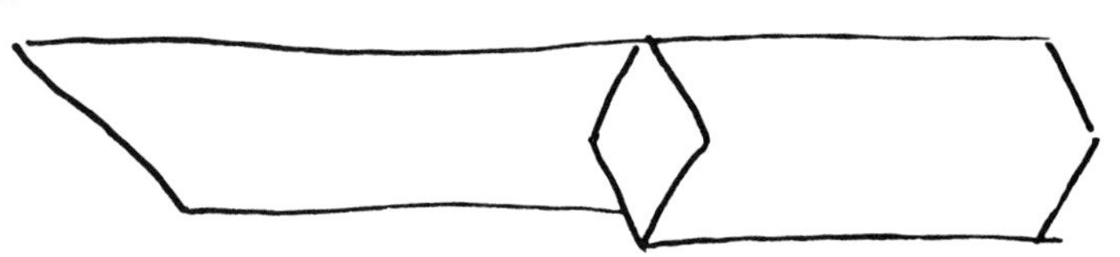

NO SCORE

9.

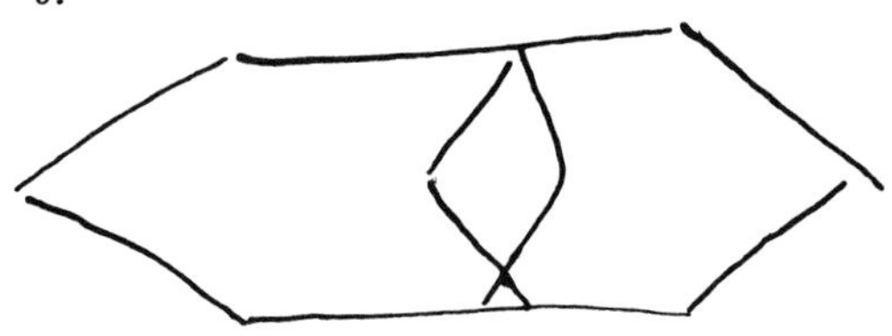

10. (Example scored for extra angles, Item 2)

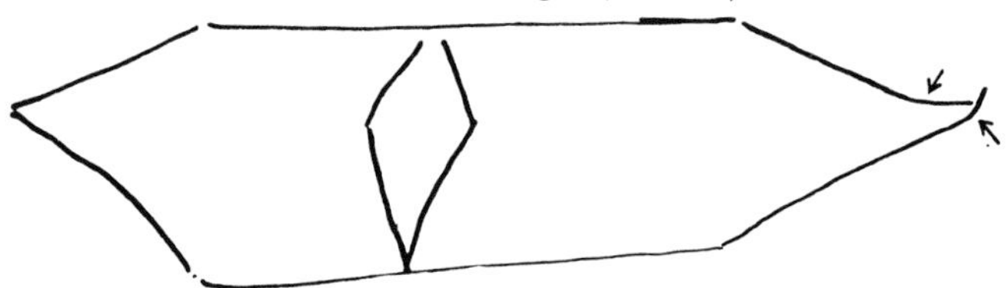

11.

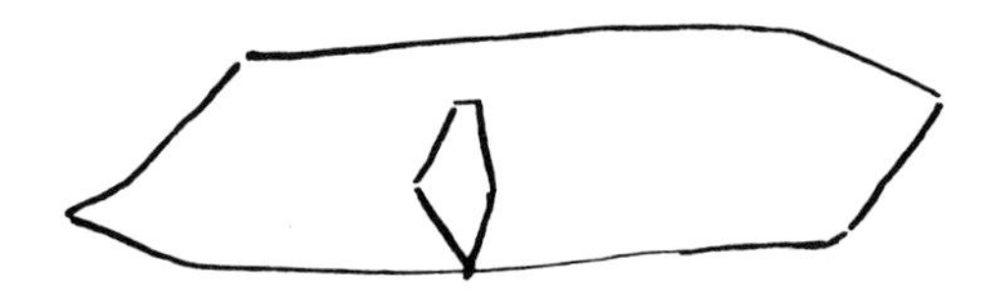

8. *Guide lines. Score 2.* The item is scored as item 10, design 4.

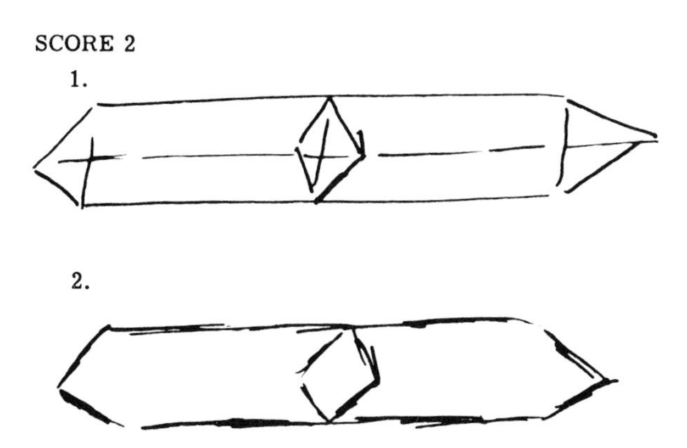

9. *Workover. Score 2.* The item is scored as item 10, design 6.

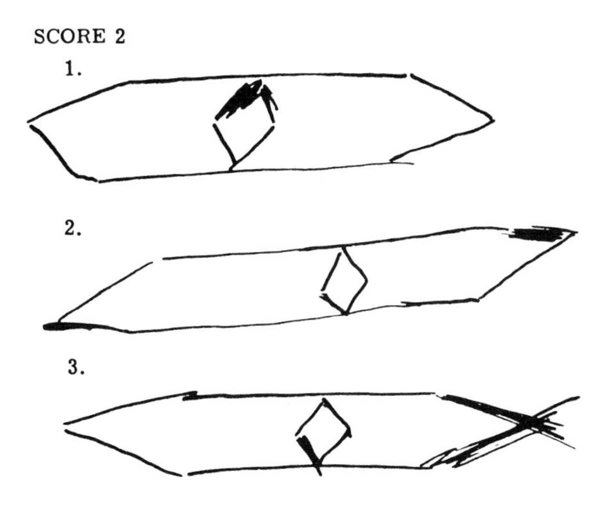

10. *Second attempt. Score 3 for each.* The item is scored as item 11, design 4.

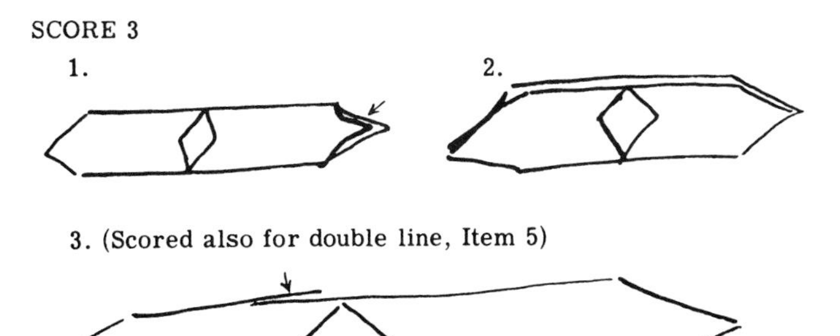

11. *Rotation. Score 8.* The item is scored when the base of the design is rotated 45° or more from the horizontal.

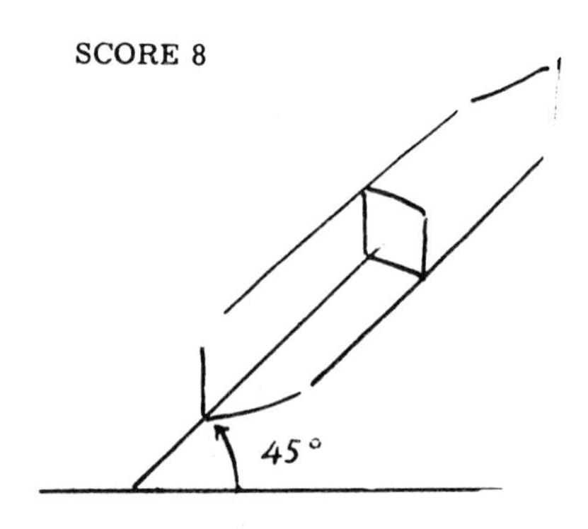

12. *Part of the design missing. Score 8.* The item is scored when the subject omits the diamond, or at least one-third of either the diamond or the hexagon.

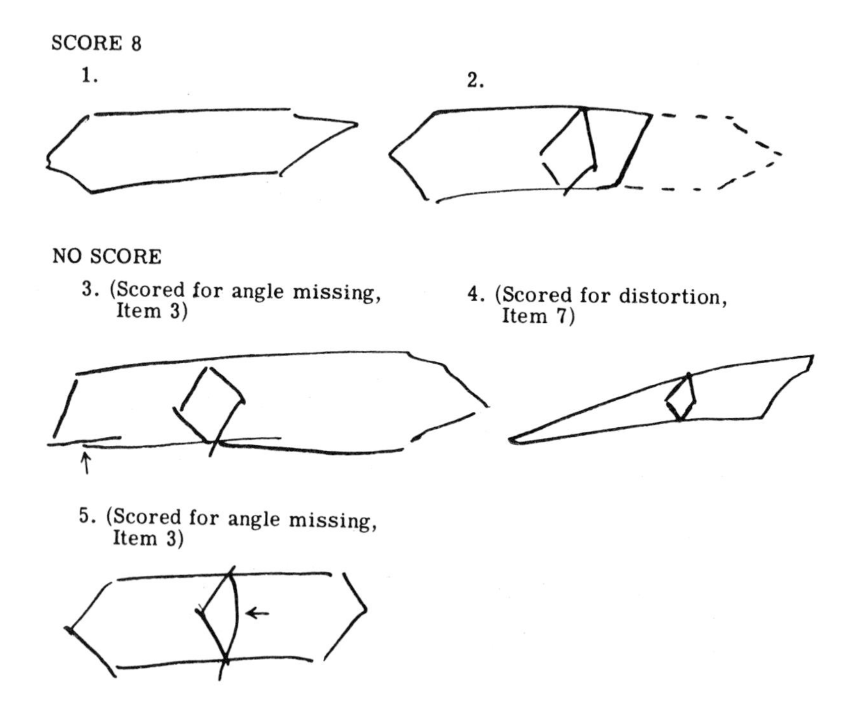

Examples of scoring for design 8. Items scored are indicated by numbers.

A.

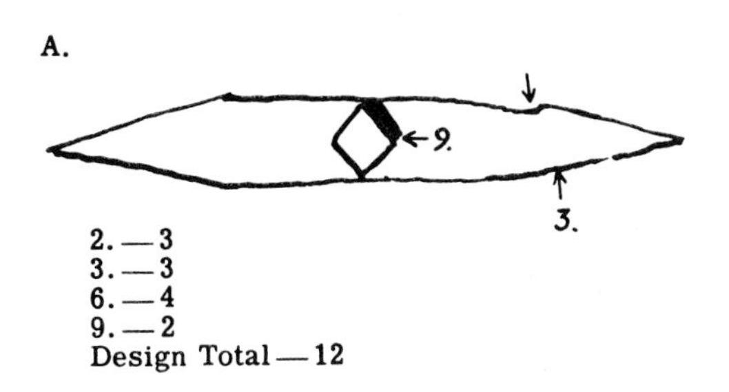

2.—3
3.—3
6.—4
9.—2
Design Total—12

B.

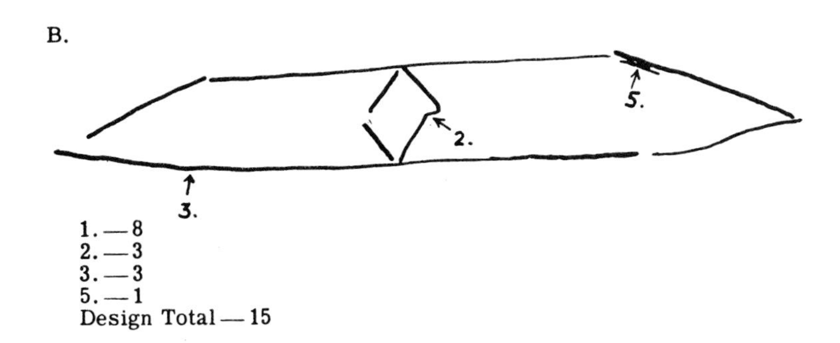

1.—8
2.—3
3.—3
5.—1
Design Total—15

C.

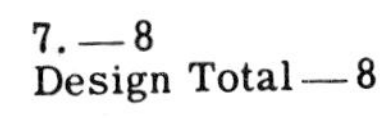

7.—8
Design Total—8

D.

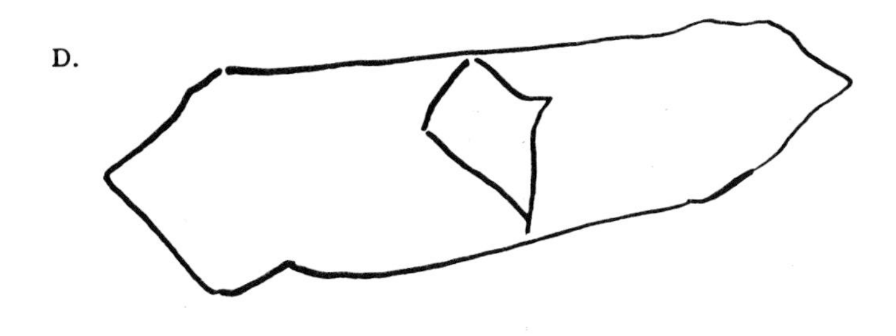

2.—3
6.—4
7.—8
Design Total—15

CONFIGURATION SCORE

1. *Placement of Design A. Score 2.* The item is scored when design A is placed in the lower two-thirds of the page. The reproduction of design A should be at least three inches from the top of the page for the deviation to be scorable. (In the examples that follow the large rectangle represents the paper.)

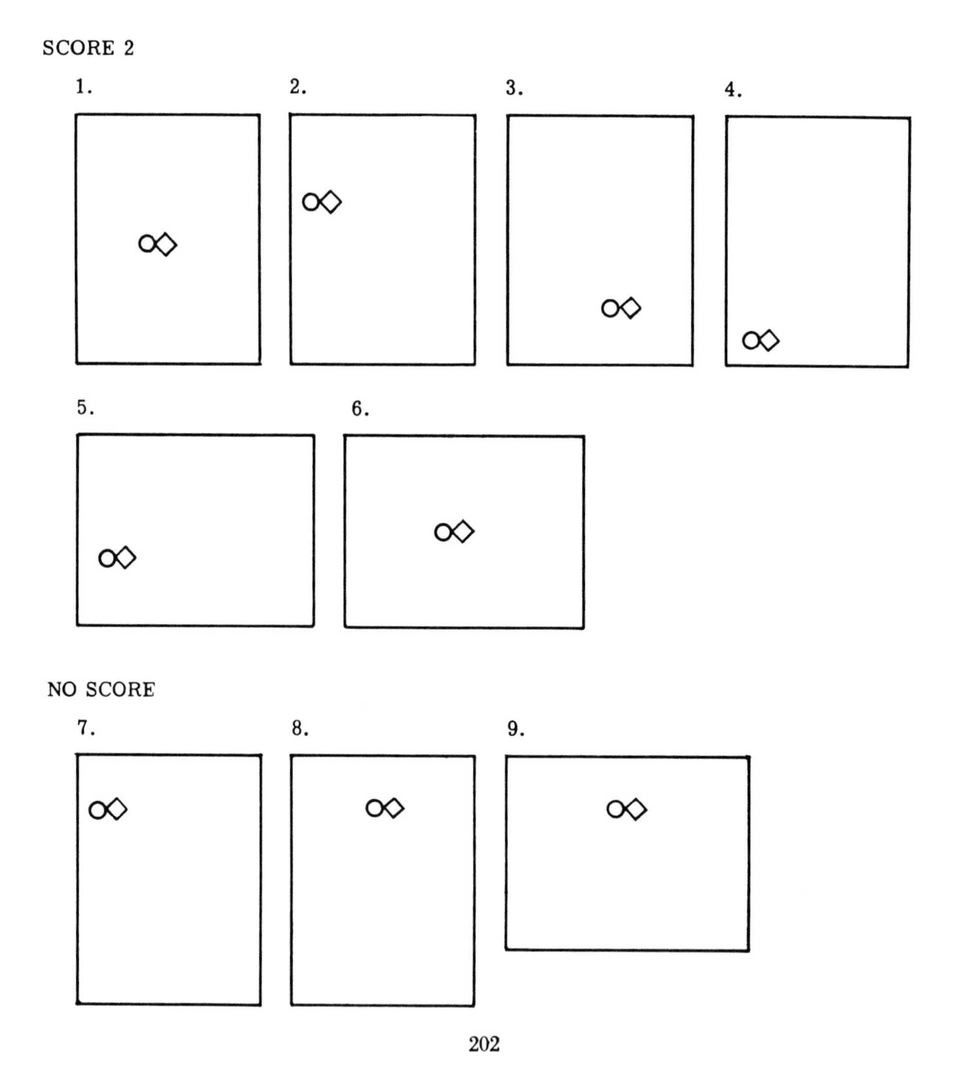

2. *Overlapping of the designs. Score 2 for each.* The item is scored when the lines of one design overlap the lines of, or run into the "enclosed space" of, another design. The item is also scored when the subject has drawn lines to separate the designs, and overlaps these lines and the reproductions, as in example 5. *Each* time overlapping occurs, the score is 2.

SCORE 2

1.

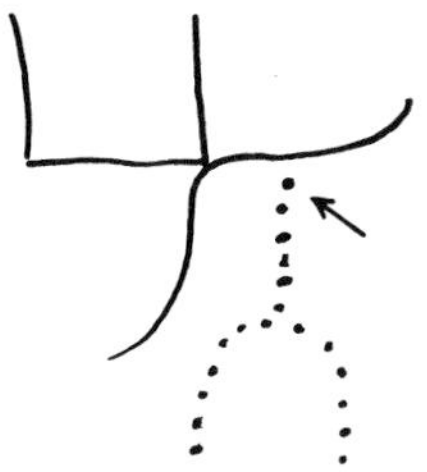

2.

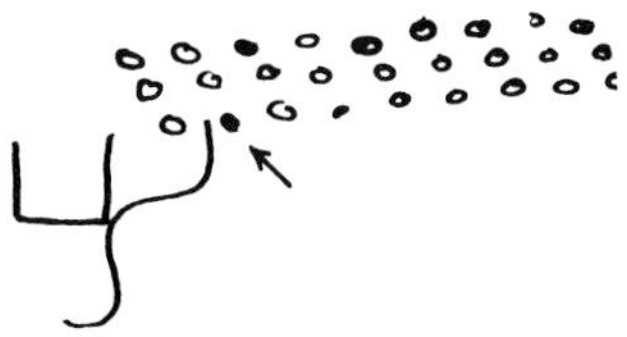

3.

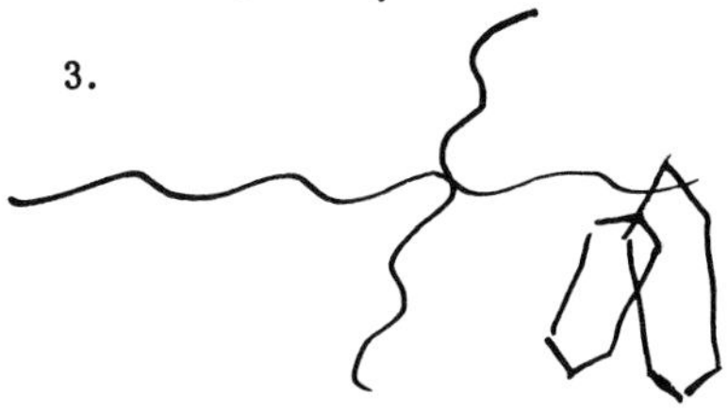

SCORE 4

4.

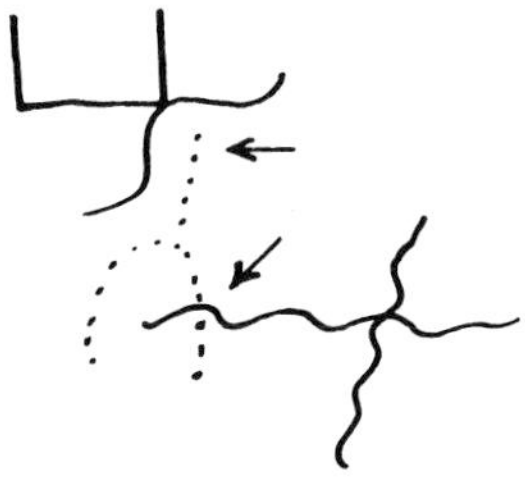

5.

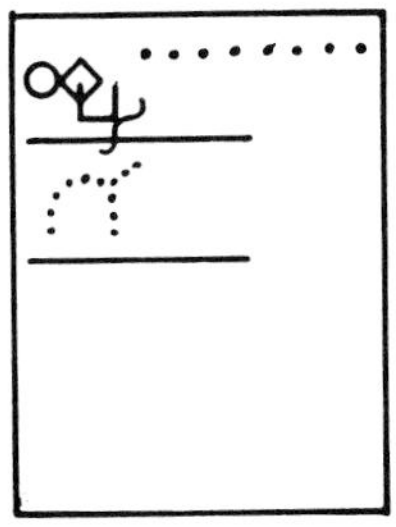

3. *Compression. Score 2.* The item is scored when the reproductions are compressed to cover approximately one-half of the page, whether the half used is the top, middle, right, or left half.

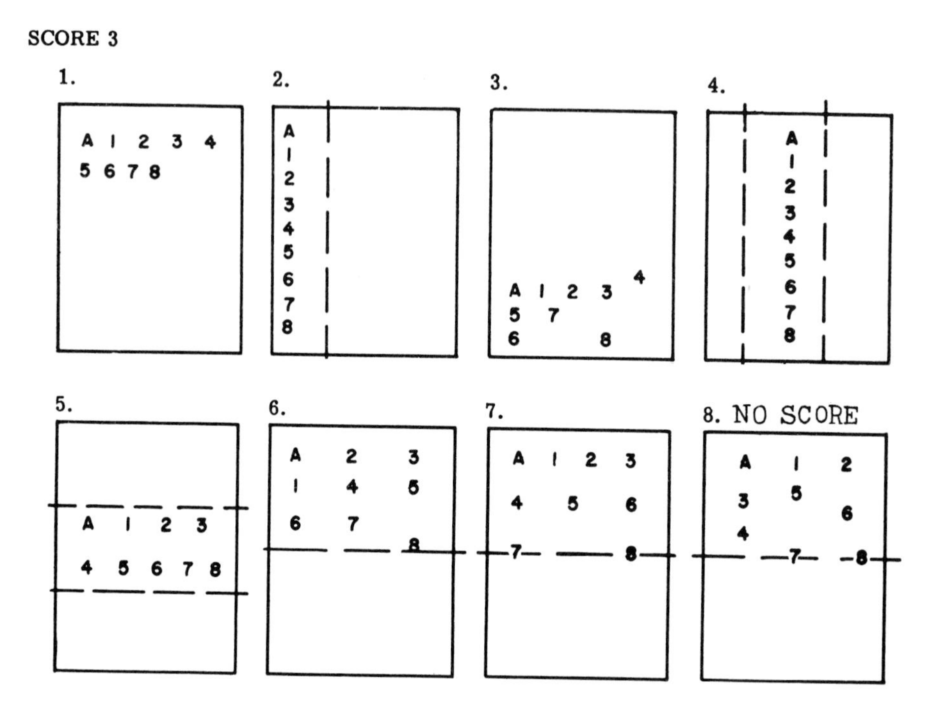

4. *Lines drawn to separate the designs. Score 8.* The item is scored when the subject draws lines to separate the reproduced designs. The deviation is scored even when only one such line is drawn.

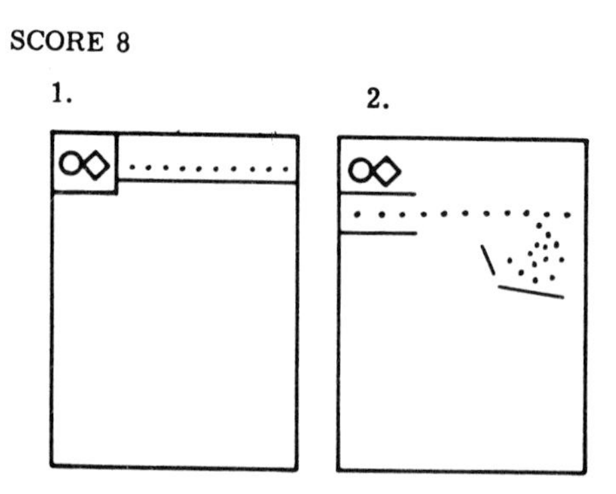

EXAMPLES OF LOGICAL ORDER

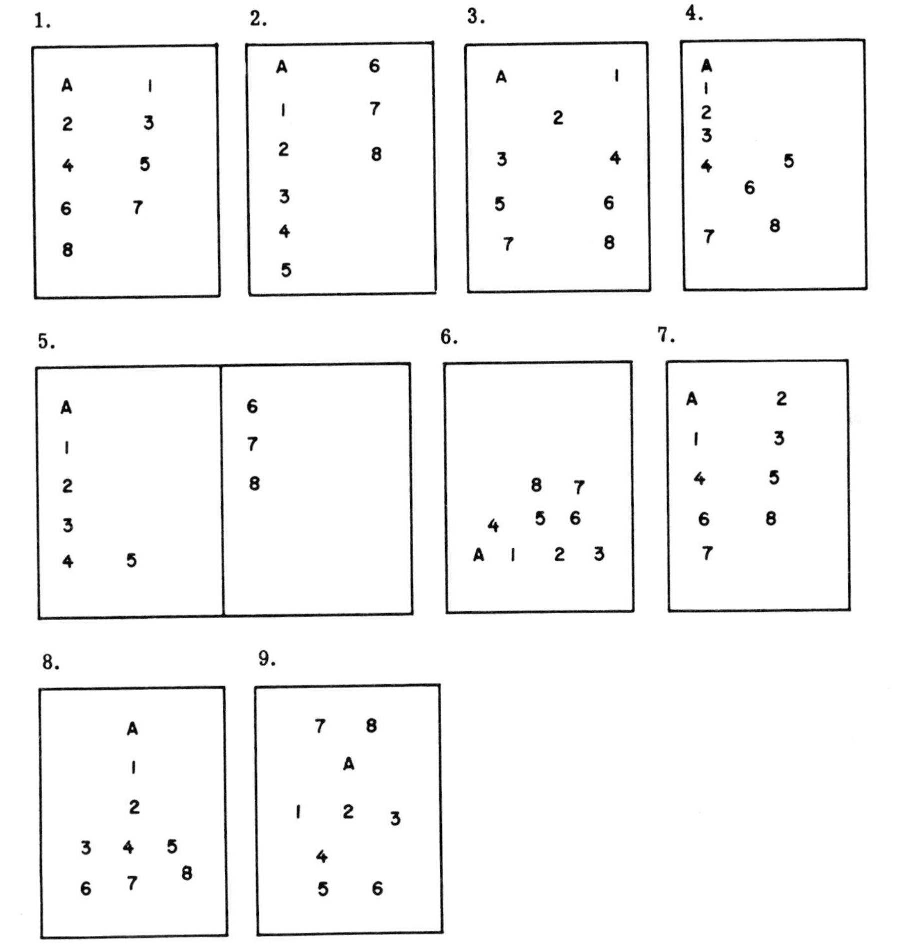

5. *Order. Score 2.* Scoring for this item is differentiated from scoring "no order," item 6. To score here, the arrangement of the drawings on the page must depart from logical order, but not markedly. Usually this type of ordering results from arbitrary placement of one or two reproductions. (See examples of logical order below.)

The examples following will clarify the scoring. The arrows indicate the basis for scoring. Thus, in example 1, design 8 is arbitrarily placed at the top of the page when sufficient space remains for its placement at the bottom.

SCORE 2

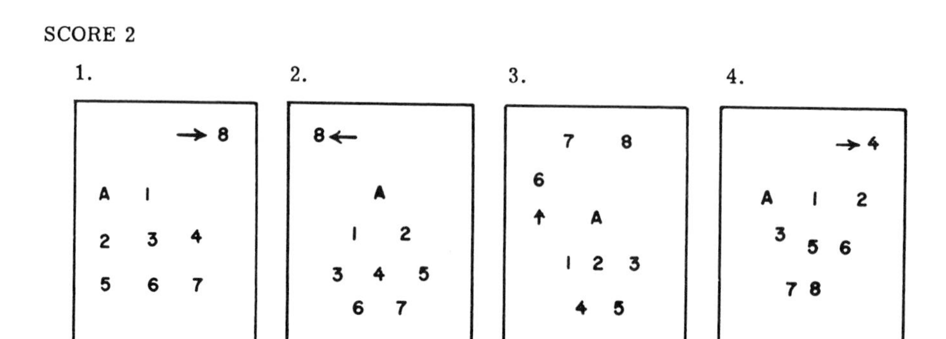

NO SCORE (Examples not scored, impossible to place 8 below 6 and 7)

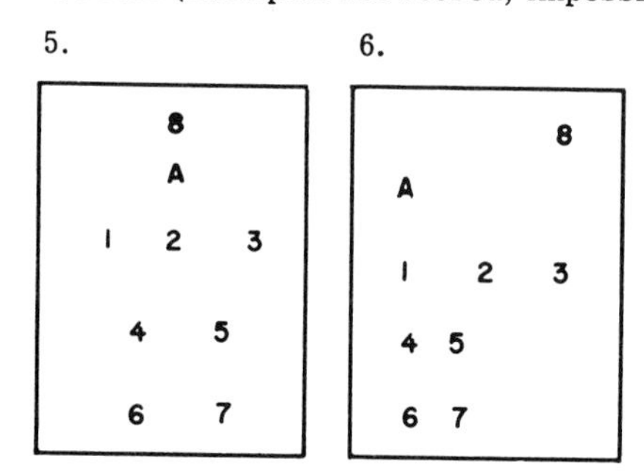

6. *No Order. Score 8.* When the ordering of the reproductions is confused, no order is scored. In cases of doubt, the item is not scored; when there is *any discernable order* the item is *not* scored.

SCORE 8

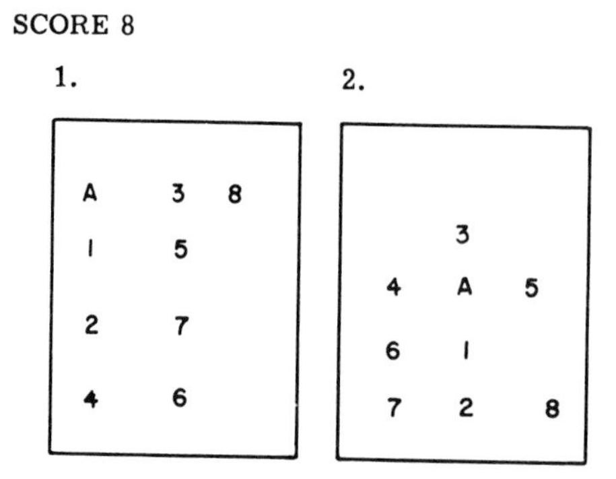

7. *Relative size of the reproductions. Score 8.* The item is scored when there occurs pronounced variations in the size of the reproductions. The deviation is scorable even when only one of the designs is disproportionately compressed or expanded. In cases of doubt, the item is not scored.

SCORE 8

1.

2.

SCORE SHEET—Bender-Gestalt Test

Name .... Age ...... Sex ......

Education .... I.Q. ...... Diagnosis ....

DESIGN 1

1. Wavy line (2) ......
2. Dot, dash, cir. (3) ......
3. Dashes (2) ......
4. Circles (8) ......
5. No. dots (2) each ......
6. Dbl. row (8) ......
7. Workover (2) ......
8. Sec. attempt (3 ea.) ......
9. Rotation (8) ......
10. Des. miss. (8) ......

Design Total ......

DESIGN 4

1. Asym. Crv. (3) ......
2. Break crv. (4) ......
3. Crv. not center. (1) ......
4. Curls (4) ......
5. Not joined (8) ......
6. Crv. rotation (3) ......
7. Touch-up (8) ......
8. Tremor (4) ......
9. Distortion (8) ......
10. Guide lines (2) ......
11. Sec. attempt (3 ea.) ......
12. Rotation (8) ......
13. Des. miss. (8) ......

Design Total ......

DESIGN 7

1. Ends no. join. (8) ......
2. Angles ext. (3) ......
3. Angles miss. (3) ......
4. Ext. scat. (3) ......
5. Dbl. line (1 ea.) ......
6. Tremor (4) ......
7. Distortion (8 ea.) ......
8. Guide lines (2) ......
9. Sec. attempt (3 ea.) ......
10. Rotation (8) ......
11. Des. miss. (8) ......

Design Total ......

DESIGN 2

1. Wavy line (2) ......
2. Dash or dots (3) ......
3. Shape cir. (3) ......
4. Cir. miss., ext. (3) ......
5. Cir. touch. (5) ......
6. Dev. slant (3) ......
7. No. col. (2 ea.) ......
8. Fig. on 2 lines (8) ......
9. Guide lines (2) ......
10. Workover (2) ......
11. Sec. attempt (3 ea.) ......
12. Rotation (8) ......
13. Des. miss. (8) ......

Design Total ......

DESIGN 5

1. Asymmetry (3) ......
2. Dot, dash, cir. (3) ......
3. Dashes (2) ......
4. Circles (8) ......
5. Ext. join. dot (2) ......
6. Ext. rotation (3) ......
7. No. dots (2) ......
8. Distortion (8) ......
9. Guide lines (2) ......
10. Workover (2) ......
11. Sec. attempt (3 ea.) ......
12. Rotation (8) ......
13. Des. miss. (8) ......

Design Total ......

DESIGN 8

1. Ends no. join. (8) ......
2. Angles ext. (3) ......
3. Angles miss. (3) ......
4. Ext. scat. (3) ......
5. Dbl. line (1 ea.) ......
6. Tremor (4) ......
7. Distortion (8 ea.) ......
8. Guide lines (2) ......
9. Workover (2) ......
10. Sec. attempt (3 ea.) ......
11. Rotation (8) ......
12. Des. miss. (8) ......

Design Total ......

DESIGN 3

1. Asymmetry (3) ......
2. Dot, dash, cir. (3) ......
3. Dashes (2) ......
4. Circles (8) ......
5. No. dots (2) ......
6. Extra row (8) ......
7. Blunting (8) ......
8. Distortion (8) ......
9. Guide lines (2) ......
10. Workover (2) ......
11. Sec. attempt (3 ea.) ......
12. Rotation (8) ......
13. Des. miss. (8) ......

Design Total ......

DESIGN 6

1. Asymmetry (3) ......
2. Angles (2) ......
3. Pt. crossing (2 ea.) ......
4. Crv. extra (8) ......
5. Dbl. line (1 ea.) ......
6. Touch-up (8) ......
7. Tremor (4) ......
8. Distortion (8) ......
9. Guide lines (2) ......
10. Workover (2) ......
11. Sec. attempt (3 ea.) ......
12. Rotation (8) ......
13. Des. miss. (8) ......

Design Total ......

CONFIG. DESIGN

1. Place. Des. A. (2) ......
2. Overlap (2 ea.) ......
3. Compression (3) ......
4. Lines drawn (8) ......
5. Order (2) ......
6. No order (8) ......
7. Rel. size (8) ......

Total ......

DESIGN TOTALS

1. ...... 5. ......
2. ...... 6. ......
3. ...... 7. ......
4. ...... 8. ......
Config. ......

Total Raw Score ......

Standard Score ......

SCORE SHEET—Bender-Gestalt Test

Name No. 4 Age 11-11 Sex F

Education .... I.Q. 40 Diagnosis Feeble-minded

DESIGN 1		DESIGN 4		DESIGN 7	
1. Wavy line (2)		1. Asym. Crv. (3)	3	1. Ends no. join. (8)	
2. Dot, dash, cir. (3)		2. Break crv. (4)		2. Angles ext. (3)	
3. Dashes (2)		3. Crv. not center. (1)		3. Angles miss. (3)	3
4. Circles (8)		4. Curls (4)		4. Ext. scat. (3)	
5. No. dots (2) each	2	5. Not joined (8)		5. Dbl. line (1 ea.)	
6. Dbl. row (8)		6. Crv. rotation (3)		6. Tremor (4)	
7. Workover (2)	2	7. Touch-up (8)		7. Distortion (8 ea.)	16
8. Sec. attempt (3 ea.)		8. Tremor (4)	4	8. Guide lines (2)	
9. Rotation (8)		9. Distortion (8)	8	9. Sec. attempt (3 ea.)	
10. Des. miss. (8)		10. Guide lines (2)		10. Rotation (8)	8
Design Total	4	11. Sec. attempt (3 ea.)		11. Des. miss. (8)	
		12. Rotation (8)		Design Total	27
		13. Des. miss. (8)			
		Design Total	15		

DESIGN 2		DESIGN 5		DESIGN 8	
1. Wavy line (2)	2	1. Asymmetry (3)		1. Ends no. join. (8)	
2. Dash or dots (3)		2. Dot, dash, cir. (3)		2. Angles ext. (3)	
3. Shape cir. (3)		3. Dashes (2)		3. Angles miss. (3)	
4. Cir. miss., ext. (3)		4. Circles (8)	8	4. Ext. scat. (3)	
5. Cir. touch. (5)		5. Ext. join. dot (2)		5. Dbl. line (1 ea.)	1
6. Dev. slant (3)		6. Ext. rotation (3)		6. Tremor (4)	4
7. No. col. (2 ea.)		7. No. dots (2)	2	7. Distortion (8 ea.)	16
8. Fig. on 2 lines (8)		8. Distortion (8)	8	8. Guide lines (2)	
9. Guide lines (2)		9. Guide lines (2)		9. Workover (2)	
10. Workover (2)		10. Workover (2)	2	10. Sec. attempt (3 ea.)	
11. Sec. attempt (3 ea.)		11. Sec. attempt (3 ea.)		11. Rotation (8)	
12. Rotation (8)		12. Rotation (8)		12. Des. miss. (8)	
13. Des. miss. (8)		13. Des. miss. (8)		Design Total	21
Design Total	2	Design Total	20		

DESIGN 3		DESIGN 6		CONFIG. DESIGN	
1. Asymmetry (3)		1. Asymmetry (3)	3	1. Place. Des. A. (2)	
2. Dot, dash, cir. (3)		2. Angles (2)	2	2. Overlap (2 ea.)	
3. Dashes (2)		3. Pt. crossing (2 ea.)		3. Compression (3)	
4. Circles (8)		4. Crv. extra (8)		4. Lines drawn (8)	
5. No. dots (2)	2	5. Dbl. line (1 ea.)		5. Order (2)	2
6. Extra row (8)		6. Touch-up (8)		6. No order (8)	
7. Blunting (8)		7. Tremor (4)		7. Rel. size (8)	
8. Distortion (8)	8	8. Distortion (8)	8	Total	2
9. Guide lines (2)		9. Guide lines (2)			
10. Workover (2)	2	10. Workover (2)			
11. Sec. attempt (3 ea.)		11. Sec. attempt (3 ea.)			
12. Rotation (8)		12. Rotation (8)			
13. Des. miss. (8)		13. Des. miss. (8)			
Design Total	12	Design Total	13		

DESIGN TOTALS

1.	4	5.	20
2.	2	6.	13
3.	12	7.	27
4.	15	8.	21
Config.	2		

Total Raw Score 116 Standard Score ......

SCORE SHEET—Bender-Gestalt Test

Name No. 5 Age 19-6 Sex M

Education .... I.Q. M.A. 6-4 (SB) 12-5 (Porteus) Diagnosis Feeble-minded

DESIGN 1		DESIGN 4		DESIGN 7	
1. Wavy line (2)	2	1. Asym. Crv. (3)	3	1. Ends no. join. (8)	
2. Dot, dash, cir. (3)	3	2. Break crv. (4)		2. Angles ext. (3)	
3. Dashes (2)		3. Crv. not center. (1)		3. Angles miss. (3)	
4. Circles (8)		4. Curls (4)		4. Ext. scat. (3)	
5. No. dots (2) each	6	5. Not joined (8)		5. Dbl. line (1 ea.)	
6. Dbl. row (8)		6. Crv. rotation (3)	3	6. Tremor (4)	4
7. Workover (2)	2	7. Touch-up (8)		7. Distortion (8 ea.)	8
8. Sec. attempt (3 ea.)		8. Tremor (4)		8. Guide lines (2)	
9. Rotation (8)		9. Distortion (8)		9. Sec. attempt (3 ea.)	
10. Des. miss. (8)		10. Guide lines (2)		10. Rotation (8)	
Design Total	13	11. Sec. attempt (3 ea.)		11. Des. miss. (8)	
		12. Rotation (8)		Design Total	12
		13. Des. miss. (8)			
		Design Total	6		

DESIGN 2		DESIGN 5		DESIGN 8	
1. Wavy line (2)	2	1. Asymmetry (3)		1. Ends no. join. (8)	
2. Dash or dots (3)		2. Dot, dash, cir. (3)		2. Angles ext. (3)	3
3. Shape cir. (3)		3. Dashes (2)		3. Angles miss. (3)	
4. Cir. miss., ext. (3)		4. Circles (8)	8	4. Ext. scat. (3)	
5. Cir. touch. (5)		5. Ext. join. dot (2)	2	5. Dbl. line (1 ea.)	
6. Dev. slant (3)		6. Ext. rotation (3)	3	6. Tremor (4)	
7. No. col. (2 ea.)	8	7. No. dots (2)		7. Distortion (8 ea.)	16
8. Fig. on 2 lines (8)		8. Distortion (8)		8. Guide lines (2)	
9. Guide lines (2)		9. Guide lines (2)		9. Workover (2)	
10. Workover (2)	2	10. Workover (2)		10. Sec. attempt (3 ea.)	
11. Sec. attempt (3 ea.)		11. Sec. attempt (3 ea.)		11. Rotation (8)	
12. Rotation (8)		12. Rotation (8)		12. Des. miss. (8)	
13. Des. miss. (8)		13. Des. miss. (8)		Design Total	19
Design Total	12	Design Total	13		

DESIGN 3		DESIGN 6		CONFIG. DESIGN	
1. Asymmetry (3)	3	1. Asymmetry (3)	3	1. Place. Des. A. (2)	2
2. Dot, dash, cir. (3)		2. Angles (2)	2	2. Overlap (2 ea.)	
3. Dashes (2)		3. Pt. crossing (2 ea.)		3. Compression (3)	
4. Circles (8)	8	4. Crv. extra (8)		4. Lines drawn (8)	
5. No. dots (2)	2	5. Dbl. line (1 ea.)		5. Order (2)	2
6. Extra row (8)		6. Touch-up (8)		6. No order (8)	
7. Blunting (8)		7. Tremor (4)	4	7. Rel. size (8)	
8. Distortion (8)		8. Distortion (8)		Total	4
9. Guide lines (2)		9. Guide lines (2)			
10. Workover (2)		10. Workover (2)			
11. Sec. attempt (3 ea.)		11. Sec. attempt (3 ea.)			
12. Rotation (8)		12. Rotation (8)			
13. Des. miss. (8)		13. Des. miss. (8)			
Design Total	13	Design Total	9		

DESIGN TOTALS

1.	13	5.	13
2.	12	6.	9
3.	13	7.	12
4.	6	8.	19
Config.	4		

Total Raw Score 109 Standard Score ......

SCORE SHEET—Bender-Gestalt Test

Name No. 6 Age 6-11 Sex M

Education .... I.Q. 101 Diagnosis Normal Child

DESIGN 1		DESIGN 4		DESIGN 7	
1. Wavy line (2)	2	1. Asym. Crv. (3)	3	1. Ends no. join. (8)	
2. Dot, dash, cir. (3)	3	2. Break crv. (4)		2. Angles ext. (3)	
3. Dashes (2)		3. Crv. not center. (1)		3. Angles miss. (3)	3
4. Circles (8)		4. Curls (4)		4. Ext. scat. (3)	
5. No. dots (2) each	26	5. Not joined (8)	8	5. Dbl. line (1 ea.)	4
6. Dbl. row (8)		6. Crv. rotation (3)		6. Tremor (4)	
7. Workover (2)	2	7. Touch-up (8)		7. Distortion (8 ea.)	8
8. Sec. attempt (3 ea.)		8. Tremor (4)		8. Guide lines (2)	
9. Rotation (8)		9. Distortion (8)		9. Sec. attempt (3 ea.)	
10. Des. miss. (8)		10. Guide lines (2)		10. Rotation (8)	
Design Total	39	11. Sec. attempt (3 ea.)		11. Des. miss. (8)	
		12. Rotation (8)	8	Design Total	15
		13. Des. miss. (8)			
		Design Total	19		

DESIGN 2		DESIGN 5		DESIGN 8	
1. Wavy line (2)	2	1. Asymmetry (3)		1. Ends no. join. (8)	
2. Dash or dots (3)		2. Dot, dash, cir. (3)		2. Angles ext. (3)	
3. Shape cir. (3)	3	3. Dashes (2)		3. Angles miss. (3)	3
4. Cir. miss., ext. (3)		4. Circles (8)		4. Ext. scat. (3)	
5. Cir. touch. (5)		5. Ext. join. dot (2)		5. Dbl. line (1 ea.)	1
6. Dev. slant (3)	3	6. Ext. rotation (3)	3	6. Tremor (4)	
7. No. col. (2 ea.)	10	7. No. dots (2)		7. Distortion (8 ea.)	8
8. Fig. on 2 lines (8)		8. Distortion (8)	8	8. Guide lines (2)	
9. Guide lines (2)		9. Guide lines (2)		9. Workover (2)	
10. Workover (2)	2	10. Workover (2)		10. Sec. attempt (3 ea.)	
11. Sec. attempt (3 ea.)		11. Sec. attempt (3 ea.)		11. Rotation (8)	
12. Rotation (8)		12. Rotation (8)		12. Des. miss. (8)	
13. Des. miss. (8)		13. Des. miss. (8)		Design Total	12
Design Total	20	Design Total	11		

DESIGN 3		DESIGN 6		CONFIG. DESIGN	
1. Asymmetry (3)	3	1. Asymmetry (3)	3	1. Place. Des. A. (2)	
2. Dot, dash, cir. (3)	3	2. Angles (2)	2	2. Overlap (2 ea.)	
3. Dashes (2)		3. Pt. crossing (2 ea.)		3. Compression (3)	
4. Circles (8)		4. Crv. extra (8)		4. Lines drawn (8)	
5. No. dots (2)		5. Dbl. line (1 ea.)		5. Order (2)	
6. Extra row (8)		6. Touch-up (8)		6. No order (8)	
7. Blunting (8)		7. Tremor (4)		7. Rel. size (8)	
8. Distortion (8)		8. Distortion (8)		Total	0
9. Guide lines (2)		9. Guide lines (2)			
10. Workover (2)	2	10. Workover (2)			
11. Sec. attempt (3 ea.)		11. Sec. attempt (3 ea.)			
12. Rotation (8)		12. Rotation (8)			
13. Des. miss. (8)		13. Des. miss. (8)	8		
Design Total	8	Design Total	13		

DESIGN TOTALS

1.	39	5.	11
2.	20	6.	13
3.	8	7.	15
4.	19	8.	12
Config.	0		

Total Raw Score 137 Standard Score ......

SCORE SHEET—Bender-Gestalt Test

Name No. 7 Age 6-3 Sex M

Education .... I.Q. 115 Diagnosis Normal Child

DESIGN 1		DESIGN 4		DESIGN 7	
1. Wavy line (2)	2	1. Asym. Crv. (3)		1. Ends no. join. (8)	
2. Dot, dash, cir. (3)	3	2. Break crv. (4)		2. Angles ext. (3)	3
3. Dashes (2)		3. Crv. not center. (1)		3. Angles miss. (3)	
4. Circles (8)		4. Curls (4)	4	4. Ext. scat. (3)	3
5. No. dots (2) each	12	5. Not joined (8)	8	5. Dbl. line (1 ea.)	1
6. Dbl. row (8)		6. Crv. rotation (3)		6. Tremor (4)	
7. Workover (2)	2	7. Touch-up (8)		7. Distortion (8 ea.)	8
8. Sec. attempt (3 ea.)		8. Tremor (4)	4	8. Guide lines (2)	
9. Rotation (8)		9. Distortion (8)		9. Sec. attempt (3 ea.)	
10. Des. miss. (8)		10. Guide lines (2)		10. Rotation (8)	8
Design Total	19	11. Sec. attempt (3 ea.)		11. Des. miss. (8)	
		12. Rotation (8)	8	Design Total	23
		13. Des. miss. (8)			
		Design Total	24		

DESIGN 2		DESIGN 5		DESIGN 8	
1. Wavy line (2)	2	1. Asymmetry (3)		1. Ends no. join. (8)	
2. Dash or dots (3)		2. Dot, dash, cir. (3)	3	2. Angles ext. (3)	
3. Shape cir. (3)		3. Dashes (2)		3. Angles miss. (3)	
4. Cir. miss., ext. (3)	5	4. Circles (8)		4. Ext. scat. (3)	
5. Cir. touch. (5)		5. Ext. join. dot (2)	2	5. Dbl. line (1 ea.)	
6. Dev. slant (3)	3	6. Ext. rotation (3)		6. Tremor (4)	
7. No. col. (2 ea.)	2	7. No. dots (2)	2	7. Distortion (8 ea.)	8
8. Fig. on 2 lines (8)		8. Distortion (8)		8. Guide lines (2)	
9. Guide lines (2)		9. Guide lines (2)		9. Workover (2)	
10. Workover (2)	2	10. Workover (2)	2	10. Sec. attempt (3 ea.)	
11. Sec. attempt (3 ea.)		11. Sec. attempt (3 ea.)		11. Rotation (8)	
12. Rotation (8)		12. Rotation (8)		12. Des. miss. (8)	
13. Des. miss. (8)		13. Des. miss. (8)		Design Total	8
Design Total	14	Design Total	9		

DESIGN 3		DESIGN 6		CONFIG. DESIGN	
1. Asymmetry (3)	3	1. Asymmetry (3)	3	1. Place. Des. A. (2)	2
2. Dot, dash, cir. (3)	3	2. Angles (2)	2	2. Overlap (2 ea.)	
3. Dashes (2)		3. Pt. crossing (2 ea.)	2	3. Compression (3)	
4. Circles (8)		4. Crv. extra (8)	8	4. Lines drawn (8)	
5. No. dots (2)	2	5. Dbl. line (1 ea.)		5. Order (2)	
6. Extra row (8)		6. Touch-up (8)		6. No order (8)	8
7. Blunting (8)		7. Tremor (4)		7. Rel. size (8)	
8. Distortion (8)		8. Distortion (8)		Total	10
9. Guide lines (2)		9. Guide lines (2)			
10. Workover (2)	2	10. Workover (2)			
11. Sec. attempt (3 ea.)		11. Sec. attempt (3 ea.)			
12. Rotation (8)	8	12. Rotation (8)			
13. Des. miss. (8)		13. Des. miss. (8)			
Design Total	18	Design Total	15		

DESIGN TOTALS

1.	19	5.	9
2.	14	6.	15
3.	18	7.	23
4.	24	8.	8
Config.	10		

Total Raw Score 140 Standard Score ......

SCORE SHEET—Bender-Gestalt Test

Name ......No. 8...... Age 8-6 Sex M

Education .... I.Q. 107 Diagnosis Normal Child

DESIGN 1
1. Wavy line (2) 2
2. Dot, dash, cir. (3) ......
3. Dashes (2) ......
4. Circles (8) ......
5. No. dots (2) each ......
6. Dbl. row (8) ......
7. Workover (2) 2
8. Sec. attempt (3 ea.) ......
9. Rotation (8) ......
10. Des. miss. (8) ......

Design Total 4

DESIGN 4
1. Asym. Crv. (3) 3
2. Break crv. (4) ......
3. Crv. not center. (1) 1
4. Curls (4) ......
5. Not joined (8) ......
6. Crv. rotation (3) ......
7. Touch-up (8) ......
8. Tremor (4) ......
9. Distortion (8) ......
10. Guide lines (2) ......
11. Sec. attempt (3 ea.) ......
12. Rotation (8) ......
13. Des. miss. (8) ......

Design Total 4

DESIGN 7
1. Ends no. join. (8) ......
2. Angles ext. (3) ......
3. Angles miss. (3) ......
4. Ext. scat. (3) ......
5. Dbl. line (1 ea.) 4
6. Tremor (4) ......
7. Distortion (8 ea.) ......
8. Guide lines (2) ......
9. Sec. attempt (3 ea.) ......
10. Rotation (8) ......
11. Des. miss. (8) ......

Design Total 4

DESIGN 2
1. Wavy line (2) 2
2. Dash or dots (3) ......
3. Shape cir. (3) ......
4. Cir. miss., ext. (3) ......
5. Cir. touch. (5) ......
6. Dev. slant (3) 3
7. No. col. (2 ea.) ......
8. Fig. on 2 lines (8) ......
9. Guide lines (2) ......
10. Workover (2) ......
11. Sec. attempt (3 ea.) ......
12. Rotation (8) ......
13. Des. miss. (8) ......

Design Total 5

DESIGN 5
1. Asymmetry (3) 3
2. Dot, dash, cir. (3) 3
3. Dashes (2) ......
4. Circles (8) ......
5. Ext. join. dot (2) ......
6. Ext. rotation (3) ......
7. No. dots (2) ......
8. Distortion (8) ......
9. Guide lines (2) ......
10. Workover (2) ......
11. Sec. attempt (3 ea.) ......
12. Rotation (8) ......
13. Des. miss. (8) ......

Design Total 6

DESIGN 8
1. Ends no. join. (8) 8
2. Angles ext. (3) 3
3. Angles miss. (3) ......
4. Ext. scat. (3) ......
5. Dbl. line (1 ea.) 3
6. Tremor (4) ......
7. Distortion (8 ea.) 8
8. Guide lines (2) ......
9. Workover (2) ......
10. Sec. attempt (3 ea.) ......
11. Rotation (8) ......
12. Des. miss. (8) ......

Design Total 22

DESIGN 3
1. Asymmetry (3) 3
2. Dot, dash, cir. (3) ......
3. Dashes (2) ......
4. Circles (8) ......
5. No. dots (2) ......
6. Extra row (8) ......
7. Blunting (8) ......
8. Distortion (8) ......
9. Guide lines (2) ......
10. Workover (2) ......
11. Sec. attempt (3 ea.) ......
12. Rotation (8) ......
13. Des. miss. (8) ......

Design Total 3

DESIGN 6
1. Asymmetry (3) ......
2. Angles (2) 2
3. Pt. crossing (2 ea.) ......
4. Crv. extra (8) ......
5. Dbl. line (1 ea.) 1
6. Touch-up (8) ......
7. Tremor (4) 4
8. Distortion (8) ......
9. Guide lines (2) ......
10. Workover (2) ......
11. Sec. attempt (3 ea.) ......
12. Rotation (8) ......
13. Des. miss. (8) ......

Design Total 7

CONFIG. DESIGN
1. Place. Des. A. (2) 2
2. Overlap (2 ea.) ......
3. Compression (3) ......
4. Lines drawn (8) ......
5. Order (2) 2
6. No order (8) ......
7. Rel. size (8) ......

Total 4

DESIGN TOTALS

1. 4 5. 6
2. 5 6. 7
3. 3 7. 4
4. 4 8. 22

Config. 4

Total Raw Score 59 Standard Score —

SCORE SHEET—Bender-Gestalt Test

Name ...No. 9...... Age 9-2 Sex M

Education .... I.Q. 137 Diagnosis Normal Child

DESIGN 1
1. Wavy line (2) ......
2. Dot, dash, cir. (3) 3
3. Dashes (2) ......
4. Circles (8) ......
5. No. dots (2) each ......
6. Dbl. row (8) ......
7. Workover (2) ......
8. Sec. attempt (3 ea.) ......
9. Rotation (8) ......
10. Des. miss. (8) ......

Design Total 3

DESIGN 4
1. Asym. Crv. (3) ......
2. Break crv. (4) ......
3. Crv. not center. (1) ......
4. Curls (4) ......
5. Not joined (8) ......
6. Crv. rotation (3) ......
7. Touch-up (8) ......
8. Tremor (4) 4
9. Distortion (8) ......
10. Guide lines (2) ......
11. Sec. attempt (3 ea.) ......
12. Rotation (8) ......
13. Des. miss. (8) ......

Design Total 4

DESIGN 7
1. Ends no. join. (8) 8
2. Angles ext. (3) ......
3. Angles miss. (3) ......
4. Ext. scat. (3) ......
5. Dbl. line (1 ea.) 3
6. Tremor (4) 4
7. Distortion (8 ea.) ......
8. Guide lines (2) ......
9. Sec. attempt (3 ea.) ......
10. Rotation (8) 8
11. Des. miss. (8) ......

Design Total 23

DESIGN 2
1. Wavy line (2) 2
2. Dash or dots (3) 3
3. Shape cir. (3) ......
4. Cir. miss., ext. (3) ......
5. Cir. touch. (5) ......
6. Dev. slant (3) ......
7. No. col. (2 ea.) ......
8. Fig. on 2 lines (8) ......
9. Guide lines (2) ......
10. Workover (2) ......
11. Sec. attempt (3 ea.) ......
12. Rotation (8) ......
13. Des. miss. (8) ......

Design Total 5

DESIGN 5
1. Asymmetry (3) 3
2. Dot, dash, cir. (3) ......
3. Dashes (2) ......
4. Circles (8) ......
5. Ext. join. dot (2) 2
6. Ext. rotation (3) ......
7. No. dots (2) ......
8. Distortion (8) ......
9. Guide lines (2) ......
10. Workover (2) ......
11. Sec. attempt (3 ea.) ......
12. Rotation (8) ......
13. Des. miss. (8) ......

Design Total 8

DESIGN 8
1. Ends no. join. (8) ......
2. Angles ext. (3) 3
3. Angles miss. (3) ......
4. Ext. scat. (3) ......
5. Dbl. line (1 ea.) ......
6. Tremor (4) 4
7. Distortion (8 ea.) ......
8. Guide lines (2) ......
9. Workover (2) ......
10. Sec. attempt (3 ea.) ......
11. Rotation (8) ......
12. Des. miss. (8) ......

Design Total 7

DESIGN 3
1. Asymmetry (3) 3
2. Dot, dash, cir. (3) ......
3. Dashes (2) 2
4. Circles (8) ......
5. No. dots (2) 2
6. Extra row (8) ......
7. Blunting (8) ......
8. Distortion (8) ......
9. Guide lines (2) ......
10. Workover (2) ......
11. Sec. attempt (3 ea.) ......
12. Rotation (8) ......
13. Des. miss. (8) ......

Design Total 7

DESIGN 6
1. Asymmetry (3) ......
2. Angles (2) ......
3. Pt. crossing (2 ea.) ......
4. Crv. extra (8) ......
5. Dbl. line (1 ea.) ......
6. Touch-up (8) ......
7. Tremor (4) 4
8. Distortion (8) ......
9. Guide lines (2) ......
10. Workover (2) ......
11. Sec. attempt (3 ea.) ......
12. Rotation (8) ......
13. Des. miss. (8) ......

Design Total 4

CONFIG. DESIGN
1. Place. Des. A. (2) ......
2. Overlap (2 ea.) 2
3. Compression (3) ......
4. Lines drawn (8) ......
5. Order (2) ......
6. No order (8) ......
7. Rel. size (8) ......

Total 2

DESIGN TOTALS

1. 3 5. 8
2. 5 6. 4
3. 7 7. 23
4. 4 8. 7

Config. 2

Total Raw Score 63 Standard Score ......

SCORE SHEET—Bender-Gestalt Test

Name ....No. 10...... Age 35 Sex F

Education Grammar I.Q. 91 Diagnosis Manic-Depressive

DESIGN 1
1. Wavy line (2) ......
2. Dot, dash, cir. (3) ......
3. Dashes (2) ......
4. Circles (8) ......
5. No. dots (2) each ......
6. Dbl. row (8) ......
7. Workover (2) ......
8. Sec. attempt (3 ea.) ......
9. Rotation (8) ......
10. Des. miss. (8) ......

Design Total 0

DESIGN 4
1. Asym. Crv. (3) ......
2. Break crv. (4) ......
3. Crv. not center. (1) ......
4. Curls (4) ......
5. Not joined (8) ......
6. Crv. rotation (3) ......
7. Touch-up (8) ......
8. Tremor (4) ......
9. Distortion (8) ......
10. Guide lines (2) ......
11. Sec. attempt (3 ea.) ......
12. Rotation (8) ......
13. Des. miss. (8) ......

Design Total 0

DESIGN 7
1. Ends no. join. (8) ......
2. Angles ext. (3) ......
3. Angles miss. (3) ......
4. Ext. scat. (3) ......
5. Dbl. line (1 ea.) ......
6. Tremor (4) ......
7. Distortion (8 ea.) ......
8. Guide lines (2) ......
9. Sec. attempt (3 ea.) ......
10. Rotation (8) ......
11. Des. miss. (8) ......

Design Total 0

DESIGN 2
1. Wavy line (2) 2
2. Dash or dots (3) ......
3. Shape cir. (3) ......
4. Cir. miss., ext. (3) ......
5. Cir. touch. (5) ......
6. Dev. slant (3) ......
7. No. col. (2 ea.) ......
8. Fig. on 2 lines (8) ......
9. Guide lines (2) ......
10. Workover (2) ......
11. Sec. attempt (3 ea.) ......
12. Rotation (8) ......
13. Des. miss. (8) ......

Design Total 2

DESIGN 5
1. Asymmetry (3) 3
2. Dot, dash, cir. (3) 3
3. Dashes (2) ......
4. Circles (8) ......
5. Ext. join. dot (2) ......
6. Ext. rotation (3) ......
7. No. dots (2) ......
8. Distortion (8) ......
9. Guide lines (2) ......
10. Workover (2) ......
11. Sec. attempt (3 ea.) ......
12. Rotation (8) ......
13. Des. miss. (8) ......

Design Total 6

DESIGN 8
1. Ends no. join. (8) ......
2. Angles ext. (3) ......
3. Angles miss. (3) ......
4. Ext. scat. (3) ......
5. Dbl. line (1 ea.) 1
6. Tremor (4) 4
7. Distortion (8 ea.) ......
8. Guide lines (2) ......
9. Workover (2) ......
10. Sec. attempt (3 ea.) ......
11. Rotation (8) ......
12. Des. miss. (8) ......

Design Total 5

DESIGN 3
1. Asymmetry (3) ......
2. Dot, dash, cir. (3) 3
3. Dashes (2) ......
4. Circles (8) ......
5. No. dots (2) ......
6. Extra row (8) ......
7. Blunting (8) ......
8. Distortion (8) ......
9. Guide lines (2) ......
10. Workover (2) 2
11. Sec. attempt (3 ea.) ......
12. Rotation (8) ......
13. Des. miss. (8) ......

Design Total 5

DESIGN 6
1. Asymmetry (3) 3
2. Angles (2) ......
3. Pt. crossing (2 ea.) ......
4. Crv. extra (8) ......
5. Dbl. line (1 ea.) ......
6. Touch-up (8) ......
7. Tremor (4) ......
8. Distortion (8) ......
9. Guide lines (2) ......
10. Workover (2) ......
11. Sec. attempt (3 ea.) ......
12. Rotation (8) ......
13. Des. miss. (8) ......

Design Total 3

CONFIG. DESIGN
1. Place. Des. A. (2) ......
2. Overlap (2 ea.) 2
3. Compression (3) ......
4. Lines drawn (8) ......
5. Order (2) 2
6. No order (8) ......
7. Rel. size (8) ......

Total 4

DESIGN TOTALS

1. 0 5. 6
2. 2 6. 3
3. 5 7. 0
4. 0 8. 5

Config. 4

Total Raw Score 25 Standard Score ......

SCORE SHEET—Bender-Gestalt Test

Name ....No. 11...... Age 38 Sex M

Education High School I.Q. 124 Diagnosis Schizo-Paranoid

DESIGN 1
1. Wavy line (2) ......
2. Dot, dash, cir. (3) ......
3. Dashes (2) ......
4. Circles (8) ......
5. No. dots (2) each ......
6. Dbl. row (8) ......
7. Workover (2) 2
8. Sec. attempt (3 ea.) ......
9. Rotation (8) ......
10. Des. miss. (8) ......

Design Total 2

DESIGN 4
1. Asym. Crv. (3) 3
2. Break crv. (4) ......
3. Crv. not center. (1) ......
4. Curls (4) ......
5. Not joined (8) ......
6. Crv. rotation (3) ......
7. Touch-up (8) ......
8. Tremor (4) 4
9. Distortion (8) ......
10. Guide lines (2) ......
11. Sec. attempt (3 ea.) ......
12. Rotation (8) ......
13. Des. miss. (8) ......

Design Total 7

DESIGN 7
1. Ends no. join. (8) ......
2. Angles ext. (3) ......
3. Angles miss. (3) ......
4. Ext. scat. (3) ......
5. Dbl. line (1 ea.) 2
6. Tremor (4) ......
7. Distortion (8 ea.) ......
8. Guide lines (2) ......
9. Sec. attempt (3 ea.) ......
10. Rotation (8) ......
11. Des. miss. (8) ......

Design Total 2

DESIGN 2
1. Wavy line (2) ......
2. Dash or dots (3) ......
3. Shape cir. (3) ......
4. Cir. miss., ext. (3) ......
5. Cir. touch. (5) ......
6. Dev. slant (3) 3
7. No. col. (2 ea.) ......
8. Fig. on 2 lines (8) ......
9. Guide lines (2) ......
10. Workover (2) ......
11. Sec. attempt (3 ea.) ......
12. Rotation (8) ......
13. Des. miss. (8) ......

Design Total 3

DESIGN 5
1. Asymmetry (3) ......
2. Dot, dash, cir. (3) ......
3. Dashes (2) ......
4. Circles (8) ......
5. Ext. join. dot (2) 2
6. Ext. rotation (3) ......
7. No. dots (2) ......
8. Distortion (8) ......
9. Guide lines (2) ......
10. Workover (2) 2
11. Sec. attempt (3 ea.) ......
12. Rotation (8) ......
13. Des. miss. (8) ......

Design Total 4

DESIGN 8
1. Ends no. join. (8) ......
2. Angles ext. (3) ......
3. Angles miss. (3) ......
4. Ext. scat. (3) ......
5. Dbl. line (1 ea.) 4
6. Tremor (4) ......
7. Distortion (8 ea.) ......
8. Guide lines (2) ......
9. Workover (2) ......
10. Sec. attempt (3 ea.) 3
11. Rotation (8) ......
12. Des. miss. (8) ......

Design Total 7

DESIGN 3
1. Asymmetry (3) ......
2. Dot, dash, cir. (3) ......
3. Dashes (2) ......
4. Circles (8) ......
5. No. dots (2) ......
6. Extra row (8) ......
7. Blunting (8) ......
8. Distortion (8) ......
9. Guide lines (2) ......
10. Workover (2) 2
11. Sec. attempt (3 ea.) ......
12. Rotation (8) ......
13. Des. miss. (8) ......

Design Total 2

DESIGN 6
1. Asymmetry (3) ......
2. Angles (2) ......
3. Pt. crossing (2 ea.) ......
4. Crv. extra (8) ......
5. Dbl. line (1 ea.) 1
6. Touch-up (8) ......
7. Tremor (4) 4
8. Distortion (8) ......
9. Guide lines (2) ......
10. Workover (2) ......
11. Sec. attempt (3 ea.) ......
12. Rotation (8) ......
13. Des. miss. (8) ......

Design Total 5

CONFIG. DESIGN
1. Place. Des. A. (2) ......
2. Overlap (2 ea.) 2
3. Compression (3) ......
4. Lines drawn (8) ......
5. Order (2) ......
6. No order (8) ......
7. Rel. size (8) ......

Total 2

DESIGN TOTALS

1. 2 5. 4
2. 3 6. 5
3. 2 7. 2
4. 7 8. 7

Config. 2

Total Raw Score 34 Standard Score 67

SCORE SHEET—Bender-Gestalt Test

Name ......No. 12...................... Age 20... Sex ..F..

Education College I.Q. ...... Diagnosis ..Schizo.-Catatonic

DESIGN 1
1. Wavy line (2) ..2..
2. Dot, dash, cir. (3) ..3..
3. Dashes (2) ......
4. Circles (8) ......
5. No. dots (2) each ......
6. Dbl. row (8) ......
7. Workover (2) ......
8. Sec. attempt (3 ea.) ......
9. Rotation (8) ......
10. Des. miss. (8) ......

Design Total ..5..

DESIGN 2
1. Wavy line (2) ......
2. Dash or dots (3) ......
3. Shape cir. (3) ..3..
4. Cir. miss., ext. (3) ......
5. Cir. touch. (5) ......
6. Dev. slant (3) ......
7. No. col. (2 ea.) ......
8. Fig. on 2 lines (8) ......
9. Guide lines (2) ......
10. Workover (2) ......
11. Sec. attempt (3 ea.) ......
12. Rotation (8) ......
13. Des. miss. (8) ......

Design Total .3..

DESIGN 3
1. Asymmetry (3) .3..
2. Dot, dash, cir. (3) .3..
3. Dashes (2) ......
4. Circles (8) ......
5. No. dots (2) .2..
6. Extra row (8) ......
7. Blunting (8) ......
8. Distortion (8) ......
9. Guide lines (2) ......
10. Workover (2) ......
11. Sec. attempt (3 ea.) ......
12. Rotation (8) ......
13. Des. miss. (8) ......

Design Total .8..

DESIGN 4
1. Asym. Crv. (3) ..3..
2. Break crv. (4) ......
3. Crv. not center. (1) ......
4. Curls (4) ......
5. Not joined (8) ......
6. Crv. rotation (3) ......
7. Touch-up (8) ......
8. Tremor (4) ......
9. Distortion (8) ......
10. Guide lines (2) ......
11. Sec. attempt (3 ea.) ......
12. Rotation (8) ......
13. Des. miss. (8) ......

Design Total ..3..

DESIGN 5
1. Asymmetry (3) ......
2. Dot, dash, cir. (3) ..3..
3. Dashes (2) ......
4. Circles (8) ......
5. Ext. join. dot (2) ..2..
6. Ext. rotation (3) ......
7. No. dots (2) ......
8. Distortion (8) ......
9. Guide lines (2) ......
10. Workover (2) ......
11. Sec. attempt (3 ea.) ......
12. Rotation (8) ......
13. Des. miss. (8) ......

Design Total ..5..

DESIGN 6
1. Asymmetry (3) ......
2. Angles (2) ......
3. Pt. crossing (2 ea.) ......
4. Crv. extra (8) ......
5. Dbl. line (1 ea.) ......
6. Touch-up (8) ......
7. Tremor (4) ..4..
8. Distortion (8) ......
9. Guide lines (2) ......
10. Workover (2) ......
11. Sec. attempt (3 ea.) ......
12. Rotation (8) ......
13. Des. miss. (8) ......

Design Total ..4..

DESIGN 7
1. Ends no. join. (8) ......
2. Angles ext. (3) ......
3. Angles miss. (3) ......
4. Ext. scat. (3) ......
5. Dbl. line (1 ea.) ......
6. Tremor (4) ..4..
7. Distortion (8 ea.) ......
8. Guide lines (2) ......
9. Sec. attempt (3 ea.) ......
10. Rotation (8) ......
11. Des. miss. (8) ......

Design Total ..4..

DESIGN 8
1. Ends no. join. (8) ..8..
2. Angles ext. (3) ......
3. Angles miss. (3) ......
4. Ext. scat. (3) ......
5. Dbl. line (1 ea.) ......
6. Tremor (4) ..4..
7. Distortion (8 ea.) ......
8. Guide lines (2) ......
9. Workover (2) ......
10. Sec. attempt (3 ea.) ......
11. Rotation (8) ......
12. Des. miss. (8) ......

Design Total ..12.

CONFIG. DESIGN
1. Place. Des. A. (2) ......
2. Overlap (2 ea.) ......
3. Compression (3) ......
4. Lines drawn (8) ......
5. Order (2) ......
6. No order (8) ......
7. Rel. size (8) ......

Total ..0..

DESIGN TOTALS

1. .5... 5. .5...
2. .3... 6. .4...
3. .8... 7. .4...
4. .3... 8. .12..

Config. .0...

Total Raw Score .44.. Standard Score 84..

SCORE SHEET—Bender-Gestalt Test

Name ....No. 13...................... Age .20.. Sex ...M.

Education ..H. S. I.Q. ...... Diagnosis Schizo-Catatonic...

DESIGN 1
1. Wavy line (2) ..2..
2. Dot, dash, cir. (3) ......
3. Dashes (2) ......
4. Circles (8) ......
5. No. dots (2) each ......
6. Dbl. row (8) ......
7. Workover (2) ......
8. Sec. attempt (3 ea.) ......
9. Rotation (8) ......
10. Des. miss. (8) ......

Design Total ..2..

DESIGN 2
1. Wavy line (2) ......
2. Dash or dots (3) ......
3. Shape cir. (3) ..3..
4. Cir. miss., ext. (3) ......
5. Cir. touch. (5) ......
6. Dev. slant (3) ......
7. No. col. (2 ea.) ......
8. Fig. on 2 lines (8) ......
9. Guide lines (2) ......
10. Workover (2) ......
11. Sec. attempt (3 ea.) ......
12. Rotation (8) ......
13. Des. miss. (8) ......

Design Total ..3..

DESIGN 3
1. Asymmetry (3) ......
2. Dot, dash, cir. (3) ..3..
3. Dashes (2) ......
4. Circles (8) ......
5. No. dots (2) ......
6. Extra row (8) ......
7. Blunting (8) ......
8. Distortion (8) ......
9. Guide lines (2) ......
10. Workover (2) ......
11. Sec. attempt (3 ea.) ......
12. Rotation (8) ......
13. Des. miss. (8) ......

Design Total ..3..

DESIGN 4
1. Asym. Crv. (3) ......
2. Break crv. (4) ......
3. Crv. not center. (1) ......
4. Curls (4) ......
5. Not joined (8) ......
6. Crv. rotation (3) ......
7. Touch-up (8) ......
8. Tremor (4) ......
9. Distortion (8) ......
10. Guide lines (2) ......
11. Sec. attempt (3 ea.) ......
12. Rotation (8) ......
13. Des. miss. (8) ......

Design Total ..0..

DESIGN 5
1. Asymmetry (3) ......
2. Dot, dash, cir. (3) ..3..
3. Dashes (2) ......
4. Circles (8) ......
5. Ext. join. dot (2) ......
6. Ext. rotation (3) ......
7. No. dots (2) ......
8. Distortion (8) ......
9. Guide lines (2) ......
10. Workover (2) ......
11. Sec. attempt (3 ea.) ......
12. Rotation (8) ......
13. Des. miss. (8) ......

Design Total ..3..

DESIGN 6
1. Asymmetry (3) ......
2. Angles (2) ......
3. Pt. crossing (2 ea.) ......
4. Crv. extra (8) ......
5. Dbl. line (1 ea.) ......
6. Touch-up (8) ......
7. Tremor (4) ......
8. Distortion (8) ......
9. Guide lines (2) ......
10. Workover (2) ......
11. Sec. attempt (3 ea.) ......
12. Rotation (8) ......
13. Des. miss. (8) ......

Design Total ...0.

DESIGN 7
1. Ends no. join. (8) ......
2. Angles ext. (3) ......
3. Angles miss. (3) ......
4. Ext. scat. (3) ......
5. Dbl. line (1 ea.) ......
6. Tremor (4) ......
7. Distortion (8 ea.) ......
8. Guide lines (2) ......
9. Sec. attempt (3 ea.) ......
10. Rotation (8) ......
11. Des. miss. (8) ......

Design Total ..0..

DESIGN 8
1. Ends no. join. (8) ......
2. Angles ext. (3) ......
3. Angles miss. (3) ......
4. Ext. scat. (3) ......
5. Dbl. line (1 ea.) ..2..
6. Tremor (4) ......
7. Distortion (8 ea.) ......
8. Guide lines (2) ......
9. Workover (2) ......
10. Sec. attempt (3 ea.) ......
11. Rotation (8) ......
12. Des. miss. (8) ......

Design Total ..2..

CONFIG. DESIGN
1. Place. Des. A. (2) ..2..
2. Overlap (2 ea.) ......
3. Compression (3) ..3..
4. Lines drawn (8) ......
5. Order (2) ......
6. No order (8) ......
7. Rel. size (8) ......

Total ..5..

DESIGN TOTALS

1. ..2.. 5. ..3..
2. ..3.. 6. ..0..
3. ..3.. 7. ..0..
4. ..0.. 8. ..2..

Config. ..5..

Total Raw Score .18.. Standard Score .50.

SCORE SHEET—Bender-Gestalt Test

Name ..No. 14........................... Age .44.. Sex ..M..

Education Grammar I.Q. 105.. Diagnosis ...Involutional Psychosis

DESIGN 1
1. Wavy line (2) ..2..
2. Dot, dash, cir. (3) ......
3. Dashes (2) ..2..
4. Circles (8) ......
5. No. dots (2) each ......
6. Dbl. row (8) ......
7. Workover (2) ......
8. Sec. attempt (3 ea.) ......
9. Rotation (8) ......
10. Des. miss. (8) ......

Design Total ..4..

DESIGN 2
1. Wavy line (2) ......
2. Dash or dots (3) ..3..
3. Shape cir. (3) ......
4. Cir. miss., ext. (3) ......
5. Cir. touch. (5) ......
6. Dev. slant (3) ......
7. No. col. (2 ea.) ......
8. Fig. on 2 lines (8) ......
9. Guide lines (2) ......
10. Workover (2) ......
11. Sec. attempt (3 ea.) ......
12. Rotation (8) ......
13. Des. miss. (8) ......

Design Total ..3..

DESIGN 3
1. Asymmetry (3) ..3..
2. Dot, dash, cir. (3) ..3..
3. Dashes (2) ......
4. Circles (8) ......
5. No. dots (2) ..2..
6. Extra row (8) ......
7. Blunting (8) ......
8. Distortion (8) ......
9. Guide lines (2) ......
10. Workover (2) ......
11. Sec. attempt (3 ea.) ......
12. Rotation (8) ......
13. Des. miss. (8) ......

Design Total ..8..

DESIGN 4
1. Asym. Crv. (3) ..3..
2. Break crv. (4) ......
3. Crv. not center. (1) ......
4. Curls (4) ......
5. Not joined (8) ......
6. Crv. rotation (3) ......
7. Touch-up (8) ......
8. Tremor (4) ......
9. Distortion (8) ......
10. Guide lines (2) ......
11. Sec. attempt (3 ea.) ..3.
12. Rotation (8) ......
13. Des. miss. (8) ......

Design Total ..6..

DESIGN 5
1. Asymmetry (3) ......
2. Dot, dash, cir. (3) ..3..
3. Dashes (2) ......
4. Circles (8) ......
5. Ext. join. dot (2) ..2..
6. Ext. rotation (3) ......
7. No. dots (2) ......
8. Distortion (8) ......
9. Guide lines (2) ......
10. Workover (2) ......
11. Sec. attempt (3 ea.) ......
12. Rotation (8) ......
13. Des. miss. (8) ......

Design Total ..5..

DESIGN 6
1. Asymmetry (3) ......
2. Angles (2) ......
3. Pt. crossing (2 ea.) ......
4. Crv. extra (8) ......
5. Dbl. line (1 ea.) ..2.
6. Touch-up (8) ......
7. Tremor (4) ......
8. Distortion (8) ......
9. Guide lines (2) ......
10. Workover (2) ......
11. Sec. attempt (3 ea.) ......
12. Rotation (8) ......
13. Des. miss. (8) ......

Design Total ..2.

DESIGN 7
1. Ends no. join. (8) ......
2. Angles ext. (3) ......
3. Angles miss. (3) ......
4. Ext. scat. (3) ......
5. Dbl. line (1 ea.) ..6.
6. Tremor (4) ......
7. Distortion (8 ea.) ..8..
8. Guide lines (2) ......
9. Sec. attempt (3 ea.) ......
10. Rotation (8) ..8..
11. Des. miss. (8) ......

Design Total .22.

DESIGN 8
1. Ends no. join. (8) ......
2. Angles ext. (3) ......
3. Angles miss. (3) ......
4. Ext. scat. (3) ......
5. Dbl. line (1 ea.) ..4..
6. Tremor (4) ..4..
7. Distortion (8 ea.) ......
8. Guide lines (2) ......
9. Workover (2) ......
10. Sec. attempt (3 ea.) ......
11. Rotation (8) ......
12. Des. miss. (8) ......

Design Total ..8...

CONFIG. DESIGN
1. Place. Des. A. (2) ......
2. Overlap (2 ea.) ..2..
3. Compression (3) ......
4. Lines drawn (8) ......
5. Order (2) ......
6. No order (8) ......
7. Rel. size (8) ......

Total ..2..

DESIGN TOTALS

1. .4... 5. .5...
2. .3... 6. .2...
3. .8... 7. .22.
4. .6... 8. ..8..

Config. .2...

Total Raw Score .60... Standard Score ......

SCORE SHEET—Bender-Gestalt Test

Name ....No. 15..................... Age ..52. Sex ..M...

Education .H.S.... I.Q. ...... Diagnosis .Involutional Psychosis

DESIGN 1
1. Wavy line (2) ......
2. Dot, dash, cir. (3) ......
3. Dashes (2) ......
4. Circles (8) ......
5. No. dots (2) each ......
6. Dbl. row (8) ......
7. Workover (2) ......
8. Sec. attempt (3 ea.) ......
9. Rotation (8) ......
10. Des. miss. (8) ......

Design Total ..0..

DESIGN 2
1. Wavy line (2) ..2..
2. Dash or dots (3) ......
3. Shape cir. (3) ......
4. Cir. miss., ext. (3) ......
5. Cir. touch. (5) ......
6. Dev. slant (3) ......
7. No. col. (2 ea.) ......
8. Fig. on 2 lines (8) ......
9. Guide lines (2) ......
10. Workover (2) ......
11. Sec. attempt (3 ea.) ......
12. Rotation (8) ......
13. Des. miss. (8) ......

Design Total ..2..

DESIGN 3
1. Asymmetry (3) ......
2. Dot, dash, cir. (3) ......
3. Dashes (2) ......
4. Circles (8) ......
5. No. dots (2) ......
6. Extra row (8) ......
7. Blunting (8) ......
8. Distortion (8) ......
9. Guide lines (2) ......
10. Workover (2) ......
11. Sec. attempt (3 ea.) ......
12. Rotation (8) ......
13. Des. miss. (8) ......

Design Total ..0...

DESIGN 4
1. Asym. Crv. (3) ......
2. Break crv. (4) ......
3. Crv. not center. (1) ......
4. Curls (4) ......
5. Not joined (8) ......
6. Crv. rotation (3) ......
7. Touch-up (8) ......
8. Tremor (4) ..4..
9. Distortion (8) ......
10. Guide lines (2) ......
11. Sec. attempt (3 ea.) ......
12. Rotation (8) ......
13. Des. miss. (8) ......

Design Total ..4..

DESIGN 5
1. Asymmetry (3) ......
2. Dot, dash, cir. (3) ..3..
3. Dashes (2) ......
4. Circles (8) ......
5. Ext. join. dot (2) ......
6. Ext. rotation (3) ......
7. No. dots (2) ......
8. Distortion (8) ......
9. Guide lines (2) ......
10. Workover (2) ......
11. Sec. attempt (3 ea.) ......
12. Rotation (8) ......
13. Des. miss. (8) ......

Design Total ..3..

DESIGN 6
1. Asymmetry (3) ......
2. Angles (2) ......
3. Pt. crossing (2 ea.) ......
4. Crv. extra (8) ......
5. Dbl. line (1 ea.) ..3..
6. Touch-up (8) ......
7. Tremor (4) ..4..
8. Distortion (8) ......
9. Guide lines (2) ......
10. Workover (2) ......
11. Sec. attempt (3 ea.) ......
12. Rotation (8) ......
13. Des. miss. (8) ......

Design Total ..7..

DESIGN 7
1. Ends no. join. (8) ......
2. Angles ext. (3) ......
3. Angles miss. (3) ......
4. Ext. scat. (3) ......
5. Dbl. line (1 ea.) ..2..
6. Tremor (4) ..4..
7. Distortion (8 ea.) ......
8. Guide lines (2) ......
9. Sec. attempt (3 ea.) ......
10. Rotation (8) ......
11. Des. miss. (8) ......

Design Total ..6..

DESIGN 8
1. Ends no. join. (8) ......
2. Angles ext. (3) ......
3. Angles miss. (3) ......
4. Ext. scat. (3) ......
5. Dbl. line (1 ea.) ..1...
6. Tremor (4) ......
7. Distortion (8 ea.) ......
8. Guide lines (2) ......
9. Workover (2) ......
10. Sec. attempt (3 ea.) ......
11. Rotation (8) ......
12. Des. miss. (8) ......

Design Total ..1...

CONFIG. DESIGN
1. Place. Des. A. (2) ......
2. Overlap (2 ea.) ......
3. Compression (3) ......
4. Lines drawn (8) ......
5. Order (2) ..2..
6. No order (8) ......
7. Rel. size (8) ......

Total ..2..

DESIGN TOTALS

1. ..0... 5. .3...
2. .2... 6. .7...
3. .0... 7. .6...
4. .4... 8. .1...

Config. .2..

Total Raw Score 25.. Standard Score .57.

SCORE SHEET—Bender-Gestalt Test

Name ....No. 16.................... Age .32.. Sex ..M..

Education .H.S.... I.Q. ...122 Diagnosis P.N. anxiety compulsion

DESIGN 1
1. Wavy line (2) ......
2. Dot, dash, cir. (3) ......
3. Dashes (2) ......
4. Circles (8) ......
5. No. dots (2) each ......
6. Dbl. row (8) ......
7. Workover (2) ......
8. Sec. attempt (3 ea.) ......
9. Rotation (8) ......
10. Des. miss. (8) ......

Design Total ..0..

DESIGN 4
1. Asym. Crv. (3) ......
2. Break crv. (4) ......
3. Crv. not center. (1) ......
4. Curls (4) ......
5. Not joined (8) ......
6. Crv. rotation (3) ......
7. Touch-up (8) ......
8. Tremor (4) ......
9. Distortion (8) ......
10. Guide lines (2) ......
11. Sec. attempt (3 ea.) ......
12. Rotation (8) ......
13. Des. miss. (8) ......

Design Total ..0..

DESIGN 7
1. Ends no. join. (8) ......
2. Angles ext. (3) ......
3. Angles miss. (3) ......
4. Ext. scat. (3) ......
5. Dbl. line (1 ea.) ..2..
6. Tremor (4) ......
7. Distortion (8 ea.) ......
8. Guide lines (2) ......
9. Sec. attempt (3 ea.) ......
10. Rotation (8) ......
11. Des. miss. (8) ......

Design Total ..2..

DESIGN 2
1. Wavy line (2) ......
2. Dash or dots (3) ......
3. Shape cir. (3) ......
4. Cir. miss., ext. (3) ......
5. Cir. touch. (5) ......
6. Dev. slant (3) ......
7. No. col. (2 ea.) ......
8. Fig. on 2 lines (8) ......
9. Guide lines (2) ......
10. Workover (2) ......
11. Sec. attempt (3 ea.) ......
12. Rotation (8) ......
13. Des. miss. (8) ......

Design Total ..0..

DESIGN 5
1. Asymmetry (3) ......
2. Dot, dash, cir. (3) ......
3. Dashes (2) ......
4. Circles (8) ......
5. Ext. join. dot (2) ......
6. Ext. rotation (3) ......
7. No. dots (2) ......
8. Distortion (8) ......
9. Guide lines (2) ......
10. Workover (2) ......
11. Sec. attempt (3 ea.) ..3..
12. Rotation (8) ......
13. Des. miss. (8) ......

Design Total ..3..

DESIGN 8
1. Ends no. join. (8) ......
2. Angles ext. (3) ......
3. Angles miss. (3) ......
4. Ext. scat. (3) ......
5. Dbl. line (1 ea.) ..2..
6. Tremor (4) ..4..
7. Distortion (8 ea.) ......
8. Guide lines (2) ......
9. Workover (2) ......
10. Sec. attempt (3 ea.) ......
11. Rotation (8) ......
12. Des. miss. (8) ......

Design Total ..6..

DESIGN 3
1. Asymmetry (3) ......
2. Dot, dash, cir. (3) ......
3. Dashes (2) ......
4. Circles (8) ......
5. No. dots (2) ......
6. Extra row (8) ......
7. Blunting (8) ......
8. Distortion (8) ......
9. Guide lines (2) ......
10. Workover (2) ......
11. Sec. attempt (3 ea.) ......
12. Rotation (8) ......
13. Des. miss. (8) ......

Design Total ..0..

DESIGN 6
1. Asymmetry (3) ......
2. Angles (2) ......
3. Pt. crossing (2 ea.) ......
4. Crv. extra (8) ......
5. Dbl. line (1 ea.) ......
6. Touch-up (8) ......
7. Tremor (4) ..4..
8. Distortion (8) ......
9. Guide lines (2) ......
10. Workover (2) ......
11. Sec. attempt (3 ea.) ......
12. Rotation (8) ......
13. Des. miss. (8) ......

Design Total ..4..

CONFIG. DESIGN
1. Place. Des. A. (2) ......
2. Overlap (2 ea.) ..2..
3. Compression (3) ......
4. Lines drawn (8) ......
5. Order (2) ......
6. No order (8) ......
7. Rel. size (8) ......

Total ..2..

DESIGN TOTALS

1. ..0.. 5. ..3..
2. ..0.. 6. ..4..
3. ..0.. 7. ..2..
4. ..0.. 8. ..6..
Config. ..2..

Total Raw Score .17.. Standard Score .49..

SCORE SHEET—Bender-Gestalt Test

Name ....No. 17.................... Age .21.. Sex .F...

Education ..College I.Q. ...... Diagnosis ..Normal............

DESIGN 1
1. Wavy line (2) ......
2. Dot, dash, cir. (3) ..3..
3. Dashes (2) ......
4. Circles (8) ......
5. No. dots (2) each ......
6. Dbl. row (8) ......
7. Workover (2) ......
8. Sec. attempt (3 ea.) ......
9. Rotation (8) ......
10. Des. miss. (8) ......

Design Total ..3..

DESIGN 4
1. Asym. Crv. (3) ......
2. Break crv. (4) ......
3. Crv. not center. (1) ......
4. Curls (4) ......
5. Not joined (8) ......
6. Crv. rotation (3) ......
7. Touch-up (8) ......
8. Tremor (4) ......
9. Distortion (8) ......
10. Guide lines (2) ......
11. Sec. attempt (3 ea.) ......
12. Rotation (8) ......
13. Des. miss. (8) ......

Design Total ..0..

DESIGN 7
1. Ends no. join. (8) ......
2. Angles ext. (3) ......
3. Angles miss. (3) ......
4. Ext. scat. (3) ......
5. Dbl. line (1 ea.) ......
6. Tremor (4) ......
7. Distortion (8 ea.) ......
8. Guide lines (2) ......
9. Sec. attempt (3 ea.) ......
10. Rotation (8) ......
11. Des. miss. (8) ......

Design Total ..0..

DESIGN 2
1. Wavy line (2) ......
2. Dash or dots (3) ......
3. Shape cir. (3) ......
4. Cir. miss., ext. (3) ......
5. Cir. touch. (5) ......
6. Dev. slant (3) ......
7. No. col. (2 ea.) ......
8. Fig. on 2 lines (8) ......
9. Guide lines (2) ......
10. Workover (2) ......
11. Sec. attempt (3 ea.) ......
12. Rotation (8) ......
13. Des. miss. (8) ......

Design Total ..0..

DESIGN 5
1. Asymmetry (3) ......
2. Dot, dash, cir. (3) ......
3. Dashes (2) ......
4. Circles (8) ......
5. Ext. join. dot (2) ..2..
6. Ext. rotation (3) ......
7. No. dots (2) ......
8. Distortion (8) ......
9. Guide lines (2) ......
10. Workover (2) ......
11. Sec. attempt (3 ea.) ......
12. Rotation (8) ......
13. Des. miss. (8) ......

Design Total ..2..

DESIGN 8
1. Ends no. join. (8) ......
2. Angles ext. (3) ......
3. Angles miss. (3) ......
4. Ext. scat. (3) ......
5. Dbl. line (1 ea.) ......
6. Tremor (4) ..4..
7. Distortion (8 ea.) ......
8. Guide lines (2) ......
9. Workover (2) ......
10. Sec. attempt (3 ea.) ......
11. Rotation (8) ......
12. Des. miss. (8) ......

Design Total ..4..

DESIGN 3
1. Asymmetry (3) ......
2. Dot, dash, cir. (3) ......
3. Dashes (2) ......
4. Circles (8) ......
5. No. dots (2) ......
6. Extra row (8) ......
7. Blunting (8) ......
8. Distortion (8) ......
9. Guide lines (2) ......
10. Workover (2) ......
11. Sec. attempt (3 ea.) ......
12. Rotation (8) ......
13. Des. miss. (8) ......

Design Total ..0..

DESIGN 6
1. Asymmetry (3) ......
2. Angles (2) ......
3. Pt. crossing (2 ea.) ......
4. Crv. extra (8) ......
5. Dbl. line (1 ea.) ......
6. Touch-up (8) ......
7. Tremor (4) ......
8. Distortion (8) ......
9. Guide lines (2) ......
10. Workover (2) ......
11. Sec. attempt (3 ea.) ......
12. Rotation (8) ......
13. Des. miss. (8) ......

Design Total ..0..

CONFIG. DESIGN
1. Place. Des. A. (2) ......
2. Overlap (2 ea.) ......
3. Compression (3) ......
4. Lines drawn (8) ......
5. Order (2) ......
6. No order (8) ......
7. Rel. size (8) ......

Total ..0..

DESIGN TOTALS

1. ..3.. 5. ..2..
2. ..0.. 6. ..0..
3. ..0.. 7. ..0..
4. ..0.. 8. ..4..
Config. ..0..

Total Raw Score .9... Standard Score .46..

SCORE SHEET—Bender-Gestalt Test

Name ..No. 18......................... Age ..26.. Sex ..M..

Education .H.S.. I.Q. ...... Diagnosis ....Normal...........

DESIGN 1
1. Wavy line (2) ......
2. Dot, dash, cir. (3) ......
3. Dashes (2) ......
4. Circles (8) ......
5. No. dots (2) each ......
6. Dbl. row (8) ......
7. Workover (2) ......
8. Sec. attempt (3 ea.) ......
9. Rotation (8) ......
10. Des. miss. (8) ......

Design Total ..0..

DESIGN 4
1. Asym. Crv. (3) ..3..
2. Break crv. (4) ......
3. Crv. not center. (1) ..1..
4. Curls (4) ......
5. Not joined (8) ......
6. Crv. rotation (3) ......
7. Touch-up (8) ......
8. Tremor (4) ......
9. Distortion (8) ......
10. Guide lines (2) ......
11. Sec. attempt (3 ea.) ......
12. Rotation (8) ......
13. Des. miss. (8) ......

Design Total ..4..

DESIGN 7
1. Ends no. join. (8) ......
2. Angles ext. (3) ......
3. Angles miss. (3) ......
4. Ext. scat. (3) ......
5. Dbl. line (1 ea.) ..2..
6. Tremor (4) ......
7. Distortion (8 ea.) ......
8. Guide lines (2) ......
9. Sec. attempt (3 ea.) ......
10. Rotation (8) ......
11. Des. miss. (8) ......

Design Total ..2..

DESIGN 2
1. Wavy line (2) ......
2. Dash or dots (3) ......
3. Shape cir. (3) ......
4. Cir. miss., ext. (3) ......
5. Cir. touch. (5) ......
6. Dev. slant (3) ......
7. No. col. (2 ea.) ......
8. Fig. on 2 lines (8) ......
9. Guide lines (2) ......
10. Workover (2) ......
11. Sec. attempt (3 ea.) ......
12. Rotation (8) ......
13. Des. miss. (8) ......

Design Total ..0..

DESIGN 5
1. Asymmetry (3) ......
2. Dot, dash, cir. (3) ......
3. Dashes (2) ......
4. Circles (8) ......
5. Ext. join. dot (2) ......
6. Ext. rotation (3) ......
7. No. dots (2) ......
8. Distortion (8) ......
9. Guide lines (2) ......
10. Workover (2) ......
11. Sec. attempt (3 ea.) ......
12. Rotation (8) ......
13. Des. miss. (8) ......

Design Total ..0..

DESIGN 8
1. Ends no. join. (8) ......
2. Angles ext. (3) ......
3. Angles miss. (3) ......
4. Ext. scat. (3) ......
5. Dbl. line (1 ea.) ......
6. Tremor (4) ......
7. Distortion (8 ea.) ......
8. Guide lines (2) ......
9. Workover (2) ......
10. Sec. attempt (3 ea.) ......
11. Rotation (8) ......
12. Des. miss. (8) ......

Design Total ..0..

DESIGN 3
1. Asymmetry (3) ......
2. Dot, dash, cir. (3) ......
3. Dashes (2) ......
4. Circles (8) ......
5. No. dots (2) ......
6. Extra row (8) ......
7. Blunting (8) ......
8. Distortion (8) ......
9. Guide lines (2) ......
10. Workover (2) ......
11. Sec. attempt (3 ea.) ......
12. Rotation (8) ..8..
13. Des. miss. (8) ......

Design Total ..8..

DESIGN 6
1. Asymmetry (3) ......
2. Angles (2) ......
3. Pt. crossing (2 ea.) ......
4. Crv. extra (8) ......
5. Dbl. line (1 ea.) ......
6. Touch-up (8) ......
7. Tremor (4) ......
8. Distortion (8) ......
9. Guide lines (2) ......
10. Workover (2) ......
11. Sec. attempt (3 ea.) ......
12. Rotation (8) ......
13. Des. miss. (8) ......

Design Total ..0..

CONFIG. DESIGN
1. Place. Des. A. (2) ......
2. Overlap (2 ea.) ......
3. Compression (3) ......
4. Lines drawn (8) ......
5. Order (2) ......
6. No order (8) ......
7. Rel. size (8) ......

Total ..0..

DESIGN TOTALS

1. ..0.. 5. ..0..
2. ..0.. 6. ..0..
3. ..8.. 7. ..2..
4. ..4.. 8. ..0..
Config. ..0..

Total Raw Score .14.. Standard Score .46..

SCORE SHEET—Bender-Gestalt Test

Name ....No. 19......................... Age .29... Sex .M..

Education College. I.Q. ...... Diagnosis .....Normal..........

DESIGN 1
1. Wavy line (2) ......
2. Dot, dash, cir. (3) ..3..
3. Dashes (2) ......
4. Circles (8) ......
5. No. dots (2) each ......
6. Dbl. row (8) ......
7. Workover (2) ......
8. Sec. attempt (3 ea.) ......
9. Rotation (8) ......
10. Des. miss. (8) ......

Design Total ..3..

DESIGN 4
1. Asym. Crv. (3) ......
2. Break crv. (4) ......
3. Crv. not center. (1) ......
4. Curls (4) ......
5. Not joined (8) ......
6. Crv. rotation (3) ......
7. Touch-up (8) ......
8. Tremor (4) ......
9. Distortion (8) ......
10. Guide lines (2) ......
11. Sec. attempt (3 ea.) ......
12. Rotation (8) ......
13. Des. miss. (8) ......

Design Total ..0..

DESIGN 7
1. Ends no. join. (8) ......
2. Angles ext. (3) ..3..
3. Angles miss. (3) ......
4. Ext. scat. (3) ......
5. Dbl. line (1 ea.) ......
6. Tremor (4) ......
7. Distortion (8 ea.) ......
8. Guide lines (2) ......
9. Sec. attempt (3 ea.) ......
10. Rotation (8) ......
11. Des. miss. (8) ......

Design Total ..3..

DESIGN 2
1. Wavy line (2) ......
2. Dash or dots (3) ......
3. Shape cir. (3) ......
4. Cir. miss., ext. (3) ......
5. Cir. touch. (5) ......
6. Dev. slant (3) ..3..
7. No. col. (2 ea.) ......
8. Fig. on 2 lines (8) ......
9. Guide lines (2) ......
10. Workover (2) ......
11. Sec. attempt (3 ea.) ......
12. Rotation (8) ......
13. Des. miss. (8) ......

Design Total ..3..

DESIGN 5
1. Asymmetry (3) ......
2. Dot, dash, cir. (3) ......
3. Dashes (2) ......
4. Circles (8) ......
5. Ext. join. dot (2) ..2..
6. Ext. rotation (3) ......
7. No. dots (2) ......
8. Distortion (8) ......
9. Guide lines (2) ......
10. Workover (2) ......
11. Sec. attempt (3 ea.) ......
12. Rotation (8) ......
13. Des. miss. (8) ......

Design Total ..2..

DESIGN 8
1. Ends no. join. (8) ......
2. Angles ext. (3) ......
3. Angles miss. (3) ......
4. Ext. scat. (3) ......
5. Dbl. line (1 ea.) ......
6. Tremor (4) ......
7. Distortion (8 ea.) ......
8. Guide lines (2) ......
9. Workover (2) ......
10. Sec. attempt (3 ea.) ......
11. Rotation (8) ......
12. Des. miss. (8) ......

Design Total ..0..

DESIGN 3
1. Asymmetry (3) ......
2. Dot, dash, cir. (3) ......
3. Dashes (2) ......
4. Circles (8) ......
5. No. dots (2) ......
6. Extra row (8) ......
7. Blunting (8) ......
8. Distortion (8) ......
9. Guide lines (2) ......
10. Workover (2) ......
11. Sec. attempt (3 ea.) ......
12. Rotation (8) ......
13. Des. miss. (8) ......

Design Total ..0..

DESIGN 6
1. Asymmetry (3) ......
2. Angles (2) ......
3. Pt. crossing (2 ea.) ......
4. Crv. extra (8) ......
5. Dbl. line (1 ea.) ......
6. Touch-up (8) ......
7. Tremor (4) ..4..
8. Distortion (8) ......
9. Guide lines (2) ......
10. Workover (2) ......
11. Sec. attempt (3 ea.) ......
12. Rotation (8) ......
13. Des. miss. (8) ......

Design Total ..4..

CONFIG. DESIGN
1. Place. Des. A. (2) ......
2. Overlap (2 ea.) ......
3. Compression (3) ......
4. Lines drawn (8) ......
5. Order (2) ......
6. No order (8) ......
7. Rel. size (8) ......

Total ..0..

DESIGN TOTALS

1. ..3.. 5. ..2..
2. ..3.. 6. ..4..
3. ..0.. 7. ..3..
4. ..0.. 8. ..0..
Config. ..0..

Total Raw Score .15... Standard Score .52.

SCORE SHEET—Bender-Gestalt Test

Name No. 20 Age 39 Sex M
Education H.S. I.Q. ...... Diagnosis Normal

DESIGN 1
1. Wavy line (2) ......
2. Dot, dash, cir. (3) ......
3. Dashes (2) ......
4. Circles (8) ......
5. No. dots (2) each ......
6. Dbl. row (8) ......
7. Workover (2) ......
8. Sec. attempt (3 ea.) ......
9. Rotation (8) ......
10. Des. miss. (8) ......

Design Total 0

DESIGN 4
1. Asym. Crv. (3) ......
2. Break crv. (4) ......
3. Crv. not center. (1) ......
4. Curls (4) ......
5. Not joined (8) ......
6. Crv. rotation (3) ......
7. Touch-up (8) ......
8. Tremor (4) ......
9. Distortion (8) ......
10. Guide lines (2) ......
11. Sec. attempt (3 ea.) ......
12. Rotation (8) ......
13. Des. miss. (8) ......

Design Total 0

DESIGN 7
1. Ends no. join. (8) ......
2. Angles ext. (3) ......
3. Angles miss. (3) ......
4. Ext. scat. (3) ......
5. Dbl. line (1 ea.) ......
6. Tremor (4) 4
7. Distortion (8 ea.) ......
8. Guide lines (2) ......
9. Sec. attempt (3 ea.) ......
10. Rotation (8) ......
11. Des. miss. (8) ......

Design Total 4

DESIGN 2
1. Wavy line (2) 2
2. Dash or dots (3) ......
3. Shape cir. (3) ......
4. Cir. miss., ext. (3) ......
5. Cir. touch. (5) ......
6. Dev. slant (3) ......
7. No. col. (2 ea.) ......
8. Fig. on 2 lines (8) ......
9. Guide lines (2) ......
10. Workover (2) ......
11. Sec. attempt (3 ea.) ......
12. Rotation (8) ......
13. Des. miss. (8) ......

Design Total 2

DESIGN 5
1. Asymmetry (3) ......
2. Dot, dash, cir. (3) 3
3. Dashes (2) ......
4. Circles (8) ......
5. Ext. join. dot (2) 2
6. Ext. rotation (3) ......
7. No. dots (2) ......
8. Distortion (8) ......
9. Guide lines (2) ......
10. Workover (2) ......
11. Sec. attempt (3 ea.) ......
12. Rotation (8) ......
13. Des. miss. (8) ......

Design Total 5

DESIGN 8
1. Ends no. join. (8) ......
2. Angles ext. (3) ......
3. Angles miss. (3) ......
4. Ext. scat. (3) ......
5. Dbl. line (1 ea.) 2
6. Tremor (4) 4
7. Distortion (8 ea.) ......
8. Guide lines (2) ......
9. Workover (2) ......
10. Sec. attempt (3 ea.) ......
11. Rotation (8) ......
12. Des. miss. (8) ......

Design Total 6

DESIGN 3
1. Asymmetry (3) ......
2. Dot, dash, cir. (3) 3
3. Dashes (2) ......
4. Circles (8) ......
5. No. dots (2) ......
6. Extra row (8) ......
7. Blunting (8) ......
8. Distortion (8) ......
9. Guide lines (2) ......
10. Workover (2) ......
11. Sec. attempt (3 ea.) ......
12. Rotation (8) ......
13. Des. miss. (8) ......

Design Total 3

DESIGN 6
1. Asymmetry (3) ......
2. Angles (2) ......
3. Pt. crossing (2 ea.) ......
4. Crv. extra (8) ......
5. Dbl. line (1 ea.) ......
6. Touch-up (8) ......
7. Tremor (4) 4
8. Distortion (8) ......
9. Guide lines (2) ......
10. Workover (2) ......
11. Sec. attempt (3 ea.) ......
12. Rotation (8) ......
13. Des. miss. (8) ......

Design Total 4

CONFIG. DESIGN
1. Place. Des. A. (2) ......
2. Overlap (2 ea.) ......
3. Compression (3) ......
4. Lines drawn (8) ......
5. Order (2) ......
6. No order (8) ......
7. Rel. size (8) ......

Total 0

DESIGN TOTALS
1. 0 5. 5
2. 2 6. 4
3. 3 7. 4
4. 0 8. 6
Config. 0

Total Raw Score 24 Standard Score 56

SCORE SHEET—Bender-Gestalt Test

Name No. 21 Age 20 Sex F
Education H.S. I.Q. ...... Diagnosis Normal

DESIGN 1
1. Wavy line (2) ......
2. Dot, dash, cir. (3) ......
3. Dashes (2) ......
4. Circles (8) ......
5. No. dots (2) each ......
6. Dbl. row (8) ......
7. Workover (2) ......
8. Sec. attempt (3 ea.) ......
9. Rotation (8) ......
10. Des. miss. (8) ......

Design Total 0

DESIGN 4
1. Asym. Crv. (3) ......
2. Break crv. (4) ......
3. Crv. not center. (1) 1
4. Curls (4) ......
5. Not joined (8) ......
6. Crv. rotation (3) ......
7. Touch-up (8) ......
8. Tremor (4) ......
9. Distortion (8) ......
10. Guide lines (2) ......
11. Sec. attempt (3 ea.) ......
12. Rotation (8) ......
13. Des. miss. (8) ......

Design Total 1

DESIGN 7
1. Ends no. join. (8) ......
2. Angles ext. (3) ......
3. Angles miss. (3) ......
4. Ext. scat. (3) ......
5. Dbl. line (1 ea.) ......
6. Tremor (4) ......
7. Distortion (8 ea.) ......
8. Guide lines (2) ......
9. Sec. attempt (3 ea.) ......
10. Rotation (8) ......
11. Des. miss. (8) ......

Design Total 0

DESIGN 2
1. Wavy line (2) ......
2. Dash or dots (3) ......
3. Shape cir. (3) ......
4. Cir. miss., ext. (3) ......
5. Cir. touch. (5) ......
6. Dev. slant (3) ......
7. No. col. (2 ea.) ......
8. Fig. on 2 lines (8) ......
9. Guide lines (2) ......
10. Workover (2) ......
11. Sec. attempt (3 ea.) ......
12. Rotation (8) ......
13. Des. miss. (8) ......

Design Total 0

DESIGN 5
1. Asymmetry (3) ......
2. Dot, dash, cir. (3) ......
3. Dashes (2) ......
4. Circles (8) ......
5. Ext. join. dot (2) 2
6. Ext. rotation (3) ......
7. No. dots (2) ......
8. Distortion (8) ......
9. Guide lines (2) ......
10. Workover (2) ......
11. Sec. attempt (3 ea.) ......
12. Rotation (8) ......
13. Des. miss. (8) ......

Design Total 2

DESIGN 8
1. Ends no. join. (8) ......
2. Angles ext. (3) ......
3. Angles miss. (3) ......
4. Ext. scat. (3) ......
5. Dbl. line (1 ea.) ......
6. Tremor (4) ......
7. Distortion (8 ea.) ......
8. Guide lines (2) ......
9. Workover (2) ......
10. Sec. attempt (3 ea.) ......
11. Rotation (8) ......
12. Des. miss. (8) ......

Design Total 0

DESIGN 3
1. Asymmetry (3) 3
2. Dot, dash, cir. (3) 3
3. Dashes (2) ......
4. Circles (8) ......
5. No. dots (2) 2
6. Extra row (8) ......
7. Blunting (8) ......
8. Distortion (8) ......
9. Guide lines (2) ......
10. Workover (2) ......
11. Sec. attempt (3 ea.) ......
12. Rotation (8) ......
13. Des. miss. (8) ......

Design Total 8

DESIGN 6
1. Asymmetry (3) ......
2. Angles (2) ......
3. Pt. crossing (2 ea.) ......
4. Crv. extra (8) ......
5. Dbl. line (1 ea.) ......
6. Touch-up (8) ......
7. Tremor (4) ......
8. Distortion (8) ......
9. Guide lines (2) ......
10. Workover (2) ......
11. Sec. attempt (3 ea.) ......
12. Rotation (8) ......
13. Des. miss. (8) ......

Design Total 0

CONFIG. DESIGN
1. Place. Des. A. (2) ......
2. Overlap (2 ea.) ......
3. Compression (3) ......
4. Lines drawn (8) ......
5. Order (2) ......
6. No order (8) ......
7. Rel. size (8) ......

Total 0

DESIGN TOTALS
1. 0 5. 2
2. 0 6. 0
3. 8 7. 0
4. 1 8. 0
Config. 0

Total Raw Score 11 Standard Score 43

SCORE SHEET—Bender-Gestalt Test

Name No. 22 Age 63 Sex M
Education Grammar I.Q. 106 Diagnosis Normal

DESIGN 1
1. Wavy line (2) ......
2. Dot, dash, cir. (3) ......
3. Dashes (2) 2
4. Circles (8) ......
5. No. dots (2) each ......
6. Dbl. row (8) ......
7. Workover (2) ......
8. Sec. attempt (3 ea.) ......
9. Rotation (8) ......
10. Des. miss. (8) ......

Design Total 2

DESIGN 4
1. Asym. Crv. (3) 3
2. Break crv. (4) ......
3. Crv. not center. (1) ......
4. Curls (4) ......
5. Not joined (8) ......
6. Crv. rotation (3) ......
7. Touch-up (8) ......
8. Tremor (4) 4
9. Distortion (8) ......
10. Guide lines (2) ......
11. Sec. attempt (3 ea.) ......
12. Rotation (8) ......
13. Des. miss. (8) ......

Design Total 7

DESIGN 7
1. Ends no. join. (8) ......
2. Angles ext. (3) ......
3. Angles miss. (3) ......
4. Ext. scat. (3) ......
5. Dbl. line (1 ea.) 1
6. Tremor (4) 4
7. Distortion (8 ea.) ......
8. Guide lines (2) ......
9. Sec. attempt (3 ea.) ......
10. Rotation (8) ......
11. Des. miss. (8) ......

Design Total 5

DESIGN 2
1. Wavy line (2) 2
2. Dash or dots (3) ......
3. Shape cir. (3) ......
4. Cir. miss., ext. (3) ......
5. Cir. touch. (5) ......
6. Dev. slant (3) ......
7. No. col. (2 ea.) ......
8. Fig. on 2 lines (8) ......
9. Guide lines (2) ......
10. Workover (2) ......
11. Sec. attempt (3 ea.) ......
12. Rotation (8) ......
13. Des. miss. (8) ......

Design Total 2

DESIGN 5
1. Asymmetry (3) ......
2. Dot, dash, cir. (3) ......
3. Dashes (2) ......
4. Circles (8) ......
5. Ext. join. dot (2) 2
6. Ext. rotation (3) ......
7. No. dots (2) ......
8. Distortion (8) ......
9. Guide lines (2) ......
10. Workover (2) ......
11. Sec. attempt (3 ea.) ......
12. Rotation (8) ......
13. Des. miss. (8) ......

Design Total 2

DESIGN 8
1. Ends no. join. (8) ......
2. Angles ext. (3) ......
3. Angles miss. (3) 3
4. Ext. scat. (3) ......
5. Dbl. line (1 ea.) 1
6. Tremor (4) 4
7. Distortion (8 ea.) ......
8. Guide lines (2) ......
9. Workover (2) ......
10. Sec. attempt (3 ea.) ......
11. Rotation (8) ......
12. Des. miss. (8) ......

Design Total 8

DESIGN 3
1. Asymmetry (3) ......
2. Dot, dash, cir. (3) 3
3. Dashes (2) ......
4. Circles (8) ......
5. No. dots (2) ......
6. Extra row (8) ......
7. Blunting (8) ......
8. Distortion (8) ......
9. Guide lines (2) ......
10. Workover (2) ......
11. Sec. attempt (3 ea.) ......
12. Rotation (8) 8
13. Des. miss. (8) ......

Design Total 11

DESIGN 6
1. Asymmetry (3) ......
2. Angles (2) ......
3. Pt. crossing (2 ea.) ......
4. Crv. extra (8) ......
5. Dbl. line (1 ea.) 1
6. Touch-up (8) ......
7. Tremor (4) 4
8. Distortion (8) ......
9. Guide lines (2) ......
10. Workover (2) ......
11. Sec. attempt (3 ea.) ......
12. Rotation (8) ......
13. Des. miss. (8) ......

Design Total 5

CONFIG. DESIGN
1. Place. Des. A. (2) ......
2. Overlap (2 ea.) ......
3. Compression (3) ......
4. Lines drawn (8) ......
5. Order (2) ......
6. No order (8) ......
7. Rel. size (8) ......

Total 0

DESIGN TOTALS
1. 2 5. 2
2. 2 6. 5
3. 11 7. 5
4. 7 8. 8
Config. 0

Total Raw Score 42 Standard Score ......

SCORE SHEET—Bender-Gestalt Test

Name No. 23 Age 67 Sex M
Education Grammar I.Q. 79 Diagnosis ......

DESIGN 1
1. Wavy line (2) ......
2. Dot, dash, cir. (3) 3
3. Dashes (2) ......
4. Circles (8) ......
5. No. dots (2) each ......
6. Dbl. row (8) ......
7. Workover (2) ......
8. Sec. attempt (3 ea.) ......
9. Rotation (8) ......
10. Des. miss. (8) ......

Design Total 3

DESIGN 4
1. Asym. Crv. (3) 3
2. Break crv. (4) ......
3. Crv. not center. (1) 1
4. Curls (4) ......
5. Not joined (8) 8
6. Crv. rotation (3) 3
7. Touch-up (8) ......
8. Tremor (4) 4
9. Distortion (8) 8
10. Guide lines (2) ......
11. Sec. attempt (3 ea.) ......
12. Rotation (8) 8
13. Des. miss. (8) ......

Design Total 35

DESIGN 7
1. Ends no. join. (8) ......
2. Angles ext. (3) ......
3. Angles miss. (3) ......
4. Ext. scat. (3) ......
5. Dbl. line (1 ea.) 1
6. Tremor (4) 4
7. Distortion (8 ea.) ......
8. Guide lines (2) ......
9. Sec. attempt (3 ea.) 6
10. Rotation (8) 8
11. Des. miss. (8) ......

Design Total 19

DESIGN 2
1. Wavy line (2) 2
2. Dash or dots (3) ......
3. Shape cir. (3) 3
4. Cir. miss., ext. (3) ......
5. Cir. touch. (5) ......
6. Dev. slant (3) ......
7. No. col. (2 ea.) ......
8. Fig. on 2 lines (8) ......
9. Guide lines (2) ......
10. Workover (2) ......
11. Sec. attempt (3 ea.) 3
12. Rotation (8) 8
13. Des. miss. (8) ......

Design Total 16

DESIGN 5
1. Asymmetry (3) 3
2. Dot, dash, cir. (3) 3
3. Dashes (2) ......
4. Circles (8) ......
5. Ext. join. dot (2) ......
6. Ext. rotation (3) ......
7. No. dots (2) ......
8. Distortion (8) ......
9. Guide lines (2) ......
10. Workover (2) ......
11. Sec. attempt (3 ea.) ......
12. Rotation (8) ......
13. Des. miss. (8) ......

Design Total 6

DESIGN 8
1. Ends no. join. (8) ......
2. Angles ext. (3) 3
3. Angles miss. (3) ......
4. Ext. scat. (3) 3
5. Dbl. line (1 ea.) 5
6. Tremor (4) 4
7. Distortion (8 ea.) ......
8. Guide lines (2) ......
9. Workover (2) ......
10. Sec. attempt (3 ea.) ......
11. Rotation (8) ......
12. Des. miss. (8) ......

Design Total 15

DESIGN 3
1. Asymmetry (3) 3
2. Dot, dash, cir. (3) 3
3. Dashes (2) ......
4. Circles (8) ......
5. No. dots (2) 2
6. Extra row (8) 8
7. Blunting (8) ......
8. Distortion (8) ......
9. Guide lines (2) ......
10. Workover (2) 2
11. Sec. attempt (3 ea.) ......
12. Rotation (8) 8
13. Des. miss. (8) ......

Design Total 26

DESIGN 6
1. Asymmetry (3) 3
2. Angles (2) ......
3. Pt. crossing (2 ea.) ......
4. Crv. extra (8) ......
5. Dbl. line (1 ea.) 3
6. Touch-up (8) ......
7. Tremor (4) 4
8. Distortion (8) ......
9. Guide lines (2) ......
10. Workover (2) 2
11. Sec. attempt (3 ea.) 9
12. Rotation (8) ......
13. Des. miss. (8) ......

Design Total 21

CONFIG. DESIGN
1. Place. Des. A. (2) ......
2. Overlap (2 ea.) ......
3. Compression (3) ......
4. Lines drawn (8) ......
5. Order (2) ......
6. No order (8) ......
7. Rel. size (8) ......

Total 0

DESIGN TOTALS
1. 3 5. 6
2. 16 6. 21
3. 26 7. 19
4. 35 8. 15
Config. 0

Total Raw Score 143 Standard Score ......

SCORE SHEET—Bender-Gestalt Test

Name No. 24 Age 68 Sex M
Education H.S. I.Q. 114 Diagnosis Normal

DESIGN 1	
1. Wavy line (2)	......
2. Dot, dash, cir. (3)	3
3. Dashes (2)	......
4. Circles (8)	......
5. No. dots (2) each	......
6. Dbl. row (8)	......
7. Workover (2)	2
8. Sec. attempt (3 ea.)	......
9. Rotation (8)	......
10. Des. miss. (8)	......
Design Total	5

DESIGN 4	
1. Asym. Crv. (3)	......
2. Break crv. (4)	......
3. Crv. not center. (1)	......
4. Curls (4)	......
5. Not joined (8)	......
6. Crv. rotation (3)	......
7. Touch-up (8)	......
8. Tremor (4)	4
9. Distortion (8)	......
10. Guide lines (2)	......
11. Sec. attempt (3 ea.)	......
12. Rotation (8)	......
13. Des. miss. (8)	......
Design Total	4

DESIGN 7	
1. Ends no. join. (8)	......
2. Angles ext. (3)	......
3. Angles miss. (3)	......
4. Ext. scat. (3)	......
5. Dbl. line (1 ea.)	2
6. Tremor (4)	4
7. Distortion (8 ea.)	......
8. Guide lines (2)	......
9. Sec. attempt (3 ea.)	......
10. Rotation (8)	......
11. Des. miss. (8)	......
Design Total	6

DESIGN 2	
1. Wavy line (2)	2
2. Dash or dots (3)	......
3. Shape cir. (3)	3
4. Cir. miss., ext. (3)	......
5. Cir. touch. (5)	......
6. Dev. slant (3)	......
7. No. col. (2 ea.)	......
8. Fig. on 2 lines (8)	......
9. Guide lines (2)	......
10. Workover (2)	......
11. Sec. attempt (3 ea.)	......
12. Rotation (8)	......
13. Des. miss. (8)	......
Design Total	5

DESIGN 5	
1. Asymmetry (3)	......
2. Dot, dash, cir. (3)	3
3. Dashes (2)	......
4. Circles (8)	......
5. Ext. join. dot (2)	2
6. Ext. rotation (3)	......
7. No. dots (2)	......
8. Distortion (8)	......
9. Guide lines (2)	......
10. Workover (2)	......
11. Sec. attempt (3 ea.)	......
12. Rotation (8)	......
13. Des. miss. (8)	......
Design Total	5

DESIGN 8	
1. Ends no. join. (8)	......
2. Angles ext. (3)	3
3. Angles miss. (3)	......
4. Ext. scat. (3)	......
5. Dbl. line (1 ea.)	......
6. Tremor (4)	4
7. Distortion (8 ea.)	......
8. Guide lines (2)	......
9. Workover (2)	......
10. Sec. attempt (3 ea.)	......
11. Rotation (8)	......
12. Des. miss. (8)	......
Design Total	7

DESIGN 3	
1. Asymmetry (3)	......
2. Dot, dash, cir. (3)	3
3. Dashes (2)	......
4. Circles (8)	......
5. No. dots (2)	......
6. Extra row (8)	......
7. Blunting (8)	......
8. Distortion (8)	......
9. Guide lines (2)	......
10. Workover (2)	2
11. Sec. attempt (3 ea.)	......
12. Rotation (8)	......
13. Des. miss. (8)	......
Design Total	5

DESIGN 6	
1. Asymmetry (3)	3
2. Angles (2)	......
3. Pt. crossing (2 ea.)	......
4. Crv. extra (8)	......
5. Dbl. line (1 ea.)	......
6. Touch-up (8)	......
7. Tremor (4)	4
8. Distortion (8)	......
9. Guide lines (2)	......
10. Workover (2)	......
11. Sec. attempt (3 ea.)	......
12. Rotation (8)	......
13. Des. miss. (8)	......
Design Total	7

CONFIG. DESIGN	
1. Place. Des. A. (2)	......
2. Overlap (2 ea.)	......
3. Compression (3)	......
4. Lines drawn (8)	......
5. Order (2)	2
6. No order (8)	......
7. Rel. size (8)	......
Total	2

DESIGN TOTALS

1.	5	5.	5
2.	5	6.	7
3.	5	7.	6
4.	4	8.	7
Config.	2		

Total Raw Score 46 Standard Score 80

SCORE SHEET—Bender-Gestalt Test

Name No. 25 Age 65 Sex M
Education H.S. I.Q. ...... Diagnosis Normal

DESIGN 1	
1. Wavy line (2)	......
2. Dot, dash, cir. (3)	3
3. Dashes (2)	......
4. Circles (8)	......
5. No. dots (2) each	......
6. Dbl. row (8)	......
7. Workover (2)	......
8. Sec. attempt (3 ea.)	......
9. Rotation (8)	......
10. Des. miss. (8)	......
Design Total	3

DESIGN 4	
1. Asym. Crv. (3)	3
2. Break crv. (4)	......
3. Crv. not center. (1)	......
4. Curls (4)	4
5. Not joined (8)	......
6. Crv. rotation (3)	......
7. Touch-up (8)	......
8. Tremor (4)	......
9. Distortion (8)	......
10. Guide lines (2)	......
11. Sec. attempt (3 ea.)	......
12. Rotation (8)	......
13. Des. miss. (8)	......
Design Total	7

DESIGN 7	
1. Ends no. join. (8)	......
2. Angles ext. (3)	......
3. Angles miss. (3)	......
4. Ext. scat. (3)	......
5. Dbl. line (1 ea.)	2
6. Tremor (4)	4
7. Distortion (8 ea.)	......
8. Guide lines (2)	......
9. Sec. attempt (3 ea.)	......
10. Rotation (8)	......
11. Des. miss. (8)	......
Design Total	6

DESIGN 2	
1. Wavy line (2)	......
2. Dash or dots (3)	3
3. Shape cir. (3)	......
4. Cir. miss., ext. (3)	......
5. Cir. touch. (5)	......
6. Dev. slant (3)	......
7. No. col. (2 ea.)	......
8. Fig. on 2 lines (8)	......
9. Guide lines (2)	......
10. Workover (2)	2
11. Sec. attempt (3 ea.)	......
12. Rotation (8)	......
13. Des. miss. (8)	......
Design Total	5

DESIGN 5	
1. Asymmetry (3)	......
2. Dot, dash, cir. (3)	3
3. Dashes (2)	......
4. Circles (8)	......
5. Ext. join. dot (2)	2
6. Ext. rotation (3)	......
7. No. dots (2)	......
8. Distortion (8)	......
9. Guide lines (2)	......
10. Workover (2)	......
11. Sec. attempt (3 ea.)	......
12. Rotation (8)	......
13. Des. miss. (8)	......
Design Total	5

DESIGN 8	
1. Ends no. join. (8)	......
2. Angles ext. (3)	......
3. Angles miss. (3)	......
4. Ext. scat. (3)	......
5. Dbl. line (1 ea.)	......
6. Tremor (4)	4
7. Distortion (8 ea.)	......
8. Guide lines (2)	......
9. Workover (2)	......
10. Sec. attempt (3 ea.)	......
11. Rotation (8)	......
12. Des. miss. (8)	......
Design Total	4

DESIGN 3	
1. Asymmetry (3)	......
2. Dot, dash, cir. (3)	3
3. Dashes (2)	......
4. Circles (8)	......
5. No. dots (2)	......
6. Extra row (8)	......
7. Blunting (8)	......
8. Distortion (8)	......
9. Guide lines (2)	......
10. Workover (2)	......
11. Sec. attempt (3 ea.)	......
12. Rotation (8)	......
13. Des. miss. (8)	......
Design Total	3

DESIGN 6	
1. Asymmetry (3)	......
2. Angles (2)	......
3. Pt. crossing (2 ea.)	......
4. Crv. extra (8)	......
5. Dbl. line (1 ea.)	......
6. Touch-up (8)	......
7. Tremor (4)	4
8. Distortion (8)	......
9. Guide lines (2)	......
10. Workover (2)	......
11. Sec. attempt (3 ea.)	......
12. Rotation (8)	......
13. Des. miss. (8)	......
Design Total	4

CONFIG. DESIGN	
1. Place. Des. A. (2)	......
2. Overlap (2 ea.)	......
3. Compression (3)	......
4. Lines drawn (8)	......
5. Order (2)	2
6. No order (8)	......
7. Rel. size (8)	......
Total	2

DESIGN TOTALS

1.	3	5.	5
2.	5	6.	4
3.	3	7.	6
4.	7	8.	4
Config.	2		

Total Raw Score 39 Standard Score 72

N.B.: The score sheets that follow are not to be consulted by the beginning scorer until he has completed his own scoring of records 26 to 45.

SCORE SHEET—Bender-Gestalt Test

Name No. 26 Age 43 Sex F

Education H.S. I.Q. ...... Diagnosis Normal

DESIGN 1
1. Wavy line (2) .. 2
2. Dot, dash, cir. (3) .. 3
3. Dashes (2) ......
4. Circles (8) ......
5. No. dots (2) each ......
6. Dbl. row (8) ......
7. Workover (2) ......
8. Sec. attempt (3 ea.) ......
9. Rotation (8) ......
10. Des. miss. (8) ......

Design Total .. 5

DESIGN 4
1. Asym. Crv. (3) ......
2. Break crv. (4) ......
3. Crv. not center. (1) ......
4. Curls (4) ......
5. Not joined (8) ......
6. Crv. rotation (3) ......
7. Touch-up (8) ......
8. Tremor (4) ......
9. Distortion (8) ......
10. Guide lines (2) ......
11. Sec. attempt (3 ea.) ......
12. Rotation (8) ......
13. Des. miss. (8) ......

Design Total .. 0

DESIGN 7
1. Ends no. join. (8) ......
2. Angles ext. (3) ......
3. Angles miss. (3) ......
4. Ext. scat. (3) ......
5. Dbl. line (1 ea.) ......
6. Tremor (4) ......
7. Distortion (8 ea.) ......
8. Guide lines (2) ......
9. Sec. attempt (3 ea.) ......
10. Rotation (8) ......
11. Des. miss. (8) ......

Design Total .. 0

DESIGN 2
1. Wavy line (2) ......
2. Dash or dots (3) ......
3. Shape cir. (3) ......
4. Cir. miss., ext. (3) ......
5. Cir. touch. (5) ......
6. Dev. slant (3) ......
7. No. col. (2 ea.) ......
8. Fig. on 2 lines (8) ......
9. Guide lines (2) ......
10. Workover (2) ......
11. Sec. attempt (3 ea.) ......
12. Rotation (8) ......
13. Des. miss. (8) ......

Design Total .. 0

DESIGN 5
1. Asymmetry (3) ......
2. Dot, dash, cir. (3) ......
3. Dashes (2) ......
4. Circles (8) ......
5. Ext. join. dot (2) ......
6. Ext. rotation (3) ......
7. No. dots (2) ......
8. Distortion (8) ......
9. Guide lines (2) ......
10. Workover (2) ......
11. Sec. attempt (3 ea.) ......
12. Rotation (8) ......
13. Des. miss. (8) ......

Design Total .. 0

DESIGN 8
1. Ends no. join. (8) ......
2. Angles ext. (3) ......
3. Angles miss. (3) ......
4. Ext. scat. (3) ......
5. Dbl. line (1 ea.) ......
6. Tremor (4) .. 4
7. Distortion (8 ea.) ......
8. Guide lines (2) ......
9. Workover (2) ......
10. Sec. attempt (3 ea.) ......
11. Rotation (8) ......
12. Des. miss. (8) ......

Design Total .. 4

DESIGN 3
1. Asymmetry (3) ......
2. Dot, dash, cir. (3) ......
3. Dashes (2) ......
4. Circles (8) ......
5. No. dots (2) ......
6. Extra row (8) ......
7. Blunting (8) ......
8. Distortion (8) ......
9. Guide lines (2) ......
10. Workover (2) ......
11. Sec. attempt (3 ea.) ......
12. Rotation (8) ......
13. Des. miss. (8) ......

Design Total .. 0

DESIGN 6
1. Asymmetry (3) ......
2. Angles (2) ......
3. Pt. crossing (2 ea.) ......
4. Crv. extra (8) ......
5. Dbl. line (1 ea.) ......
6. Touch-up (8) ......
7. Tremor (4) ......
8. Distortion (8) ......
9. Guide lines (2) ......
10. Workover (2) ......
11. Sec. attempt (3 ea.) ......
12. Rotation (8) ......
13. Des. miss. (8) ......

Design Total .. 0

CONFIG. DESIGN
1. Place. Des. A. (2) ......
2. Overlap (2 ea.) ......
3. Compression (3) ......
4. Lines drawn (8) ......
5. Order (2) ......
6. No order (8) ......
7. Rel. size (8) ......

Total .. 0

DESIGN TOTALS
1. 5 5. 0
2. 0 6. 0
3. 0 7. 0
4. 0 8. 4

Config. 0

Total Raw Score 9 Standard Score 40

SCORE SHEET—Bender-Gestalt Test

Name No. 27 Age 26 Sex M

Education H.S. I.Q. 124 Diagnosis Pl. sex. perversion

DESIGN 1
1. Wavy line (2) ......
2. Dot, dash, cir. (3) ......
3. Dashes (2) ......
4. Circles (8) ......
5. No. dots (2) each ......
6. Dbl. row (8) ......
7. Workover (2) ......
8. Sec. attempt (3 ea.) ......
9. Rotation (8) ......
10. Des. miss. (8) ......

Design Total .. 0

DESIGN 4
1. Asym. Crv. (3) ......
2. Break crv. (4) ......
3. Crv. not center. (1) .. 1
4. Curls (4) ......
5. Not joined (8) ......
6. Crv. rotation (3) ......
7. Touch-up (8) ......
8. Tremor (4) .. 4
9. Distortion (8) ......
10. Guide lines (2) ......
11. Sec. attempt (3 ea.) ......
12. Rotation (8) ......
13. Des. miss. (8) ......

Design Total .. 5

DESIGN 7
1. Ends no. join. (8) ......
2. Angles ext. (3) .. 3
3. Angles miss. (3) ......
4. Ext. scat. (3) ......
5. Dbl. line (1 ea.) .. 1
6. Tremor (4) ......
7. Distortion (8 ea.) ......
8. Guide lines (2) ......
9. Sec. attempt (3 ea.) ......
10. Rotation (8) ......
11. Des. miss. (8) ......

Design Total .. 4

DESIGN 2
1. Wavy line (2) .. 2
2. Dash or dots (3) ......
3. Shape cir. (3) ......
4. Cir. miss., ext. (3) ......
5. Cir. touch. (5) ......
6. Dev. slant (3) .. 3
7. No. col. (2 ea.) ......
8. Fig. on 2 lines (8) ......
9. Guide lines (2) ......
10. Workover (2) ......
11. Sec. attempt (3 ea.) ......
12. Rotation (8) ......
13. Des. miss. (8) ......

Design Total .. 5

DESIGN 5
1. Asymmetry (3) ......
2. Dot, dash, cir. (3) .. 3
3. Dashes (2) ......
4. Circles (8) ......
5. Ext. join. dot (2) ......
6. Ext. rotation (3) ......
7. No. dots (2) ......
8. Distortion (8) ......
9. Guide lines (2) ......
10. Workover (2) ......
11. Sec. attempt (3 ea.) ......
12. Rotation (8) ......
13. Des. miss. (8) ......

Design Total .. 3

DESIGN 8
1. Ends no. join. (8) ......
2. Angles ext. (3) ......
3. Angles miss. (3) ......
4. Ext. scat. (3) ......
5. Dbl. line (1 ea.) ......
6. Tremor (4) .. 4
7. Distortion (8 ea.) ......
8. Guide lines (2) ......
9. Workover (2) ......
10. Sec. attempt (3 ea.) ......
11. Rotation (8) ......
12. Des. miss. (8) ......

Design Total .. 4

DESIGN 3
1. Asymmetry (3) ......
2. Dot, dash, cir. (3) .. 3
3. Dashes (2) ......
4. Circles (8) ......
5. No. dots (2) ......
6. Extra row (8) ......
7. Blunting (8) ......
8. Distortion (8) ......
9. Guide lines (2) ......
10. Workover (2) ......
11. Sec. attempt (3 ea.) ......
12. Rotation (8) ......
13. Des. miss. (8) ......

Design Total .. 3

DESIGN 6
1. Asymmetry (3) ......
2. Angles (2) ......
3. Pt. crossing (2 ea.) ......
4. Crv. extra (8) ......
5. Dbl. line (1 ea.) ......
6. Touch-up (8) ......
7. Tremor (4) .. 4
8. Distortion (8) ......
9. Guide lines (2) ......
10. Workover (2) ......
11. Sec. attempt (3 ea.) ......
12. Rotation (8) ......
13. Des. miss. (8) ......

Design Total .. 4

CONFIG. DESIGN
1. Place. Des. A. (2) ......
2. Overlap (2 ea.) .. 2
3. Compression (3) .. 3
4. Lines drawn (8) ......
5. Order (2) ......
6. No order (8) ......
7. Rel. size (8) ......

Total .. 5

DESIGN TOTALS
1. 0 5. 3
2. 5 6. 4
3. 3 7. 4
4. 5 8. 4

Config. 5

Total Raw Score 33 Standard Score 66

SCORE SHEET—Bender-Gestalt Test

Name No. 28 Age 46 Sex M

Education H.S. I.Q. ...... Diagnosis Invol. Psychosis.

DESIGN 1
1. Wavy line (2) ......
2. Dot, dash, cir. (3) .. 3
3. Dashes (2) ......
4. Circles (8) ......
5. No. dots (2) each ......
6. Dbl. row (8) ......
7. Workover (2) .. 2
8. Sec. attempt (3 ea.) ......
9. Rotation (8) ......
10. Des. miss. (8) ......

Design Total .. 5

DESIGN 4
1. Asym. Crv. (3) .. 3
2. Break crv. (4) ......
3. Crv. not center. (1) .. 1
4. Curls (4) .. 4
5. Not joined (8) ......
6. Crv. rotation (3) ......
7. Touch-up (8) ......
8. Tremor (4) .. 4
9. Distortion (8) ......
10. Guide lines (2) ......
11. Sec. attempt (3 ea.) ......
12. Rotation (8) ......
13. Des. miss. (8) ......

Design Total .. 12

DESIGN 7
1. Ends no. join. (8) ......
2. Angles ext. (3) .. 3
3. Angles miss. (3) ......
4. Ext. scat. (3) ......
5. Dbl. line (1 ea.) .. 3
6. Tremor (4) .. 4
7. Distortion (8 ea.) ......
8. Guide lines (2) ......
9. Sec. attempt (3 ea.) ......
10. Rotation (8) ......
11. Des. miss. (8) ......

Design Total .. 10

DESIGN 2
1. Wavy line (2) .. 2
2. Dash or dots (3) ......
3. Shape cir. (3) ......
4. Cir. miss., ext. (3) ......
5. Cir. touch. (5) ......
6. Dev. slant (3) ......
7. No. col. (2 ea.) ......
8. Fig. on 2 lines (8) ......
9. Guide lines (2) ......
10. Workover (2) .. 2
11. Sec. attempt (3 ea.) ......
12. Rotation (8) ......
13. Des. miss. (8) ......

Design Total .. 4

DESIGN 5
1. Asymmetry (3) ......
2. Dot, dash, cir. (3) ......
3. Dashes (2) ......
4. Circles (8) .. 8
5. Ext. join. dot (2) ......
6. Ext. rotation (3) ......
7. No. dots (2) ......
8. Distortion (8) ......
9. Guide lines (2) ......
10. Workover (2) .. 2
11. Sec. attempt (3 ea.) ......
12. Rotation (8) ......
13. Des. miss. (8) ......

Design Total .. 10

DESIGN 8
1. Ends no. join. (8) ......
2. Angles ext. (3) .. 3
3. Angles miss. (3) ......
4. Ext. scat. (3) ......
5. Dbl. line (1 ea.) .. 5
6. Tremor (4) ......
7. Distortion (8 ea.) ......
8. Guide lines (2) .. 2
9. Workover (2) ......
10. Sec. attempt (3 ea.) .. 3
11. Rotation (8) ......
12. Des. miss. (8) ......

Design Total .. 13

DESIGN 3
1. Asymmetry (3) ......
2. Dot, dash, cir. (3) ......
3. Dashes (2) ......
4. Circles (8) .. 8
5. No. dots (2) ......
6. Extra row (8) ......
7. Blunting (8) ......
8. Distortion (8) ......
9. Guide lines (2) ......
10. Workover (2) .. 2
11. Sec. attempt (3 ea.) ......
12. Rotation (8) ......
13. Des. miss. (8) ......

Design Total .. 10

DESIGN 6
1. Asymmetry (3) ......
2. Angles (2) ......
3. Pt. crossing (2 ea.) .. 2
4. Crv. extra (8) ......
5. Dbl. line (1 ea.) ......
6. Touch-up (8) ......
7. Tremor (4) .. 4
8. Distortion (8) ......
9. Guide lines (2) ......
10. Workover (2) ......
11. Sec. attempt (3 ea.) ......
12. Rotation (8) ......
13. Des. miss. (8) ......

Design Total .. 6

CONFIG. DESIGN
1. Place. Des. A. (2) ......
2. Overlap (2 ea.) ......
3. Compression (3) ......
4. Lines drawn (8) ......
5. Order (2) ......
6. No order (8) ......
7. Rel. size (8) ......

Total .. 0

DESIGN TOTALS
1. 3 5. 10
2. 4 6. 6
3. 10 7. 10
4. 12 8. 13

Config. 0

Total Raw Score 68 Standard Score 103

SCORE SHEET—Bender-Gestalt Test

Name No. 29 Age 30 Sex M

Education College I.Q. ...... Diagnosis Normal

DESIGN 1
1. Wavy line (2) ......
2. Dot, dash, cir. (3) ......
3. Dashes (2) ......
4. Circles (8) ......
5. No. dots (2) each ......
6. Dbl. row (8) ......
7. Workover (2) ......
8. Sec. attempt (3 ea.) ......
9. Rotation (8) ......
10. Des. miss. (8) ......

Design Total .. 0

DESIGN 4
1. Asym. Crv. (3) ......
2. Break crv. (4) ......
3. Crv. not center. (1) ......
4. Curls (4) ......
5. Not joined (8) ......
6. Crv. rotation (3) ......
7. Touch-up (8) ......
8. Tremor (4) ......
9. Distortion (8) ......
10. Guide lines (2) ......
11. Sec. attempt (3 ea.) ......
12. Rotation (8) ......
13. Des. miss. (8) ......

Design Total .. 0

DESIGN 7
1. Ends no. join. (8) ......
2. Angles ext. (3) ......
3. Angles miss. (3) ......
4. Ext. scat. (3) ......
5. Dbl. line (1 ea.) ......
6. Tremor (4) ......
7. Distortion (8 ea.) ......
8. Guide lines (2) ......
9. Sec. attempt (3 ea.) ......
10. Rotation (8) ......
11. Des. miss. (8) ......

Design Total .. 0

DESIGN 2
1. Wavy line (2) .. 2
2. Dash or dots (3) ......
3. Shape cir. (3) ......
4. Cir. miss., ext. (3) ......
5. Cir. touch. (5) ......
6. Dev. slant (3) ......
7. No. col. (2 ea.) ......
8. Fig. on 2 lines (8) ......
9. Guide lines (2) ......
10. Workover (2) ......
11. Sec. attempt (3 ea.) ......
12. Rotation (8) ......
13. Des. miss. (8) ......

Design Total .. 2

DESIGN 5
1. Asymmetry (3) ......
2. Dot, dash, cir. (3) ......
3. Dashes (2) ......
4. Circles (8) ......
5. Ext. join. dot (2) .. 2
6. Ext. rotation (3) ......
7. No. dots (2) ......
8. Distortion (8) ......
9. Guide lines (2) ......
10. Workover (2) ......
11. Sec. attempt (3 ea.) ......
12. Rotation (8) ......
13. Des. miss. (8) ......

Design Total .. 2

DESIGN 8
1. Ends no. join. (8) ......
2. Angles ext. (3) ......
3. Angles miss. (3) ......
4. Ext. scat. (3) ......
5. Dbl. line (1 ea.) .. 1
6. Tremor (4) ......
7. Distortion (8 ea.) ......
8. Guide lines (2) ......
9. Workover (2) ......
10. Sec. attempt (3 ea.) ......
11. Rotation (8) ......
12. Des. miss. (8) ......

Design Total .. 1

DESIGN 3
1. Asymmetry (3) ......
2. Dot, dash, cir. (3) ......
3. Dashes (2) ......
4. Circles (8) ......
5. No. dots (2) ......
6. Extra row (8) ......
7. Blunting (8) ......
8. Distortion (8) ......
9. Guide lines (2) ......
10. Workover (2) ......
11. Sec. attempt (3 ea.) ......
12. Rotation (8) ......
13. Des. miss. (8) ......

Design Total .. 0

DESIGN 6
1. Asymmetry (3) .. 3
2. Angles (2) .. 2
3. Pt. crossing (2 ea.) ......
4. Crv. extra (8) ......
5. Dbl. line (1 ea.) ......
6. Touch-up (8) ......
7. Tremor (4) ......
8. Distortion (8) ......
9. Guide lines (2) ......
10. Workover (2) ......
11. Sec. attempt (3 ea.) ......
12. Rotation (8) ......
13. Des. miss. (8) ......

Design Total .. 5

CONFIG. DESIGN
1. Place. Des. A. (2) ......
2. Overlap (2 ea.) ......
3. Compression (3) ......
4. Lines drawn (8) ......
5. Order (2) ......
6. No order (8) ......
7. Rel. size (8) ......

Total .. 0

DESIGN TOTALS
1. 0 5. 2
2. 2 6. 5
3. 0 7. 0
4. 0 8. 1

Config. 0

Total Raw Score 10 Standard Score 47

SCORE SHEET—Bender-Gestalt Test

Name No. 30 Age 24 Sex M
Education College I.Q. ...... Diagnosis Schizo-Catatonic

DESIGN 1
1. Wavy line (2) 2
2. Dot, dash, cir. (3) 3
3. Dashes (2) ......
4. Circles (8) ......
5. No. dots (2) each ......
6. Dbl. row (8) ......
7. Workover (2) ......
8. Sec. attempt (3 ea.) ......
9. Rotation (8) ......
10. Des. miss. (8) ......

Design Total 5

DESIGN 4
1. Asym. Crv. (3) 3
2. Break crv. (4) ......
3. Crv. not center. (1) ......
4. Curls (4) 4
5. Not joined (8) ......
6. Crv. rotation (3) ......
7. Touch-up (8) ......
8. Tremor (4) ......
9. Distortion (8) ......
10. Guide lines (2) ......
11. Sec. attempt (3 ea.) ......
12. Rotation (8) ......
13. Des. miss. (8) ......

Design Total 7

DESIGN 7
1. Ends no. join. (8) ......
2. Angles ext. (3) ......
3. Angles miss. (3) ......
4. Ext. scat. (3) ......
5. Dbl. line (1 ea.) ......
6. Tremor (4) ......
7. Distortion (8 ea.) ......
8. Guide lines (2) ......
9. Sec. attempt (3 ea.) ......
10. Rotation (8) ......
11. Des. miss. (8) ......

Design Total 0

DESIGN 2
1. Wavy line (2) 2
2. Dash or dots (3) ......
3. Shape cir. (3) ......
4. Cir. miss., ext. (3) ......
5. Cir. touch. (5) ......
6. Dev. slant (3) 3
7. No. col. (2 ea.) ......
8. Fig. on 2 lines (8) ......
9. Guide lines (2) ......
10. Workover (2) ......
11. Sec. attempt (3 ea.) ......
12. Rotation (8) ......
13. Des. miss. (8) ......

Design Total 5

DESIGN 5
1. Asymmetry (3) 3
2. Dot, dash, cir. (3) 3
3. Dashes (2) ......
4. Circles (8) ......
5. Ext. join. dot (2) 2
6. Ext. rotation (3) ......
7. No. dots (2) ......
8. Distortion (8) ......
9. Guide lines (2) ......
10. Workover (2) ......
11. Sec. attempt (3 ea.) ......
12. Rotation (8) ......
13. Des. miss. (8) ......

Design Total 8

DESIGN 8
1. Ends no. join. (8) ......
2. Angles ext. (3) ......
3. Angles miss. (3) ......
4. Ext. scat. (3) ......
5. Dbl. line (1 ea.) 1
6. Tremor (4) 4
7. Distortion (8 ea.) ......
8. Guide lines (2) ......
9. Workover (2) ......
10. Sec. attempt (3 ea.) ......
11. Rotation (8) ......
12. Des. miss. (8) ......

Design Total 5

DESIGN 3
1. Asymmetry (3) ......
2. Dot, dash, cir. (3) 3
3. Dashes (2) ......
4. Circles (8) ......
5. No. dots (2) ......
6. Extra row (8) ......
7. Blunting (8) ......
8. Distortion (8) ......
9. Guide lines (2) ......
10. Workover (2) ......
11. Sec. attempt (3 ea.) ......
12. Rotation (8) ......
13. Des. miss. (8) ......

Design Total 3

DESIGN 6
1. Asymmetry (3) ......
2. Angles (2) ......
3. Pt. crossing (2 ea.) ......
4. Crv. extra (8) ......
5. Dbl. line (1 ea.) ......
6. Touch-up (8) ......
7. Tremor (4) ......
8. Distortion (8) ......
9. Guide lines (2) ......
10. Workover (2) ......
11. Sec. attempt (3 ea.) ......
12. Rotation (8) ......
13. Des. miss. (8) ......

Design Total 0

CONFIG. DESIGN
1. Place. Des. A. (2) 2
2. Overlap (2 ea.) 2
3. Compression (3) ......
4. Lines drawn (8) 8
5. Order (2) 2
6. No order (8) ......
7. Rel. size (8) ......

Total 14

DESIGN TOTALS
1. 5 5. 8
2. 5 6. 0
3. 3 7. 0
4. 7 8. 5
Config. 14

Total Raw Score 47 Standard Score 87

SCORE SHEET—Bender-Gestalt Test

Name No. 31 Age 37 Sex M
Education College I.Q. ...... Diagnosis PN

DESIGN 1
1. Wavy line (2) ......
2. Dot, dash, cir. (3) ......
3. Dashes (2) ......
4. Circles (8) ......
5. No. dots (2) each ......
6. Dbl. row (8) ......
7. Workover (2) ......
8. Sec. attempt (3 ea.) ......
9. Rotation (8) ......
10. Des. miss. (8) ......

Design Total 0

DESIGN 4
1. Asym. Crv. (3) ......
2. Break crv. (4) ......
3. Crv. not center. (1) ......
4. Curls (4) 4
5. Not joined (8) ......
6. Crv. rotation (3) ......
7. Touch-up (8) 8
8. Tremor (4) ......
9. Distortion (8) ......
10. Guide lines (2) ......
11. Sec. attempt (3 ea.) ......
12. Rotation (8) ......
13. Des. miss. (8) ......

Design Total 12

DESIGN 7
1. Ends no. join. (8) ......
2. Angles ext. (3) ......
3. Angles miss. (3) ......
4. Ext. scat. (3) ......
5. Dbl. line (1 ea.) 1
6. Tremor (4) 4
7. Distortion (8 ea.) ......
8. Guide lines (2) ......
9. Sec. attempt (3 ea.) ......
10. Rotation (8) ......
11. Des. miss. (8) ......

Design Total 5

DESIGN 2
1. Wavy line (2) ......
2. Dash or dots (3) ......
3. Shape cir. (3) ......
4. Cir. miss., ext. (3) ......
5. Cir. touch. (5) ......
6. Dev. slant (3) ......
7. No. col. (2 ea.) ......
8. Fig. on 2 lines (8) ......
9. Guide lines (2) ......
10. Workover (2) ......
11. Sec. attempt (3 ea.) ......
12. Rotation (8) ......
13. Des. miss. (8) ......

Design Total 0

DESIGN 5
1. Asymmetry (3) ......
2. Dot, dash, cir. (3) ......
3. Dashes (2) ......
4. Circles (8) ......
5. Ext. join. dot (2) 2
6. Ext. rotation (3) ......
7. No. dots (2) ......
8. Distortion (8) ......
9. Guide lines (2) ......
10. Workover (2) ......
11. Sec. attempt (3 ea.) ......
12. Rotation (8) ......
13. Des. miss. (8) ......

Design Total 2

DESIGN 8
1. Ends no. join. (8) ......
2. Angles ext. (3) ......
3. Angles miss. (3) ......
4. Ext. scat. (3) ......
5. Dbl. line (1 ea.) ......
6. Tremor (4) ......
7. Distortion (8 ea.) ......
8. Guide lines (2) ......
9. Workover (2) ......
10. Sec. attempt (3 ea.) 3
11. Rotation (8) ......
12. Des. miss. (8) ......

Design Total 3

DESIGN 3
1. Asymmetry (3) ......
2. Dot, dash, cir. (3) ......
3. Dashes (2) ......
4. Circles (8) ......
5. No. dots (2) ......
6. Extra row (8) ......
7. Blunting (8) ......
8. Distortion (8) ......
9. Guide lines (2) 2
10. Workover (2) ......
11. Sec. attempt (3 ea.) ......
12. Rotation (8) ......
13. Des. miss. (8) ......

Design Total 2

DESIGN 6
1. Asymmetry (3) 3
2. Angles (2) ......
3. Pt. crossing (2 ea.) ......
4. Crv. extra (8) ......
5. Dbl. line (1 ea.) ......
6. Touch-up (8) ......
7. Tremor (4) 4
8. Distortion (8) ......
9. Guide lines (2) ......
10. Workover (2) 2
11. Sec. attempt (3 ea.) ......
12. Rotation (8) ......
13. Des. miss. (8) ......

Design Total 9

CONFIG. DESIGN
1. Place. Des. A. (2) ......
2. Overlap (2 ea.) ......
3. Compression (3) ......
4. Lines drawn (8) ......
5. Order (2) ......
6. No order (8) ......
7. Rel. size (8) ......

Total 0

DESIGN TOTALS
1. 0 5. 2
2. 0 6. 9
3. 2 7. 5
4. 12 8. 3
Config. 0

Total Raw Score 33 Standard Score 72

SCORE SHEET—Bender-Gestalt Test

Name No. 32 Age 43 Sex F
Education H.S. I.Q. ...... Diagnosis Normal

DESIGN 1
1. Wavy line (2) ......
2. Dot, dash, cir. (3) 3
3. Dashes (2) ......
4. Circles (8) ......
5. No. dots (2) each ......
6. Dbl. row (8) ......
7. Workover (2) ......
8. Sec. attempt (3 ea.) ......
9. Rotation (8) ......
10. Des. miss. (8) ......

Design Total 3

DESIGN 4
1. Asym. Crv. (3) ......
2. Break crv. (4) ......
3. Crv. not center. (1) 1
4. Curls (4) ......
5. Not joined (8) ......
6. Crv. rotation (3) ......
7. Touch-up (8) ......
8. Tremor (4) ......
9. Distortion (8) ......
10. Guide lines (2) ......
11. Sec. attempt (3 ea.) ......
12. Rotation (8) ......
13. Des. miss. (8) ......

Design Total 1

DESIGN 7
1. Ends no. join. (8) ......
2. Angles ext. (3) ......
3. Angles miss. (3) ......
4. Ext. scat. (3) ......
5. Dbl. line (1 ea.) ......
6. Tremor (4) ......
7. Distortion (8 ea.) ......
8. Guide lines (2) ......
9. Sec. attempt (3 ea.) ......
10. Rotation (8) ......
11. Des. miss. (8) ......

Design Total 0

DESIGN 2
1. Wavy line (2) 2
2. Dash or dots (3) ......
3. Shape cir. (3) ......
4. Cir. miss., ext. (3) ......
5. Cir. touch. (5) ......
6. Dev. slant (3) ......
7. No. col. (2 ea.) ......
8. Fig. on 2 lines (8) ......
9. Guide lines (2) ......
10. Workover (2) ......
11. Sec. attempt (3 ea.) ......
12. Rotation (8) ......
13. Des. miss. (8) ......

Design Total 2

DESIGN 5
1. Asymmetry (3) 3
2. Dot, dash, cir. (3) 3
3. Dashes (2) ......
4. Circles (8) ......
5. Ext. join. dot (2) 2
6. Ext. rotation (3) ......
7. No. dots (2) ......
8. Distortion (8) ......
9. Guide lines (2) ......
10. Workover (2) ......
11. Sec. attempt (3 ea.) ......
12. Rotation (8) ......
13. Des. miss. (8) ......

Design Total 8

DESIGN 8
1. Ends no. join. (8) ......
2. Angles ext. (3) ......
3. Angles miss. (3) ......
4. Ext. scat. (3) ......
5. Dbl. line (1 ea.) ......
6. Tremor (4) ......
7. Distortion (8 ea.) ......
8. Guide lines (2) ......
9. Workover (2) ......
10. Sec. attempt (3 ea.) ......
11. Rotation (8) ......
12. Des. miss. (8) ......

Design Total 0

DESIGN 3
1. Asymmetry (3) ......
2. Dot, dash, cir. (3) ......
3. Dashes (2) ......
4. Circles (8) ......
5. No. dots (2) ......
6. Extra row (8) ......
7. Blunting (8) ......
8. Distortion (8) ......
9. Guide lines (2) ......
10. Workover (2) ......
11. Sec. attempt (3 ea.) ......
12. Rotation (8) ......
13. Des. miss. (8) ......

Design Total 0

DESIGN 6
1. Asymmetry (3) 3
2. Angles (2) ......
3. Pt. crossing (2 ea.) ......
4. Crv. extra (8) ......
5. Dbl. line (1 ea.) ......
6. Touch-up (8) ......
7. Tremor (4) ......
8. Distortion (8) ......
9. Guide lines (2) ......
10. Workover (2) ......
11. Sec. attempt (3 ea.) ......
12. Rotation (8) ......
13. Des. miss. (8) ......

Design Total 3

CONFIG. DESIGN
1. Place. Des. A. (2) ......
2. Overlap (2 ea.) ......
3. Compression (3) ......
4. Lines drawn (8) ......
5. Order (2) ......
6. No order (8) ......
7. Rel. size (8) ......

Total 0

DESIGN TOTALS
1. 3 5. 8
2. 2 6. 3
3. 0 7. 0
4. 1 8. 0
Config. 0

Total Raw Score 17 Standard Score 47

SCORE SHEET—Bender-Gestalt Test

Name No. 33 Age 16 Sex M
Education H.S. 1 I.Q. ...... Diagnosis Schizo-Catatonic

DESIGN 1
1. Wavy line (2) ......
2. Dot, dash, cir. (3) ......
3. Dashes (2) ......
4. Circles (8) ......
5. No. dots (2) each ......
6. Dbl. row (8) ......
7. Workover (2) ......
8. Sec. attempt (3 ea.) ......
9. Rotation (8) ......
10. Des. miss. (8) ......

Design Total 0

DESIGN 4
1. Asym. Crv. (3) ......
2. Break crv. (4) ......
3. Crv. not center. (1) ......
4. Curls (4) ......
5. Not joined (8) ......
6. Crv. rotation (3) ......
7. Touch-up (8) ......
8. Tremor (4) 4
9. Distortion (8) ......
10. Guide lines (2) ......
11. Sec. attempt (3 ea.) ......
12. Rotation (8) ......
13. Des. miss. (8) ......

Design Total 4

DESIGN 7
1. Ends no. join. (8) ......
2. Angles ext. (3) 3
3. Angles miss. (3) 3
4. Ext. scat. (3) ......
5. Dbl. line (1 ea.) ......
6. Tremor (4) 4
7. Distortion (8 ea.) ......
8. Guide lines (2) ......
9. Sec. attempt (3 ea.) ......
10. Rotation (8) ......
11. Des. miss. (8) ......

Design Total 10

DESIGN 2
1. Wavy line (2) 2
2. Dash or dots (3) ......
3. Shape cir. (3) 3
4. Cir. miss., ext. (3) ......
5. Cir. touch. (5) ......
6. Dev. slant (3) 3
7. No. col. (2 ea.) ......
8. Fig. on 2 lines (8) ......
9. Guide lines (2) ......
10. Workover (2) ......
11. Sec. attempt (3 ea.) ......
12. Rotation (8) ......
13. Des. miss. (8) ......

Design Total 8

DESIGN 5
1. Asymmetry (3) 3
2. Dot, dash, cir. (3) ......
3. Dashes (2) ......
4. Circles (8) ......
5. Ext. join. dot (2) ......
6. Ext. rotation (3) ......
7. No. dots (2) ......
8. Distortion (8) ......
9. Guide lines (2) ......
10. Workover (2) ......
11. Sec. attempt (3 ea.) ......
12. Rotation (8) ......
13. Des. miss. (8) ......

Design Total 3

DESIGN 8
1. Ends no. join. (8) ......
2. Angles ext. (3) 3
3. Angles miss. (3) ......
4. Ext. scat. (3) ......
5. Dbl. line (1 ea.) 1
6. Tremor (4) 4
7. Distortion (8 ea.) ......
8. Guide lines (2) ......
9. Workover (2) ......
10. Sec. attempt (3 ea.) ......
11. Rotation (8) ......
12. Des. miss. (8) ......

Design Total 8

DESIGN 3
1. Asymmetry (3) ......
2. Dot, dash, cir. (3) 3
3. Dashes (2) ......
4. Circles (8) ......
5. No. dots (2) ......
6. Extra row (8) ......
7. Blunting (8) ......
8. Distortion (8) ......
9. Guide lines (2) ......
10. Workover (2) ......
11. Sec. attempt (3 ea.) ......
12. Rotation (8) ......
13. Des. miss. (8) ......

Design Total 3

DESIGN 6
1. Asymmetry (3) 3
2. Angles (2) 2
3. Pt. crossing (2 ea.) ......
4. Crv. extra (8) ......
5. Dbl. line (1 ea.) ......
6. Touch-up (8) ......
7. Tremor (4) 4
8. Distortion (8) ......
9. Guide lines (2) ......
10. Workover (2) ......
11. Sec. attempt (3 ea.) ......
12. Rotation (8) ......
13. Des. miss. (8) ......

Design Total 9

CONFIG. DESIGN
1. Place. Des. A. (2) ......
2. Overlap (2 ea.) ......
3. Compression (3) ......
4. Lines drawn (8) ......
5. Order (2) ......
6. No order (8) ......
7. Rel. size (8) ......

Total 0

DESIGN TOTALS
1. 0 5. 3
2. 8 6. 9
3. 3 7. 10
4. 4 8. 8
Config. 0

Total Raw Score 45 Standard Score 79

SCORE SHEET—BENDER-GESTALT TEST

Name No. 34 Age 24 Sex M

Education College I.Q. ...... Diagnosis Normal

DESIGN 1		*DESIGN 4*		*DESIGN 7*	
1. Wavy line (2)		1. Asym. Crv. (3)		1. Ends no. join. (8)	
2. Dot, dash, cir. (3)		2. Break crv. (4)		2. Angles ext. (3)	
3. Dashes (2)		3. Crv. not center. (1)		3. Angles miss. (3)	
4. Circles (8)		4. Curls (4)		4. Ext. scat. (3)	
5. No. dots (2) each		5. Not joined (8)		5. Dbl. line (1 ea.)	
6. Dbl. row (8)		6. Crv. rotation (3)		6. Tremor (4)	
7. Workover (2)		7. Touch-up (8)		7. Distortion (8 ea.)	
8. Sec. attempt (3 ea.)		8. Tremor (4)		8. Guide lines (2)	
9. Rotation (8)		9. Distortion (8)		9. Sec. attempt (3 ea.)	
10. Des. miss. (8)		10. Guide lines (2)		10. Rotation (8)	
Design Total	0	11. Sec. attempt (3 ea.)		11. Des. miss. (8)	
		12. Rotation (8)		Design Total	0
		13. Des. miss. (8)			
		Design Total	0		

DESIGN 2		*DESIGN 5*		*DESIGN 8*	
1. Wavy line (2)		1. Asymmetry (3)		1. Ends no. join. (8)	
2. Dash or dots (3)		2. Dot, dash, cir. (3)		2. Angles ext. (3)	
3. Shape cir. (3)		3. Dashes (2)		3. Angles miss. (3)	
4. Cir. miss., ext. (3)		4. Circles (8)		4. Ext. scat. (3)	
5. Cir. touch. (5)		5. Ext. join. dot (2)	2	5. Dbl. line (1 ea.)	
6. Dev. slant (3)		6. Ext. rotation (3)		6. Tremor (4)	
7. No. col. (2 ea.)		7. No. dots (2)		7. Distortion (8 ea.)	
8. Fig. on 2 lines (8)		8. Distortion (8)		8. Guide lines (2)	
9. Guide lines (2)		9. Guide lines (2)		9. Workover (2)	
10. Workover (2)		10. Workover (2)		10. Sec. attempt (3 ea.)	
11. Sec. attempt (3 ea.)		11. Sec. attempt (3 ea.)		11. Rotation (8)	
12. Rotation (8)		12. Rotation (8)		12. Des. miss. (8)	
13. Des. miss. (8)		13. Des. miss. (8)		Design Total	0
Design Total	0	Design Total	2		

DESIGN 3		*DESIGN 6*		*CONFIG. DESIGN*	
1. Asymmetry (3)		1. Asymmetry (3)		1. Place. Des. A. (2)	
2. Dot, dash, cir. (3)		2. Angles (2)		2. Overlap (2 ea.)	
3. Dashes (2)		3. Pt. crossing (2 ea.)		3. Compression (3)	
4. Circles (8)		4. Crv. extra (8)		4. Lines drawn (8)	
5. No. dots (2)		5. Dbl. line (1 ea.)		5. Order (2)	
6. Extra row (8)		6. Touch-up (8)		6. No order (8)	
7. Blunting (8)		7. Tremor (4)	4	7. Rel. size (8)	
8. Distortion (8)		8. Distortion (8)		Total	0
9. Guide lines (2)		9. Guide lines (2)		*DESIGN TOTALS*	
10. Workover (2)	2	10. Workover (2)		1. 0	5. 2
11. Sec. attempt (3 ea.)		11. Sec. attempt (3 ea.)		2. 0	6. 4
12. Rotation (8)		12. Rotation (8)		3. 2	7. 0
13. Des. miss. (8)		13. Des. miss. (8)		4. 0	8. 0
Design Total	2	Design Total	4	Config.	0

Total Raw Score 8 Standard Score 45

SCORE SHEET—BENDER-GESTALT TEST

Name No. 35 Age 33 Sex M

Education College I.Q. ...... Diagnosis Normal

DESIGN 1		*DESIGN 4*		*DESIGN 7*	
1. Wavy line (2)		1. Asym. Crv. (3)		1. Ends no. join. (8)	
2. Dot, dash, cir. (3)		2. Break crv. (4)		2. Angles ext. (3)	
3. Dashes (2)		3. Crv. not center. (1)		3. Angles miss. (3)	
4. Circles (8)		4. Curls (4)		4. Ext. scat. (3)	
5. No. dots (2) each		5. Not joined (8)		5. Dbl. line (1 ea.)	
6. Dbl. row (8)		6. Crv. rotation (3)		6. Tremor (4)	
7. Workover (2)		7. Touch-up (8)		7. Distortion (8 ea.)	
8. Sec. attempt (3 ea.)		8. Tremor (4)		8. Guide lines (2)	
9. Rotation (8)		9. Distortion (8)		9. Sec. attempt (3 ea.)	
10. Des. miss. (8)		10. Guide lines (2)		10. Rotation (8)	
Design Total	0	11. Sec. attempt (3 ea.)		11. Des. miss. (8)	
		12. Rotation (8)		Design Total	0
		13. Des. miss. (8)			
		Design Total	0		

DESIGN 2		*DESIGN 5*		*DESIGN 8*	
1. Wavy line (2)		1. Asymmetry (3)		1. Ends no. join. (8)	
2. Dash or dots (3)		2. Dot, dash, cir. (3)		2. Angles ext. (3)	
3. Shape cir. (3)		3. Dashes (2)		3. Angles miss. (3)	
4. Cir. miss., ext. (3)		4. Circles (8)		4. Ext. scat. (3)	
5. Cir. touch. (5)		5. Ext. join. dot (2)		5. Dbl. line (1 ea.)	
6. Dev. slant (3)		6. Ext. rotation (3)		6. Tremor (4)	
7. No. col. (2 ea.)		7. No. dots (2)		7. Distortion (8 ea.)	
8. Fig. on 2 lines (8)		8. Distortion (8)		8. Guide lines (2)	
9. Guide lines (2)		9. Guide lines (2)		9. Workover (2)	
10. Workover (2)		10. Workover (2)		10. Sec. attempt (3 ea.)	
11. Sec. attempt (3 ea.)		11. Sec. attempt (3 ea.)		11. Rotation (8)	
12. Rotation (8)		12. Rotation (8)		12. Des. miss. (8)	
13. Des. miss. (8)		13. Des. miss. (8)		Design Total	0
Design Total	0	Design Total	0		

DESIGN 3		*DESIGN 6*		*CONFIG. DESIGN*	
1. Asymmetry (3)		1. Asymmetry (3)		1. Place. Des. A. (2)	
2. Dot, dash, cir. (3)		2. Angles (2)		2. Overlap (2 ea.)	
3. Dashes (2)		3. Pt. crossing (2 ea.)		3. Compression (3)	
4. Circles (8)		4. Crv. extra (8)		4. Lines drawn (8)	
5. No. dots (2)		5. Dbl. line (1 ea.)		5. Order (2)	
6. Extra row (8)		6. Touch-up (8)		6. No order (8)	
7. Blunting (8)		7. Tremor (4)		7. Rel. size (8)	
8. Distortion (8)		8. Distortion (8)		Total	0
9. Guide lines (2)		9. Guide lines (2)		*DESIGN TOTALS*	
10. Workover (2)		10. Workover (2)		1. 0	5. 0
11. Sec. attempt (3 ea.)		11. Sec. attempt (3 ea.)		2. 0	6. 0
12. Rotation (8)		12. Rotation (8)		3. 0	7. 0
13. Des. miss. (8)		13. Des. miss. (8)		4. 0	8. 0
Design Total	0	Design Total	0	Config.	0

Total Raw Score 1 Standard Score 37

SCORE SHEET—BENDER-GESTALT TEST

Name No. 36 Age 38 Sex M

Education H.S. I.Q. ...... Diagnosis Schizo- Paranoid

DESIGN 1		*DESIGN 4*		*DESIGN 7*	
1. Wavy line (2)		1. Asym. Crv. (3)	3	1. Ends no. join. (8)	
2. Dot, dash, cir. (3)		2. Break crv. (4)	4	2. Angles ext. (3)	
3. Dashes (2)		3. Crv. not center. (1)		3. Angles miss. (3)	
4. Circles (8)		4. Curls (4)		4. Ext. scat. (3)	
5. No. dots (2) each		5. Not joined (8)		5. Dbl. line (1 ea.)	
6. Dbl. row (8)		6. Crv. rotation (3)		6. Tremor (4)	
7. Workover (2)	2	7. Touch-up (8)		7. Distortion (8 ea.)	
8. Sec. attempt (3 ea.)		8. Tremor (4)		8. Guide lines (2)	
9. Rotation (8)		9. Distortion (8)		9. Sec. attempt (3 ea.)	
10. Des. miss. (8)		10. Guide lines (2)		10. Rotation (8)	
Design Total	2	11. Sec. attempt (3 ea.)		11. Des. miss. (8)	
		12. Rotation (8)		Design Total	0
		13. Des. miss. (8)			
		Design Total	7		

DESIGN 2		*DESIGN 5*		*DESIGN 8*	
1. Wavy line (2)	2	1. Asymmetry (3)	3	1. Ends no. join. (8)	
2. Dash or dots (3)		2. Dot, dash, cir. (3)		2. Angles ext. (3)	3
3. Shape cir. (3)		3. Dashes (2)		3. Angles miss. (3)	
4. Cir. miss., ext. (3)		4. Circles (8)		4. Ext. scat. (3)	
5. Cir. touch. (5)		5. Ext. join. dot (2)	2	5. Dbl. line (1 ea.)	
6. Dev. slant (3)		6. Ext. rotation (3)		6. Tremor (4)	
7. No. col. (2 ea.)		7. No. dots (2)		7. Distortion (8 ea.)	
8. Fig. on 2 lines (8)		8. Distortion (8)		8. Guide lines (2)	
9. Guide lines (2)		9. Guide lines (2)		9. Workover (2)	2
10. Workover (2)		10. Workover (2)	2	10. Sec. attempt (3 ea.)	
11. Sec. attempt (3 ea.)		11. Sec. attempt (3 ea.)		11. Rotation (8)	
12. Rotation (8)		12. Rotation (8)		12. Des. miss. (8)	
13. Des. miss. (8)		13. Des. miss. (8)		Design Total	5
Design Total	2	Design Total	7		

DESIGN 3		*DESIGN 6*		*CONFIG. DESIGN*	
1. Asymmetry (3)	3	1. Asymmetry (3)		1. Place. Des. A. (2)	2
2. Dot, dash, cir. (3)		2. Angles (2)		2. Overlap (2 ea.)	
3. Dashes (2)		3. Pt. crossing (2 ea.)		3. Compression (3)	
4. Circles (8)		4. Crv. extra (8)		4. Lines drawn (8)	
5. No. dots (2)	2	5. Dbl. line (1 ea.)		5. Order (2)	
6. Extra row (8)		6. Touch-up (8)		6. No order (8)	8
7. Blunting (8)		7. Tremor (4)		7. Rel. size (8)	
8. Distortion (8)		8. Distortion (8)		Total	10
9. Guide lines (2)		9. Guide lines (2)		*DESIGN TOTALS*	
10. Workover (2)	2	10. Workover (2)	2	1. 2	5. 7
11. Sec. attempt (3 ea.)		11. Sec. attempt (3 ea.)		2. 2	6. 2
12. Rotation (8)		12. Rotation (8)		3. 7	7. 0
13. Des. miss. (8)		13. Des. miss. (8)		4. 7	8. 5
Design Total	7	Design Total	2	Config.	10

Total Raw Score 42 Standard Score 75

SCORE SHEET—BENDER-GESTALT TEST

Name No. 37 Age 19 Sex M

Education Normal I.Q. ...... Diagnosis Normal

DESIGN 1		*DESIGN 4*		*DESIGN 7*	
1. Wavy line (2)		1. Asym. Crv. (3)		1. Ends no. join. (8)	
2. Dot, dash, cir. (3)		2. Break crv. (4)		2. Angles ext. (3)	
3. Dashes (2)		3. Crv. not center. (1)		3. Angles miss. (3)	
4. Circles (8)		4. Curls (4)		4. Ext. scat. (3)	
5. No. dots (2) each		5. Not joined (8)		5. Dbl. line (1 ea.)	
6. Dbl. row (8)		6. Crv. rotation (3)		6. Tremor (4)	
7. Workover (2)		7. Touch-up (8)		7. Distortion (8 ea.)	
8. Sec. attempt (3 ea.)		8. Tremor (4)		8. Guide lines (2)	
9. Rotation (8)		9. Distortion (8)		9. Sec. attempt (3 ea.)	
10. Des. miss. (8)		10. Guide lines (2)		10. Rotation (8)	
Design Total	0	11. Sec. attempt (3 ea.)		11. Des. miss. (8)	
		12. Rotation (8)		Design Total	0
		13. Des. miss. (8)			
		Design Total	0		

DESIGN 2		*DESIGN 5*		*DESIGN 8*	
1. Wavy line (2)	2	1. Asymmetry (3)		1. Ends no. join. (8)	
2. Dash or dots (3)		2. Dot, dash, cir. (3)		2. Angles ext. (3)	
3. Shape cir. (3)		3. Dashes (2)		3. Angles miss. (3)	
4. Cir. miss., ext. (3)		4. Circles (8)		4. Ext. scat. (3)	
5. Cir. touch. (5)		5. Ext. join. dot (2)	2	5. Dbl. line (1 ea.)	1
6. Dev. slant (3)		6. Ext. rotation (3)		6. Tremor (4)	4
7. No. col. (2 ea.)		7. No. dots (2)		7. Distortion (8 ea.)	
8. Fig. on 2 lines (8)		8. Distortion (8)		8. Guide lines (2)	
9. Guide lines (2)		9. Guide lines (2)		9. Workover (2)	
10. Workover (2)	2	10. Workover (2)		10. Sec. attempt (3 ea.)	
11. Sec. attempt (3 ea.)		11. Sec. attempt (3 ea.)		11. Rotation (8)	
12. Rotation (8)		12. Rotation (8)		12. Des. miss. (8)	
13. Des. miss. (8)		13. Des. miss. (8)		Design Total	5
Design Total	4	Design Total	2		

DESIGN 3		*DESIGN 6*		*CONFIG. DESIGN*	
1. Asymmetry (3)		1. Asymmetry (3)		1. Place. Des. A. (2)	
2. Dot, dash, cir. (3)		2. Angles (2)		2. Overlap (2 ea.)	
3. Dashes (2)		3. Pt. crossing (2 ea.)		3. Compression (3)	
4. Circles (8)		4. Crv. extra (8)		4. Lines drawn (8)	
5. No. dots (2)		5. Dbl. line (1 ea.)	1	5. Order (2)	
6. Extra row (8)		6. Touch-up (8)		6. No order (8)	
7. Blunting (8)		7. Tremor (4)		7. Rel. size (8)	
8. Distortion (8)		8. Distortion (8)		Total	0
9. Guide lines (2)		9. Guide lines (2)		*DESIGN TOTALS*	
10. Workover (2)		10. Workover (2)		1. 0	5. 2
11. Sec. attempt (3 ea.)		11. Sec. attempt (3 ea.)		2. 4	6. 1
12. Rotation (8)		12. Rotation (8)		3. 0	7. 0
13. Des. miss. (8)		13. Des. miss. (8)		4. 0	8. 5
Design Total	0	Design Total	1	Config.	0

Total Raw Score 12 Standard Score 49

SCORE SHEET—Bender-Gestalt Test

Name No. 38 Age 26 Sex M

Education College I.Q. 129 Diagnosis Manic-Depressive

DESIGN 1	
1. Wavy line (2)	
2. Dot, dash, cir. (3)	
3. Dashes (2)	
4. Circles (8)	
5. No. dots (2) each	
6. Dbl. row (8)	
7. Workover (2)	
8. Sec. attempt (3 ea.)	
9. Rotation (8)	
10. Des. miss. (8)	
Design Total	0

DESIGN 4	
1. Asym. Crv. (3)	
2. Break crv. (4)	
3. Crv. not center. (1)	
4. Curls (4)	
5. Not joined (8)	
6. Crv. rotation (3)	
7. Touch-up (8)	
8. Tremor (4)	
9. Distortion (8)	
10. Guide lines (2)	
11. Sec. attempt (3 ea.)	
12. Rotation (8)	
13. Des. miss. (8)	
Design Total	0

DESIGN 7	
1. Ends no. join. (8)	
2. Angles ext. (3)	3
3. Angles miss. (3)	
4. Ext. scat. (3)	
5. Dbl. line (1 ea.)	6
6. Tremor (4)	
7. Distortion (8 ea.)	
8. Guide lines (2)	
9. Sec. attempt (3 ea.)	
10. Rotation (8)	
11. Des. miss. (8)	
Design Total	9

DESIGN 2	
1. Wavy line (2)	2
2. Dash or dots (3)	
3. Shape cir. (3)	
4. Cir. miss., ext. (3)	
5. Cir. touch. (5)	
6. Dev. slant (3)	
7. No. col. (2 ea.)	
8. Fig. on 2 lines (8)	
9. Guide lines (2)	
10. Workover (2)	
11. Sec. attempt (3 ea.)	
12. Rotation (8)	
13. Des. miss. (8)	
Design Total	2

DESIGN 5	
1. Asymmetry (3)	
2. Dot, dash, cir. (3)	3
3. Dashes (2)	
4. Circles (8)	
5. Ext. join. dot (2)	2
6. Ext. rotation (3)	3
7. No. dots (2)	
8. Distortion (8)	
9. Guide lines (2)	
10. Workover (2)	
11. Sec. attempt (3 ea.)	
12. Rotation (8)	
13. Des. miss. (8)	
Design Total	8

DESIGN 8	
1. Ends no. join. (8)	
2. Angles ext. (3)	
3. Angles miss. (3)	
4. Ext. scat. (3)	
5. Dbl. line (1 ea.)	
6. Tremor (4)	4
7. Distortion (8 ea.)	
8. Guide lines (2)	
9. Workover (2)	
10. Sec. attempt (3 ea.)	
11. Rotation (8)	
12. Des. miss. (8)	
Design Total	4

DESIGN 3	
1. Asymmetry (3)	
2. Dot, dash, cir. (3)	3
3. Dashes (2)	
4. Circles (8)	
5. No. dots (2)	
6. Extra row (8)	
7. Blunting (8)	
8. Distortion (8)	
9. Guide lines (2)	
10. Workover (2)	
11. Sec. attempt (3 ea.)	
12. Rotation (8)	
13. Des. miss. (8)	
Design Total	3

DESIGN 6	
1. Asymmetry (3)	
2. Angles (2)	
3. Pt. crossing (2 ea.)	
4. Crv. extra (8)	
5. Dbl. line (1 ea.)	
6. Touch-up (8)	
7. Tremor (4)	4
8. Distortion (8)	
9. Guide lines (2)	
10. Workover (2)	
11. Sec. attempt (3 ea.)	
12. Rotation (8)	
13. Des. miss. (8)	
Design Total	4

CONFIG. DESIGN	
1. Place. Des. A. (2)	
2. Overlap (2 ea.)	
3. Compression (3)	
4. Lines drawn (8)	8
5. Order (2)	
6. No order (8)	
7. Rel. size (8)	
Total	8

DESIGN TOTALS			
1.	0	5.	8
2.	2	6.	4
3.	3	7.	9
4.	0	8.	4
Config.	8		

Total Raw Score 38 Standard Score 77

SCORE SHEET—Bender-Gestalt Test

Name No. 39 Age 21 Sex M

Education H. S. I.Q. ...... Diagnosis Schizo- Paranoid

DESIGN 1	
1. Wavy line (2)	2
2. Dot, dash, cir. (3)	3
3. Dashes (2)	
4. Circles (8)	
5. No. dots (2) each	
6. Dbl. row (8)	
7. Workover (2)	
8. Sec. attempt (3 ea.)	
9. Rotation (8)	
10. Des. miss. (8)	
Design Total	5

DESIGN 4	
1. Asym. Crv. (3)	3
2. Break crv. (4)	4
3. Crv. not center. (1)	
4. Curls (4)	4
5. Not joined (8)	
6. Crv. rotation (3)	
7. Touch-up (8)	
8. Tremor (4)	
9. Distortion (8)	
10. Guide lines (2)	
11. Sec. attempt (3 ea.)	3
12. Rotation (8)	
13. Des. miss. (8)	
Design Total	14

DESIGN 7	
1. Ends no. join. (8)	
2. Angles ext. (3)	
3. Angles miss. (3)	
4. Ext. scat. (3)	
5. Dbl. line (1 ea.)	2
6. Tremor (4)	
7. Distortion (8 ea.)	
8. Guide lines (2)	
9. Sec. attempt (3 ea.)	
10. Rotation (8)	
11. Des. miss. (8)	
Design Total	2

DESIGN 2	
1. Wavy line (2)	2
2. Dash or dots (3)	
3. Shape cir. (3)	
4. Cir. miss., ext. (3)	
5. Cir. touch. (5)	
6. Dev. slant (3)	3
7. No. col. (2 ea.)	
8. Fig. on 2 lines (8)	
9. Guide lines (2)	
10. Workover (2)	
11. Sec. attempt (3 ea.)	
12. Rotation (8)	
13. Des. miss. (8)	
Design Total	5

DESIGN 5	
1. Asymmetry (3)	
2. Dot, dash, cir. (3)	3
3. Dashes (2)	
4. Circles (8)	
5. Ext. join. dot (2)	2
6. Ext. rotation (3)	
7. No. dots (2)	
8. Distortion (8)	
9. Guide lines (2)	
10. Workover (2)	
11. Sec. attempt (3 ea.)	
12. Rotation (8)	
13. Des. miss. (8)	
Design Total	5

DESIGN 8	
1. Ends no. join. (8)	
2. Angles ext. (3)	
3. Angles miss. (3)	
4. Ext. scat. (3)	
5. Dbl. line (1 ea.)	4
6. Tremor (4)	
7. Distortion (8 ea.)	
8. Guide lines (2)	
9. Workover (2)	
10. Sec. attempt (3 ea.)	
11. Rotation (8)	
12. Des. miss. (8)	
Design Total	4

DESIGN 3	
1. Asymmetry (3)	
2. Dot, dash, cir. (3)	3
3. Dashes (2)	
4. Circles (8)	
5. No. dots (2)	2
6. Extra row (8)	
7. Blunting (8)	
8. Distortion (8)	
9. Guide lines (2)	
10. Workover (2)	2
11. Sec. attempt (3 ea.)	
12. Rotation (8)	
13. Des. miss. (8)	
Design Total	7

DESIGN 6	
1. Asymmetry (3)	3
2. Angles (2)	
3. Pt. crossing (2 ea.)	
4. Crv. extra (8)	
5. Dbl. line (1 ea.)	3
6. Touch-up (8)	
7. Tremor (4)	
8. Distortion (8)	
9. Guide lines (2)	
10. Workover (2)	2
11. Sec. attempt (3 ea.)	
12. Rotation (8)	
13. Des. miss. (8)	
Design Total	8

CONFIG. DESIGN	
1. Place. Des. A. (2)	2
2. Overlap (2 ea.)	
3. Compression (3)	
4. Lines drawn (8)	
5. Order (2)	
6. No order (8)	8
7. Rel. size (8)	
Total	10

DESIGN TOTALS			
1.	5	5.	5
2.	5	6.	8
3.	7	7.	2
4.	14	8.	4
Config.	10		

Total Raw Score 60 Standard Score 95

SCORE SHEET—Bender-Gestalt Test

Name No. 40 Age 48 Sex M

Education H.S. I.Q. 125 Diagnosis PN anxiety

DESIGN 1	
1. Wavy line (2)	
2. Dot, dash, cir. (3)	3
3. Dashes (2)	
4. Circles (8)	
5. No. dots (2) each	
6. Dbl. row (8)	
7. Workover (2)	
8. Sec. attempt (3 ea.)	
9. Rotation (8)	
10. Des. miss. (8)	
Design Total	3

DESIGN 4	
1. Asym. Crv. (3)	
2. Break crv. (4)	
3. Crv. not center. (1)	
4. Curls (4)	
5. Not joined (8)	
6. Crv. rotation (3)	
7. Touch-up (8)	
8. Tremor (4)	
9. Distortion (8)	
10. Guide lines (2)	
11. Sec. attempt (3 ea.)	
12. Rotation (8)	
13. Des. miss. (8)	
Design Total	0

DESIGN 7	
1. Ends no. join. (8)	
2. Angles ext. (3)	
3. Angles miss. (3)	
4. Ext. scat. (3)	
5. Dbl. line (1 ea.)	1
6. Tremor (4)	
7. Distortion (8 ea.)	
8. Guide lines (2)	
9. Sec. attempt (3 ea.)	
10. Rotation (8)	
11. Des. miss. (8)	
Design Total	1

DESIGN 2	
1. Wavy line (2)	2
2. Dash or dots (3)	
3. Shape cir. (3)	
4. Cir. miss., ext. (3)	
5. Cir. touch. (5)	
6. Dev. slant (3)	
7. No. col. (2 ea.)	
8. Fig. on 2 lines (8)	
9. Guide lines (2)	
10. Workover (2)	
11. Sec. attempt (3 ea.)	
12. Rotation (8)	
13. Des. miss. (8)	
Design Total	2

DESIGN 5	
1. Asymmetry (3)	
2. Dot, dash, cir. (3)	3
3. Dashes (2)	
4. Circles (8)	
5. Ext. join. dot (2)	
6. Ext. rotation (3)	
7. No. dots (2)	
8. Distortion (8)	
9. Guide lines (2)	2
10. Workover (2)	
11. Sec. attempt (3 ea.)	3
12. Rotation (8)	
13. Des. miss. (8)	
Design Total	8

DESIGN 8	
1. Ends no. join. (8)	
2. Angles ext. (3)	
3. Angles miss. (3)	
4. Ext. scat. (3)	
5. Dbl. line (1 ea.)	2
6. Tremor (4)	4
7. Distortion (8 ea.)	
8. Guide lines (2)	
9. Workover (2)	
10. Sec. attempt (3 ea.)	
11. Rotation (8)	
12. Des. miss. (8)	
Design Total	6

DESIGN 3	
1. Asymmetry (3)	
2. Dot, dash, cir. (3)	3
3. Dashes (2)	
4. Circles (8)	
5. No. dots (2)	
6. Extra row (8)	
7. Blunting (8)	
8. Distortion (8)	
9. Guide lines (2)	
10. Workover (2)	
11. Sec. attempt (3 ea.)	
12. Rotation (8)	
13. Des. miss. (8)	
Design Total	3

DESIGN 6	
1. Asymmetry (3)	
2. Angles (2)	
3. Pt. crossing (2 ea.)	
4. Crv. extra (8)	
5. Dbl. line (1 ea.)	
6. Touch-up (8)	
7. Tremor (4)	
8. Distortion (8)	
9. Guide lines (2)	
10. Workover (2)	
11. Sec. attempt (3 ea.)	
12. Rotation (8)	
13. Des. miss. (8)	
Design Total	0

CONFIG. DESIGN	
1. Place. Des. A. (2)	
2. Overlap (2 ea.)	2
3. Compression (3)	
4. Lines drawn (8)	
5. Order (2)	
6. No order (8)	
7. Rel. size (8)	
Total	2

DESIGN TOTALS			
1.	3	5.	8
2.	2	6.	0
3.	3	7.	1
4.	0	8.	6
Config.	2		

Total Raw Score 25 Standard Score 57

SCORE SHEET—Bender-Gestalt Test

Name No. 41 Age 19 Sex F

Education College I.Q. ...... Diagnosis Normal

DESIGN 1	
1. Wavy line (2)	
2. Dot, dash, cir. (3)	3
3. Dashes (2)	
4. Circles (8)	
5. No. dots (2) each	
6. Dbl. row (8)	
7. Workover (2)	
8. Sec. attempt (3 ea.)	
9. Rotation (8)	
10. Des. miss. (8)	
Design Total	3

DESIGN 4	
1. Asym. Crv. (3)	
2. Break crv. (4)	
3. Crv. not center. (1)	
4. Curls (4)	
5. Not joined (8)	
6. Crv. rotation (3)	
7. Touch-up (8)	
8. Tremor (4)	
9. Distortion (8)	
10. Guide lines (2)	
11. Sec. attempt (3 ea.)	
12. Rotation (8)	
13. Des. miss. (8)	
Design Total	0

DESIGN 7	
1. Ends no. join. (8)	
2. Angles ext. (3)	
3. Angles miss. (3)	
4. Ext. scat. (3)	
5. Dbl. line (1 ea.)	
6. Tremor (4)	
7. Distortion (8 ea.)	
8. Guide lines (2)	
9. Sec. attempt (3 ea.)	
10. Rotation (8)	
11. Des. miss. (8)	
Design Total	0

DESIGN 2	
1. Wavy line (2)	2
2. Dash or dots (3)	
3. Shape cir. (3)	
4. Cir. miss., ext. (3)	
5. Cir. touch. (5)	
6. Dev. slant (3)	
7. No. col. (2 ea.)	
8. Fig. on 2 lines (8)	
9. Guide lines (2)	
10. Workover (2)	
11. Sec. attempt (3 ea.)	
12. Rotation (8)	
13. Des. miss. (8)	
Design Total	2

DESIGN 5	
1. Asymmetry (3)	
2. Dot, dash, cir. (3)	
3. Dashes (2)	
4. Circles (8)	
5. Ext. join. dot (2)	
6. Ext. rotation (3)	
7. No. dots (2)	
8. Distortion (8)	
9. Guide lines (2)	
10. Workover (2)	
11. Sec. attempt (3 ea.)	
12. Rotation (8)	
13. Des. miss. (8)	
Design Total	0

DESIGN 8	
1. Ends no. join. (8)	
2. Angles ext. (3)	
3. Angles miss. (3)	
4. Ext. scat. (3)	
5. Dbl. line (1 ea.)	1
6. Tremor (4)	
7. Distortion (8 ea.)	
8. Guide lines (2)	
9. Workover (2)	
10. Sec. attempt (3 ea.)	
11. Rotation (8)	
12. Des. miss. (8)	
Design Total	1

DESIGN 3	
1. Asymmetry (3)	
2. Dot, dash, cir. (3)	
3. Dashes (2)	
4. Circles (8)	
5. No. dots (2)	
6. Extra row (8)	
7. Blunting (8)	
8. Distortion (8)	
9. Guide lines (2)	
10. Workover (2)	
11. Sec. attempt (3 ea.)	
12. Rotation (8)	
13. Des. miss. (8)	
Design Total	0

DESIGN 6	
1. Asymmetry (3)	
2. Angles (2)	
3. Pt. crossing (2 ea.)	
4. Crv. extra (8)	
5. Dbl. line (1 ea.)	
6. Touch-up (8)	
7. Tremor (4)	
8. Distortion (8)	
9. Guide lines (2)	
10. Workover (2)	
11. Sec. attempt (3 ea.)	
12. Rotation (8)	
13. Des. miss. (8)	
Design Total	0

CONFIG. DESIGN	
1. Place. Des. A. (2)	
2. Overlap (2 ea.)	
3. Compression (3)	
4. Lines drawn (8)	
5. Order (2)	
6. No order (8)	
7. Rel. size (8)	
Total	0

DESIGN TOTALS			
1.	3	5.	0
2.	2	6.	0
3.	0	7.	0
4.	0	8.	1
Config.	0		

Total Raw Score 6 Standard Score 42

SCORE SHEET—BENDER-GESTALT TEST

Name No. 42 Age 24 Sex M

Education H.S. I.Q. ...... Diagnosis Normal

DESIGN 1
1. Wavy line (2) ......
2. Dot, dash, cir. (3) ......
3. Dashes (2) ......
4. Circles (8) ......
5. No. dots (2) each ......
6. Dbl. row (8) ......
7. Workover (2) 2
8. Sec. attempt (3 ea.) ......
9. Rotation (8) ......
10. Des. miss. (8) ......

Design Total 2

DESIGN 2
1. Wavy line (2) 2
2. Dash or dots (3) ......
3. Shape cir. (3) ......
4. Cir. miss., ext. (3) ......
5. Cir. touch. (5) ......
6. Dev. slant (3) ......
7. No. col. (2 ea.) ......
8. Fig. on 2 lines (8) ......
9. Guide lines (2) ......
10. Workover (2) ......
11. Sec. attempt (3 ea.) ......
12. Rotation (8) ......
13. Des. miss. (8) ......

Design Total 2

DESIGN 3
1. Asymmetry (3) 3
2. Dot, dash, cir. (3) ......
3. Dashes (2) ......
4. Circles (8) ......
5. No. dots (2) ......
6. Extra row (8) ......
7. Blunting (8) ......
8. Distortion (8) ......
9. Guide lines (2) ......
10. Workover (2) ......
11. Sec. attempt (3 ea.) ......
12. Rotation (8) ......
13. Des. miss. (8) ......

Design Total 3

DESIGN 4
1. Asym. Crv. (3) ......
2. Break crv. (4) ......
3. Crv. not center. (1) ......
4. Curls (4) ......
5. Not joined (8) ......
6. Crv. rotation (3) ......
7. Touch-up (8) ......
8. Tremor (4) ......
9. Distortion (8) ......
10. Guide lines (2) ......
11. Sec. attempt (3 ea.) ......
12. Rotation (8) ......
13. Des. miss. (8) ......

Design Total 0

DESIGN 5
1. Asymmetry (3) ......
2. Dot, dash, cir. (3) ......
3. Dashes (2) ......
4. Circles (8) ......
5. Ext. join. dot (2) 2
6. Ext. rotation (3) ......
7. No. dots (2) ......
8. Distortion (8) ......
9. Guide lines (2) ......
10. Workover (2) ......
11. Sec. attempt (3 ea.) ......
12. Rotation (8) ......
13. Des. miss. (8) ......

Design Total 2

DESIGN 6
1. Asymmetry (3) ......
2. Angles (2) ......
3. Pt. crossing (2 ea.) ......
4. Crv. extra (8) ......
5. Dbl. line (1 ea.) ......
6. Touch-up (8) ......
7. Tremor (4) ......
8. Distortion (8) ......
9. Guide lines (2) ......
10. Workover (2) ......
11. Sec. attempt (3 ea.) ......
12. Rotation (8) ......
13. Des. miss. (8) ......

Design Total 0

DESIGN 7
1. Ends no. join. (8) ......
2. Angles ext. (3) ......
3. Angles miss. (3) ......
4. Ext. scat. (3) ......
5. Dbl. line (1 ea.) ......
6. Tremor (4) ......
7. Distortion (8 ea.) ......
8. Guide lines (2) ......
9. Sec. attempt (3 ea.) ......
10. Rotation (8) ......
11. Des. miss. (8) ......

Design Total 0

DESIGN 8
1. Ends no. join. (8) ......
2. Angles ext. (3) 3
3. Angles miss. (3) ......
4. Ext. scat. (3) ......
5. Dbl. line (1 ea.) ......
6. Tremor (4) ......
7. Distortion (8 ea.) ......
8. Guide lines (2) ......
9. Workover (2) ......
10. Sec. attempt (3 ea.) ......
11. Rotation (8) ......
12. Des. miss. (8) ......

Design Total 3

CONFIG. DESIGN
1. Place. Des. A. (2) ......
2. Overlap (2 ea.) ......
3. Compression (3) ......
4. Lines drawn (8) ......
5. Order (2) ......
6. No order (8) ......
7. Rel. size (8) ......

Total 0

DESIGN TOTALS

1. 2 5. 2
2. 2 6. 0
3. 3 7. 0
4. 0 8. 0

Config. 12

Total Raw Score 12 Standard Score 44

SCORE SHEET—BENDER-GESTALT TEST

Name No. 43 Age 21 Sex M

Education H.S. I.Q. ...... Diagnosis Schizo-Catatonic

DESIGN 1
1. Wavy line (2) ......
2. Dot, dash, cir. (3) ......
3. Dashes (2) ......
4. Circles (8) ......
5. No. dots (2) each ......
6. Dbl. row (8) ......
7. Workover (2) 2
8. Sec. attempt (3 ea.) ......
9. Rotation (8) ......
10. Des. miss. (8) ......

Design Total 2

DESIGN 2
1. Wavy line (2) 2
2. Dash or dots (3) ......
3. Shape cir. (3) ......
4. Cir. miss., ext. (3) ......
5. Cir. touch. (5) ......
6. Dev. slant (3) ......
7. No. col. (2 ea.) ......
8. Fig. on 2 lines (8) ......
9. Guide lines (2) ......
10. Workover (2) ......
11. Sec. attempt (3 ea.) ......
12. Rotation (8) ......
13. Des. miss. (8) ......

Design Total 2

DESIGN 3
1. Asymmetry (3) ......
2. Dot, dash, cir. (3) ......
3. Dashes (2) ......
4. Circles (8) ......
5. No. dots (2) ......
6. Extra row (8) ......
7. Blunting (8) ......
8. Distortion (8) ......
9. Guide lines (2) ......
10. Workover (2) 2
11. Sec. attempt (3 ea.) ......
12. Rotation (8) ......
13. Des. miss. (8) ......

Design Total 2

DESIGN 4
1. Asym. Crv. (3) 3
2. Break crv. (4) 4
3. Crv. not center. (1) ......
4. Curls (4) ......
5. Not joined (8) ......
6. Crv. rotation (3) ......
7. Touch-up (8) ......
8. Tremor (4) ......
9. Distortion (8) ......
10. Guide lines (2) ......
11. Sec. attempt (3 ea.) ......
12. Rotation (8) ......
13. Des. miss. (8) ......

Design Total 7

DESIGN 5
1. Asymmetry (3) 3
2. Dot, dash, cir. (3) ......
3. Dashes (2) ......
4. Circles (8) ......
5. Ext. join. dot (2) ......
6. Ext. rotation (3) ......
7. No. dots (2) ......
8. Distortion (8) ......
9. Guide lines (2) ......
10. Workover (2) 2
11. Sec. attempt (3 ea.) ......
12. Rotation (8) ......
13. Des. miss. (8) ......

Design Total 5

DESIGN 6
1. Asymmetry (3) ......
2. Angles (2) ......
3. Pt. crossing (2 ea.) ......
4. Crv. extra (8) ......
5. Dbl. line (1 ea.) 4
6. Touch-up (8) ......
7. Tremor (4) ......
8. Distortion (8) ......
9. Guide lines (2) ......
10. Workover (2) ......
11. Sec. attempt (3 ea.) 6
12. Rotation (8) ......
13. Des. miss. (8) ......

Design Total 10

DESIGN 7
1. Ends no. join. (8) ......
2. Angles ext. (3) ......
3. Angles miss. (3) ......
4. Ext. scat. (3) ......
5. Dbl. line (1 ea.) 4
6. Tremor (4) ......
7. Distortion (8 ea.) ......
8. Guide lines (2) ......
9. Sec. attempt (3 ea.) 3
10. Rotation (8) ......
11. Des. miss. (8) ......

Design Total 7

DESIGN 8
1. Ends no. join. (8) ......
2. Angles ext. (3) ......
3. Angles miss. (3) ......
4. Ext. scat. (3) ......
5. Dbl. line (1 ea.) 5
6. Tremor (4) 4
7. Distortion (8 ea.) ......
8. Guide lines (2) ......
9. Workover (2) ......
10. Sec. attempt (3 ea.) ......
11. Rotation (8) ......
12. Des. miss. (8) ......

Design Total 9

CONFIG. DESIGN
1. Place. Des. A. (2) 2
2. Overlap (2 ea.) 4
3. Compression (3) ......
4. Lines drawn (8) ......
5. Order (2) ......
6. No order (8) 8
7. Rel. size (8) ......

Total 14

DESIGN TOTALS

1. 2 5. 5
2. 2 6. 10
3. 2 7. 7
4. 7 8. 9

Config. 14

Total Raw Score 58 Standard Score 92

SCORE SHEET—BENDER-GESTALT TEST

Name No. 44 Age 22 Sex M

Education College I.Q. ...... Diagnosis Normal

DESIGN 1
1. Wavy line (2) ......
2. Dot, dash, cir. (3) 3
3. Dashes (2) ......
4. Circles (8) ......
5. No. dots (2) each ......
6. Dbl. row (8) ......
7. Workover (2) ......
8. Sec. attempt (3 ea.) ......
9. Rotation (8) ......
10. Des. miss. (8) ......

Design Total 3

DESIGN 2
1. Wavy line (2) ......
2. Dash or dots (3) ......
3. Shape cir. (3) ......
4. Cir. miss., ext. (3) ......
5. Cir. touch. (5) ......
6. Dev. slant (3) 3
7. No. col. (2 ea.) ......
8. Fig. on 2 lines (8) ......
9. Guide lines (2) ......
10. Workover (2) ......
11. Sec. attempt (3 ea.) ......
12. Rotation (8) ......
13. Des. miss. (8) ......

Design Total 3

DESIGN 3
1. Asymmetry (3) ......
2. Dot, dash, cir. (3) 3
3. Dashes (2) ......
4. Circles (8) ......
5. No. dots (2) ......
6. Extra row (8) ......
7. Blunting (8) ......
8. Distortion (8) ......
9. Guide lines (2) ......
10. Workover (2) ......
11. Sec. attempt (3 ea.) ......
12. Rotation (8) ......
13. Des. miss. (8) ......

Design Total 3

DESIGN 4
1. Asym. Crv. (3) 3
2. Break crv. (4) ......
3. Crv. not center. (1) ......
4. Curls (4) ......
5. Not joined (8) ......
6. Crv. rotation (3) ......
7. Touch-up (8) ......
8. Tremor (4) ......
9. Distortion (8) ......
10. Guide lines (2) ......
11. Sec. attempt (3 ea.) ......
12. Rotation (8) ......
13. Des. miss. (8) ......

Design Total 3

DESIGN 5
1. Asymmetry (3) ......
2. Dot, dash, cir. (3) ......
3. Dashes (2) ......
4. Circles (8) ......
5. Ext. join. dot (2) 2
6. Ext. rotation (3) ......
7. No. dots (2) ......
8. Distortion (8) ......
9. Guide lines (2) ......
10. Workover (2) ......
11. Sec. attempt (3 ea.) ......
12. Rotation (8) ......
13. Des. miss. (8) ......

Design Total 2

DESIGN 6
1. Asymmetry (3) ......
2. Angles (2) ......
3. Pt. crossing (2 ea.) ......
4. Crv. extra (8) ......
5. Dbl. line (1 ea.) ......
6. Touch-up (8) ......
7. Tremor (4) ......
8. Distortion (8) ......
9. Guide lines (2) ......
10. Workover (2) ......
11. Sec. attempt (3 ea.) ......
12. Rotation (8) ......
13. Des. miss. (8) ......

Design Total 0

DESIGN 7
1. Ends no. join. (8) ......
2. Angles ext. (3) ......
3. Angles miss. (3) ......
4. Ext. scat. (3) ......
5. Dbl. line (1 ea.) ......
6. Tremor (4) ......
7. Distortion (8 ea.) ......
8. Guide lines (2) ......
9. Sec. attempt (3 ea.) ......
10. Rotation (8) ......
11. Des. miss. (8) ......

Design Total 0

DESIGN 8
1. Ends no. join. (8) ......
2. Angles ext. (3) ......
3. Angles miss. (3) ......
4. Ext. scat. (3) ......
5. Dbl. line (1 ea.) ......
6. Tremor (4) ......
7. Distortion (8 ea.) ......
8. Guide lines (2) ......
9. Workover (2) ......
10. Sec. attempt (3 ea.) ......
11. Rotation (8) ......
12. Des. miss. (8) ......

Design Total 0

CONFIG. DESIGN
1. Place. Des. A. (2) 2
2. Overlap (2 ea.) ......
3. Compression (3) ......
4. Lines drawn (8) ......
5. Order (2) ......
6. No order (8) ......
7. Rel. size (8) ......

Total 2

DESIGN TOTALS

1. 3 5. 2
2. 3 6. 0
3. 3 7. 0
4. 3 8. 0

Config. 2

Total Raw Score 16 Standard Score 53

SCORE SHEET—BENDER-GESTALT TEST

Name No. 45 Age 36 Sex M

Education College I.Q. ...... Diagnosis Normal

DESIGN 1
1. Wavy line (2) ......
2. Dot, dash, cir. (3) ......
3. Dashes (2) ......
4. Circles (8) ......
5. No. dots (2) each ......
6. Dbl. row (8) ......
7. Workover (2) ......
8. Sec. attempt (3 ea.) ......
9. Rotation (8) ......
10. Des. miss. (8) ......

Design Total 0

DESIGN 2
1. Wavy line (2) ......
2. Dash or dots (3) ......
3. Shape cir. (3) ......
4. Cir. miss., ext. (3) ......
5. Cir. touch. (5) ......
6. Dev. slant (3) ......
7. No. col. (2 ea.) ......
8. Fig. on 2 lines (8) ......
9. Guide lines (2) ......
10. Workover (2) ......
11. Sec. attempt (3 ea.) ......
12. Rotation (8) ......
13. Des. miss. (8) ......

Design Total 0

DESIGN 3
1. Asymmetry (3) ......
2. Dot, dash, cir. (3) ......
3. Dashes (2) ......
4. Circles (8) ......
5. No. dots (2) ......
6. Extra row (8) ......
7. Blunting (8) ......
8. Distortion (8) ......
9. Guide lines (2) ......
10. Workover (2) ......
11. Sec. attempt (3 ea.) ......
12. Rotation (8) ......
13. Des. miss. (8) ......

Design Total 0

DESIGN 4
1. Asym. Crv. (3) ......
2. Break crv. (4) ......
3. Crv. not center. (1) ......
4. Curls (4) ......
5. Not joined (8) ......
6. Crv. rotation (3) ......
7. Touch-up (8) ......
8. Tremor (4) ......
9. Distortion (8) ......
10. Guide lines (2) ......
11. Sec. attempt (3 ea.) ......
12. Rotation (8) ......
13. Des. miss. (8) ......

Design Total 0

DESIGN 5
1. Asymmetry (3) ......
2. Dot, dash, cir. (3) ......
3. Dashes (2) ......
4. Circles (8) ......
5. Ext. join. dot (2) ......
6. Ext. rotation (3) ......
7. No. dots (2) ......
8. Distortion (8) ......
9. Guide lines (2) ......
10. Workover (2) ......
11. Sec. attempt (3 ea.) ......
12. Rotation (8) ......
13. Des. miss. (8) ......

Design Total 0

DESIGN 6
1. Asymmetry (3) ......
2. Angles (2) ......
3. Pt. crossing (2 ea.) ......
4. Crv. extra (8) ......
5. Dbl. line (1 ea.) ......
6. Touch-up (8) ......
7. Tremor (4) 4
8. Distortion (8) ......
9. Guide lines (2) ......
10. Workover (2) ......
11. Sec. attempt (3 ea.) ......
12. Rotation (8) ......
13. Des. miss. (8) ......

Design Total 4

DESIGN 7
1. Ends no. join. (8) ......
2. Angles ext. (3) ......
3. Angles miss. (3) ......
4. Ext. scat. (3) ......
5. Dbl. line (1 ea.) ......
6. Tremor (4) ......
7. Distortion (8 ea.) ......
8. Guide lines (2) ......
9. Sec. attempt (3 ea.) ......
10. Rotation (8) ......
11. Des. miss. (8) ......

Design Total 0

DESIGN 8
1. Ends no. join. (8) ......
2. Angles ext. (3) ......
3. Angles miss. (3) ......
4. Ext. scat. (3) ......
5. Dbl. line (1 ea.) ......
6. Tremor (4) 4
7. Distortion (8 ea.) ......
8. Guide lines (2) ......
9. Workover (2) ......
10. Sec. attempt (3 ea.) ......
11. Rotation (8) ......
12. Des. miss. (8) ......

Design Total 4

CONFIG. DESIGN
1. Place. Des. A. (2) ......
2. Overlap (2 ea.) ......
3. Compression (3) ......
4. Lines drawn (8) ......
5. Order (2) ......
6. No order (8) ......
7. Rel. size (8) ......

Total 0

DESIGN TOTALS

1. 0 5. 0
2. 0 6. 4
3. 0 7. 0
4. 0 8. 4

Config. 0

Total Raw Score 8 Standard Score 45

ATLAS OF SCORED RECORDS

Record 1. Male feeble-minded, M.A. 5-3, C.A. 9-11 (not scored).

Record 2. Male, feeble-minded, M.A. 4-4, C.A. 19-9 (not scored).

Record 3. Male, feeble-minded, M.A. 6-2, C.A. 20 (not scored).

Records 4–25. Practice—to be scored and checked against completed score sheet after scoring *each* record.

Records 26–45. All twenty records are to be scored before checking against completed score sheets to check scorer's reliability and validity..

Record 1

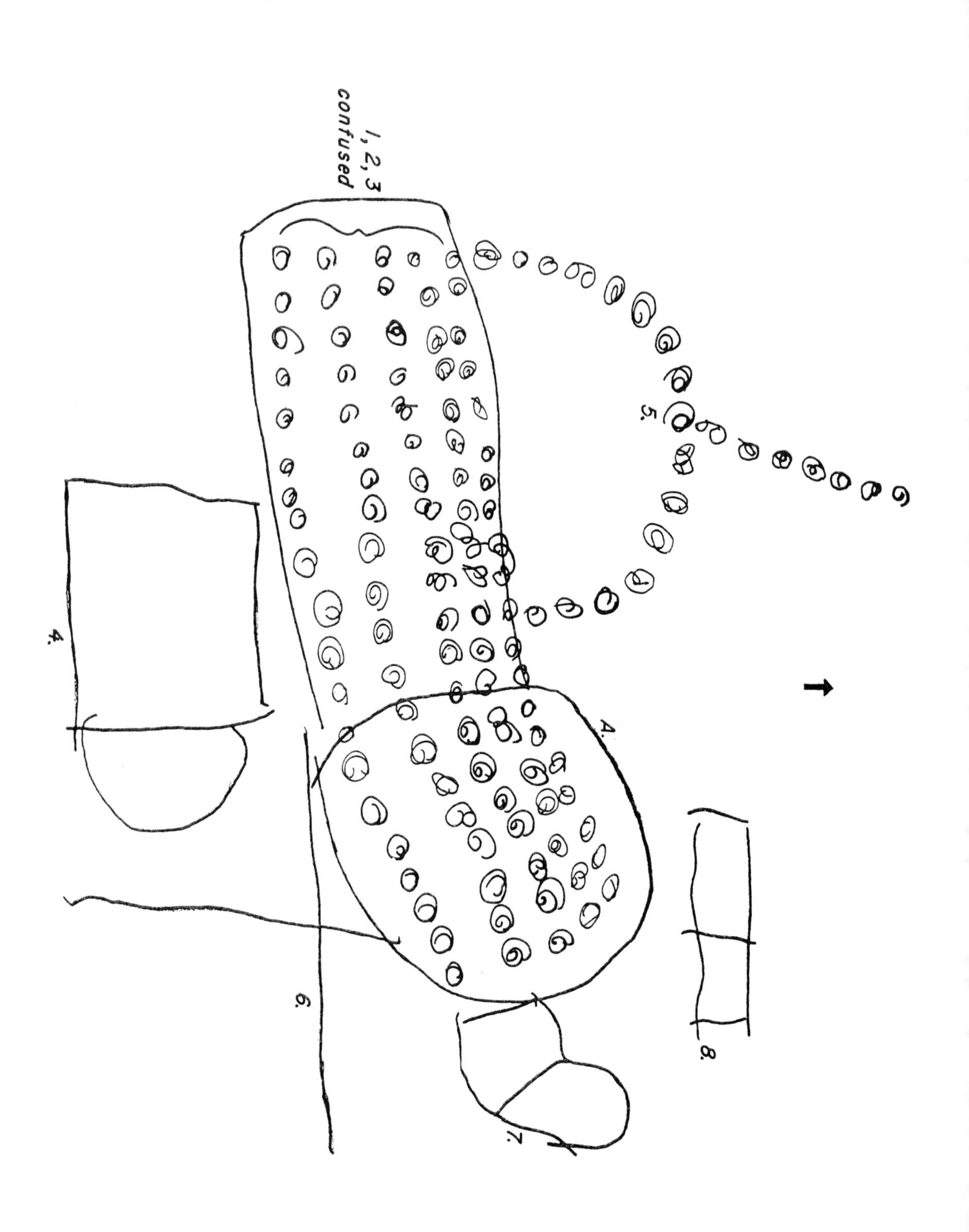

Record 2

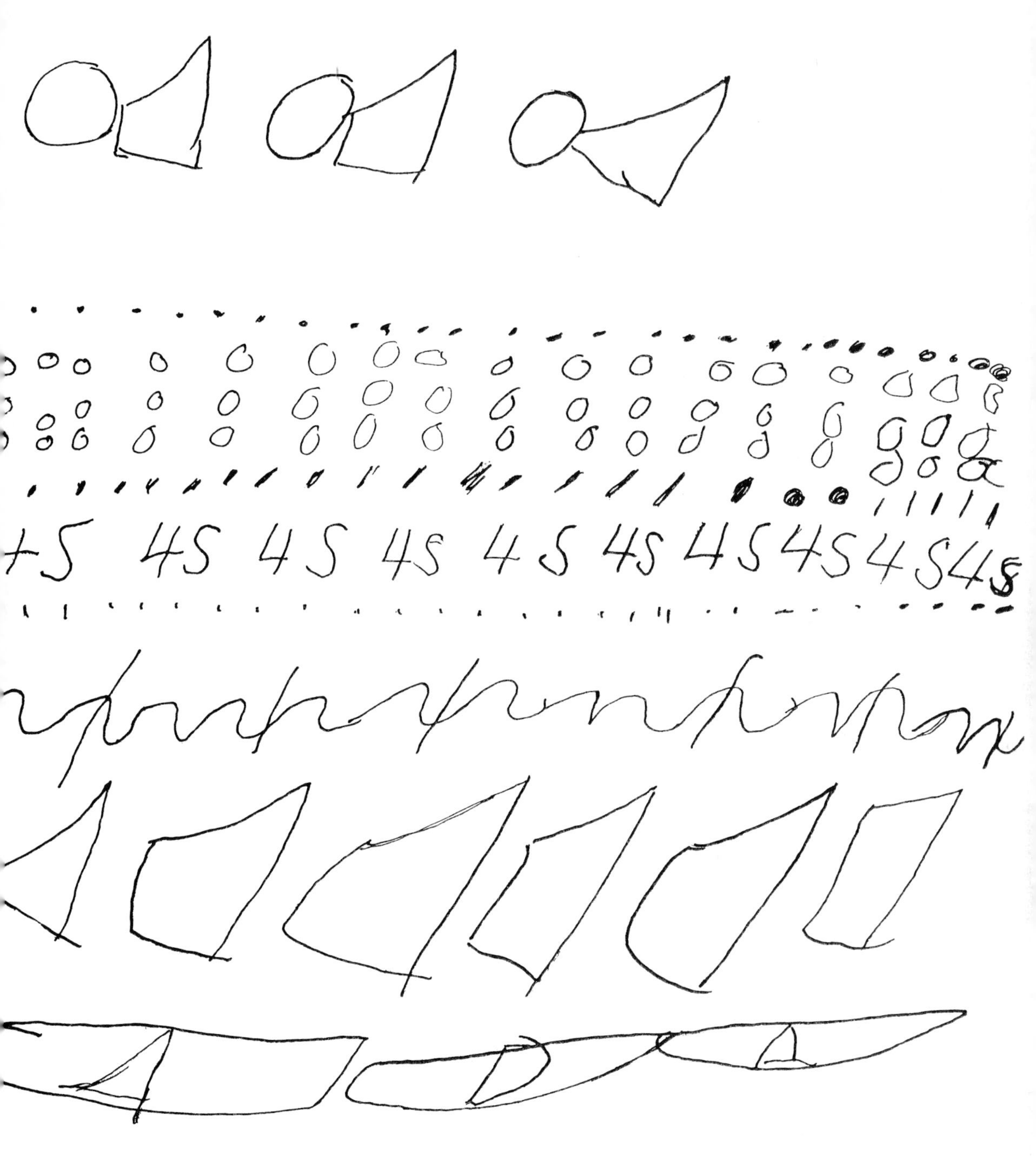

Record 3

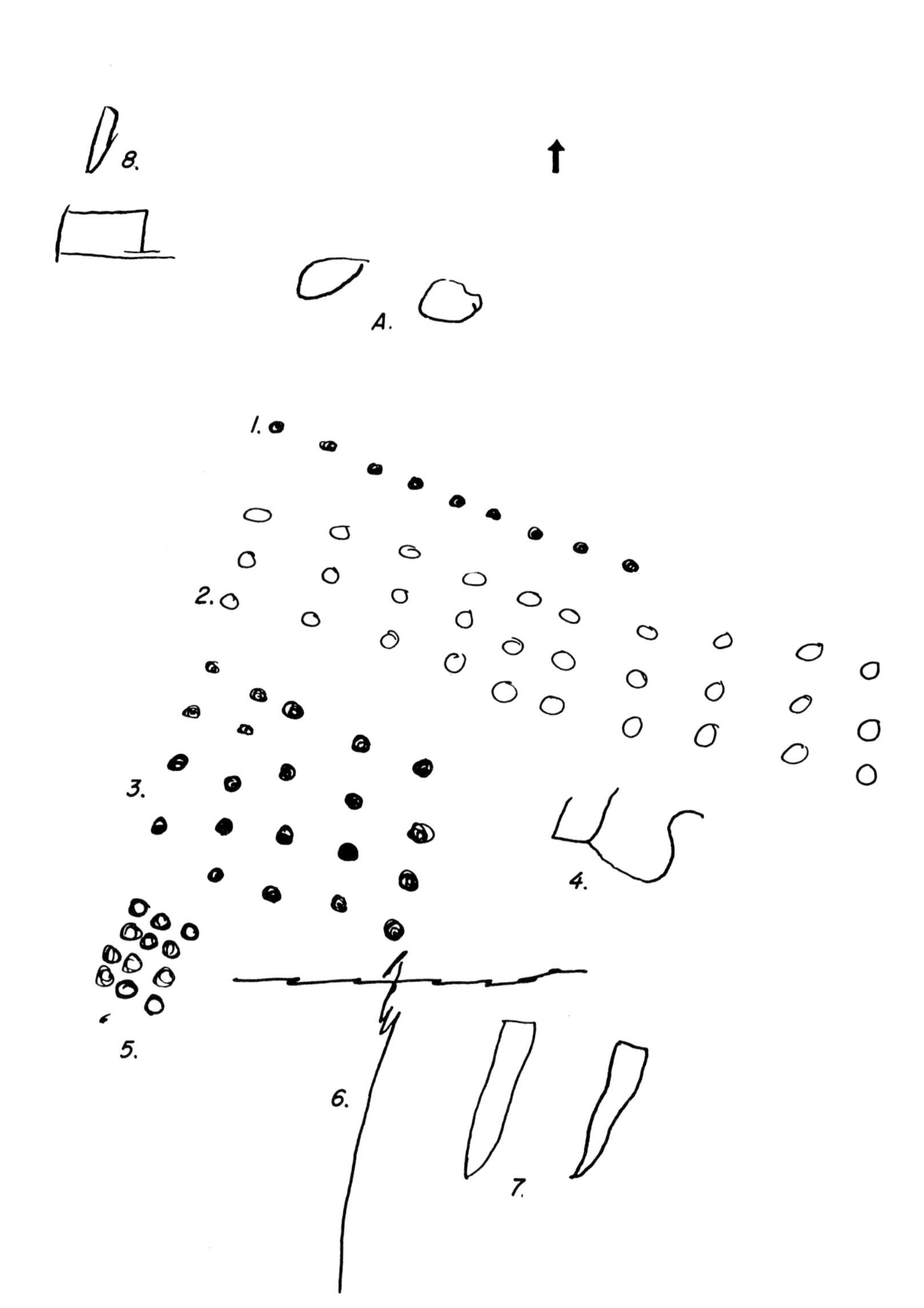

Record 4

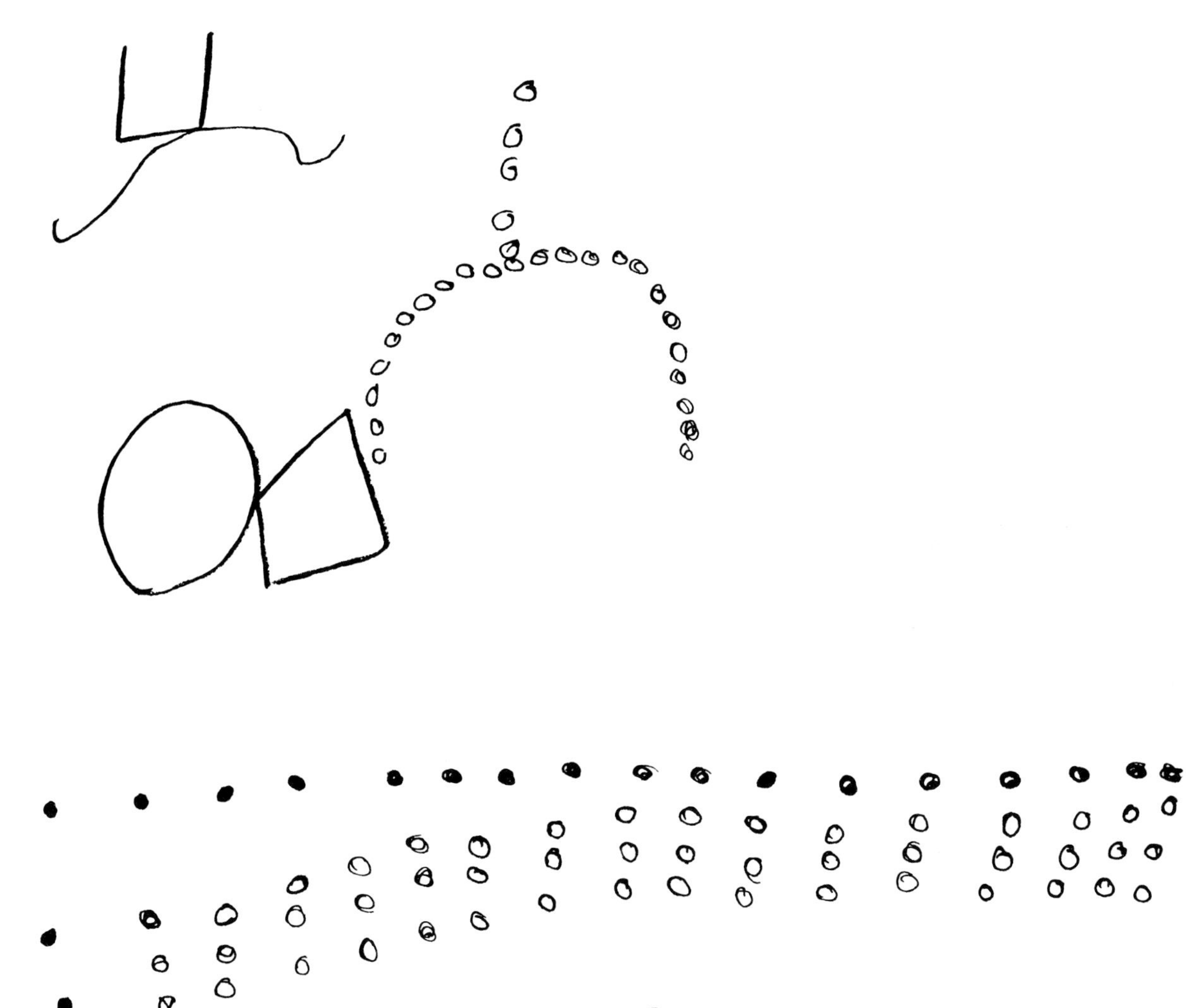

Record 5: first sheet

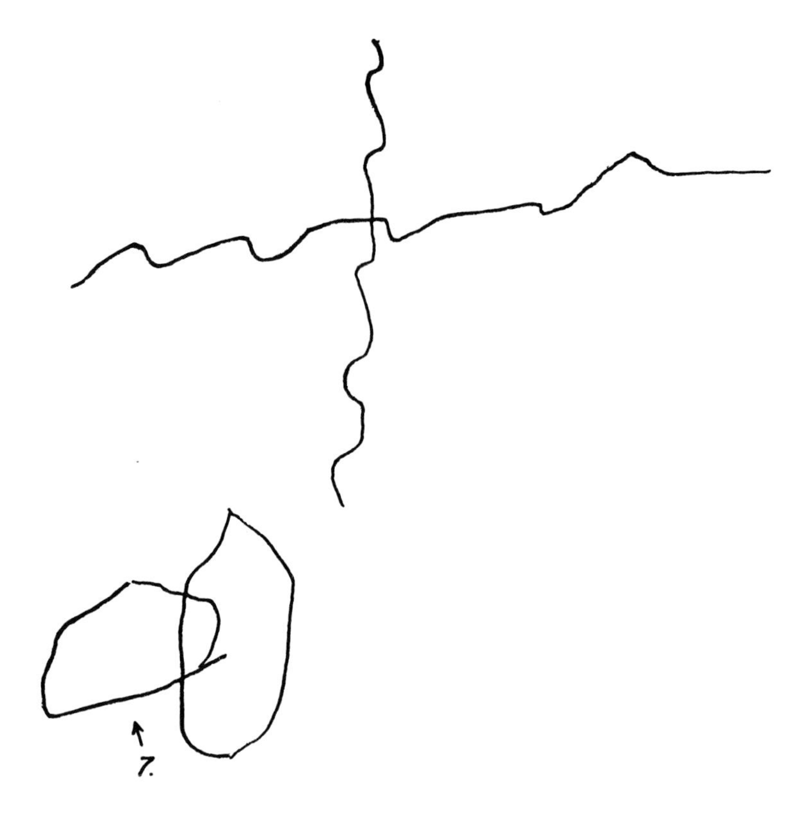

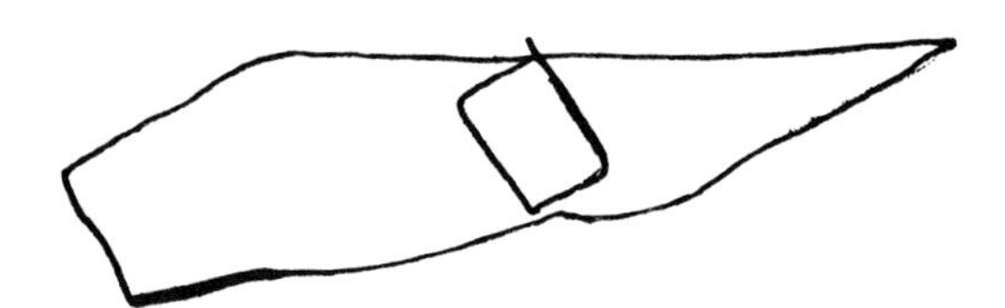

Record 5: second sheet

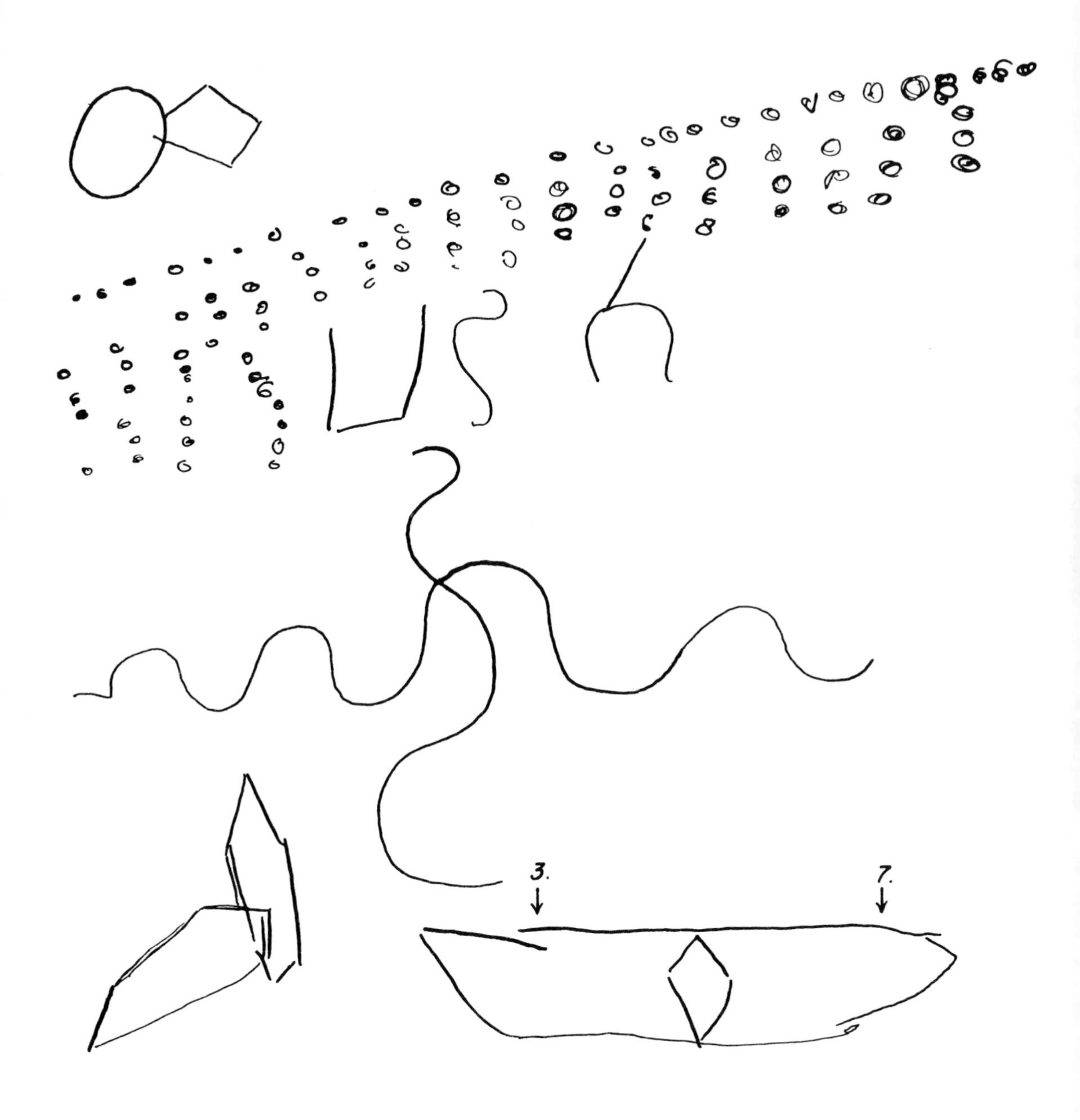
3.
7.

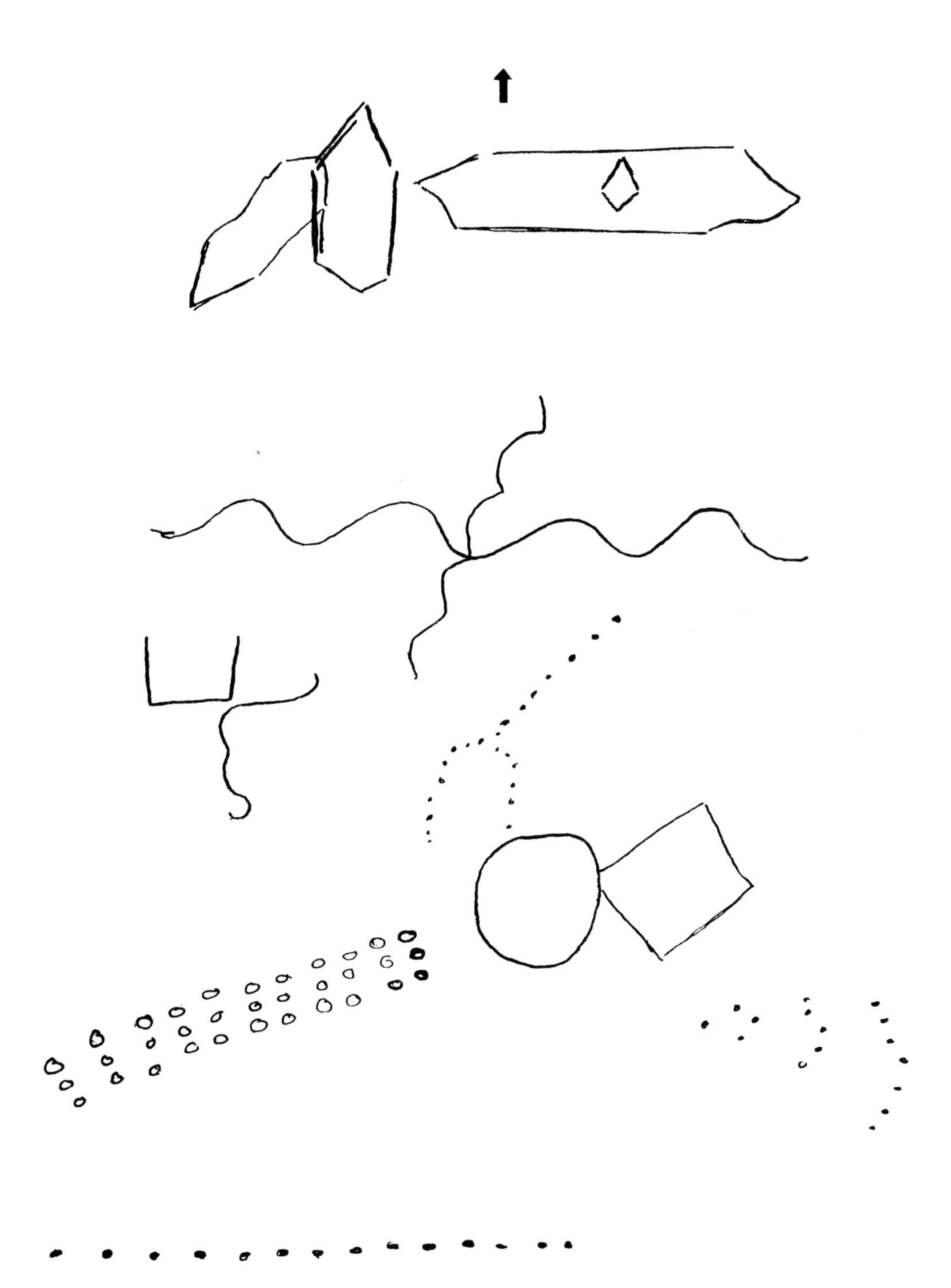

Record 8

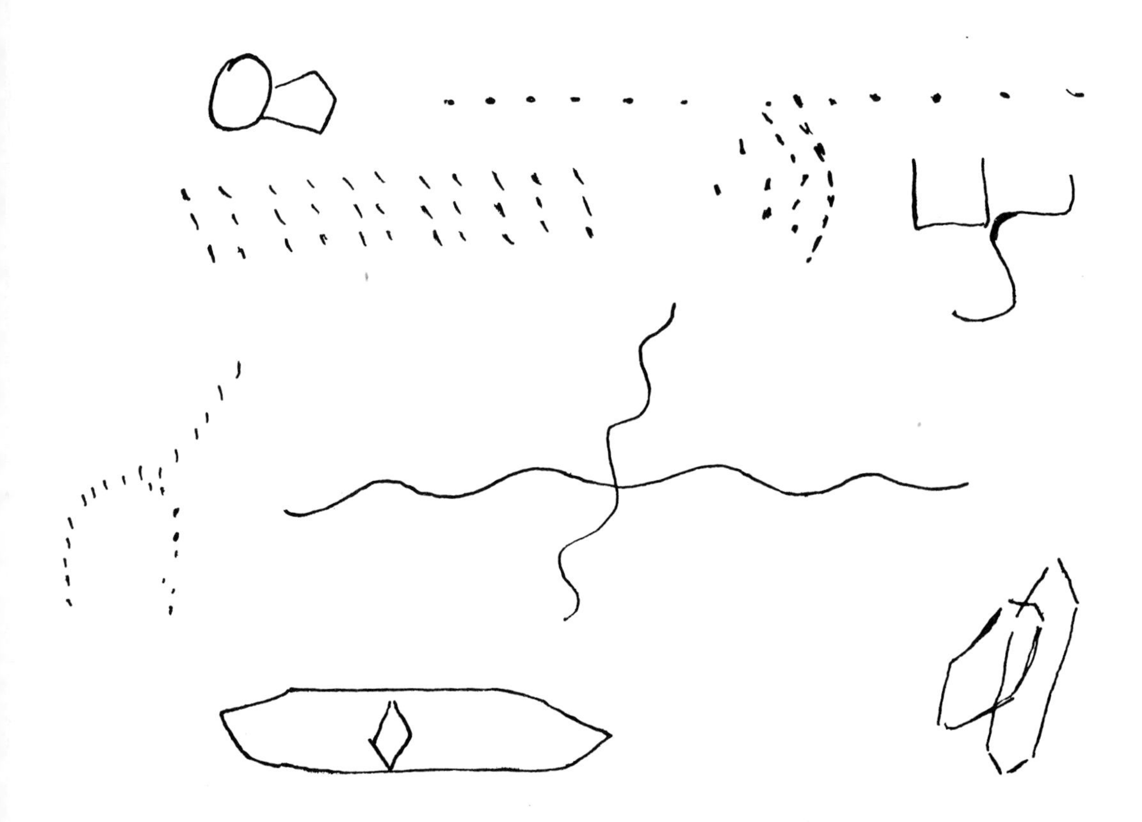

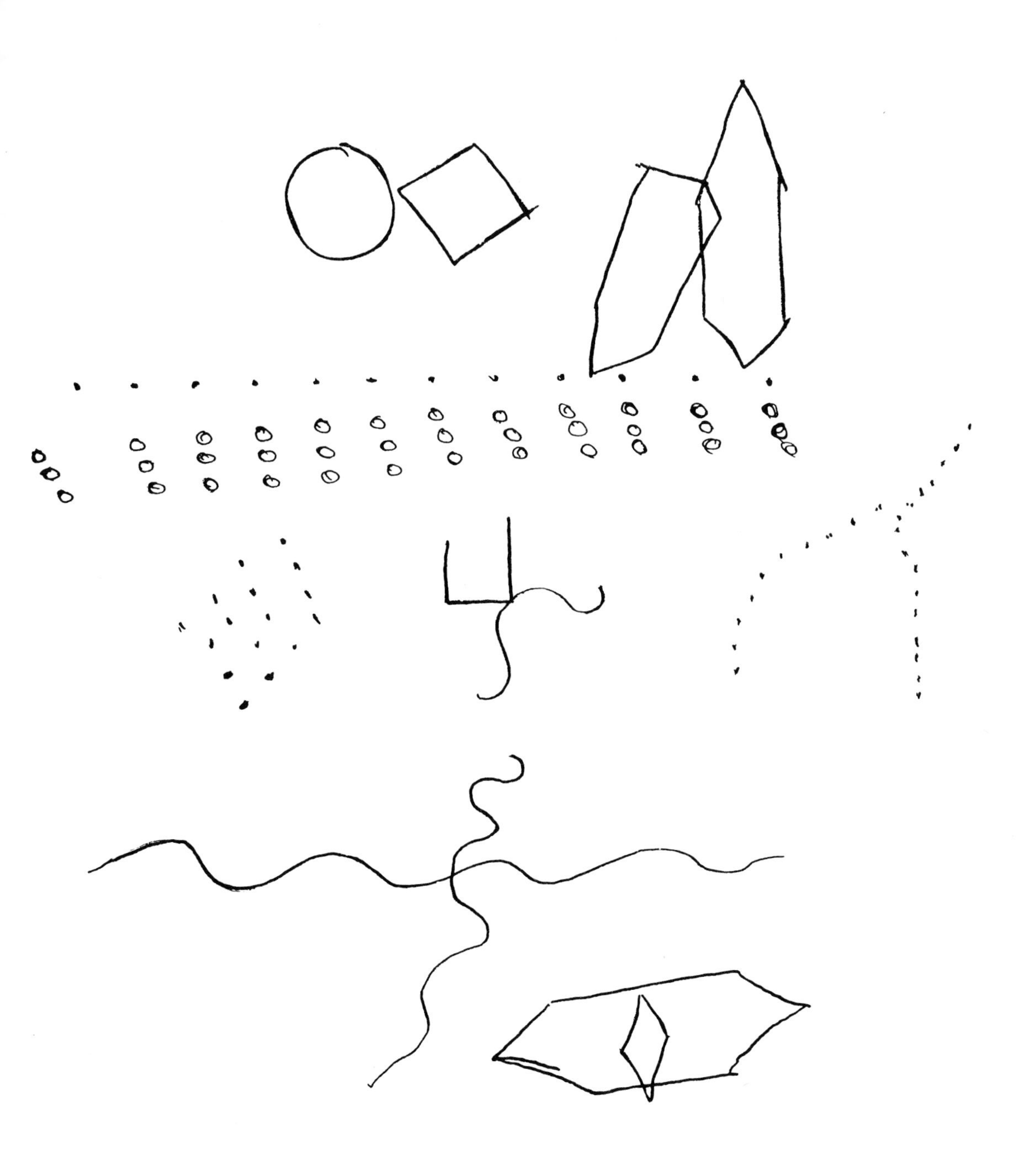

Record 10

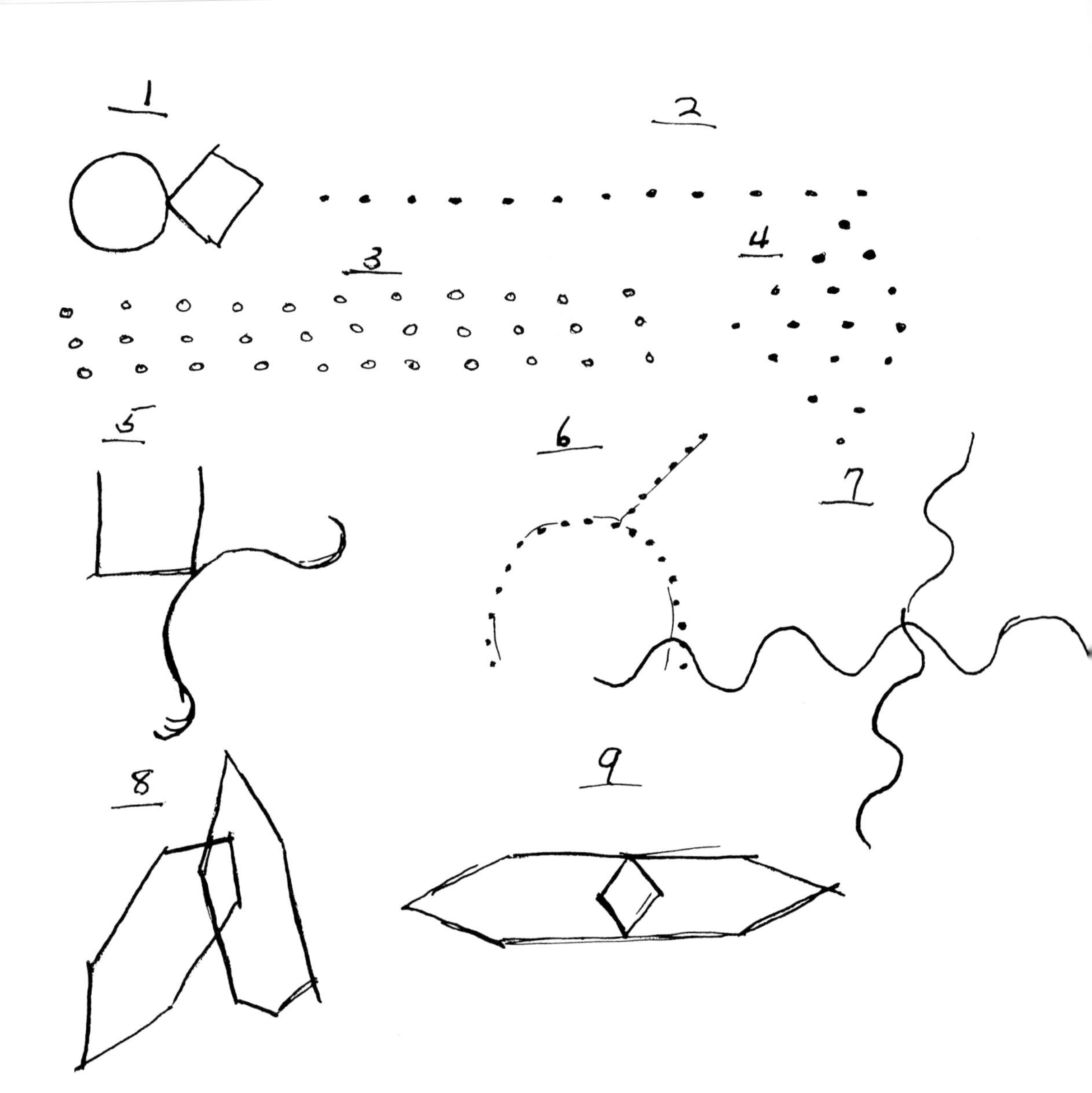

Record 11

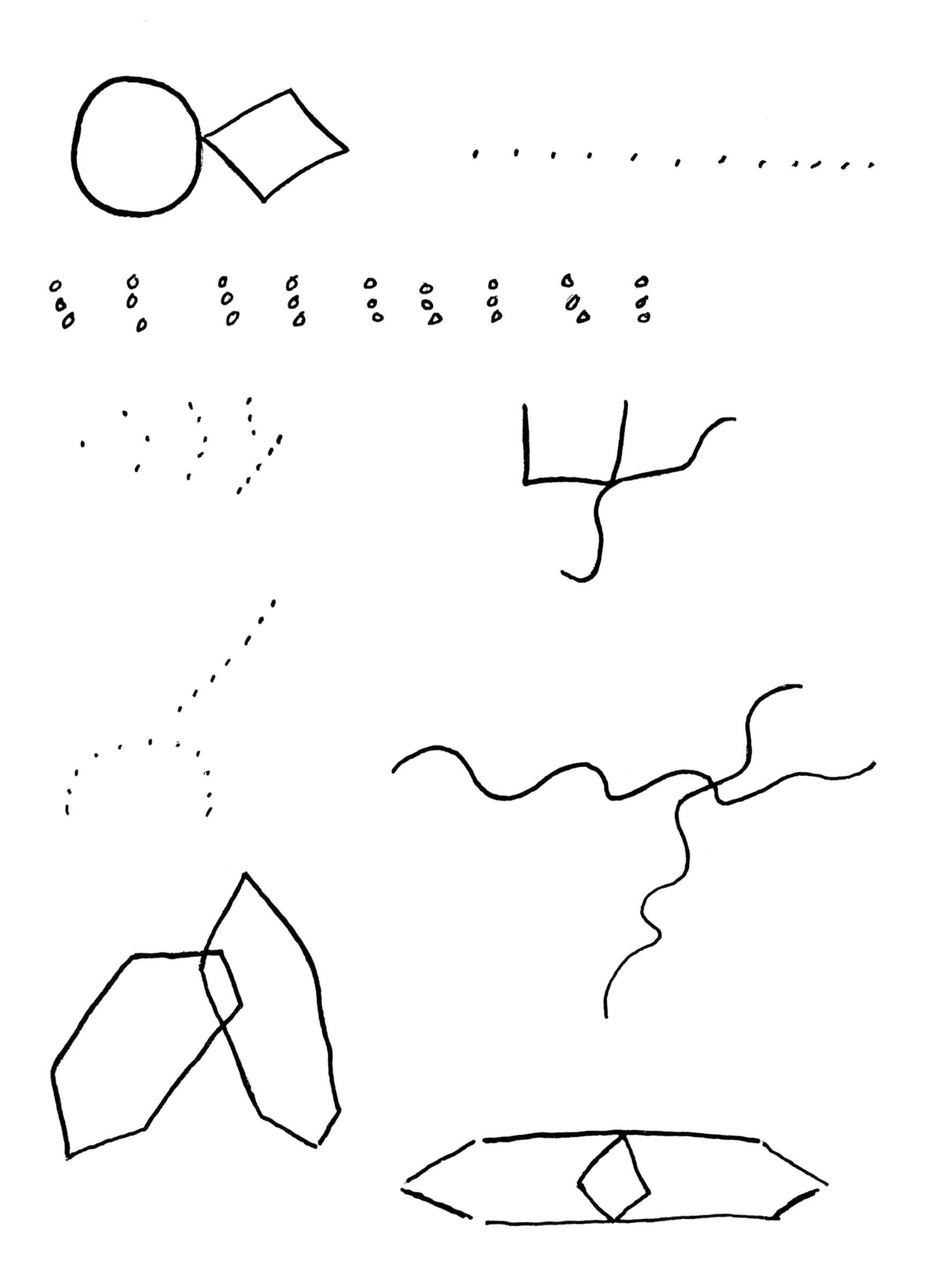

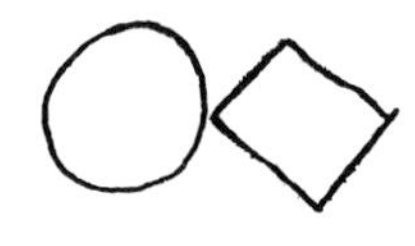

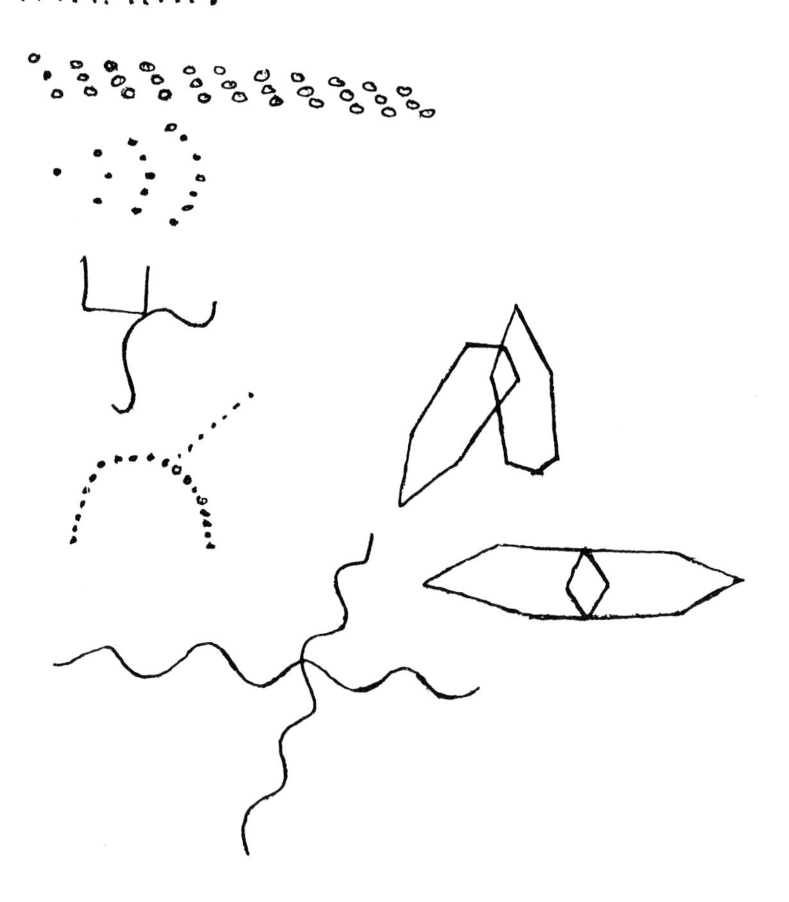

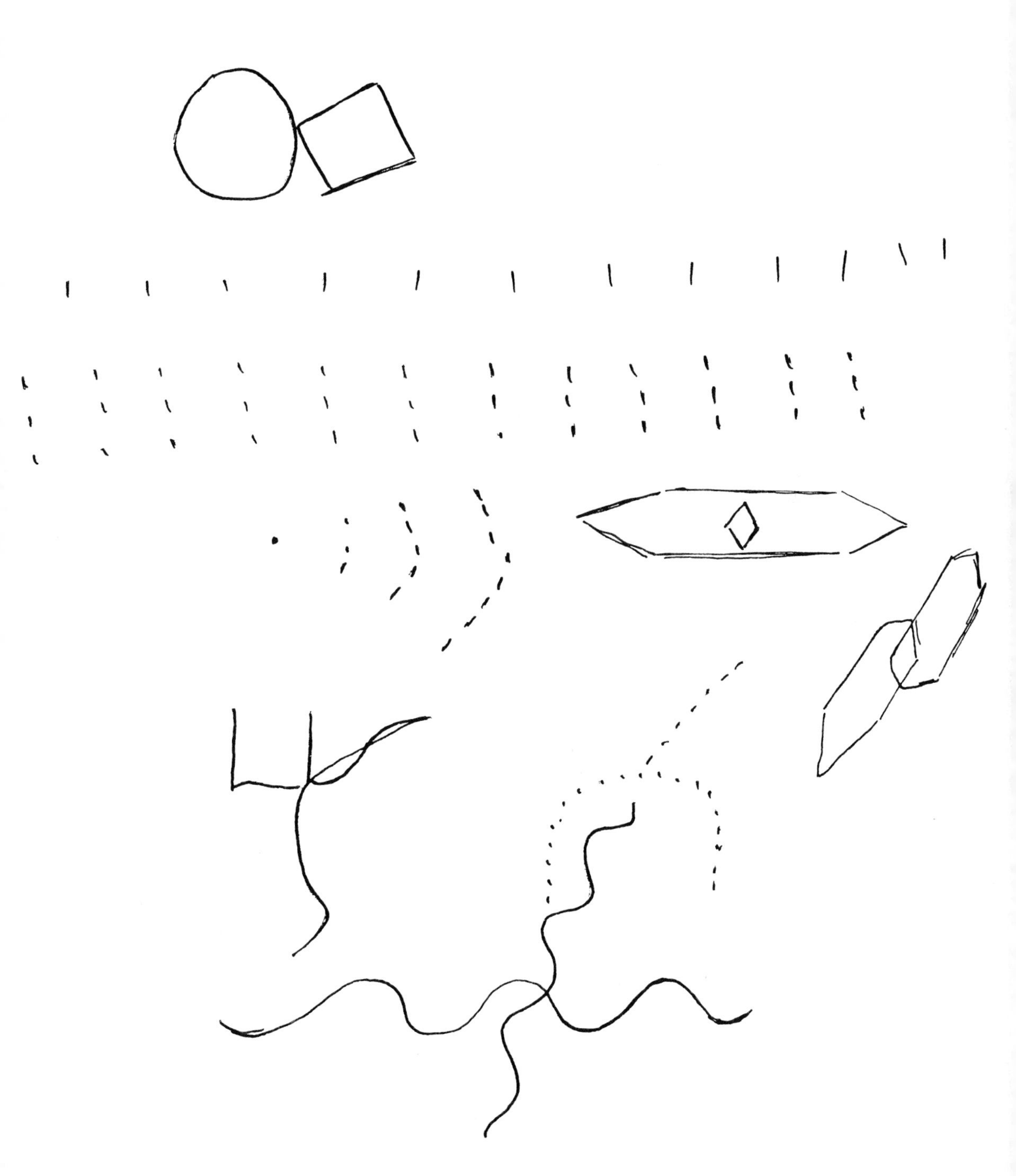

Record 14

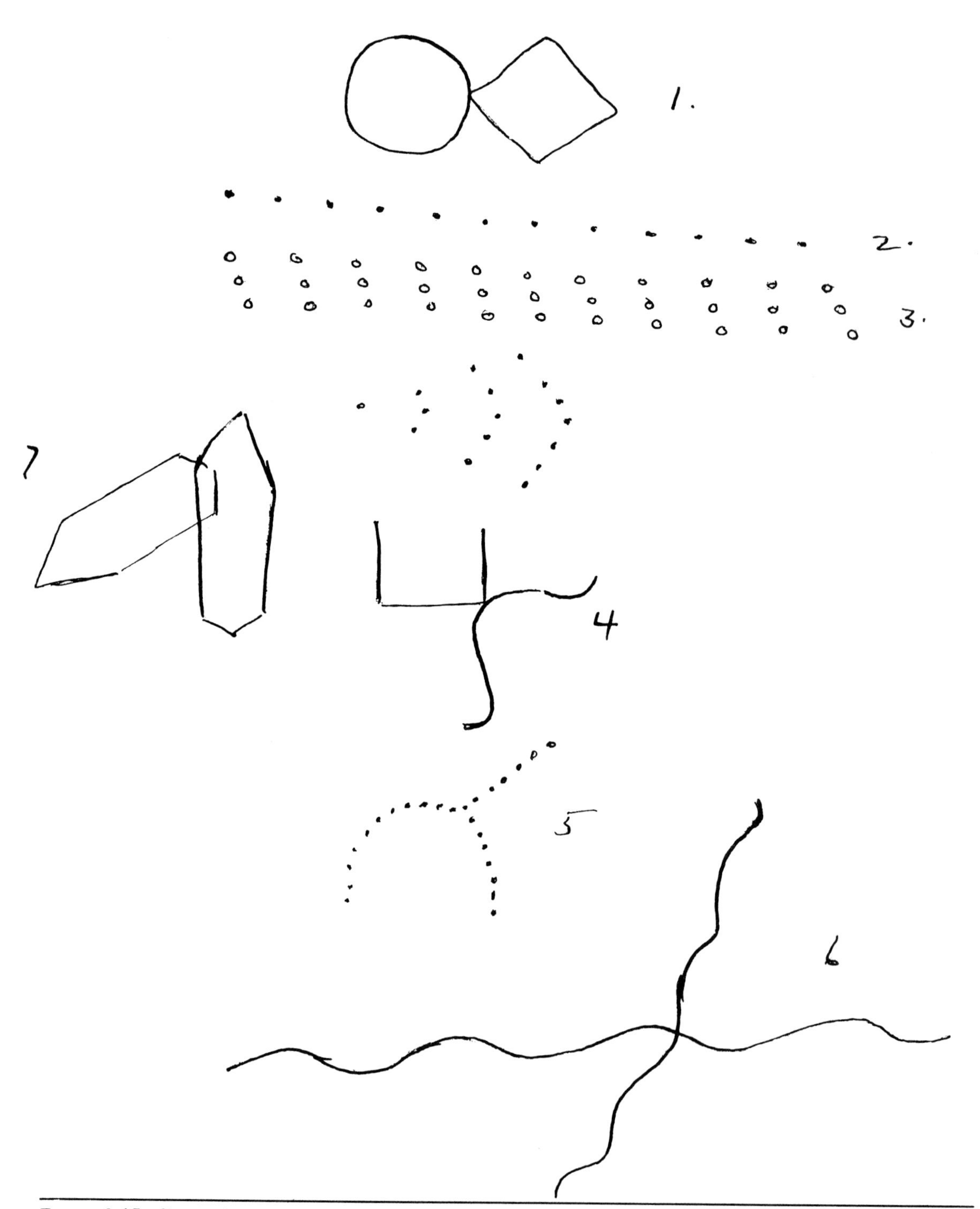

Record 15: first sheet

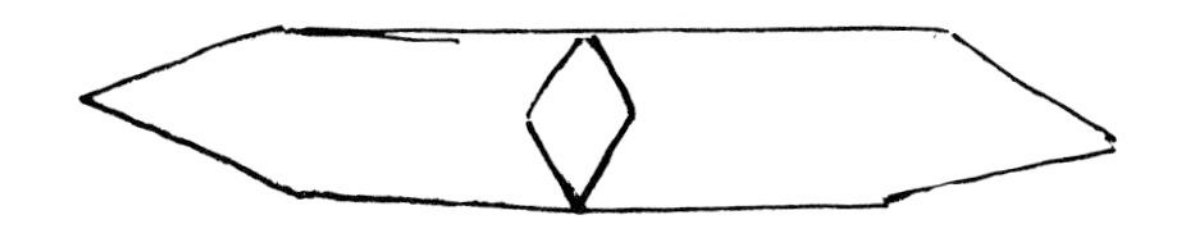

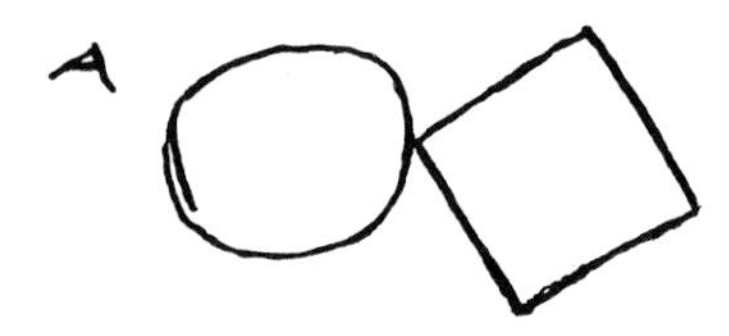

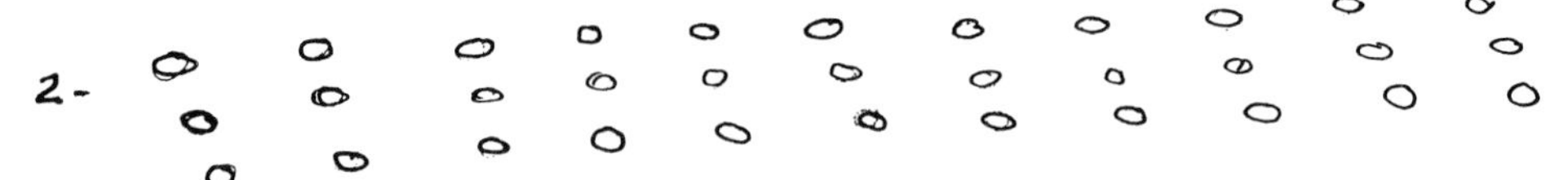

3-

4-

5 -

7

8

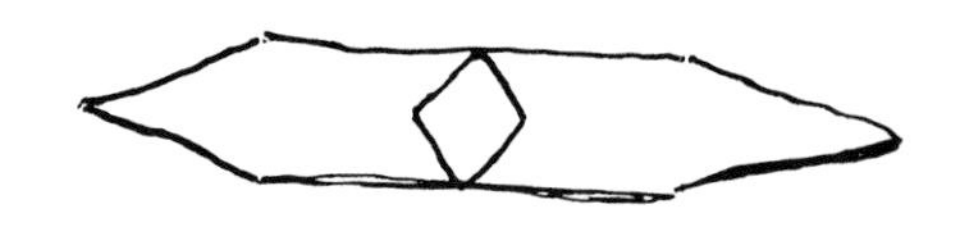

Record 16

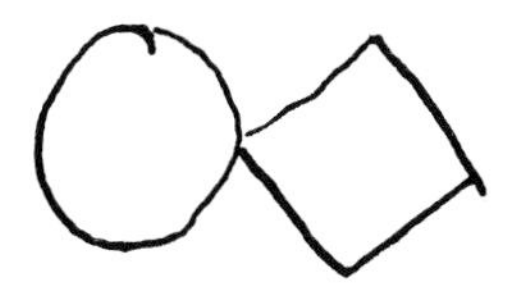

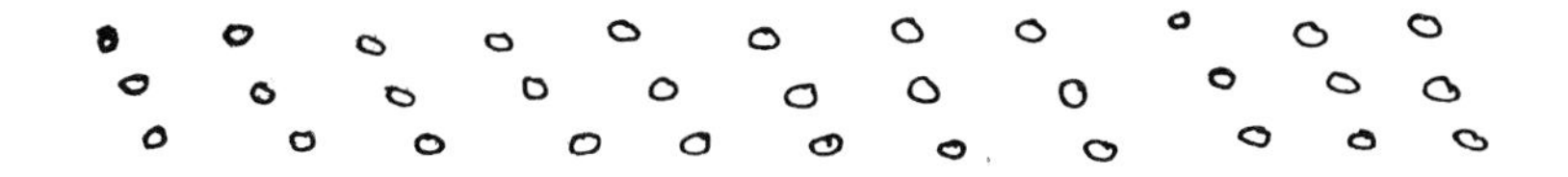

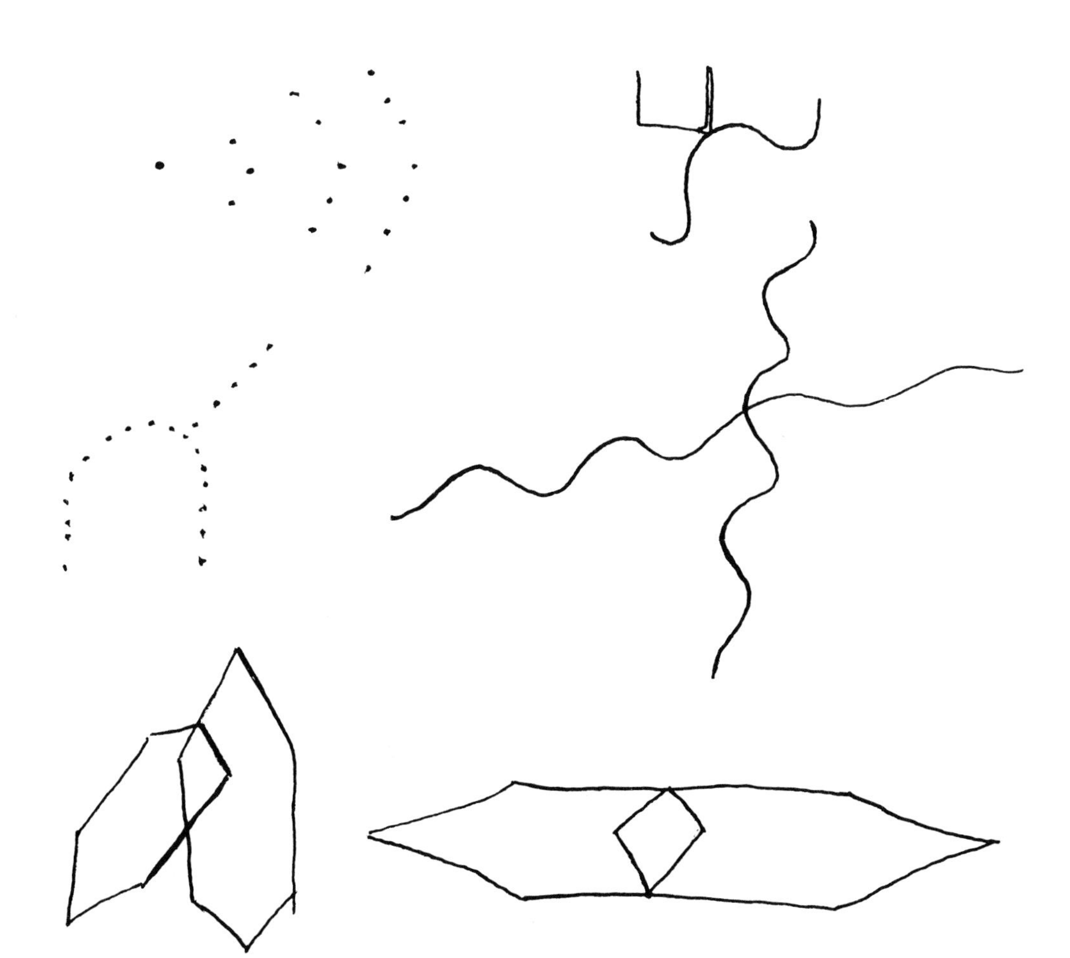

Record 17

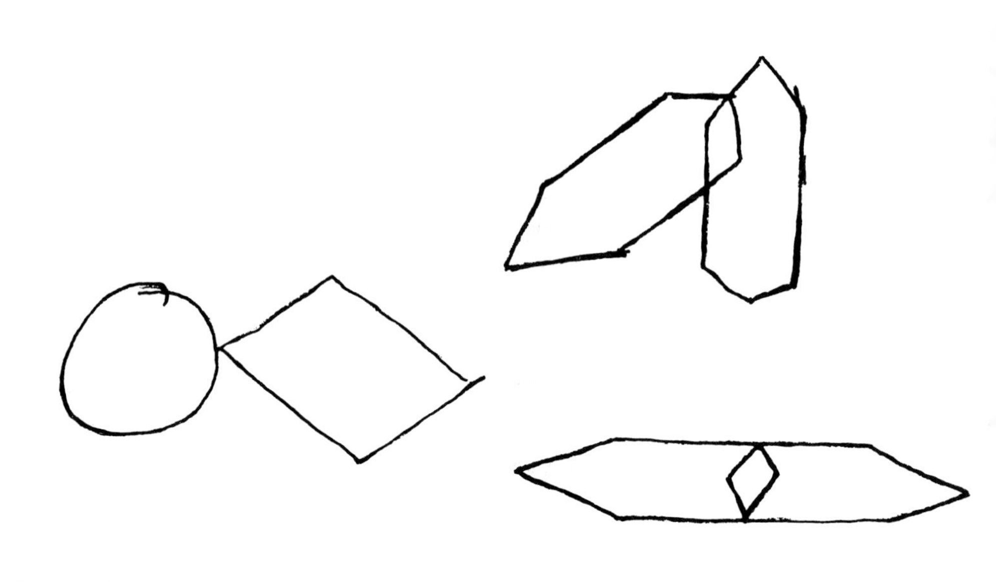

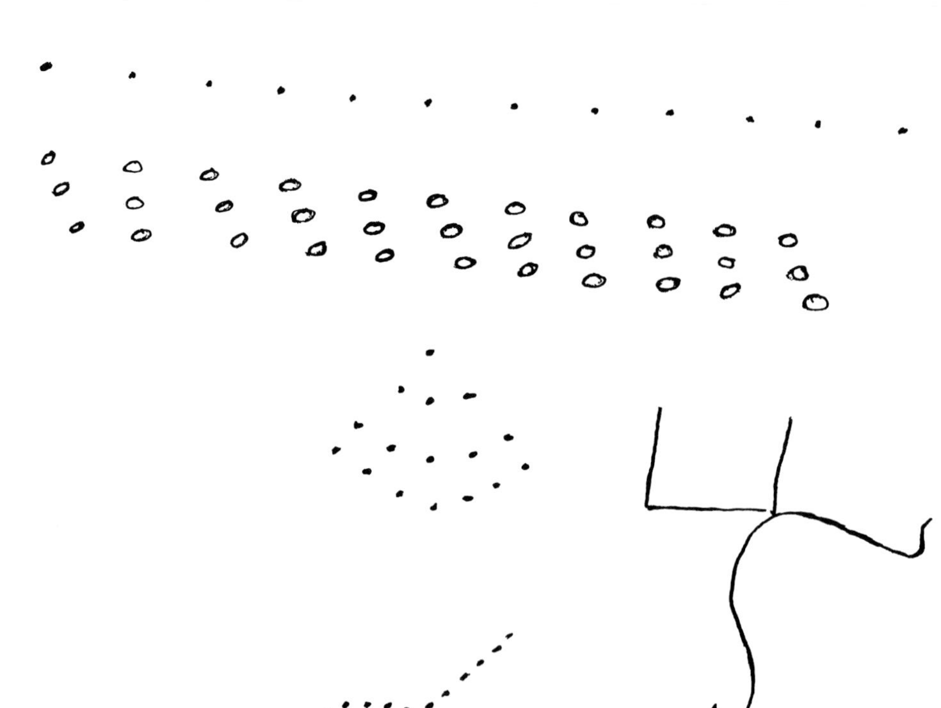

Record 18

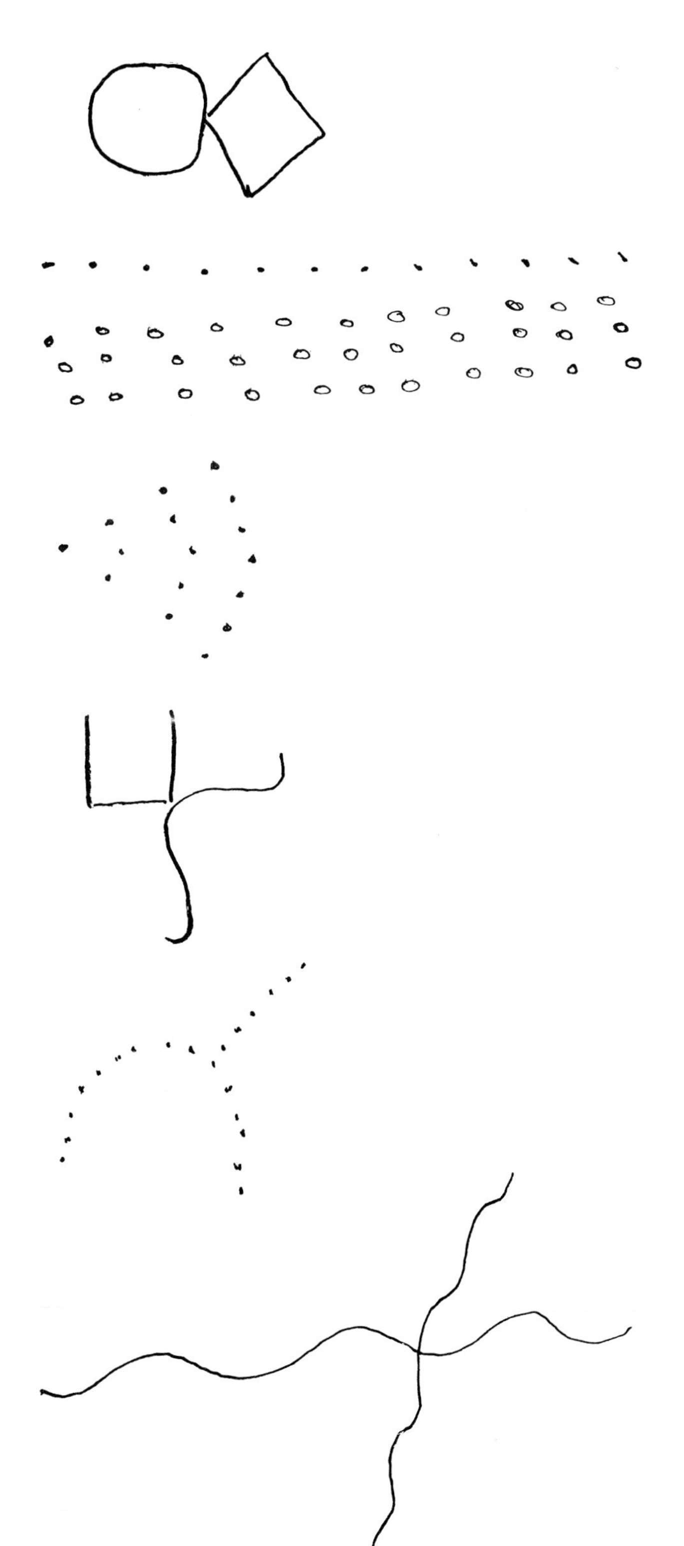

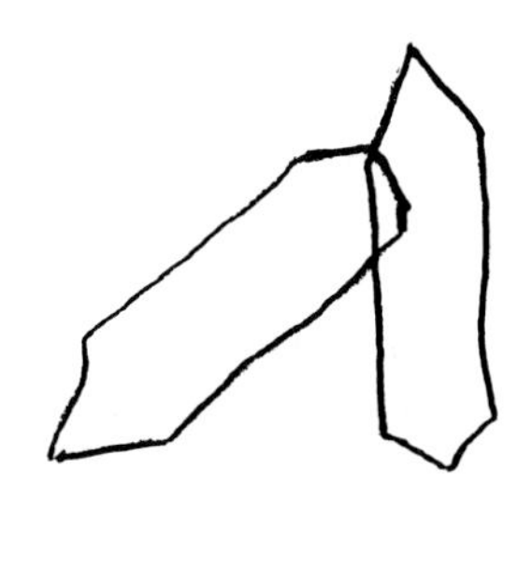

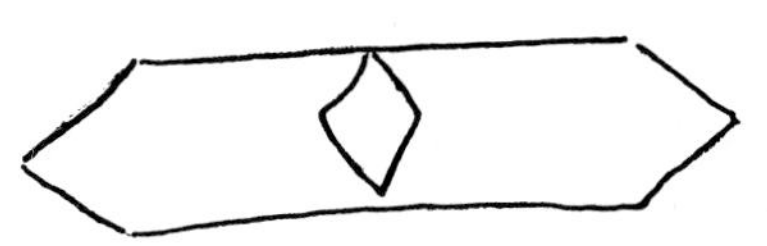

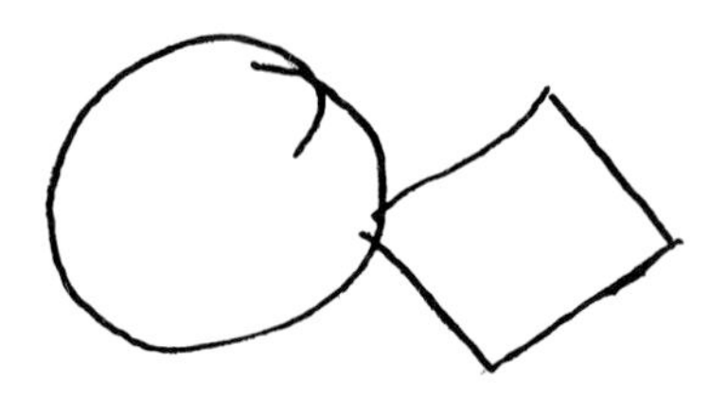

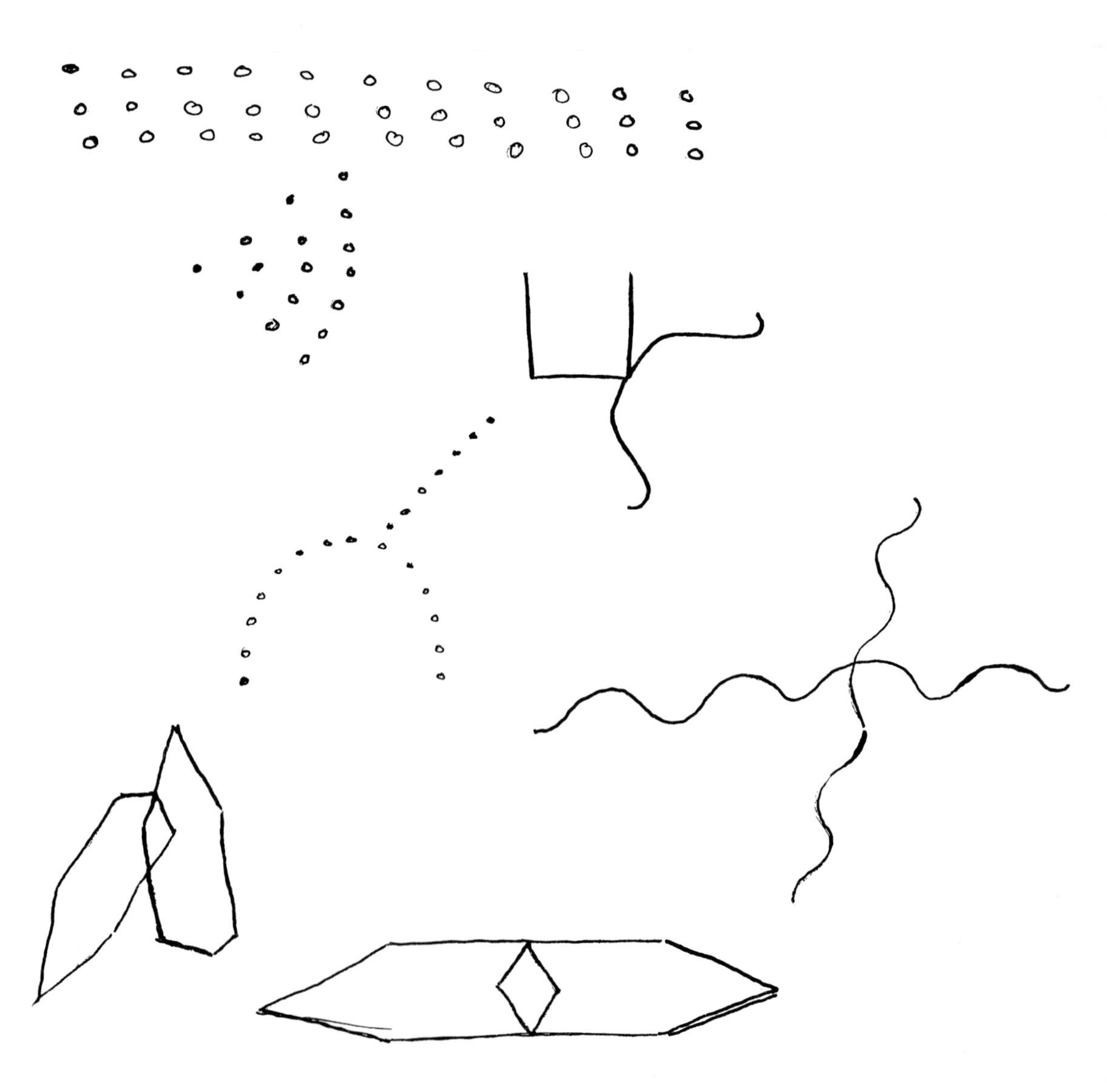

Record 20

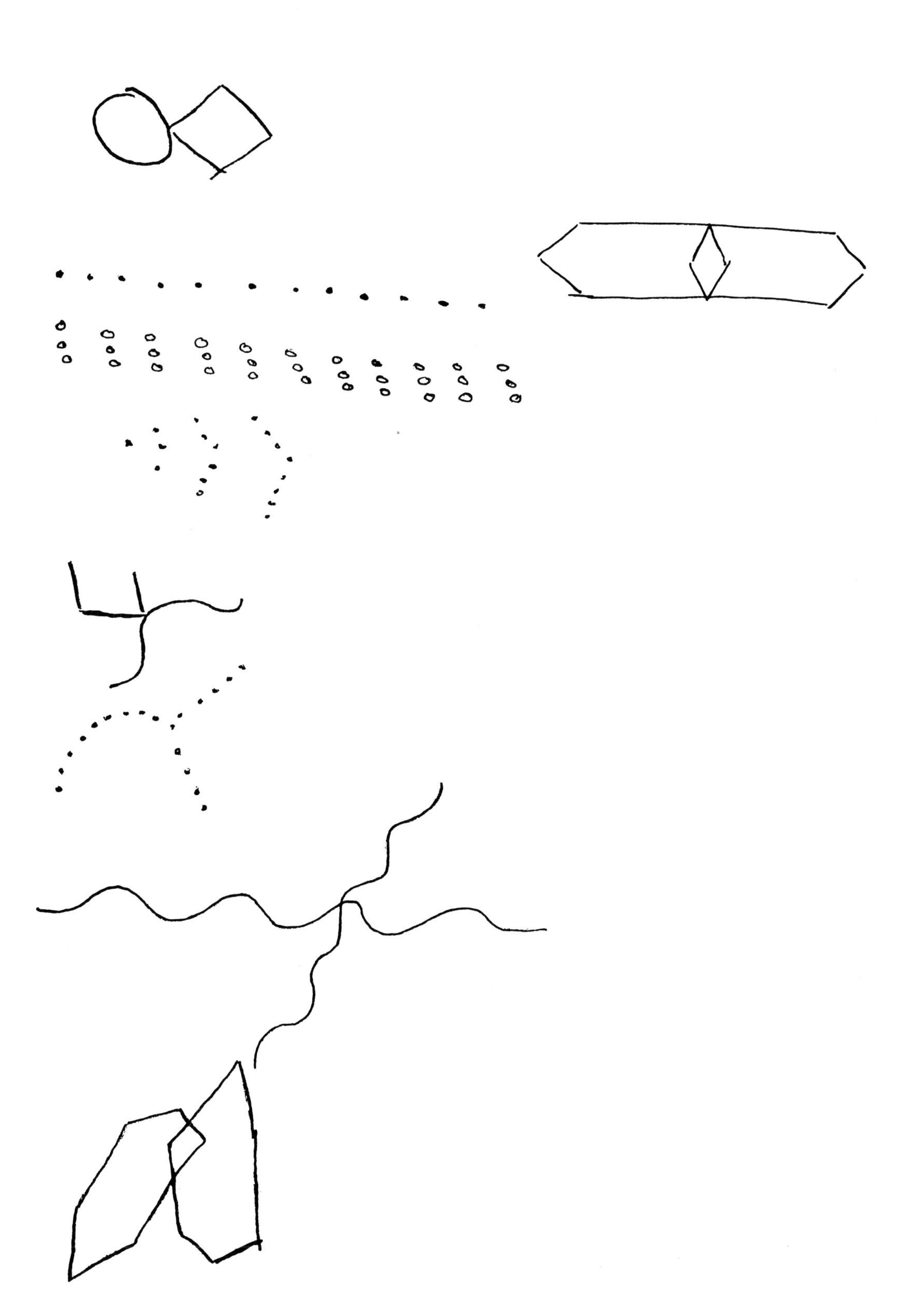

Record 21

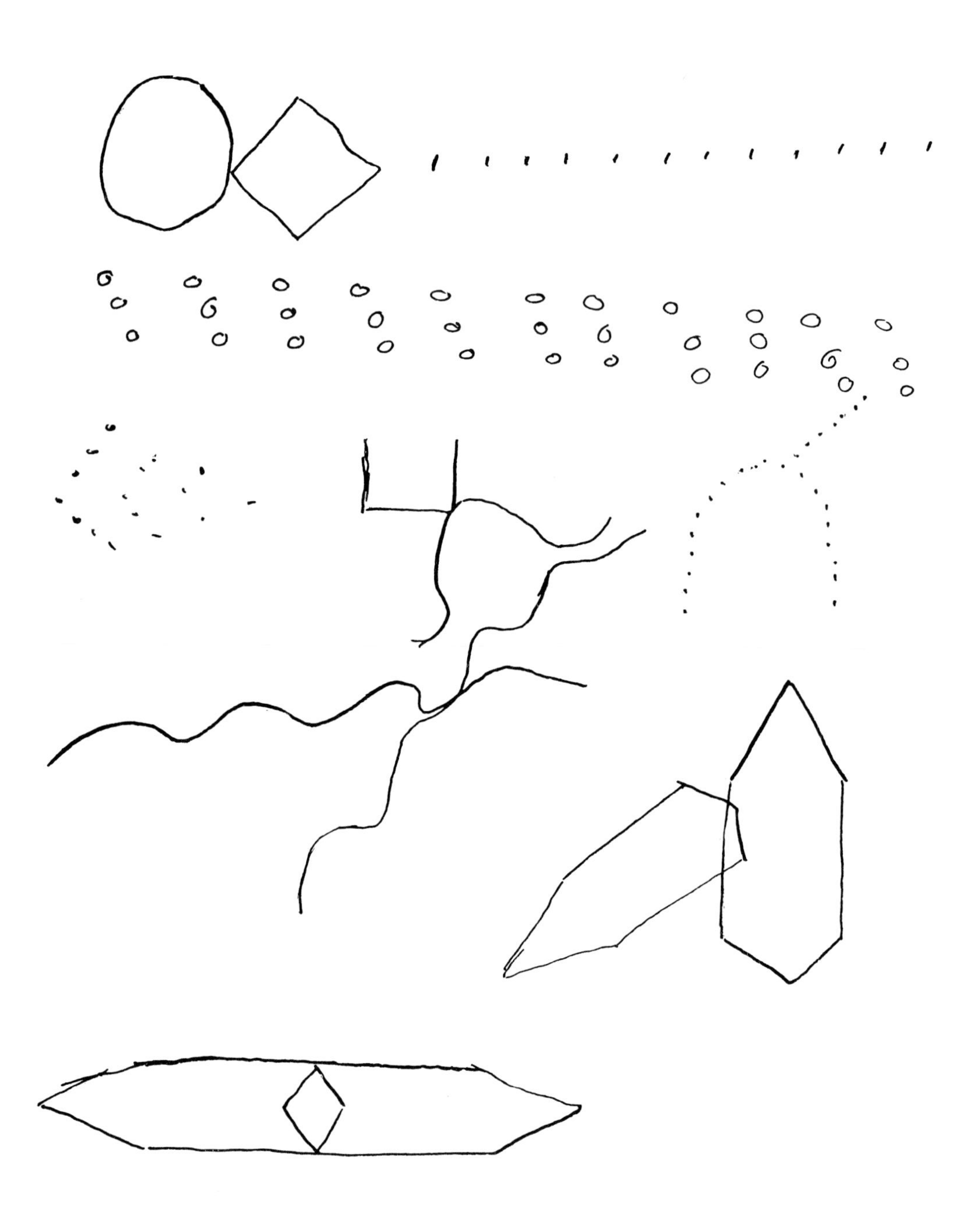

Record 22

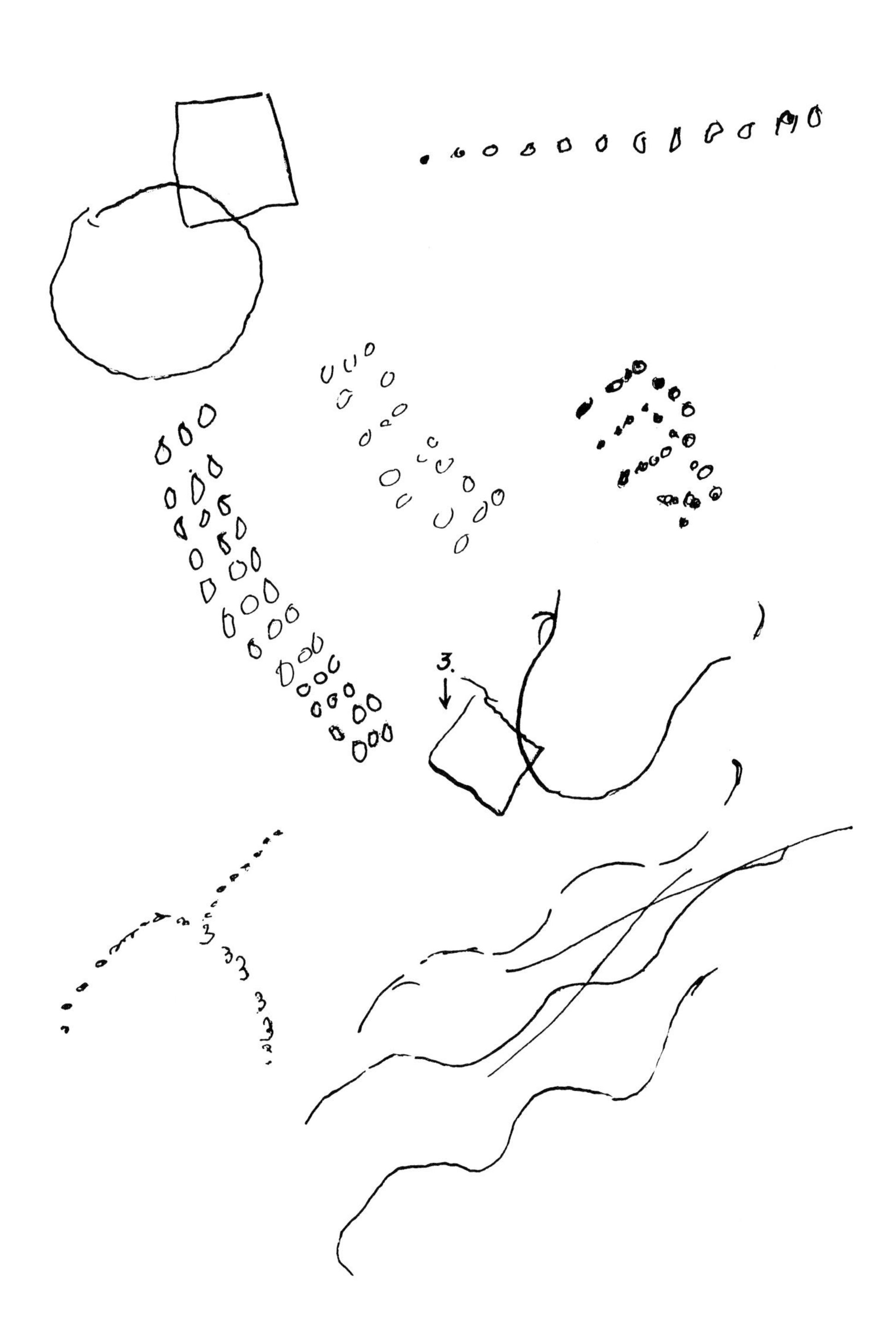

Record 23: first sheet

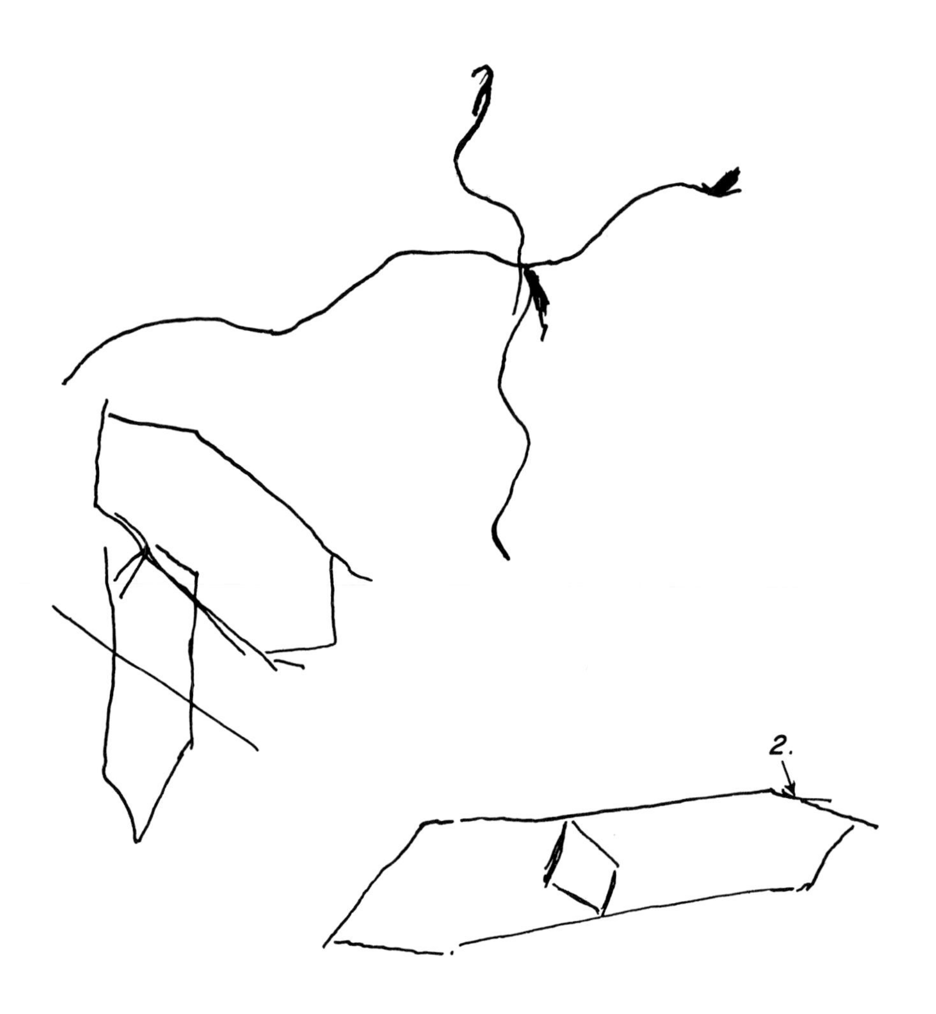

Record 23: second sheet

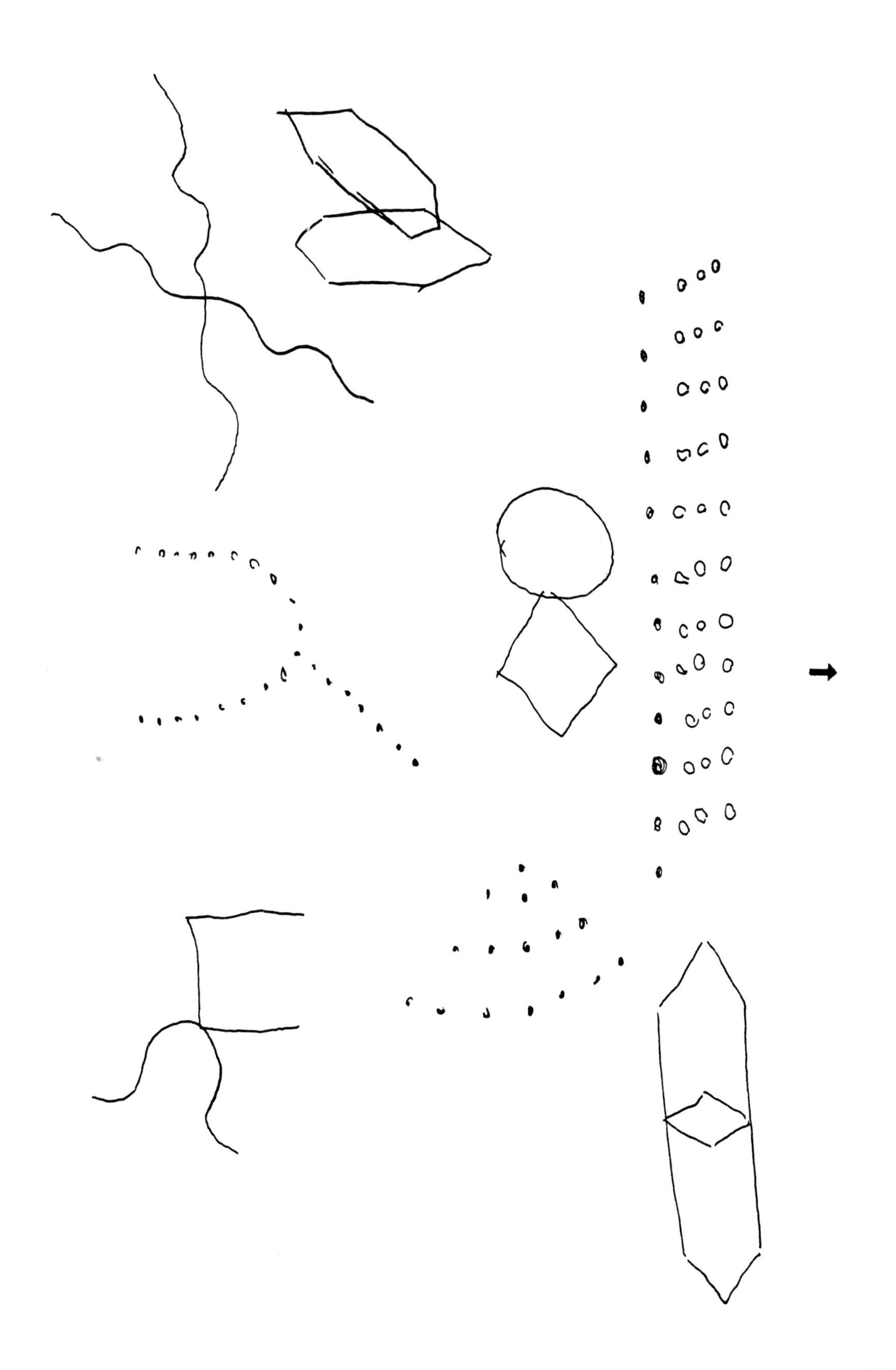

Record 24

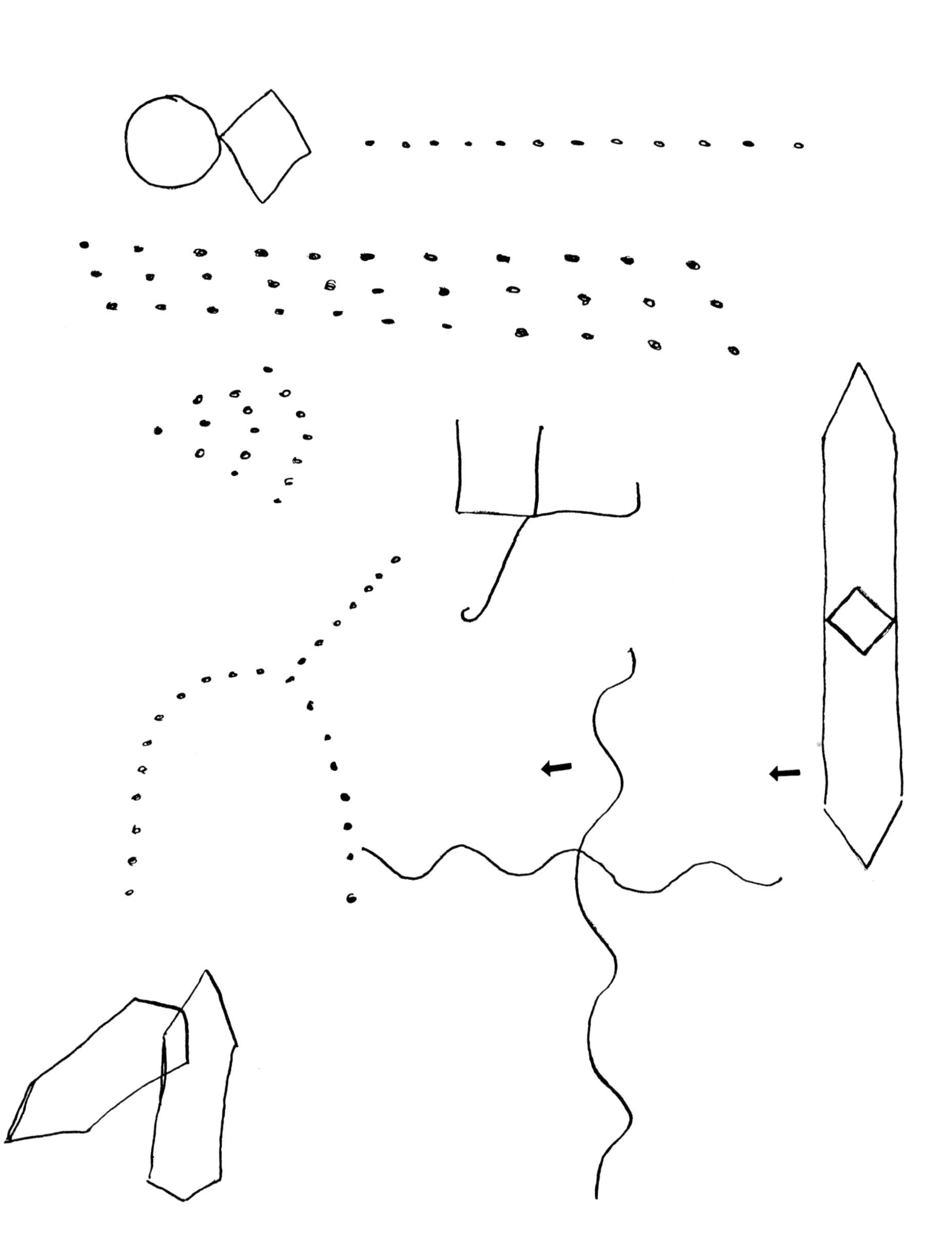

Record 25

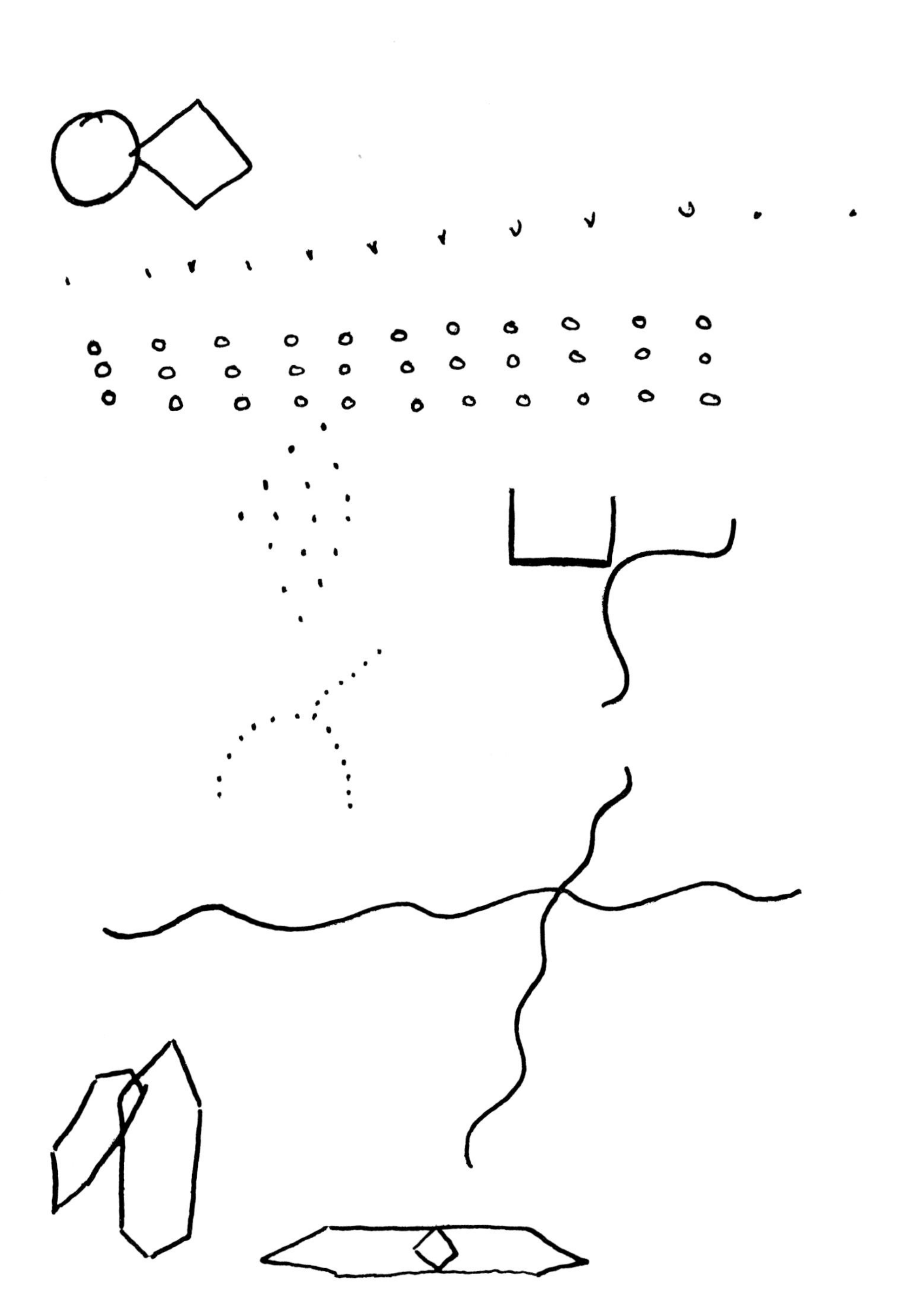

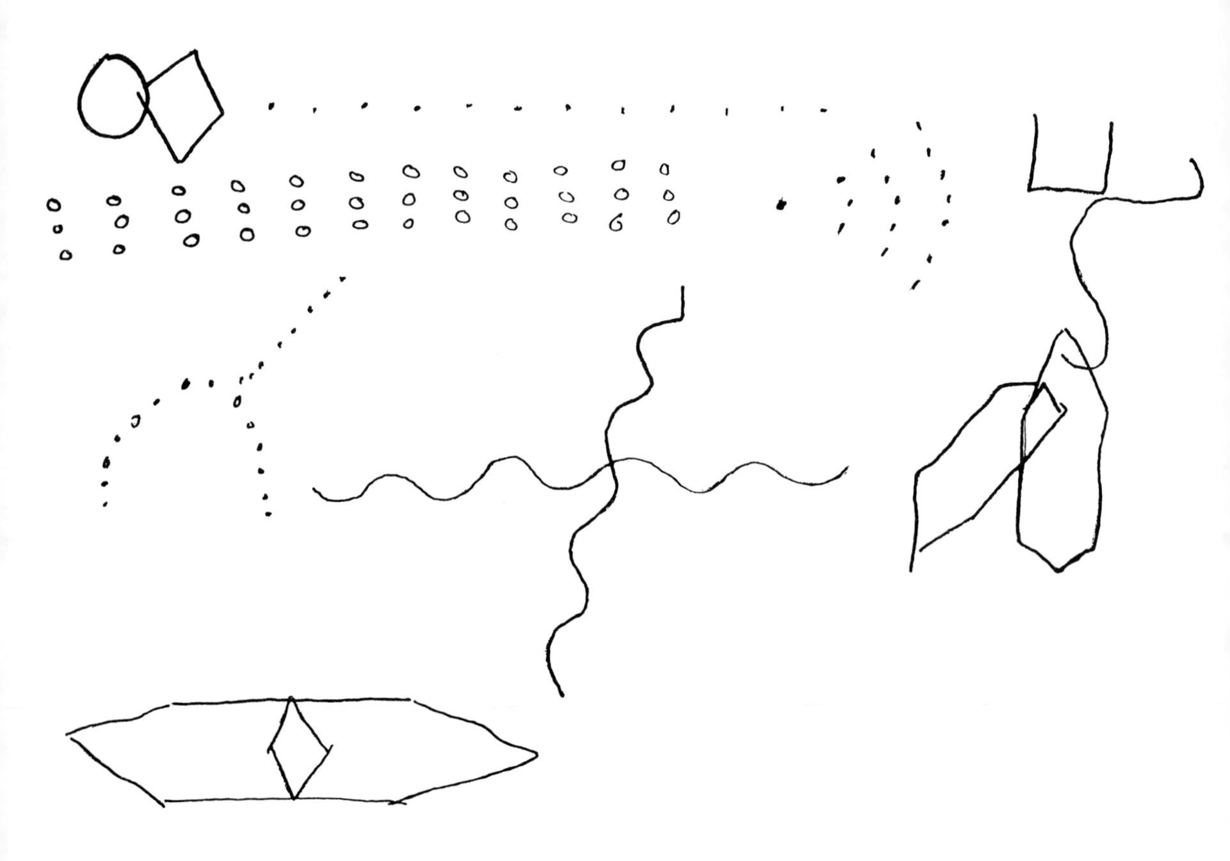

Record 27

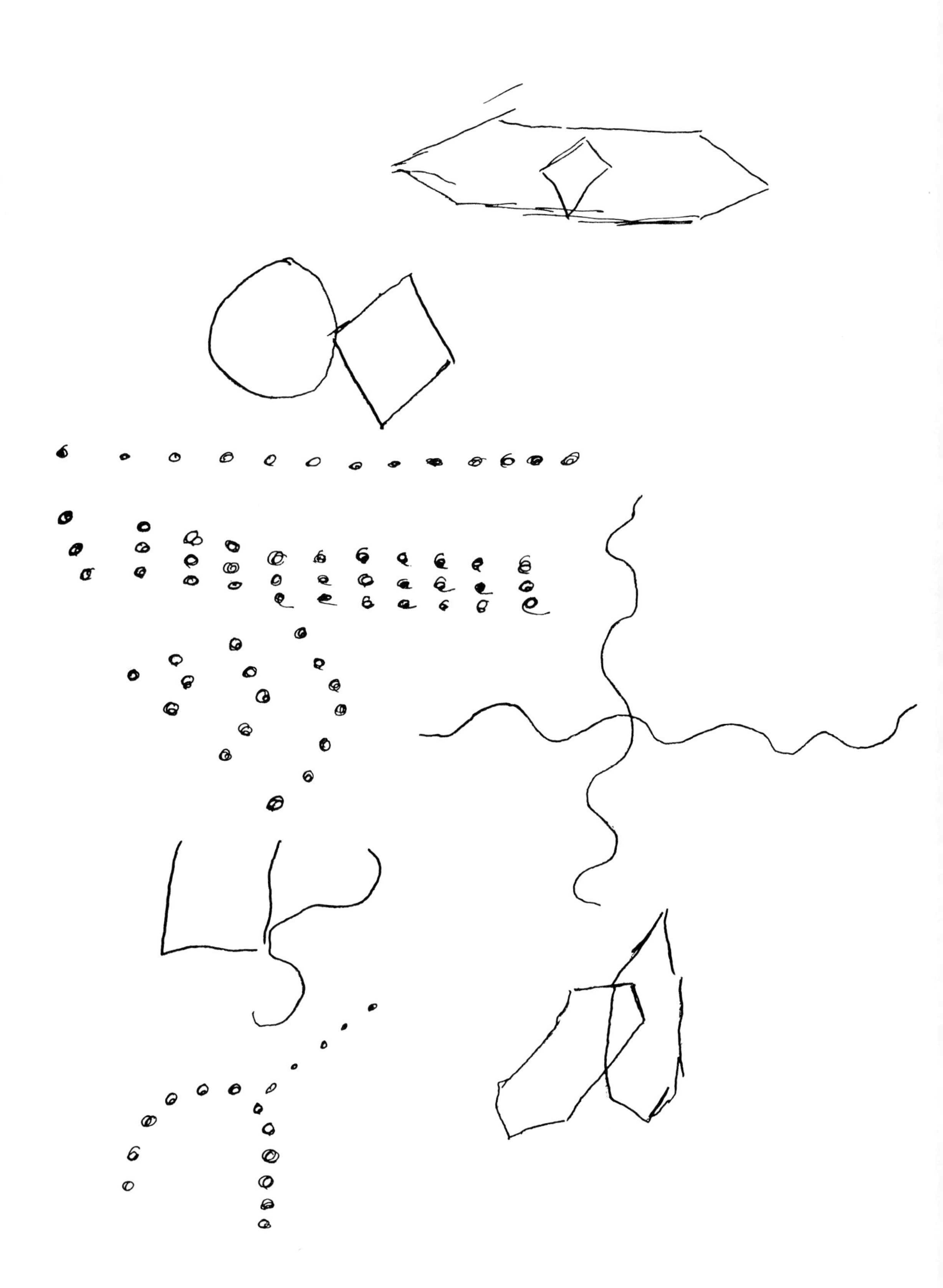

1)

2)

3)

4)

5)

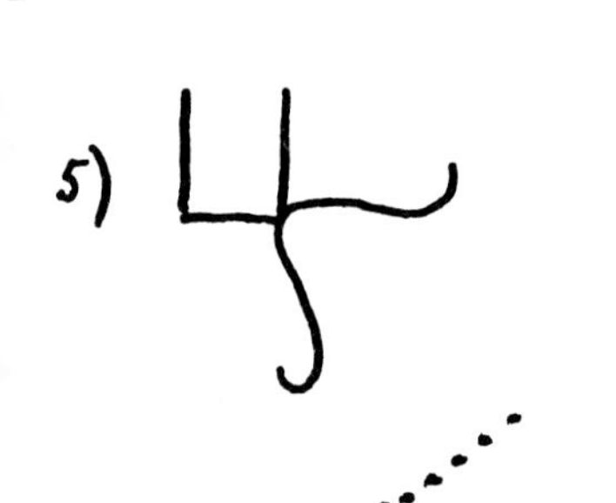

6)

7)

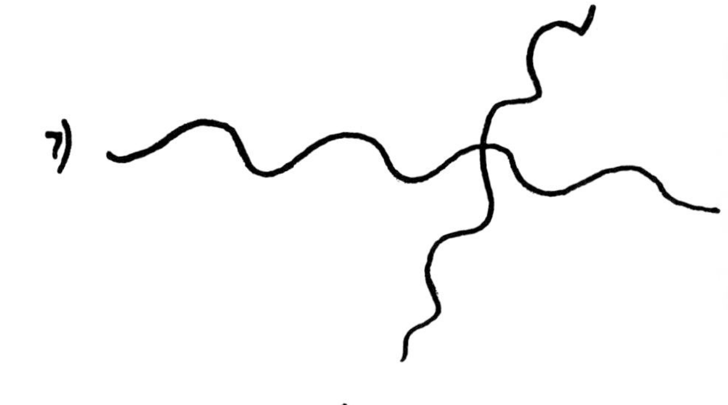

8)

9)

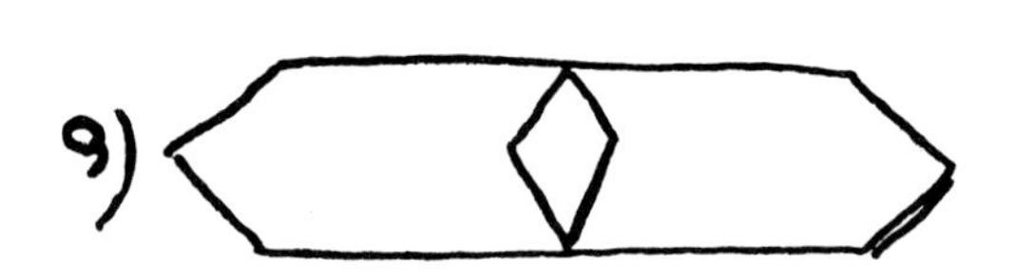

Record 29

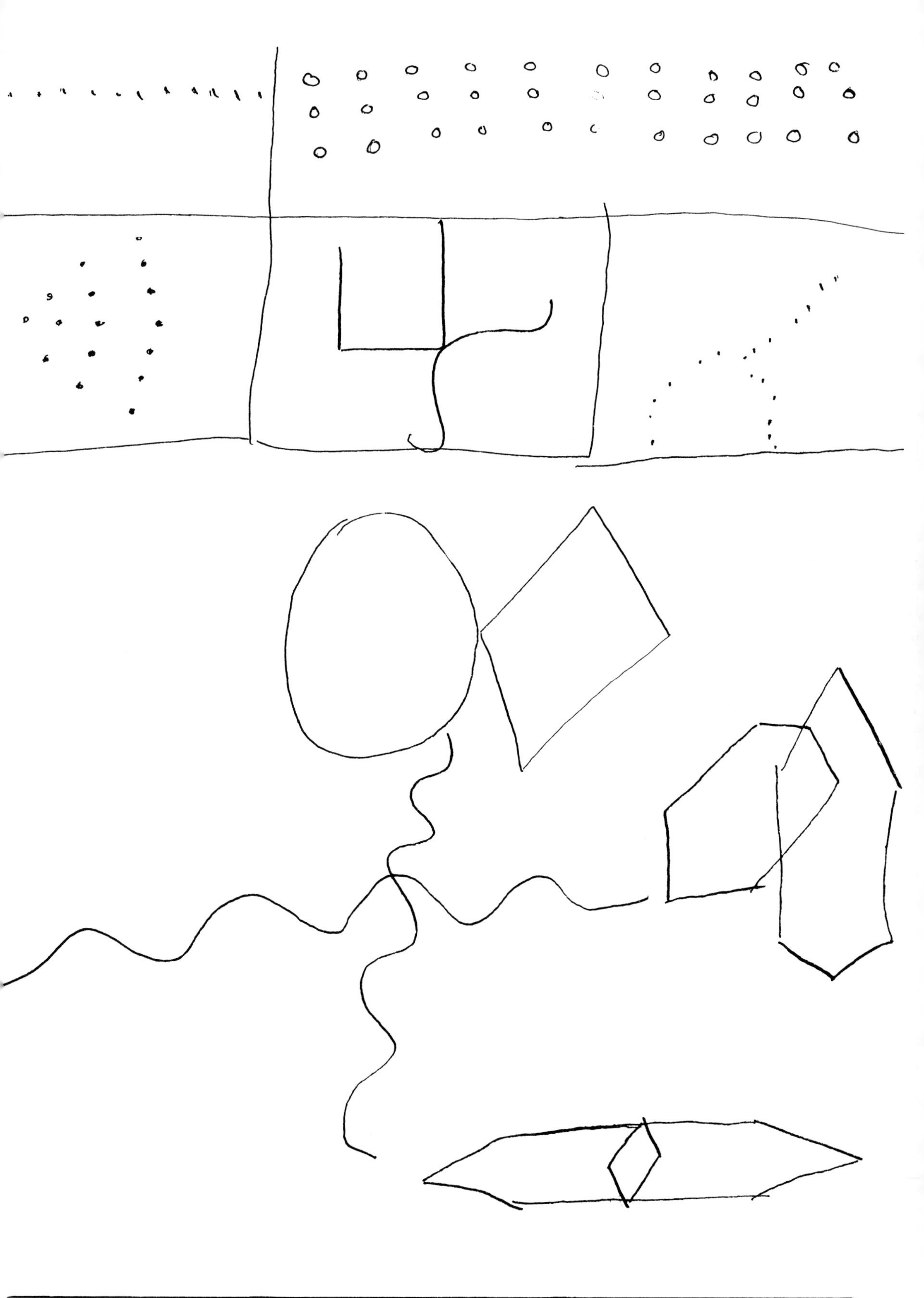

Record 30

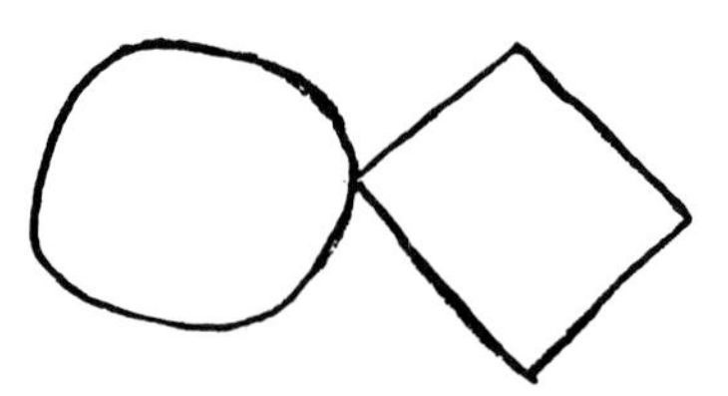

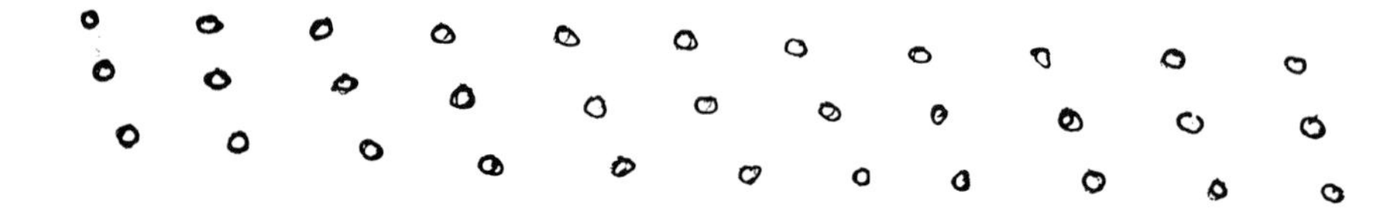

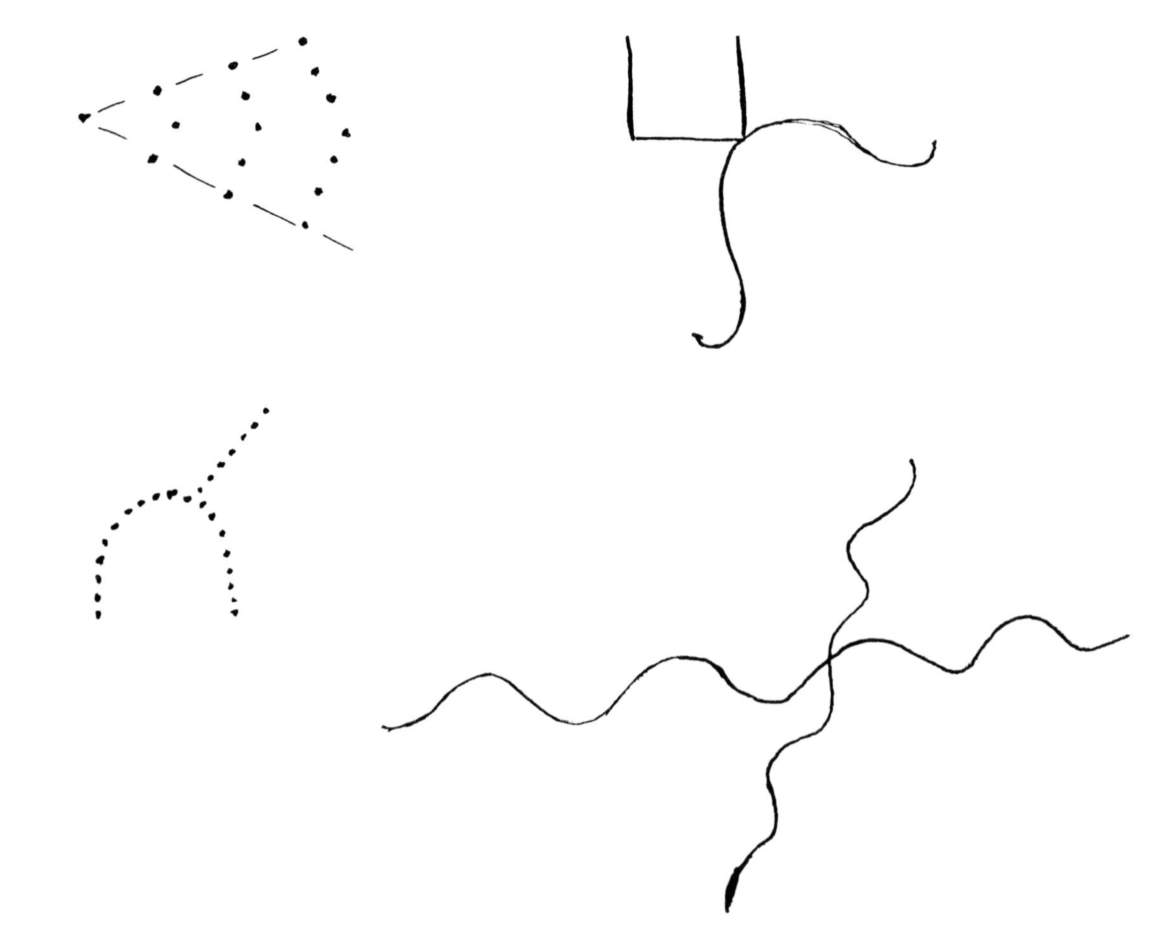

Record 31: first sheet

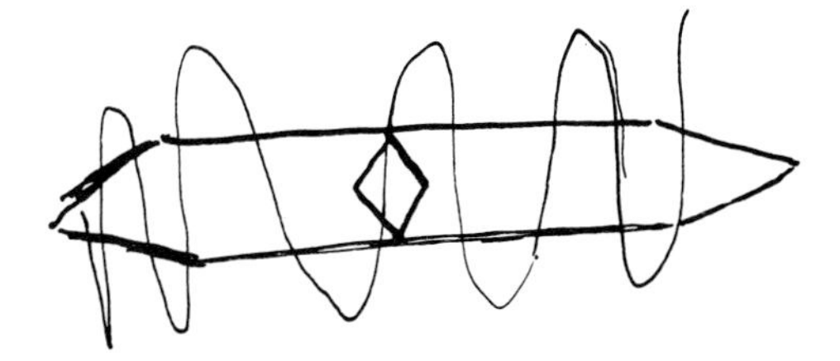

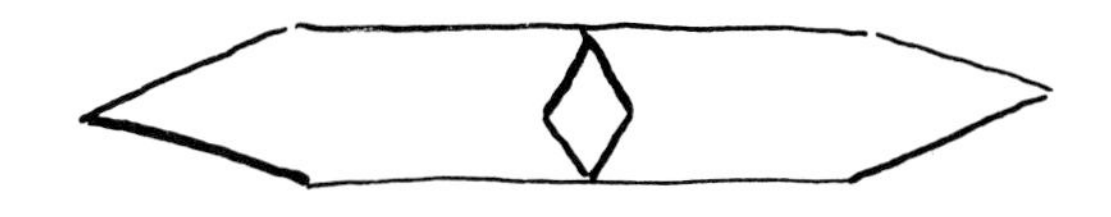

Record 31: second sheet

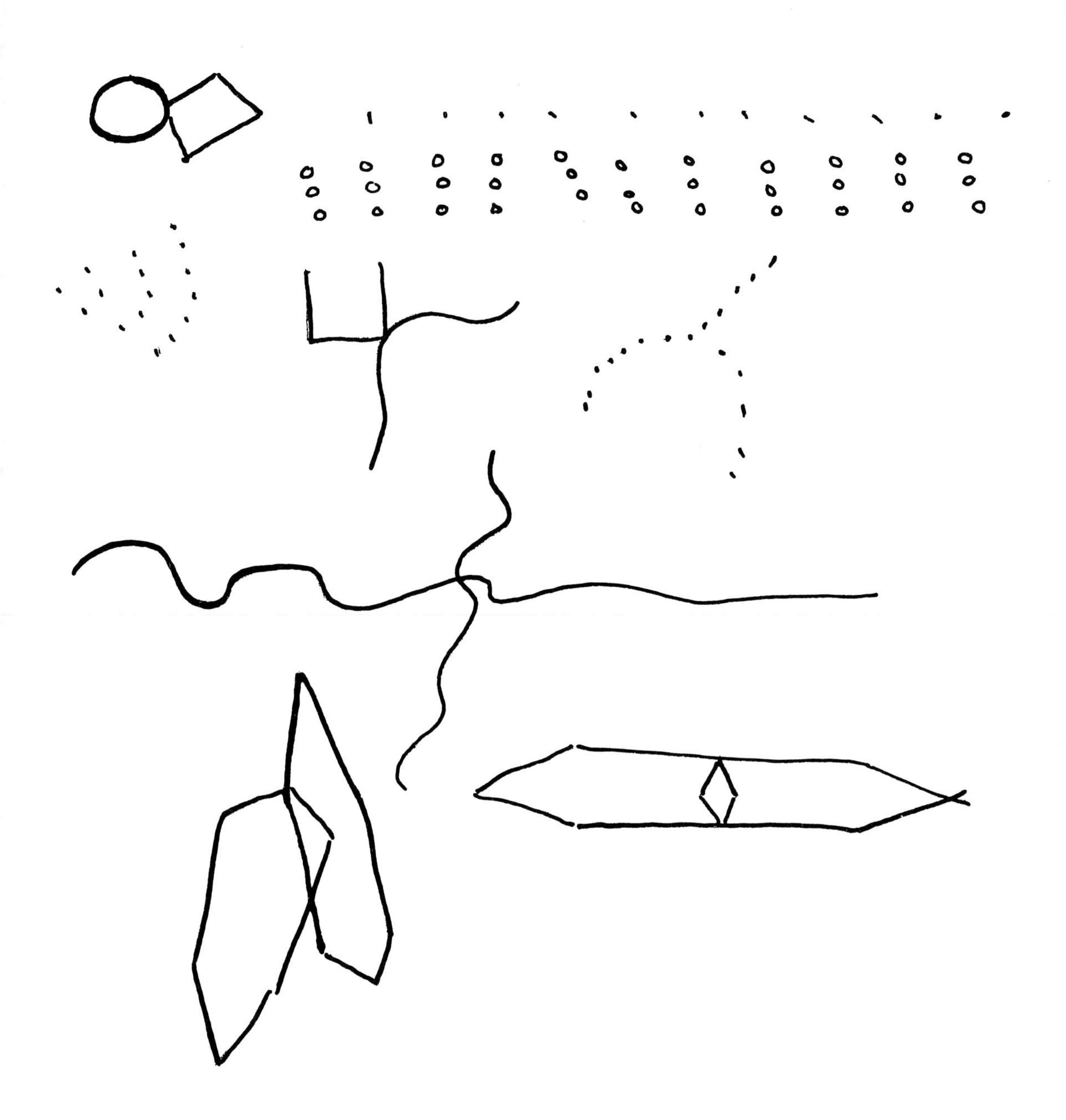

Record 32

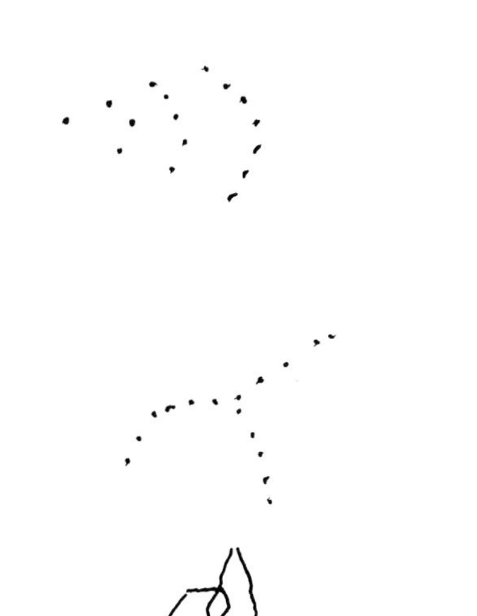

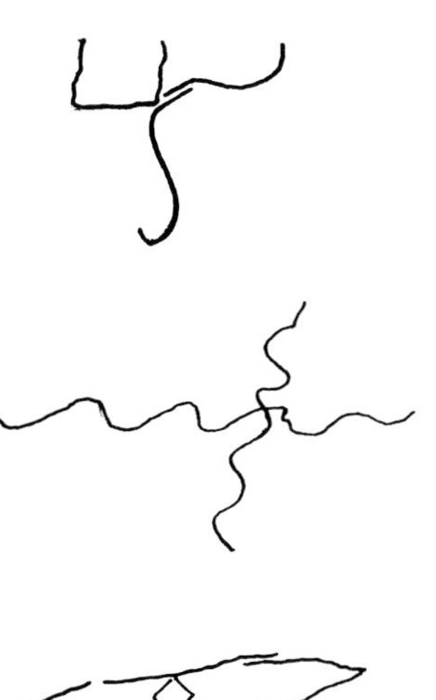

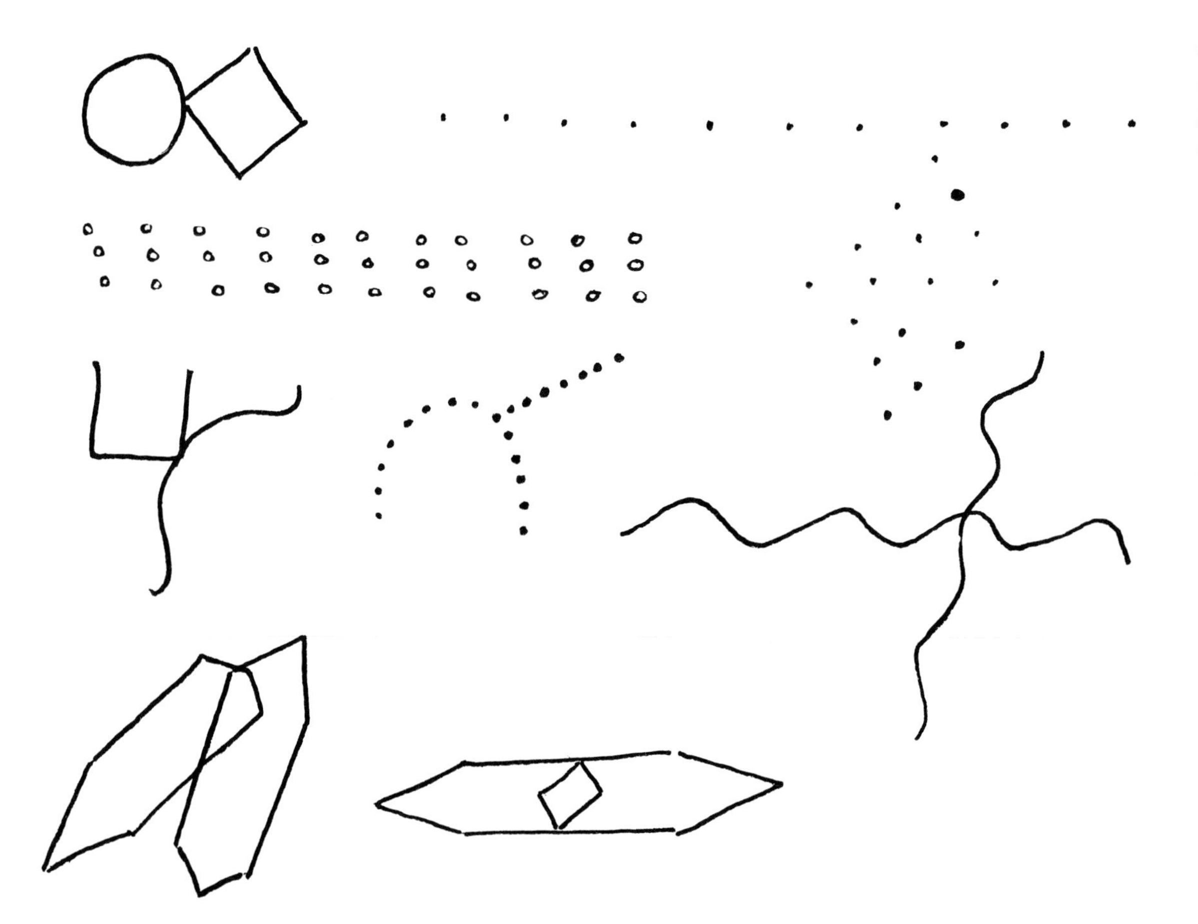

Record 34

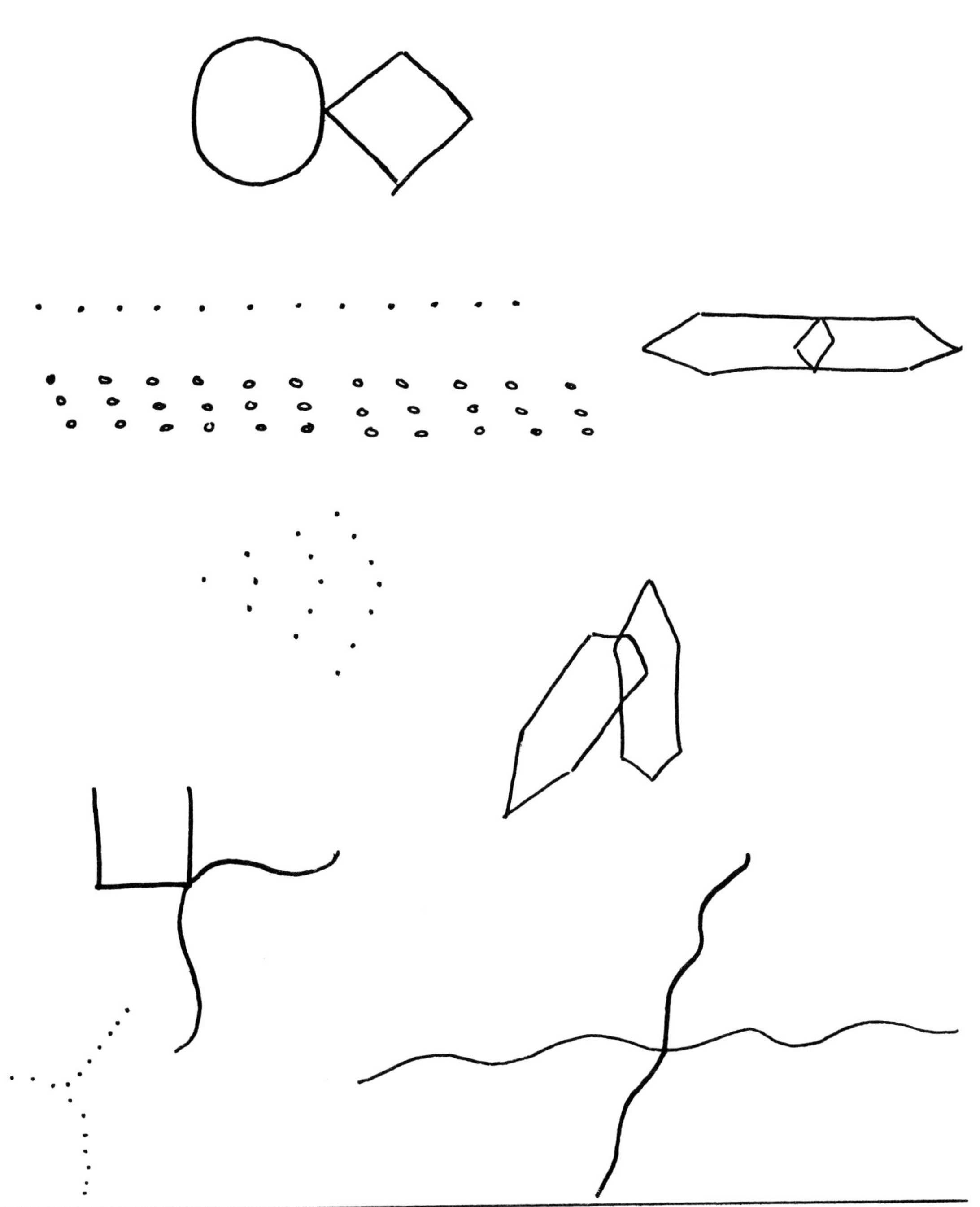

Record 35

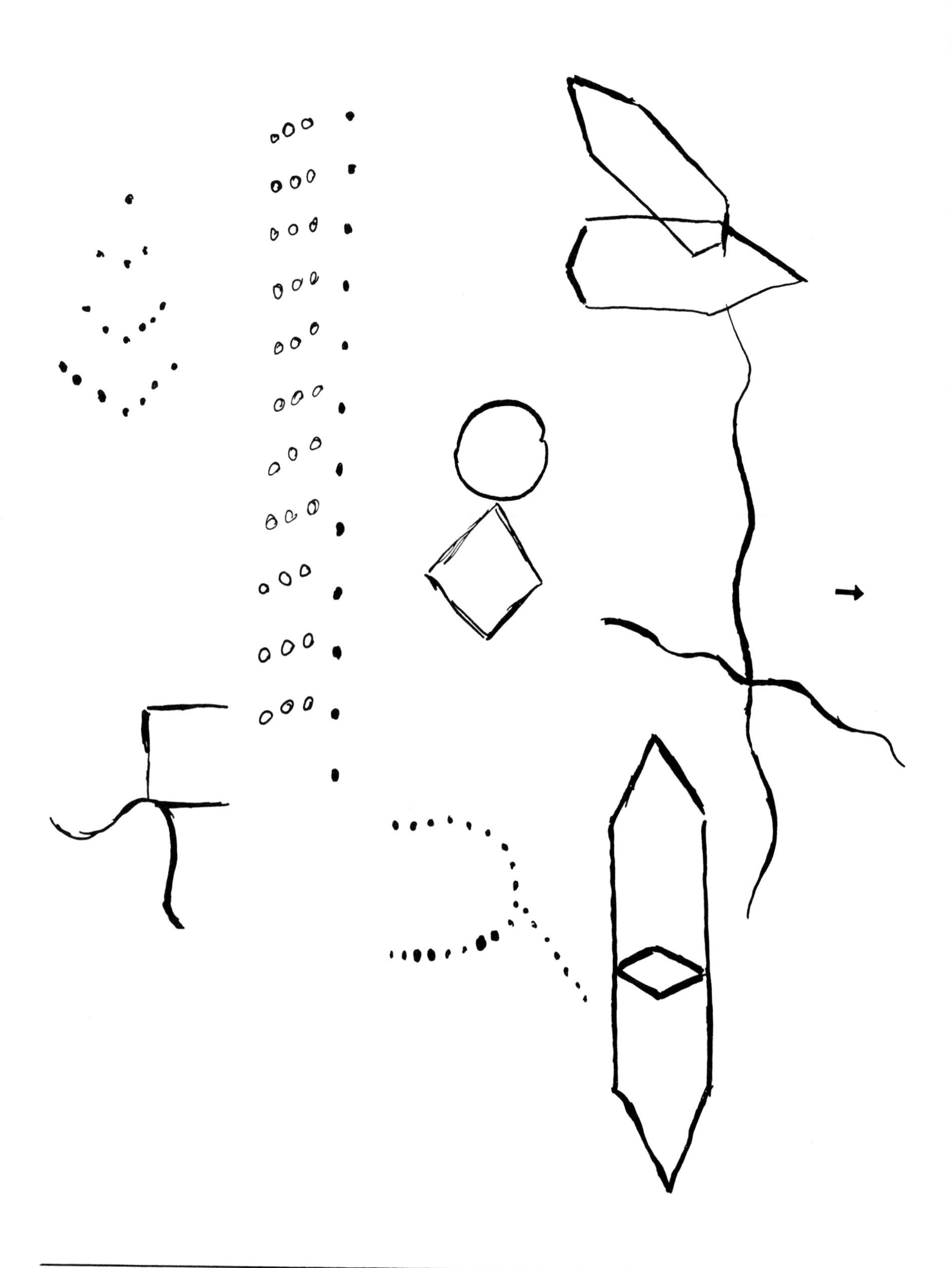

Record 36

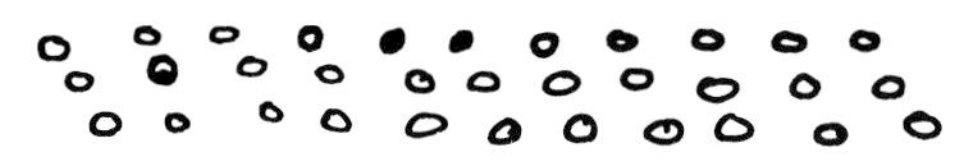

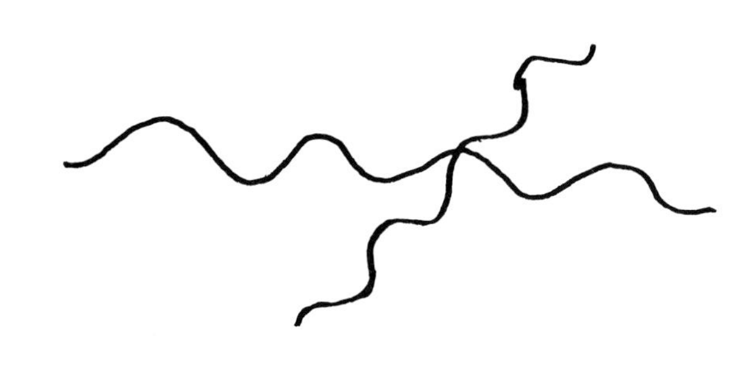

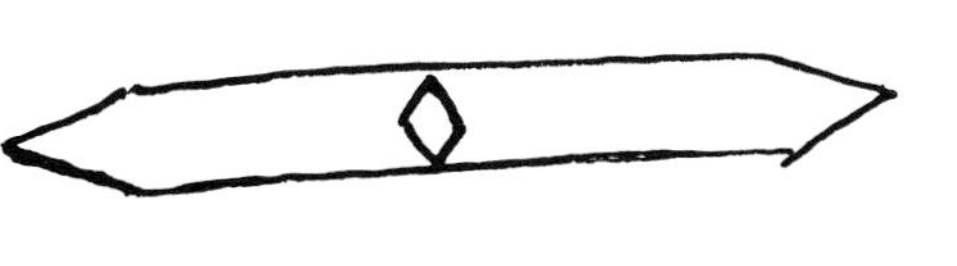

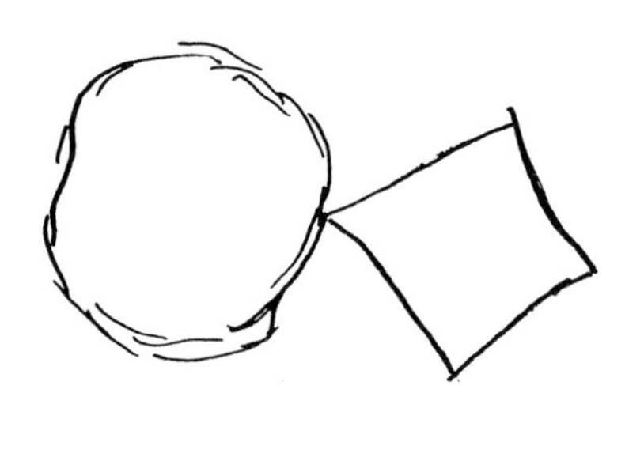

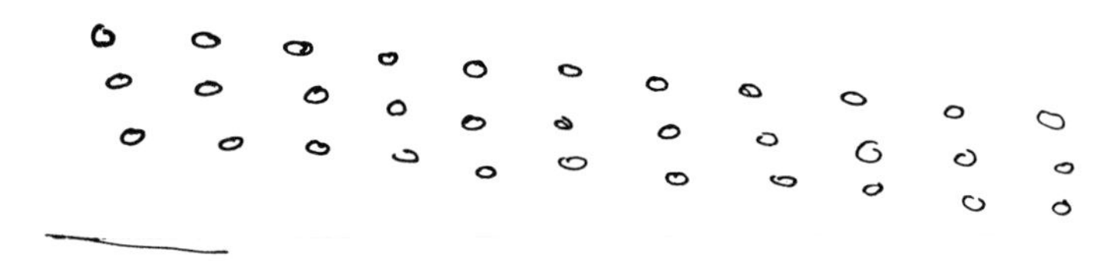

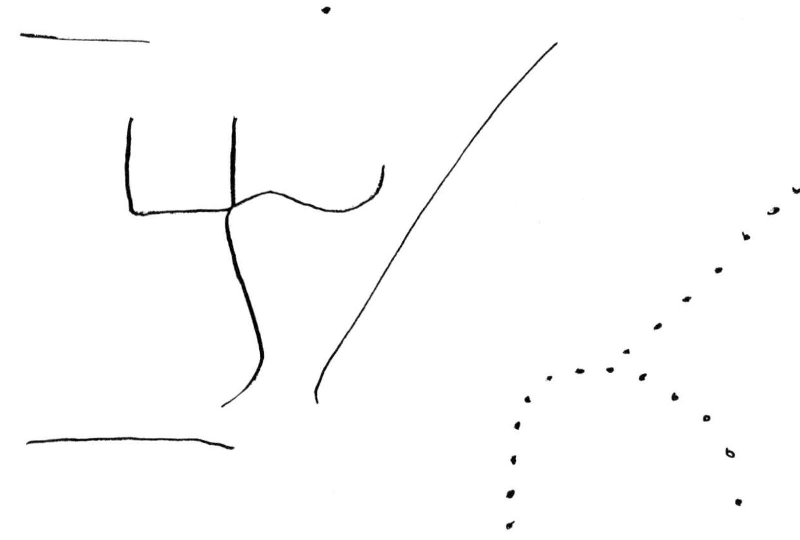

Record 38: first sheet

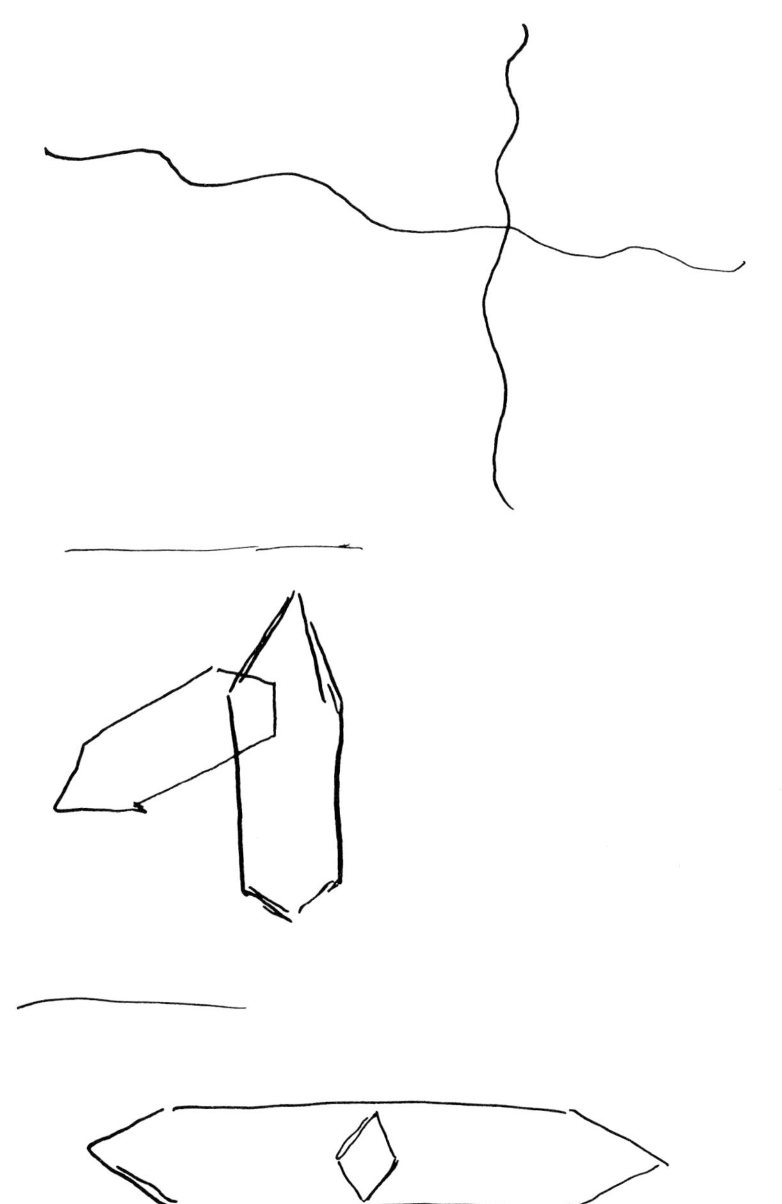

Record 38: second sheet

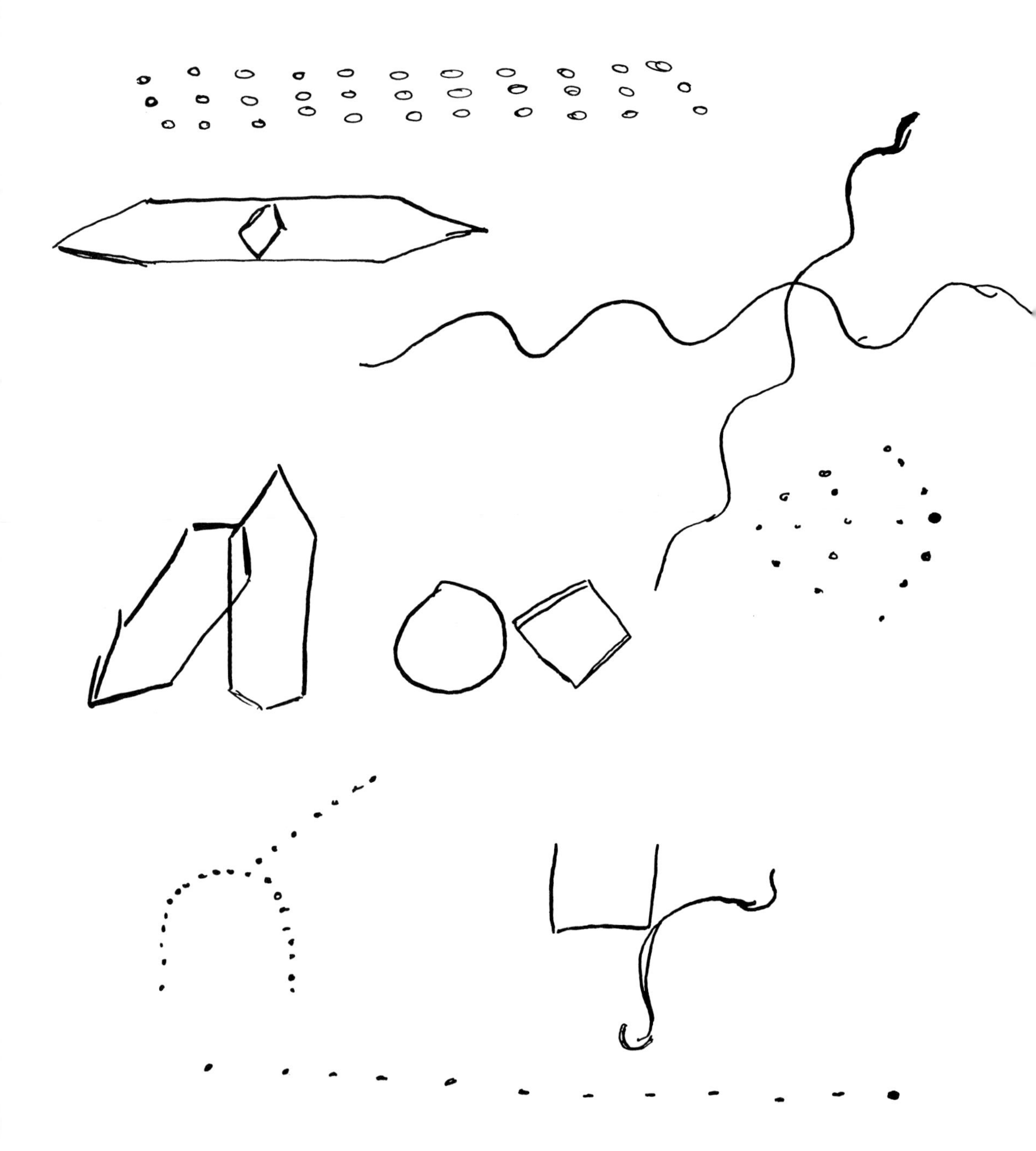

Record 39

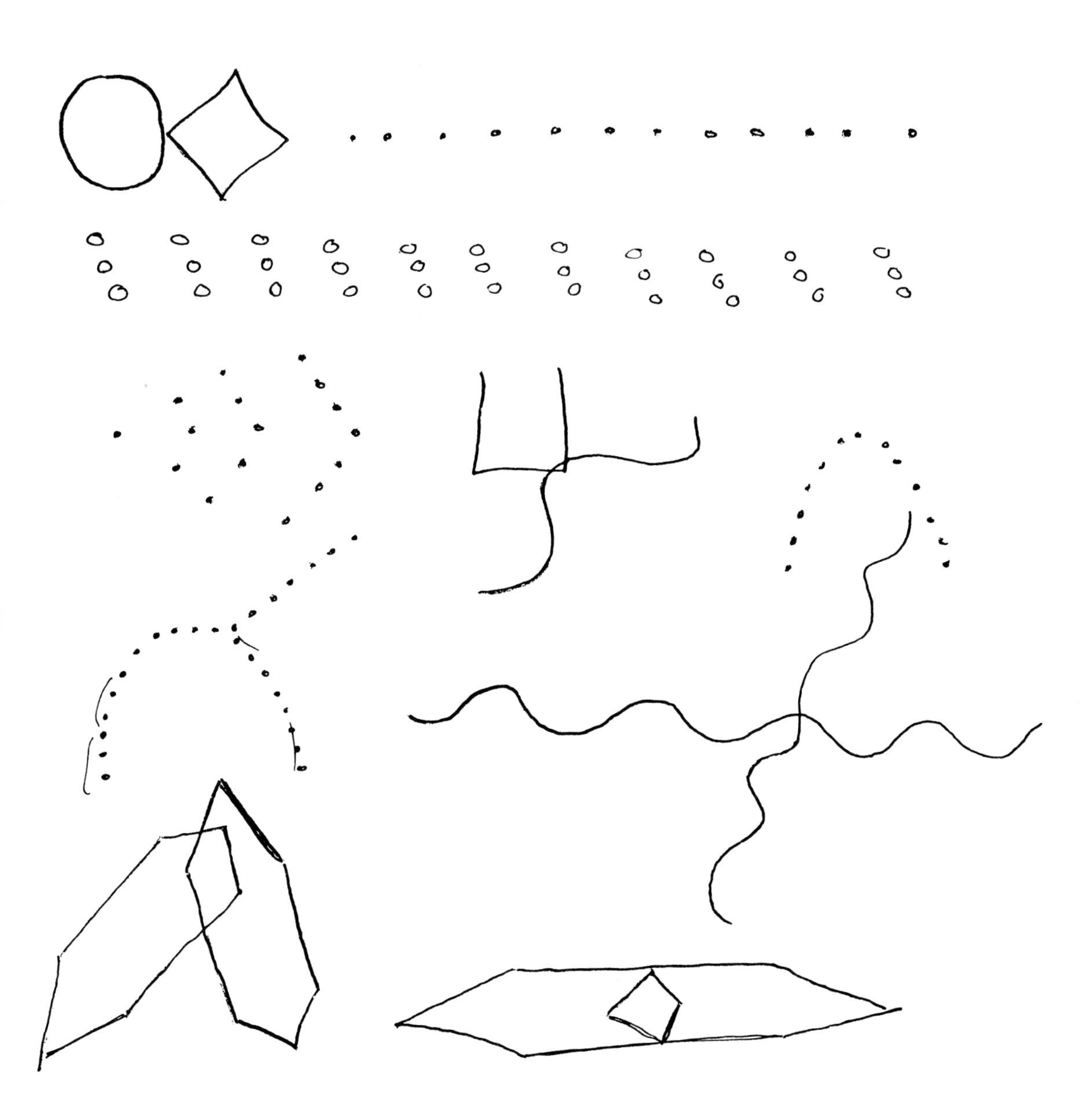

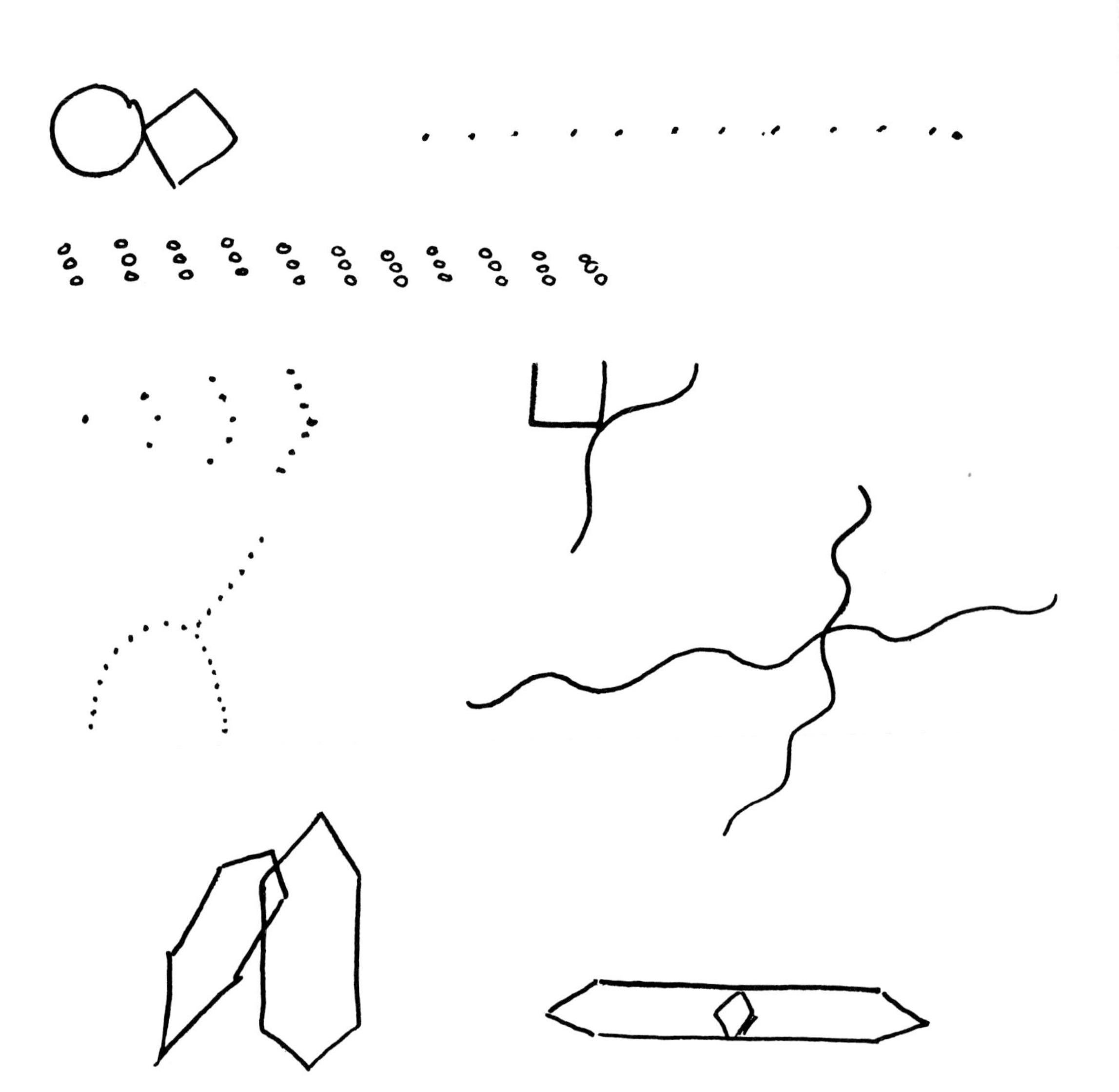

Record 41

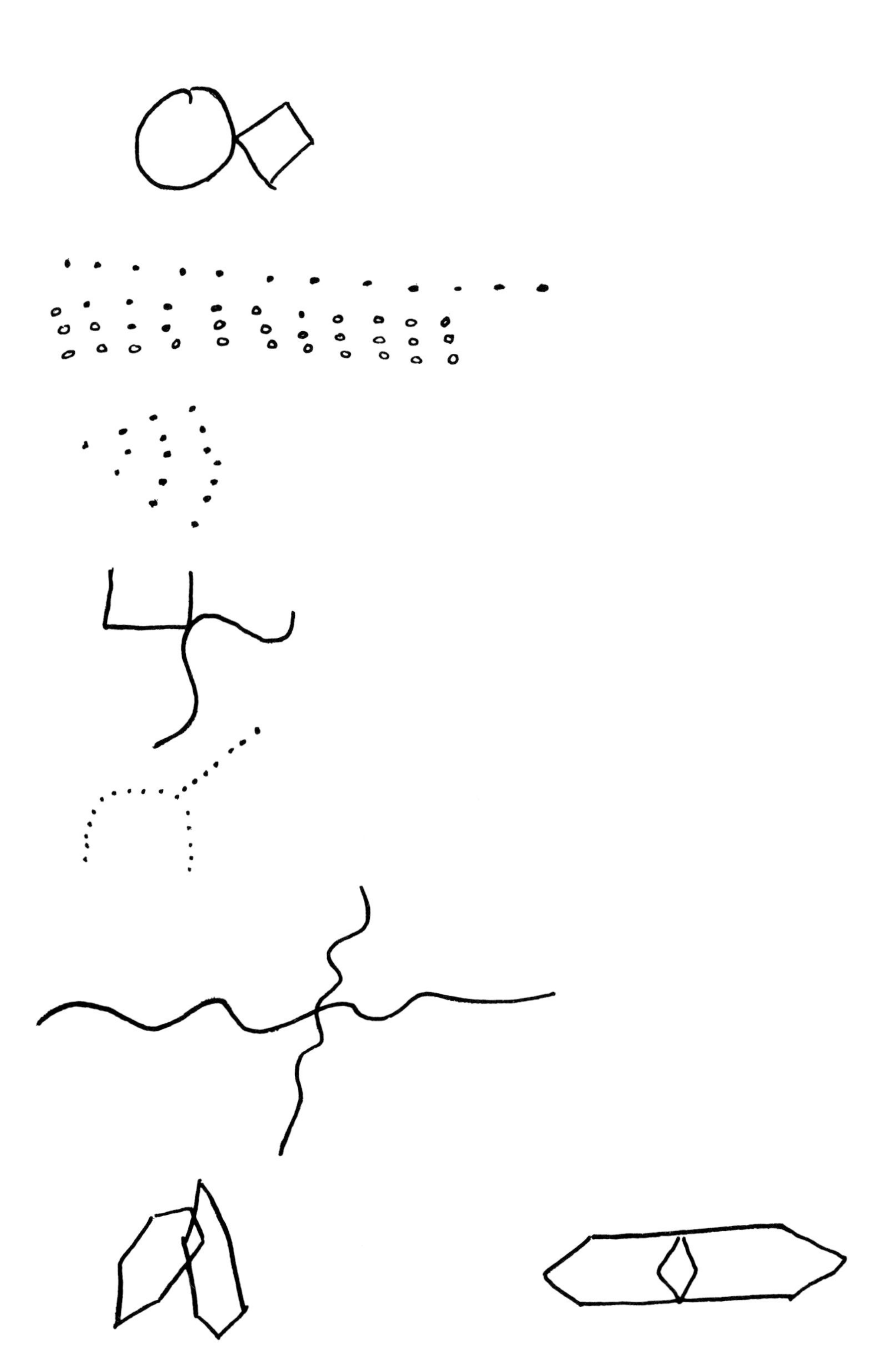

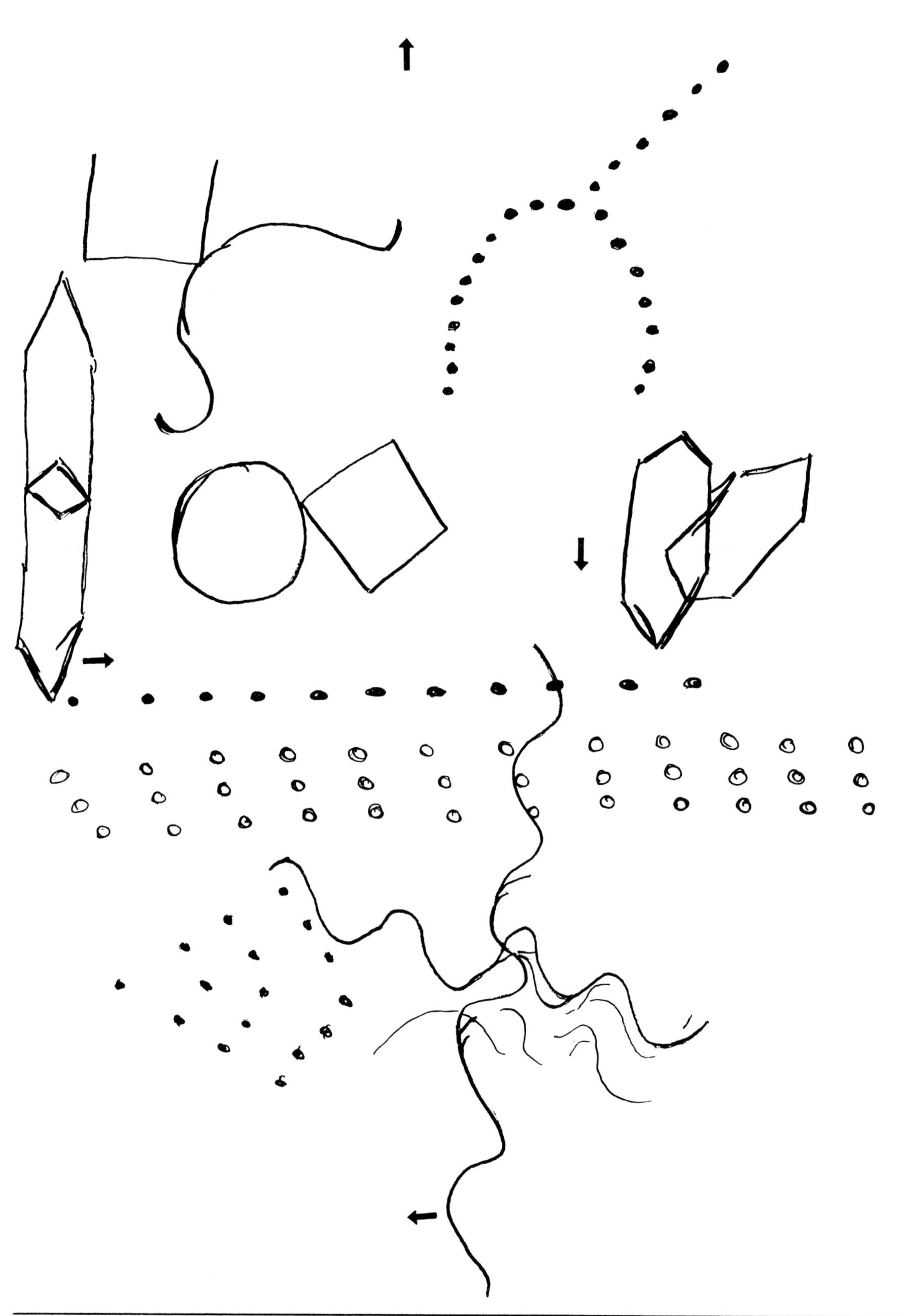

Record 43

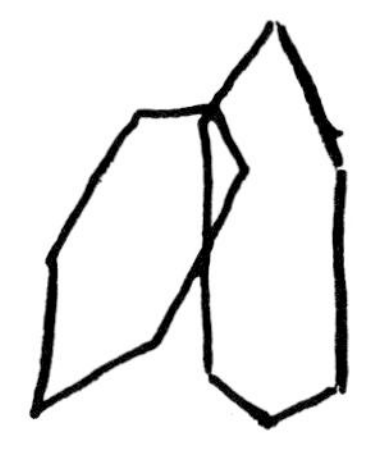

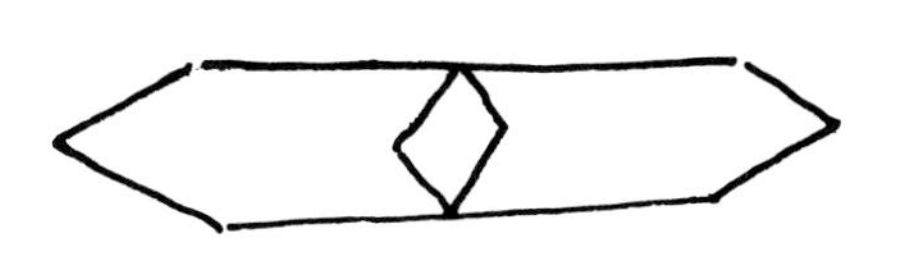

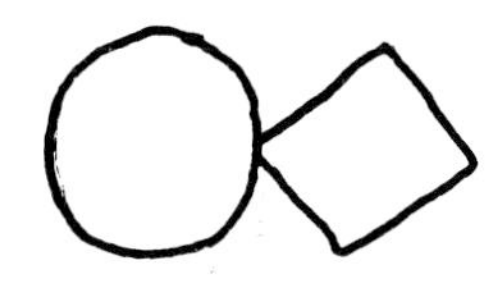

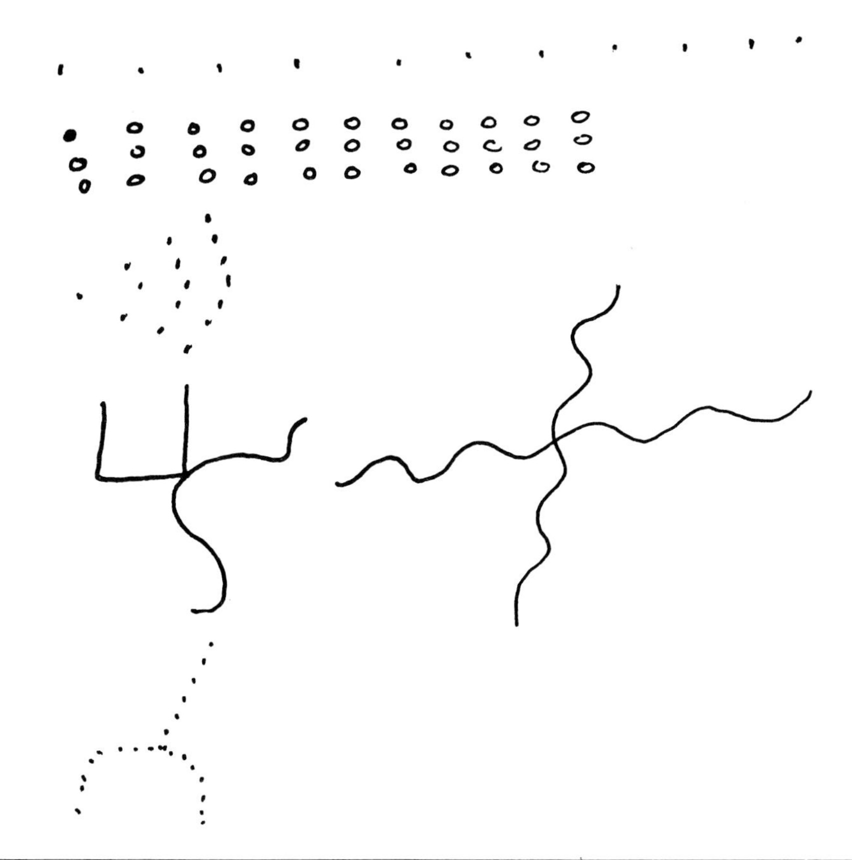

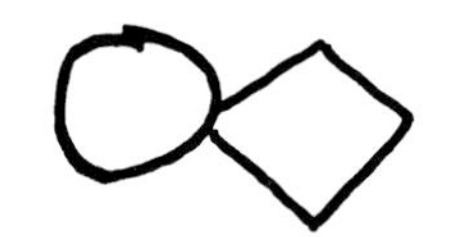

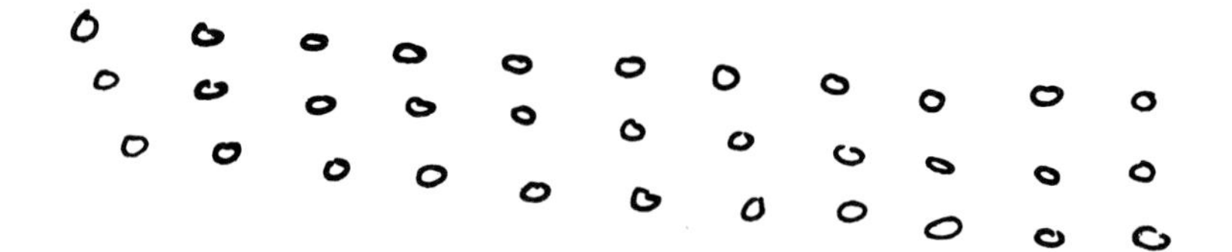

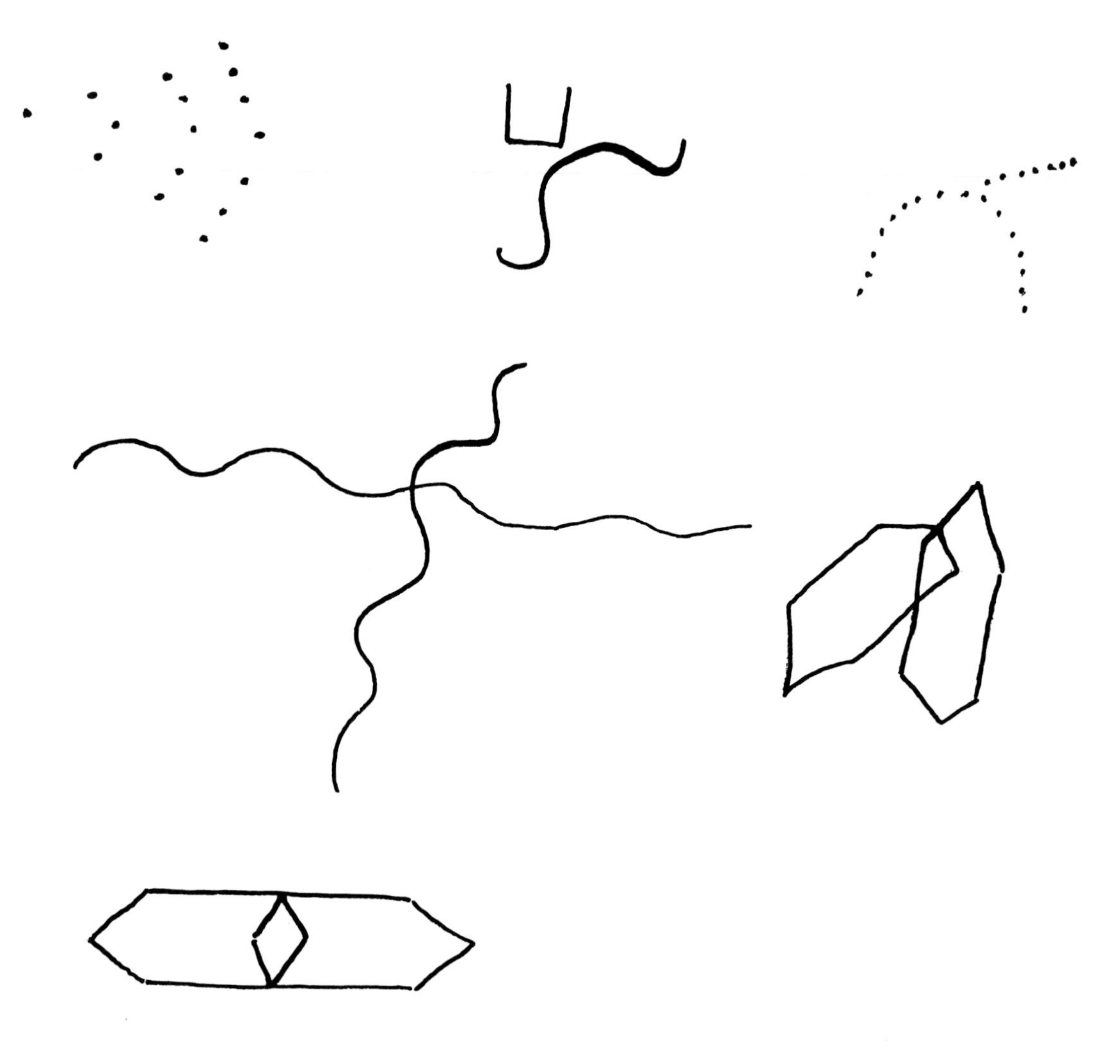

Record 45

INDEX

3
4
5
6 n
7 o
8 p
9 q
0 r
1 s
82 t